A YEAR IN THE LIFE OF
STUART BRITAIN

A YEAR IN THE LIFE OF
STUART BRITAIN

ANDREA ZUVICH

AMBERLEY

This book is dedicated with love to my husband Gavin. For his continuing encouragement and support of me and of *The Seventeenth Century Lady*, I am truly grateful.

First published 2016

Amberley Publishing
The Hill, Stroud
Gloucestershire, GL5 4EP

www.amberley-books.com

British Library Cataloguing in Publication Data.
A catalogue record for this book is available from the British Library.

ISBN 978 1 4456 4742 5 (print)
ISBN 978 1 4456 4743 2 (ebook)

Typesetting and Origination by Amberley Publishing.
Printed in the UK.

CONTENTS

Author's Note	7
Introduction	8
Chronology of Events	15
January	20
February	47
March	71
April	95
May	119
June	144
July	168
August	192
September	217
October	241
November	264
December	292
Glossary	319
Select Bibliography	323
Acknowledgements	335

AUTHOR'S NOTE

In Stuart Britain, most people were still using the Julian calendar, now mainly known as the Old Style Calendar. Under this system, 25 March was the beginning of the New Year. This is why when we look at dates in history books there is typically a N.S. or New Style date (based on the Gregorian calendar, which had begun to be used throughout Continental Europe in the late sixteenth century), and an O.S. date, which was still being used in Britain during the seventeenth century. The only exception in Britain was Scotland, which began using the Gregorian calendar in 1600. In some contemporary letters, one often finds a date with both years. For example, 1688/9, which signifies a date that falls in both 1688 (O.S.) and 1689 (N.S.) – another example of this is the date of King Charles I's execution: 30 January 1648/9. For the purposes of this book, I use the popular date format for each given event, be it O.S. or N.S.

Please also note that this book focuses on the Stuarts from 1603 to 1714, so uses the English series of regnal numbers (also known as ordinal numbers). Therefore James VII is simply James II, and so on.

Next, the Netherlands is referred to as the *Dutch Republic* as this (along with the United Provinces) is how it was known during the Stuart era.

Finally, the digitisation of many ancient books greatly aids the contemporary historian in researching the past. Many of the documents from which I have excerpted, including primary sources, are now available in the public domain for any readers with an Internet connection to examine and appreciate in their entirety.

INTRODUCTION

Hold on to your periwigs, I'm going to start you off with a whirlwind tour of the history of Stuart Britain; a time that encompassed the vast majority of the seventeenth century and the first fourteen years of the eighteenth. This period, which is sometimes overlooked in favour of the earlier Tudors, was one of the most complex periods in British history. A time in which Britain began to shake off the superstitious remnants of its medieval past, while new and sometimes radical ideologies sent shockwaves throughout England, Wales, Scotland, and Ireland. These kingdoms differed from each other greatly in some respects and this sometimes made compromise between them difficult, if not impossible. One of the institutions hit the hardest during the Stuart era was that of monarchy. In 2015, Queen Elizabeth II broke the record set by her great-great-grandmother Queen Victoria to become the longest-serving monarch in British history. Although we have a constitutional monarchy today, in which the sovereign is mostly a ceremonial figurehead, its existence was by no means assured during the Stuart era – something which I'll explain shortly.

So, who were the Stuarts? The House of Stewart was the ruling royal family in Scotland. That family became linked to that of the Tudors through the marriage of Henry VII's daughter Margaret Tudor to King James IV of Scotland (a Stewart). Queen Elizabeth I, the last of the Tudors, died in March 1603 leaving her cousin, King James VI of Scotland (who belonged to the House of Stewart), as heir to the English throne. This was a major turning point in British history, for although the Stewarts had ruled Scotland for hundreds of years, they had never ruled England – a country which was (and to some eyes still is) a rival. When James became King of England, the Union of Crowns took place, but the actual union between Scotland and England came over a hundred years later with the Union of 1707 during the reign of the last Stuart monarch, James's great-granddaughter, Queen Anne. It was as controversial a topic then as it is now. In 2014, a referendum was held wherein Scots decided whether they wished to stay in the United Kingdom or leave and become an independent country, as they had been before the Union. The voters chose the former. Although united and bound together by shared customs (and in many cases, family), Scotland and England had a long and sometimes hostile history with one another (a remnant of which might sometimes be observed at football matches even today!). Throughout this book, I will be using the Gallicised spelling of Stewart, which is Stuart. This helps differentiate between the time in which the Stewarts ruled Scotland and that in which they ruled Scotland and England together, beginning in 1603.

There were seven Stuart monarchs during the period 1603–1714, and two Lords Protector during the Commonwealth period in the 1650s:

James I: Ruled 1603–25;
Charles I: Ruled 1625–49 (executed);
Interregnum/Commonwealth under Lord Protector Oliver
    Cromwell: 1649–59;
Lord Protector Richard Cromwell: 1658–59;
Charles II: Ruled 1660–85;
James II: Ruled 1685–88 (exiled);
William & Mary: Ruled 1689–94 (Mary's death);
William III: Ruled alone 1689–1702;
Anne: Ruled 1702–14.

James I's mother was none other than Mary Queen of Scots, who lived from 1542 to 1587, when she was beheaded at Fotheringhay Castle, Northamptonshire. Mary was descended from Margaret Tudor, Henry VIII's sister, which made her Queen Elizabeth I's cousin. When Mary was found guilty of treason after the Babington Plot had been uncovered, the English queen agonised over the signing of her execution warrant.

Mary wasn't the last Stuart to lose her head. Her grandson, Charles I, lost his in the winter of 1649 after two devastating civil wars. Charles I's grandson, the dashing but doomed Duke of Monmouth, was the eldest illegitimate son of Charles II. When he invaded England in 1685 he led the Monmouth Rebellion, which sought to overthrow his uncle, King James II, in order to take the throne for himself. He and what remained of his rag-tag army suffered a substantial defeat in early July at the Battle of Sedgemoor, following which he was captured, brought to London and imprisoned in the Tower of London. Monmouth's grisly execution was botched and remains one of the ghastliest executions in British history. It wasn't only to the executioner's axe that Stuarts lost heads, either. The Duke of Monmouth's cousin, James FitzJames, Duke of Berwick, was decapitated by a cannonball at the Siege of Philipsbourg in 1734.

During the seventeenth century, British influence was not limited to the European continent but spread to other regions, especially North America. This book will focus mainly upon events and people in and from the British Isles and the Continent, but occasionally also on the colonies of the New World. Manual labour was used here to run the sugar cane and tobacco plantations, and European and Arabic traders, as well as native African tribal leaders, bought and sold their fellow human beings into bondage. Slavery, which has plagued mankind since ancient times, was during the Stuart period not just inflicted upon Africans but upon Europeans, as well. The Barbary pirates sailed from the Barbary States (the coastal areas of North Africa comprising the modern-day countries of Morocco, Libya, Tunisia, and Algeria) to coastal towns in Italy, France, Spain, the British Isles, and Iceland, where they would attack coastal villages and abduct men, women, and children. These prisoners were then taken to the slave markets in Salé (in Morocco), Algiers, Tunis, or Tripoli. For example, Jeffrey Hudson, Queen Henrietta Maria's white dwarf, was captured by Barbary pirates and sold – ultimately enduring over twenty years as a slave (according to him, a sex slave). Captive male slaves were expected to convert to Islam, and those who resisted were beaten or killed. Female slaves were converted to Islam and sold, many finding themselves in a harem.

Religion, as you might imagine, was an extremely important aspect of life in the Stuart era, and wars between Catholics and Protestants as well as wars between Christians and Muslims were a fact of life in that time. Jews, who had been expelled from England in the thirteenth century by the Edict of Expulsion of 1290, were welcomed back under Lord Protector Oliver Cromwell in 1656. Religion went hand in hand with politics, and several notable political upheavals occurred during the Stuart era. For example, there were no less than three civil wars, involving England, Scotland, Wales, and Ireland. These occurred between 1642 and 1651 and have been given various names throughout history, including The Great Rebellion, the British Civil Wars, the Wars of the Three Kingdoms, and the English Civil Wars. As most of the key battles, such as Naseby, Marston Moor, etc., were fought on English soil, this book will use the latter appellation.

Perhaps one of the most important aspects of the Stuart era is the emergence of some very radical political movements. The most important of these were the Levellers and the Diggers. The Levellers were especially important because many soldiers in the New Model Army sympathised with them, thus making them a problem for people like Oliver Cromwell. Among the most influential Levellers was one Colonel Thomas Rainsborow, who famously said that 'the poorest he that is in England hath a life to live as the greatest he'. Another vocal Leveller was 'Freeborn' John Lilburne, who was imprisoned frequently, and was later to become a Quaker. The Quakers were yet another radical group to emerge in the Stuart era, and some – such as William Penn – went on to establish communities in America, such as Pennsylvania. The Quakers, also known as the Society of Friends, were a Protestant Christian movement begun in the 1640s by George Fox. Included among their beliefs was the notion that the sexes were equal, and that slavery should be abolished – both extraordinary ideas during the Stuart era. Gerrard Winstanley founded the Diggers, also known as the True Levellers, a group who believed that the earth was a public treasury. The Diggers formed a commune in Surrey where they dug the earth in the hope of creating a common agricultural community. This whole experiment was met with hostility from both the government and the neighbouring area, and was destroyed.

By the end of the English Civil Wars, Parliament ultimately took control and Charles I was executed in 1649; soon after that, the monarchy and the House of Lords were abolished. However, it transpired that living under a Cromwellian Protectorate was not the idyll so many had thought it would be. When Oliver Cromwell died in 1658, his son Richard became the second Lord Protector, and, to cut a long story short, he was not very good at the job and resigned in 1659. As for Parliament, internal bickering ultimately brought the whole new system crumbling down. General Monck invaded London at the head of the army, and it was decided that England would welcome King Charles II from his exile. Upon the Restoration in 1660, the monarchy changed to become less absolute and more constitutional.

The second period of crucial importance during the Stuart era is the invasion of 1688, popularly referred to as the Glorious Revolution. This had lasting effects on both monarchical and parliamentary power in Britain, as the reader will discover. Mary Stuart was the daughter of James, Duke of York, and his first wife, Anne Hyde. Following the Glorious Revolution of 1688, Mary became Queen

Mary II and ruled together with her husband, William III. The most well-known, successful invasion by a foreign power was the Norman Conquest of 1066, which saw William the Conqueror invade Britain with his forces. In 1688, Britain was once again successfully invaded – this time by the Dutch, and by invitation. Prince William III of Orange, Stadtholder of the Dutch Republic, had a reputation for being one of the great heroes of Protestant Europe. He was always battling it out with his arch-nemesis, the Catholic King Louis XIV of France, whose megalomaniacal attempts to conquer more territories made him a constant foe to be reckoned with. When Louis' cousin, King James II of England (James VII of Scotland), became king after the death of his elder brother Charles II, concern spread that the new king would return his kingdoms to Roman Catholicism. When his wife, Mary of Modena, gave birth to a healthy son in the summer of 1688, rumours and fears of a Catholic succession led to the verge of rebellion. The so-called 'Immortal Seven' – seven of the most influential and powerful men in the kingdom – invited William of Orange to invade England. Why? William had royal blood connections (he was a half-Stuart through his mother, Mary, Princess Royal) and he was married to James's eldest daughter, also named Mary. William landed in Torbay in November 1688; James II fled; and in early 1689, William and Mary became the first diarchy in British history.

But in the end it was fertility troubles that plagued the late Stuarts. Combined with a dread of allowing a Catholic succession to take place, this ultimately ended the dynastic line and paved the way for the Hanoverians to ascend to the thrones of Britain. Mary II had at least two miscarriages and ultimately was unable to have children. Her sister, who became Queen Anne, had between sixteen and eighteen pregnancies which ended in stillbirth, miscarriage, or death in childhood. When Anne's only remaining child, William Henry, died in 1700 at the tragically young age of eleven, the Act of Settlement (1701) was passed in order to ensure a Protestant succession. This is why the throne passed to the Hanoverians, who were descended from King James I through his daughter Elizabeth of Bohemia.

The Stuart era coincided with a period of global cooling, known as the Little Ice Age. As such, winters were incredibly cold and the River Thames sometimes became so frozen solid that people were able to go out onto the ice and take part in a wide variety of entertainments. These frost fairs must have been magnificent, featuring ice skating, music playing, and hot food being sold and eaten on the ice. Theatres were very popular in the Elizabethan and Jacobean periods, but were done away with during the time of the puritanical Commonwealth. At the Restoration, however, the theatres were re-opened; but then something even better happened. Women were allowed to act on stage for the first time and the first actresses – Elizabeth Barry, Peg Hughes, Nell Gwynn, Moll Davis, Anne Bracegirdle, etc. – stole the show. One of the other popular entertainments of the day was an execution. Vast crowds of people would gather to see a nobleman beheaded or a common thief hanged from the Tyburn tree (which wasn't a tree, by the way, but a large wooden scaffold used for executions). Street vendors would sell food, people would cheer – it was all very similar to what we see today at spectacles like football matches, minus all the death, of course!

With the entertaining and enlightening diaries of Samuel Pepys, John Evelyn, and the more overtly political records of people like Narcissus Luttrell, not to mention the works by a wave of new female authors such as Aphra Behn, Margaret Cavendish, Katherine Philips, and Mary Astell, Stuart-era literature is as rich as it is Fascinating. Mathematicians and scientists such as Isaac Newton, Robert Hooke, Christopher Wren, Robert Boyle and other learned men formed the Royal Society. The extremes of a simultaneous superstitiousness and a spirit of scientific endeavour during the Stuart age made for a remarkable contrast.

There are countless Stuart-era buildings dotted around the United Kingdom – from stately homes and churches to taverns and more. There were several dominant architectural trends from 1603 to 1714, namely the Jacobean, neo-Palladian, and English Baroque idioms. Bolsover Castle in Derbyshire, Wroxton Abbey in the Cotswolds, Blenheim Palace in Oxfordshire, Aston Hall in Birmingham, Ham House in Surrey, Dyrham Park in South Gloucestershire, Boscobel House near Wolverhampton, and Kensington Palace are just some of the various historical buildings that figure into the immense history of the Stuart period. There were some very appetising new foods to be enjoyed. Global trade to foreign lands meant that exotic foods such as bananas, pineapples, ice cream, hot chocolate, coffee, and tea were enjoyed in Stuart Britain.

Those who have read and enjoyed *The Stuarts in 100 Facts* will find slightly longer entries about specific events in the Stuart period. During the course of this book, however, the reader will learn about an important event – such as a birth, death, publication, or battle – that occurred on a specific day in Stuart Britain. This is largely in keeping with the popular 'On This Day in the 17th Century' series that I have maintained as a Twitter feature over the past few years. Most entries include an excerpt from a play, letter, diary, poem, sermon, etc., and I've often added a mini biography in the vein of John Aubrey's *Brief Lives*. Each day and entry will be from a different year in the Stuart era, so in order to avoid confusion, please have a look at the accompanying timeline and images.

Please be aware that there may be many extracts that jar with modern-day sensibilities; I trust the reader will respect that there were sometimes substantial differences in ideology in the Stuart age compared with today. Indeed, I believe it essential for the reader to put aside their modern beliefs and morals to try to see the world through the eyes of a Stuart-era person. This time period was riddled with assassination plots and political intrigues, sex scandals, murder, duels, family rifts – you name it, it probably happened. I hope you enjoy this journey through the good, the profane, the dirty, the pestilential, the scandalous, and the utterly delightful in *A Year in the Life of Stuart Britain*.

CHRONOLOGY
OF EVENTS

1603   Death of Elizabeth I.
James VI of Scotland becomes James I of England.

1605   The Gunpowder Plot is foiled.

1606   The remaining Gunpowder Plotters are executed.

1607   Jamestown is founded in Virginia.

1610   King Henri IV is assassinated in France.

1612   Death of Henry Frederick Stuart, Prince of Wales.

1613   Elizabeth Stuart marries Frederick V, Elector Palatine.

1614   The Addle Parliament.

1616   Death of English playwright, William Shakespeare.
Death of Spanish playwright Miguel de Cervantes.

1617   Louis XIII takes power in France.
Death of Pocahontas in England.

1618   Execution of Sir Walter Raleigh.

1619   Birth of Prince Rupert of the Rhine.

1620   The Mayflower ship carrying puritans leaves England bound for the New World.

1625   Death of King James I, Charles I becomes king.
Charles I marries Louis XIII of France's sister Henrietta Maria.

1628   The assassination of George Villiers, Duke of Buckingham.

1629   Charles I dissolves Parliament, begins Personal Rule.

1630   John Winthrop leads many Puritans to the New World.
The birth of the future Charles II of England.

1631   The Sack of Baltimore by the Barbary pirates.

1635   Ship Money tax is extended to inland counties.

1638   Birth of the future Louis XIV of France.

The First Bishops' War Begins.

1639   The First Bishops' War Ends with the Truce of Berwick.

1640   The Short Parliament, from April to May.

The Second Bishops' War Begins.

The Scots capture Newcastle.

The Second Bishops' War ends with Treaty of Ripon.

The Long Parliament met.

1641   The Army Plot is foiled.

The Earl of Strafford is executed.

The Irish Rebellion/Ulster Uprising.

1642   King Charles I raises his standard at Nottingham, beginning First English Civil War.

The Battle of Edgehill.

1643   Habernfeld's Plot.

The First Battle of Newbury.

1644   The Battle of Marston Moor.

The Battle of Cropredy Bridge.

The Second Battle of Newbury.

1645   The Battle of Auldearn.

The Battle of Naseby. Parliamentarian victory.

The Battle of Langport. Parliamentarian victory.

1647   Head of Proposals created.

The Putney Debates are held.

1648   The Peace of Westphalia ends the Thirty Years War on the Continent.

The Second English Civil War, April to September.

Pride's Purge of Parliament.

1649   The trial and execution of Charles I.

The House of Lords is abolished.

Leveller movement is crushed.

Birth of James, later Duke of Monmouth.

England becomes a Commonwealth.

Drogheda Massacre during Cromwellian Conquest of Ireland.

Wexford Massacre during Cromwellian Conquest of Ireland.

1650   The Battle of Dunbar.

Death of William II of Orange.

Birth of William III of Orange, later King William III.

1651   Battle of Worcester ends the Third Civil War with a Parliamentary victory.

Sale of confiscated Royalist estates.

1653   Cromwell installed as Lord Protector.

The Rump Parliament dismissed, and 'Barebones' Parliament begins.

1658 The death of Lord Protector Oliver Cromwell.

1660 The Restoration of the Stuart monarchy.
The Convention Parliament begins.
Charles II becomes King of England.
Louis XIV of France marries Maria Theresa, Infanta of Spain.
Death of Mary Stuart, Princess of Orange.

1661 Death of Cardinal Mazarin in France.

1662 Birth of Mary, later Queen Mary II.
Marriage between King Charles II and Catherine of Braganza.

1663 The Farnley Wood/Derwentdale Plot uncovered.

1665 The Great Plague of London.

1666 The Great Fire of London.
The Pentland Rising.

1668 The Triple Alliance.

1670 The Secret Treaty of Dover between Charles II of England and Louis XIV of France.

1672 The Dutch *Rampjaar* (Disaster Year).
Cornelius and Jan de Witt are murdered by a mob.

1673 The Test Act.

1677 Marriage between William of Orange and Mary of York.

1678 Titus Oates and Israel Tonge concoct the Popish Plot.

1679 The Exclusion Bill is first introduced.
The Battle of Bothwell Brig.

1680 The Black Box is investigated under Charles II's orders.

1682 Death of Rupert of the Rhine.

1683 Death of Shaftesbury.
The Rye House Plot is foiled.
Execution of William, Lord Russell, for the Rye House Plot.
The Battle of Vienna thwarts Islamic invasion of Europe.

1685 Death of Charles II, James II becomes king.
Monmouth Rebellion.
Execution of James, Duke of Monmouth.

1686 Death of Lady Henrietta Wentworth, Duke of Monmouth's last mistress.

1687 James receives papal nuncio Cardinal Adda.

1688 Queen Mary (of Modena) gives birth to a son, James Francis Edward Stuart.

	The 'Immortal Seven' invite William of Orange to invade England.
	War of League of Augsburg begins.
1689	William and Mary are crowned joint sovereigns of England, Scotland, Ireland.
	Battle of Killiecrankie is fought.
1690	Battle of the Boyne is fought and results in a Williamite victory.
1691	The Battle of Aughrim is fought.
1692	The Glencoe Massacre takes place in Scotland.
	The Salem Witch Trials take place in Massachusetts.
	Earthquake devastates Port Royal, Jamaica.
1693	The College of William & Mary in Virginia is founded.
	Gold is discovered in Brazil.
1694	The Bank of England is founded.
	Death of Queen Mary II at Kensington Palace.
1695	The Darien Company is founded.
1696	The Scottish Education Act.
	Plot to assassinate William III is uncovered.
1697	Peace of Rijswijk: Louis XIV recognizes William III as King of England.
1698	The Darien Colony is founded by Scottish emigrants in Panama.
	The Great Recoinage begins to stop counterfeit money.
	Peter the Great of Russia visits England.
1700	Death of William Henry, Duke of Gloucester.
	Death of Carlos II, King of Spain.
	Darien Scheme collapses.
1701	Death of the exiled James II.
	The Act of Settlement in created to ensure a Protestant succession.
1702	Death of King William III at Kensington Palace.
1703	The Great Storm hits Britain.
1704	The Battle of Blenheim is fought.
	England captures Gibraltar.
1705	The Alien Act is passed by the English Parliament.
1706	The Battle of Ramillies between French and English is fought.
1707	The Act of Union is accepted, creating the United Kingdom of Great Britain.
	The Scilly Naval Disaster occurs.
1708	The Jacobite invasion of Scotland fails.
1709	The Battle of Malplaquet.
1711	The *Spectator* Magazine is launched.

1713   The War of the Spanish Succession ends with Treaty of Utrecht.

1714   Death of Queen Anne, the end of the Stuart dynasty.

1715   Death of Louis XIV of France.

          The Earl of Mar starts the Jacobite rising of 1715.

1718   Death of Mary of Modena, exiled Queen consort of England.

JANUARY

1st – A King of Scotland First

When people think about King Charles II of England, they usually think of him as the 'Merry Monarch' with his gaggle of floppy-eared spaniels and bevy of beautiful mistresses. They also connect him with the Restoration of the monarchy in 1660, when he finally reclaimed his father's throne. When he was crowned King of England on 23 April 1661, that was not the first time he had taken part in a coronation ceremony. The reality was that Charles had been crowned King of Scotland at Scone a decade earlier on 1 January 1651 (the Scottish Parliament had proclaimed him king in 1649 following his father's execution). The second King Charles's father was executed only two years before, following almost a decade of bloodshed in the English Civil Wars (also known as the Wars of the Three Kingdoms). The young prince, now king-in-exile, journeyed to Scotland in order to raise an army to attempt to take back his country from Oliver Cromwell and the Parliamentarians. The young King of Scots and his supporters made one last attempt against the Parliamentarians, which, although valiantly fought, ended in unmitigated defeat at the Battle of Worcester. It was from this bloody scene of defeat that he narrowly escaped with his life (with the help of an oak tree near Boscobel House, the help of royalist Jane Lane, and no small amount of luck). Charles would not be crowned King of England until 1661, at the Restoration of the monarchy following Cromwell's death and the downfall of the Puritan regime. According to David Hilliam in *Crown, Orb, & Sceptre: The True Stories of English Coronations*, Charles became the last monarch to take part in the tradition of living in the Tower of London before his coronation.

*

It was also on this day in 1716 that the Restoration playwright William Wycherley died. Wycherley is believed to have been born in England in

1641, lived in India for some time, converted to Roman Catholicism in France, and was imprisoned in the Fleet Prison for a number of years. While his life seems like a play in itself, Wycherley's most famous works include *The Country Wife, The Plain Dealer, Gentleman Dancing Master,* and *Love in a Wood.* When *The Country Wife* was acted at the Theatre Royal some of the most popular actors of the day performed in it, such as Charles Hart as Mr Horner and Ned Kynaston as Mr Harcourt.

Horner: Well, my dear Doctor, hast thou done what I desir'd?
Quack: I have undone you for ever with the Women, and reported you thro'out the whole Town as bad as an Eunuch, with as much Trouble as if I had made you one in earnest.
Horner: But have you told all the Midwives you know, the Orange Wenches at the Playhouses, the City Husbands, and old fumbling Keepers of this end of the Town? For they'll be the readiest to report it.
Quack: I have told all the Chamber-maids, Waiting-women, Tyre-women, and old Women of my Acquaintance; nay, and whisper'd it as a Secret to 'em, and to the Whisperers of Whitehall; so that you need not doubt 'twill spread, and you will be as odious to the handsome young Women, as -
Horner: - As the Small Pox.

Act I: Scene I, *The Country Wife,* from *Plays Written by Mr. William Wycherley: Containing The Plain Dealer, The Country Wife, Gentleman Dancing Master, Love in a Wood,* 1731

In the opening scene, excerpted above, a lothario (Horner) enlists the help of a quack to spread the fake rumour that he is impotent (hence the 'as bad as an Eunuch' line). The idea is that this will make husbands think him perfectly harmless, and then he can cunningly seduce their wives. This backfires spectacularly. Wycherley's controversial use of double entendre and the amount of sexual content in his productions made him a sort of *persona non grata* during the Victorian era.

2nd – A Naval Meeting

Attended the King and the Duke of York in the Duke of York's lodgings, with the rest of the officers and many of the commanders of the fleet, and some of our master shipwrights, to discourse the business of having topmasts of ships made to lower abaft of the mainmast; a business I understand not, and so can give no good account, but I do see that by how much greater the Council and the number of councilors is, the more confused the issue is of their councils, so that little was said to the purpose regularly, and but little use was made of it, they coming to a very broken conclusion upon it to make trial in a ship or two.

From this they fell to other talk about the fleet's fighting this late war, and how the King's ships have been shattered; though the King said that the world would not have it that above ten or twenty ships in any fight did do any service, and that this hath been told so to him himself by ignorant people. The Prince, who was there, was mightily surprised at it, and seemed troubled; but the King told him that is was only discourse of the world. But Mr. Wren whispered me in the war, and said that the Duke of Albemarle had put it into his Narrative for the House, that not above twenty-five ships fought in the engagement wherein he was, but was advised to leave it out; but this he did write from sea, I am sure, or words to that effect: and did displease many commanders, among others Captain Batts, who the Duke of York said was a very stout man, all the world knew; and that another ship was brought into his ship that had been turned out of his place when he was a boatswain, not long before for being a drunkard. This Prince Rupert took notice of, and would have been angry, I think, but they let their discourse fall, but the Duke of York was earnest in it.

Entry for 2 January 1667/8, *The Diary of Samuel Pepys*

It's from the little descriptions of daily life that we can glean much about Pepys's time. It should come as no surprise that Samuel Pepys (1633–1703) will show up throughout the course of our year in Stuart Britain because of scenes like the one described above. Pepys, the son of John and Margaret Pepys, was one of the greatest diarists of Stuart Britain. With his diaries he left us a great insight into his daily life and life in general during the Restoration, and covered such major events as the Great Plague of London of 1665, and the Great Fire of 1666. He was the Secretary to the Admiralty, which put him in close proximity to notables such as James, Duke of York, and Prince Rupert of the Rhine (both mentioned in the above entry). In his personal life Pepys was a great lover of food, music, theatre, and women. We'll look at his life in some more detail later on in our year.

3rd – The Transit of Venus

When our illustrious countryman Mr Horrox first applied himself to astronomy, he computed ephemerides for several years, from Langsbergius's tables. After continuing his labours for some time, he was enabled to discover the imperfection of these tables; upon which he laid aside his work, intending to determine the positions of the stars from his own observations ...

Hence he was encouraged to wait for the important observation of the transit of Venus in the year 1639; and no longer thought the former part of his time misspent, since his attention to Lansbergius's tables had enabled him to discover that the transit would certainly happen on the 24th of November, However, as these tables had so often deceived him, he was unwilling to reply on them entirely, but consulted other tables, and particularly those of Kepler: accordingly in a letter to his friend William Crabtree, of Manchester, dated Hoole, October 26, 1639, he communicated his discovery to him, and earnestly desired him to make whatever observation he possibly could with his telescope, particularly to measure the diameter of the planet Venus.

> *Astronomy explained upon Sir Isaac Newton's Principles: and*
> *made easy to those who have not studied mathematics,*
> James Ferguson, 1639

Jeremiah Horrocks, an English astronomer, died on this day on 3 January 1641, during the reign of King Charles I. Originally from Toxteth, near Liverpool, Horrocks (sometimes spelled Horrox) studied at Emmanuel College, Cambridge, and in 1639 became the first person to observe the transit of the planet Venus – the other being his correspondent and fellow astronomer William Crabtree. What is a transit of Venus? It is a rare phenomenon in which Venus passes across the face of the sun and can be seen briefly from Earth. According to NASA, only the transits of planets Mercury and Venus can be seen from Earth. The most recent transits of Venus occurred in 2004 and 2012.

Horrocks' observations and calculations are the reasons why he is known as the 'Father of British Astronomy'. Horrocks died unmarried, and a collection of his works was published posthumously in *Opera Posthuma* in 1673. A beautiful memorial in Westminster Abbey was created for him, but over two centuries after his death! It faces Isaac Newton's monument and was placed there in December of 1874. In April 2014, Much Hoole Parish Church held a commemorative memorial service for Horrocks. For more about Horrocks, I recommend reading Peter Aughton's *The Transit of Venus: The Brief, Brilliant Life of Jeremiah Horrocks, Father of Astronomy*, published in 2004.

4th – Five Members of Parliament

On this day, 4 January 1642, King Charles I entered the House of Commons accompanied by armed soldiers in an attempt to arrest five Members of Parliament. The five MPs were John Hampden, Arthur Haselrig, Denzil Holles,

John Pym, and William Strode; all five men were absent from the room. Henrietta Maria, in a sort of excitable mood, had blurted out what was about to happen – and Lucy Hay, Countess of Carlisle, quickly went to inform the men of the impending arrest. The Speaker of the House, William Lenthall, replied:

May it please your Majesty; I have neither eyes to see nor tongue to speak in this place, but as the house is pleased to direct me, whose servant I am here; and humbly beg your Majesty's pardon, that I cannot give any other answer than this to what your Majesty is pleased to demand of me.

5th – Political Intrigues

To the Earl of Manchester:

My Lord,
We have no letter from France since my last to you. I have spoken to the king concerning what you mention in yours of the 12/22, about the payment agreed to, in relation to Hudson's Bay. His Majesty will give orders in that affair, as soon as his meets his treasury here; this, as it may happen in discourse, your Excellency will intimate to Monsieur de Torcy. They will tell you from the Office that His Majesty returns from Hampton-Court on Thursday. I wish your Excellency a happy New-Year, and am, &c.
Jersey

Letter dated 5 January 1700, from *Memoirs of Affairs of State, Containing Letters,* ed. Christian Cole, London, 1733

The Earl of Jersey was Edward Villiers, part of the powerful Villiers family. The king whom Villiers refers to in the above letter is King William III. Edward had served in the Prince of Orange's household since the latter's marriage to the English princess Lady Mary of York in 1677. Edward was created a viscount in 1691 under William and Mary. Indeed, Villiers did very well for himself under William: on 1 June 1699, according to the *Calendar of Treasury Books, Volume 14, 1698–1699,* Villiers received £1,500 as 'King's gift and royal bounty'. In a Royal Warrant from August 1701, William granted Villiers 5,701 ounces of white plate and 1,192 ounces of gilt plate. What can be the reason for such generosity? Well, Villiers was a dutiful servant, but it's commonly believed that Edward's sister Elizabeth Villiers was William's long-term mistress, although by the time this letter was written the king had broken up with her and she had been married off to Lord George Hamilton and become the Countess of Orkney.

6th – Twelfth Night and Venner's Rebellion

In the Stuart era, 5 or 6 January would be celebrated as Twelfth Night, which is the traditional end to the Christmas period. As the early Stuart era was generally a great deal more superstitious than the latter, many believed that Christmas decorations should be taken down on this day – not to do so would be tantamount to courting bad luck.

Several popular seventeenth-century plays were written and performed based on the festival, including William Shakespeare's *Twelfth Night* (1602), and Ben Jonson's masque *The Masque of Blackness* (1605). Twelfth Night was also the inspiration for Pieter Brueghel the Younger's 1619 oil-on-oak work, *Twelfth Night*. Jan Miense Molenaer's *Twelfth Night* from 1660–65 is, at first glance, a more subdued depiction – until you notice the couple in the background snogging each other's faces off!

David Teniers the Younger's *Twelfth-night,* also known as *The King Drinks,* from 1634–40, and today housed in the Museo del Prado, Madrid, revisits the more boisterous tavern scene in keeping with Brueghel the Younger's work.

*

It was on this day in 1661 that a Fifth Monarchist rebellion headed by Thomas Venner began. Who was this Thomas Venner and what was his purpose in rebelling? In his book, *The Later Stuarts 1660–1714*, Sir George Clark amusingly referred to Venner as 'a crack-brained enthusiast' who led a group of some fifty men into London. The insurrection came to be known as Venner's Uprising. Venner was executed a few days later on 19 January 1661 by being hanged, drawn, and quartered. Even though this rebellion was crushed, it didn't stop the threat of the Fifth Monarchist subversion from causing concern later. From a note addressed to Lord Arlington, dated January 1666 in the *Calendar of State Papers Domestic: Charles II, 1665–6*, Gregory Phillipps warned that the most radical Fifth Monarchists were just waiting to begin 'the work', i.e. to get everything ready for the reign of their King Jesus.

7th – Gloriana's Limner

Nicholas Hilliard, English miniature painter, died on this day, during the reign of King James I. Hilliard was born in 1547 and his works are most often associated with the Elizabethan and Jacobean eras. According to historian G. M. Trevelyan, Hilliard founded the school of English miniature. He painted some of the most important people of the Elizabethan eras, including Queen Elizabeth herself several times, but also her favourite, Robert Dudley, 1st Earl of Leicester, her rival and cousin, Mary Queen of

Scots, and major courtiers including Sir Francis Drake, Sir Walter Raleigh, Robert Devereux, 2nd Earl of Essex, Sir Christopher Hatton, and Francis Bacon, 1st Viscount St Alban. It was during Elizabeth's reign that Hilliard became the monarch's official limner (miniature painter) – a role he kept through the end of Elizabeth's reign and into that of her successor, James I. Indeed, it is believed that Hilliard was the artist who depicted King James in the *Liber Ceruleus*, or Blue Book of the Order of the Garter. Usually painted on vellum (a kind of parchment made from calf skin) on card, the detail displayed in Hilliard's miniatures is breathtaking. The dress worn by courtiers during the period was elaborate, with exquisite lace, cabochons, lush colours, and sumptuous fabrics – and these are all to be found in his portraits. Hilliard's work is on display at museums throughout the world, including the National Portrait Gallery in London.

8th – Executed for Blasphemy

A student of eighteen, named Thomas Aikenhead, whose habits were studious and whose morals were irreproachable, had in the course of his reading met with some of the ordinary arguments against the Bible. He fancied that he had lighted on a mine of wisdom which had been hidden from the rest of mankind, and, with the conceit from which half-educated lads of quick parts are seldom free, proclaimed his discoveries to four or five of his companions. Trinity in unity, he said, was as much a contradiction as a square circle. Ezra was the author of the Pentateuch. The Apocalypse was an allegorical book about the philosopher's stone. Moses had learnt magic in Egypt. Christianity was a delusion which would not last till the year 1800. For this wild talk, of which, in all probability, he would himself have been ashamed long before he was five-and-twenty, he was prosecuted by the Lord Advocate.

Thomas Aikenhead, a twenty-year-old Scottish student, was hanged on this day in 1697, becoming the last person executed for blasphemy in Britain. 'The poor youth at the bar had no counsel. He was altogether unable to do justice to his own cause. He was convicted, and sentenced to be hanged and buried at the foot of the gallows. It was in vain that he with tears abjured his errors and begged piteously for mercy.'

9th – Counterfeit Money

Thursday, 9th Jan. - Yesterday the House of Lords debated the Commons reasons for not agreeing to the Lords' amendments to the

Coinage bill, particularly for making good the deficiency of the clipped money, which the Commons say is equivalent to the raising money, which they will not admit the Lords to do; and after a long debate, the Lords adjourned the further consideration of it till this day, and were upon it again, and adhered to their amendments; so that bill will be lost.

The Commons yesterday in a committee of the whole House upon the coin came to 6 resolutions:

1. That in order to the remedying the ill state of the coin of this kingdom, the recompense to be given for supplying the deficiency of the clipped money shall extend to all clipped money which is silver, though of a coarser alloy than standard.
2. That the collectors and receivers of His Majesty's aids and revenues be enjoined to receive all such moneys.
3. That a reward of 5l. per cent be given to all such as shall bring in either milled or broad unclipped monies to be applied in exchange for the clipped money throughout the kingdom.
4. That a reward of 3d. per ounce be given to all such as shall bring in wrought plate to the mint to be coined.
5. That for the sooner bringing in clipped monies to be recoined, any person may pay in their whole next year's tax of 4s. per pound in the said clipped money at one convenient time to be appointed for that purpose.
6. That commissioners be appointed in every county to pay and distribute the new coined monies, and receive in the clipped monies.

Which resolutions were this day reported to the House and agreed to, and a bill ordered to be brought in thereon.

The election of East Grinstead was also reported this day, and the House agreed with the committee that Sir Thomas Dyke and Mr. Conyers were duly elected.

The bill for laying a duty on windows was read the first time and ordered a second reading.

The Diary of Narcissus Luttrell, Narcissus Luttrell, 1696

Narcissus Luttrell lived from 1657 to 1732, and was an English historian and Minister of Parliament. Luttrell is most well known now for writing *A brief historical relation of state affairs, from September 1678 to April 1714*, from which the above was excerpted. The 'laying a duty on windows' was the Window tax of 1696, which would lead to the infamous 'daylight robbery' in which people with more windows were taxed more – thus leading many to brick up their windows, blocking out daylight.

10th – Laud's Will and Execution

Thus I forgive all the world, and heartily desire forgiveness of God and the world: and so again commend and commit my soul into the hands of God the Father, who gave it, in the merits and mercies of my Blessed Saviour Jesus Christ who redeemed it, and in the peace and comfort of the Holy Ghost who blessed it; and in the truth and unity of his Holy Catholic Church, and in the Communion of the Church of England, as it yet stands established by law.

I most willingly leave the world, being weary at my very heart of the vanities of it, and of my own sins many and great, and of the grievous distractions of the Church of Christ almost in all parts of Christendom, and particularly in this kingdom: which distraction God in his good time make up, who well knows upon what many of them are grounded.

And in token that this is my last will and testament, I have subscribed my name to every page of it, and sealed it in the presence of those whose names are under written.

'William Laud's Will', in *Original letters and other documents relating to the benefactions of William Laud, Archbishop of Canterbury*, 1841

And so ended Archbishop William Laud, who was executed on Tower Hill on this day. Born on 7 October 1573, he became President of St John's College, Oxford in 1611, Bishop of St David's in 1621, Bishop of Bath and Wells in 1626, and Bishop of London in 1628. Laud became one of the most hated men during the reign of King Charles I because of reforms he pushed for within the church that came to be known as Laudianism. This was seen as a step away from Arminianism, which was considered a dangerous and seditious form of Protestantism because of its perceived similarities to Roman Catholicism, for it included a great deal of ritual and ceremony. As such, Arminianism was probably one of the most divisive religious movements in the early Stuart period. King Charles I quite liked High Church rituals and in 1633 he controversially selected William Laud to be the Archbishop of Canterbury – a major position. John Pym was one of the leading critics of Arminianism and he argued for the need to reform the episcopacy. In June of 1640, an angry mob attacked Lambeth Palace – the Archbishop's home in London – with perhaps the intent of killing him. Laud died and remains a controversial figure to this day.

11th – Sloane's Inquisitive Mind

Sir,

I wrote a pretty while ago to you about the Hockesdon earth; which, because I fear it miscarried, I now repeat, desiring your opinion of it ...

The workmen having dug a pit about 6 foot deep, at about 3 yards distance from that end of the cellar which smelt so strong, I there found three several layers of earth one over another, all of them, more or less, having the same scent. The upper-most stratum was clay, or as the workmen call it, Loom. It did not smell till 3 foot deep, but then was very strong, and something noisome. If one look earnestly on some pieces of this clay, there are easily discernable several small quantities of a bituminous substance: brownish colour, and tough consistency.

The second layer was gravel, which reached from 3 and a half to about 4 and a half deep ... the third layer was an earthy sand, which smells stronger than the other two, and withal is much more fragrant.

Letter by Hans Sloane to Mr Ray dated 10 November 1685, from
*Philosophical Letters Between the Late John Ray and Several of His
Correspondents, Natives and Foreigners,* 1718

Sir Hans Sloane, 1st Baronet, a physician and collector, died on this day in 1753. While this date certainly does not fall anywhere near the Stuart period, Sloane was born in 1660 and had a substantial enough impact upon Late Stuart-era history that his inclusion is definitely warranted. The passage above is a good example of the inquisitive cast of Sloane's mind. His name was given to upmarket places such as Sloane Square and Sloane Street. As for drinking chocolate, we have Sloane to thank for that, too, for he first tried the beverage in Jamaica and subsequently brought it to England. He added milk to the mixture instead of water, finding this much more palatable.

*

It was also on this day in 1591 that Robert Devereux, 3rd Earl of Essex, was born to Robert and Frances – both historically important personages. The third earl's father was none other than Robert Devereux, 2nd Earl of Essex, who was once Queen Elizabeth's favourite – and the one who later led the Essex Rebellion against the queen. Frances Walsingham was the daughter of Queen Elizabeth I's spymaster, Francis Walsingham.

12th – Winthrop's Requests

Sweet Heart,

I was unwillingly hindered from coming to thee, nor am I like to see thee before the last day of this week: therefore I shall want a band or 2 & cuffs. I pray thee also send me 6 or 7 leaves of Tobacco dried & powdered. Have care of thy self this cold weather, & speak to the folks to keep the goats well out of the Garden; & if my brother Peter hath not fetched away the sheep ram, let them look him up & give him meat, the green peas in the Garden &c are good for him: If any letters be come for me send them by this bearer. I will trouble thee no further, the Lord blesse & keep thee my sweet wife & all of family: & send us a comfortable meeting, so I kiss thee & love thee ever & rest.

Thy faithful husband, Jo. Winthrop

Letter from John Winthrop to his wife, from *Life and Letters of John Winthrop: Governor of the Massachusetts-Bay Company at Their Emigration to New England, 1630; Vol. 1, 1869*

John Winthrop, one of the founders of the Massachusetts Bay Colony, was born on this day in 1588. In 1630, Winthrop led a large group of fellow Puritans to the New World. Not everything was smooth sailing, however. Winthrop had a difficult time with fellow Puritan Anne Hutchinson, who was excommunicated and later murdered by Native Americans. Although the Puritans in the colony had left England in order to make a new, purer life for themselves and their families, many went back to fight against King Charles I when the English Civil Wars broke out in the 1640s. Winthrop died in Boston, Massachusetts Bay Colony in April 1649.

13th – A Wedding Fit for a Princess

The marriage between Elizabeth Cromwell and John Claypole took place on this day in 1646. Several sources claim that Elizabeth was Cromwell's favourite child, and that she possessed a sweet disposition, although she seems to have suffered from what Cromwell referred to as 'vanity and a carnal mind'. Indeed, she became known for having a very high opinion of herself. Born in July 1629, Elizabeth was the fourth youngest of Cromwell's children, having followed several siblings; she was then herself followed by three more. She was truly the apple of her father's eye. John Michael Wright painted a portrait of Bettie in which she is pictured in a sumptuous dress, with long pearl earrings dangling from her ears and a string of costly pearls encircling her throat. It may amuse the reader to note that John

Michael Wright was also a popular portrait painter during the subsequent Restoration. Wright's most famous portrait is arguably that of Charles II's volatile mistress, Barbara Palmer (*née* Villiers), Lady Castlemaine.

By the time she was sixteen years old, Bettie had fallen in love with the mild-mannered, twenty-two-year-old Parliamentarian soldier – and also her father's Master of the Horse – John Claypole; she was lucky to have been able to marry for love. She and John were happy in each other's embrace and in the showers of gifts they received from her father. Cromwell made Claypole a peer, thus making his daughter Lady Claypole. The couple had several children. In 1655, however, the then twenty-six-year-old Bettie's health began to deteriorate.

In August 1658, and after a horrendously painful ordeal, Bettie died. She was only twenty-nine. Cromwell was inconsolable. The poet Andrew Marvell wrote a beautiful long poem, 'A Poem on the Death of Oliver Cromwell', about the Lord Protector. In this, he alluded to Cromwell's devotion to his daughter when she was on her deathbed. For such a would-be hardman, the death of his favourite child was almost too much for him to bear. His health went into rapid decline, and he died only a few months after Bettie. His son, Richard, became the next Lord Protector.

Bettie was laid to rest in Westminster Abbey, where other members of her family, including her paternal grandmother Elizabeth, were buried. Cromwell would be buried in the abbey as well, but his body was later disinterred and put through a posthumous execution during the Restoration. All other Cromwell family bodies were also disinterred and thrown into a pit outside the abbey. As luck would have it, however, Bettie's tomb remained unnoticed, for it was in another part of the building, and was therefore spared the Stuart revenge.

As for her husband, John, he went on to live until 1688.

*

It was also on this day in 1689 that Thomas Bellingham, a soldier under William III, wrote the following entry in his journal: 'A frost and a thaw. About two this morning Nabby fell into labour, and so continued in much pain till past nine at night, at which time she was delivered of a lusty daughter.' Nabby was Thomas's wife, and childbirth was certainly no walk in the park – it was often fatal for both mother and child. Luckily in this case all seems to have gone well.

14th – Halley's River Calculations

The Mediterranean receives these considerable Rivers: the Iberus, the Rhone, the Tiber, the To, the Danube, the Dneister, the Borysthenes, the Tanais, and the Nile; all the rest being of no great Note, and their Quantity of Water inconsiderable: These nine Rivers, we will suppose each of them to bring down ten times as much Water as the River Thames; not that any of them is so great in reality, but to comprehend with them all the small Rivulets that fell into the Sea, which otherwise I know not how to allow for.

To calculate the Water of the Thames, I assume that at Kingston Bridge where the Flood never reaches, and the Water always runs down, the breadth of the Chanel is 100 Yards, and its Depth 3, it being reduced to an Equality (in both which Suppositions I am sure I take with the most) hence the Profile of the Water in this Place is 300 square Yards: This multiplied by 48 Miles (which I allow the Water to run in 24 hours, at 2 Miles an hour) or 84,480 Yards, gives 25,344,000 Cubic yards of Water to be evacuated every day; that is, 20,300,000 Tons per diem; and I doubt not, but in the excels of my Measures of the Chanel of the River, I have made more than sufficient allowance for the Waters of the Brent, the Wandel, the Lea, and Darwent, which are all worth notice, that fall into the Thames below Kingston.

Miscellanea Curiosa: Being a Collection of Some of the Principal Phænomena in Nature, Accounted for by the Greatest Philosophers of this Age. Together with Several Discourses Read Before the Royal Society, for the Advancement of Physical and Mathematical Knowledge; Vol. 1, Edmond Halley, 1705

Edmond Halley, an English astronomer and physicist, died in Greenwich on this day in 1742. Born in 1656, Halley (pronounced Hal-ee, not Hay-lee) was a major scientist of the Stuart epoch and is best known today for 'Halley's Comet'. As a Fellow and Secretary of the Royal Society, Halley was often collaborating upon and discussing a wide variety of scientific topics with his equally erudite and bright colleagues, including Isaac Newton and Robert Hooke.

15th – Abraham de la Pryme's Dutch Heritage

My father, whose name was Mathias Pryme, was the son of Charles Pryme, my grandfather; he was one of those that came over in King Charles the First days from Flanders, from a city called Eper, upon the draining of the great fens in the Level of Hatfield Chase, but they were most of them undone by their great undertaking, as my grandfather lost many hundred of pounds by it.

My father being grown up to man's estate married Sara the daughter of Mr. Peter Smagge, who was a rich Frenchman, that with his whole family was forced from Paris by persecution for his faith, and was come to live also on these Levels.

They were married April 3rd, in the year 1670, in the Dutch congregation in the chapel at Santoft, for these foreigners had divine service there for many years together, before their chapel was built at Santoft.

I was the first born, and was born the 15th of January in the year 1671 (to all the miseries of life) at a house about the middle of the Levels, about the middle way on the high road side on the left hand as you come straight from the Isle of Axholme, or Haxyhom, from Epworth to the little neat town of Hatfield in Yorkshire, in which parish and which county I was born.

My father can speak Dutch and my mother French, but I nothing yet but English.

The Diary of Abraham de la Pryme,
The British Library Board, Ac.8045/44

Abraham de la Pryme was an English archaeologist and historian, born on this day in 1671. In the late 1690s Pryme became an ordained priest at Holy Trinity Church, in Kingston upon Hull in the East Riding of Yorkshire. Pryme was elected a Fellow of the Royal Society in 1702. He died in 1704, during Queen Anne's reign, at the young age of thirty-three.

16th – Union between England and Scotland

It particularly concerns us in Scotland to act in this matter with the utmost circumspection; for by the Union of the Crowns, which was rash and improvident on our part, we have lost so much of our freedom, substance, and reputation, that if we don't take more care of our interest in the Union of the Nations, we may not only be irrevocably lost as a sovereign and independent kingdom, but brought under the subjection of England, without being allowed the benefit of csubjects.

I don't speak thus to oppose the design of a Union, or to dissuade from a treaty on that head; for I am fully satisfied, that were the nations in a temper fit to engage in the work, with that equanimity and sedateness which the nature of the thing requires, they might both be made happy by an Union; and such a scheme might be agreed upon, as would rectify what is amiss in either of our constitutions, makes us impregnable against usurpations at home, and secure us against invasions from abroad.

My reasons for it are, that our neighbours of England proposed much fairer terms to us before the Union of the Crowns, than ever they have done since; and that from the time of King James VI's accession to their throne, to the beginning of the present reign, there has been a prevalent party in that court, who have been for imposing upon us, in relation both to Church and State.

A Discourse upon the Union of Scotland and England; Humbly submitted to the Parliament of Scotland by a Lover of his Country, Scotland, 1702

Under Queen Anne, the last Stuart monarch, the Scottish Parliament ratified the Act of Union on this day in 1707. From the pamphlet above, which was published anonymously, we can see that the unnamed individual author has some concerns about the union. These sentiments haven't changed, for the union between Scotland and England still remains contentious for many.

17th – Ben Franklin's Stuart-Era Birth

Indeed, from the marriages that have fallen under my observation, I am rather inclined to think that early ones stand the best chance of happiness. The temper and habits of the young are not yet become so stiff and uncomplying, as when more advanced in life; they form more easily to each other, and hence many occasions of disgust are removed. And if youth has less of that prudence which is necessary to manage a family, yet the parents and elder friends of young married persons are generally at hand to afford their advice, which amply supplies that defect; and by early marriage, youth is sooner formed to regular and useful life; and possibly some of those accidents or connections, that might have injured the constitution, or reputation, or both, are thereby happily prevented.

'On Early Marriage', from *Works of the Late Doctor Benjamin Franklin: Consisting of His Life Written by Himself, Together with Essays, Humorous, Moral & Literary, Chiefly in the Manner of the Spectator*, Benjamin Franklin, 1793

One of America's Founding Fathers, Benjamin Franklin was born in Boston on 17 January 1706, during the reign of Queen Anne. Franklin enjoyed a precocious childhood and became a great inventor, author, and statesman – indeed, he was polymath. Franklin moved from Boston to Philadelphia, before moving to London; while there, he attended lectures at the Royal Society – a Stuart-era creation. In 1756, Franklin was awarded an honourary Master's degree from the College of William and Mary, which was founded by Stuart monarchs William and Mary in 1693. A year later he returned to London and resided at 36 Craven Street until 1775. This residence is now the only surviving Franklin home and has been made into a museum. The American War of Independence, or Revolutionary War, took place from 1775 to 1783, ending in independence for the former British colonies – not something the Stuarts would ever have expected.

18th – Admiral Morgan's Capture of Panama

The next morning being the eighteenth, our Admiral (Morgan) gave out very early his orders, to draw out his men in battalia; which was accordingly performed, and they were drawn up in the form of a Tertia. The vanguard, which was led by Lieutenant Colonel Prince, and Major John Morris, was in number three hundred men. The main body, containing six hundred men, the right wing thereof was led by the Admiral, and the left by Colonel Edward Collier ...

At three o'clock in the afternoon, we had quiet possession of the city, although in flames, with no more loss on our side in this day's work than five men killed, and ten wounded, but of the enemy four hundred. And now were we forced to put all hands to work for the quenching the fire of our enemy's houses, which they themselves had kindled to disappoint us of the plunder, but all our labour was in vain, for by twelve o'clock at night, the whole city was burnt, except a part of the suburbs, which with our great industry, we made a shift to save, being two churches, and about three hundred houses.

Excerpt from *Admiral Morgan's Expedition against Panama*,
The British Library Board, 278.c.6

And so it was that Admiral Henry Morgan, the notorious Welsh privateer, captured Panama on this day in 1671. Although we now tend to think of him as a pirate, Morgan himself was strongly against being referred to as such. He successfully sued a publisher in the 1680s after it stated he was a 'pirate' instead of 'privateer' and won £200 in damages. Morgan died a very wealthy man in 1688. In modern times, Henry Morgan is most associated with a brand of rum that is named after him, which is rather appropriate given how much he loved to drink.

19th – Marcus Gheeraerts the Younger

Marcus Gheeraerts the Younger, court portraitist during the Elizabethan and Jacobean periods, died on 19 January 1636. Marcus was the son of Marcus Gheeraerts the Elder (*c.* 1520/21– *c.* 1586), a Flemish painter best known for his painting of Queen Elizabeth I entitled *The Peace Portrait* (1580–5). Some other examples of his work from the Tudor period include *Portrait of a Woman* (*c.* 1590–1600), Portrait of Mary Rogers, Lady Harington (1592), and the *Ditchley Portrait* of Queen Elizabeth I (*c.* 1592).

The younger Gheeraerts became better known and gained fame as a portraitist with the Stuarts, in particular Queen Anne of Denmark, who sat for him several times. One of the most striking portraits of Anne by Gheeraerts is the half-length portrait from 1614 in which she wears an embroidered cream dress with flashes of crimson in her hair, at her breasts, and on her left arm. Gheeraerts also painstakingly added not only the lace on Anne's dress, but also the many strands of pearls which graced her wrist, bodice, and neck. This portrait, now kept in the Royal Collection, is magnificent to behold in person.

In 1620, Gheeraerts painted *Portrait of a Woman in Red*, a depiction of a heavily pregnant woman who, according to the Tate, where the portrait now resides, is currently believed to be Anne, wife of Sir Philip Constable Baronet, of Everingham, Yorkshire.

*

Also on this day in 1676, John Weldon, the English Baroque composer, was born. The Chichester-born Weldon was educated at Eton, where he was a chorister. Arguably his most popular piece of music was 'Take, O take those Lips away' with lyrics from William Shakespeare's play *Measure for Measure*.

20th – 'Jesuits in Their Dark Cells'

To Mr En. P. at Paris.
Sir,
    That which the plots of the Jesuits in their dark cells, and the policy of the greatest Roman Catholic princes have driven at these many years, is now done to their hands, which was to divide and break the strength of these three kingdoms, because they held it to be too great a glory and power to be in one heretical Prince's hands, (as they esteemed the King of Great Britain) because he was in a capacity to be umpire, if not arbiter of this part of the world, as many of our kings have been.
    You write thence, that in regard of the sad condition of our Queen, their countrywoman, they are sensible of our calamities; but

I believe, it is the populace only, who see no further than the rind of things: your cabinet-council rather rejoiceth at it, who, or I am much deceived, contributed much in the time of the late sanguine Cardinal, to set a-foot these distractions, beginning first with Scotland, who, you know, hath always served that nation for a brand to set England a-fire for the advancement of their own ends. I am afraid we have seen our best days: we knew not when we were well, so that the Italian saying may be well applied to poor England, I was well, I would be better, I took physic and died. No more now, but that I rest still

Yours entirely to serve you, J.H. (James Howell).

Letter LXXVII, from Familiar letters on Important Subjects, wrote from the year 1618 to 1650, James Howell, 1753

If the above seems miserable and downright depressing, there is certainly good cause for it. James Howell, an Anglo-Welsh historian, was living in one of the most tumultuous times in the whole of the Stuart era – the English Civil Wars. He survived this period, although it included an eight-year stint in the Fleet prison, and died in 1666 – six years after the Restoration. During his lifetime he published several books and pamphlets, including, but not limited to, *Casuall Discourses, and Interlocutions betwixt Patricius and Peregrin* (1642), and *Poems on Severall Choice and Various Subjects* (1663).

21st – Shaftesbury's Speech

My Lord, I hear of a bargain in the House of Commons, and an address made to the king; but this I know, and must boldly say it and plainly, that the nation is betray'd if upon any terms we part with our money till we are sure the king is ours; have what laws you will, and what conditions you will, they will be of no use but wastepaper before Easter, if the Court have money to set up for Popery and Arbitrary Designs in the meanwhile.

On the other hand give me leave to tell you, my Lords, the King hath no reason to distrust his people; no man can go home and say, that if the King comply with his people they will do nothing for him, but tear all up from him. We want a government and we want a prince that we may trust, even with the spending of half our Annual Revenues, for some time, for the preservation of these nations.

The growing greatness of the French cannot be stopped with a little expense, not without a real and hearty union of the King and his people.

A speech lately made by a noble peer of the realm, Anthony Ashley Cooper, 1st Earl of Shaftesbury, 1681

Anthony Ashley Cooper, 1st Earl of Shaftesbury, died on this day in 1683, during the reign of Charles II. Shaftesbury is notable for his strong resistance to having James, Duke of York, as Charles II's heir, and for the Exclusion Bill, which he supported. This bill was an attempt to exclude James from the line of succession on the grounds of his Catholicism. Shaftesbury was adamantly opposed to a possible Catholic succession.

22nd – The Distempers of Learning

Here therefore [is] the first distemper of learning, when men study words and not matter; whereof, though I have represented an example of late times, yet it hath been and will be *secundum majus et minus* in all time. And how is it possible but this should have an operation to discredit learning, even with vulgar capacities, when they see learned men's works like the first letter of a patent, or limned book; which though it hath large flourishes, yet it is but a letter? It seems to me that Pygmalion's frenzy is a good emblem or portraiture of this vanity: for words are but the images of matter; and except they have life of reason and invention, to fall in love with them is all one as to fall in love with a picture.

But yet notwithstanding it is a thing not hastily to be condemned, to clothe and adorn the obscurity even of philosophy itself with sensible and plausible elocution. For hereof we have great examples in Xenophon, Cicero, Seneca, Plutarch, and of Plato also in some degree; and hereof likewise there is great use: for surely, to the severe inquisition of truth and the deep progress into philosophy, it is some hindrance; because it is too early satisfactory to the mind of man, and quencheth the de sire of further search, before we come to a just period. But then if a man be to have any use of such knowledge in civil occasions, of conference, counsel, persuasion, discourse, or the like, then shall he find it prepared to his hands in those authors which write in that manner. But the excess of this is so justly contemptible, that as Hercules, when he saw the image of Adonis, Venus' minion, in a temple, said in disdain, *Nil sacri es*; so there is none of Hercules' followers in learning, that is, the more severe and laborious sort of inquirers into truth, but will despise those delicacies and affectations, as indeed capable of no divineness. And thus much of the first disease or distemper of learning.

The second which followeth is in nature worse than the former: for as substance of matter is better than beauty of words, so contrariwise vain matter is worse than vain words: wherein it seemeth the reprehension of Saint Paul was not only proper for those times, but prophetical for the times following; and not only respective to divinity, but extensive to all knowledge: *Devita profanas vocum novitates, et oppositiones falsi nominis scientice.*

The Advancement of Learning, Francis Bacon, 1605

Francis Bacon, Viscount St Alban, was born on this day in 1561. Although this date falls firmly within the Tudor period, Bacon's life and influence continued on into the age of the Stuarts; he died in 1626. Bacon was a learned philosopher and scientist who developed the Baconian method; he was so talented that some people impute to his authorship the works of William Shakespeare.

Controversy entered his life when he was accused of corruption, causing his resignation from office. The manner in which Bacon died has been a source of much mirth in the centuries since his death. 'He caught cold after freezing a chicken' is an oft-told story for children. Indeed, Bacon was in the process of running an experiment on the preservation of meat and he did in fact catch a chill which led to pneumonia. As for his wife, within less than a fortnight she remarried.

23rd – Baffin's Adventures

Now was the land, both mountainous and plain, wholly covered with snow, so that almost all men's minds were possessed with a desire of returning for England. But to prevent a sudden resolution for a homeward voyage, without further satisfaction, I made mention that once again we might go forth with our shallops, to see what alterations there might be found along the shore. It fell out that I was to go in one shallop for this purpose, so I took with me eight men, and went from our ship the fifteenth day of August.

We rowed to Red-cliffe Sound, where we passed through much ice that was newly congealed, being thicker than a half crown piece of silver, notwithstanding we broke away through it; then we proceeded to Red-beach, where, finding the shore clear of ice (which, at my last being there, was wonderfully pestered), I conceived good hope to find passage to the futherest land from thence in sight, bearing east half a point southerly, nine or ten leagues distant; to this end we put off from the shore of Red-beach, and rowed a league and more in an open sea, and was no hindrance to our proceeding, so that we continued rowing the space of six hours, in which time we had gotten more than halfway over; but then we found the ice to lie very thick thronged together, so that it caused us much to alter our course, sometimes southward, and sometimes northward. And even in this time, when we thought we stood in most need of clear weather, it pleased God to send us the contrary, for it began to snow very fast ...

The Third Recorded Voyage of William Baffin: A Voyage of Discovery to Greenland, etc., R. O. Fotherbye, 1614

William Baffin, a major English navigator and explorer, died from a gunshot wound near Qeshm (in Iran) on this day in 1622. Baffin was born around 1584, possibly in the London area, and was a member of Captain James Hall's 1612 expedition to discover the highly sought-after Northwest Passage around the North American continent. According to the same work cited above, the native Inuit murdered Captain Hall. Baffin's own attempts to discover a Northwest Passage ended with his discovery of the bay, which lies between Greenland to the north and an island in the Nunavet territory of modern Canada. The bay was named Baffin's Bay, and the island, which is the largest in Canada, became Baffin's Island.

24th – Congreve's Love for Love

The husbandman in vain renews his toil
To cultivate each year a hungry soil;
And fondly hopes for rich and generous fruit,
When what should feed the tree devours the root
Th' unladen boughs, he sees, bode certain dearth,
Unless transplanted to more kindly earth.
So the poor husbands of the stage, who found
Their labours lost upon ungrateful ground,
This last and only remedy have proved,
And hope new fruit from ancient stocks removed.
Well may they hope, when you so kindly aid,
Well plant a soil which you so rich have made.
As Nature gave the world to man's first age,
So from your bounty, we receive this stage;
The freedom man was born to, you've restored,
And to our world such plenty you afford,
It seems like Eden, fruitful of its own accord.
But since in Paradise frail flesh gave way,
And when but two were made, both went astray;
Forbear your wonder, and the fault forgive,
If in our larger family we grieve
One falling Adam and one tempted Eve.
We who remain would gratefully repay
What our endeavours can, and bring this day

The first-fruit offering of a virgin play.
We hope there's something that may please each taste,
And though of homely fare we make the feast,
Yet you will find variety at least.
There's humour, which for cheerful friends we got,
And for the thinking party there's a plot.
We've something, too, to gratify ill-nature,
(If there be any here), and that is satire.
Though satire scarce dares grin, 'tis grown so mild
Or only shows its teeth, as if it smiled.
As asses thistles, poets mumble wit,
And dare not bite for fear of being bit:
They hold their pens, as swords are held by fools,
And are afraid to use their own edge-tools.
Since the Plain-Dealer's scenes of manly rage,
Not one has dared to lash this crying age.
This time, the poet owns the bold essay,
Yet hopes there's no ill-manners in his play;
And he declares, by me, he has designed
Affront to none, but frankly speaks his mind.
And should th' ensuing scenes not chance to hit,
He offers but this one excuse, 'twas writ
Before your late encouragement of wit.

'Prologue', *Love for Love*, William Congreve (1670–1729)

William Congreve, an English playwright and poet, was born in Yorkshire, England, on this day in 1670. Although born in England, he was educated in Dublin, before moving to London to study law. It was in London, however, that he turned his hand to writing, and in 1692 he used a nom de plume, Cleophil, to publish *Incognita*. His comedic works include the above excerpted piece, *Love for Love* (1695), but also *The Old Bachelor* (1693), and *The Double Dealer* (1694). Congreve had his portrait painted by Sir Godfrey Kneller in 1709, and for it he wore a rather sizeable dirty blond periwig. Congreve didn't only write comedy; he wrote a rather popular tragedy in 1697 entitled *The Mourning Bride*. William never married, but he did have a relationship with Henrietta, Lady Godolphin, the daughter of John and Sarah Churchill, 1st Duke and Duchess of Marlborough; this illicit romance resulted in a daughter. Congreve died in 1729, possibly as a result of internal injuries sustained following a coach accident in late 1728, and left Henrietta's husband as the executor of his estate.

25th – Boyle and the Cartesian Argument

To begin with the first question; Those that would exclude final causes from the consideration of the naturalist, are wont to do it (for ought I have observ'd) upon one of these two accounts: Either, that with Epicurus they think the world was the production of atoms and chance, without any intervention of a deity, and that consequently 'tis improper and in vain to seek for final causes in the effects of chance. Or, that they judge with Descartes, that God being an omniscient agent, 'tis rash and presumptuous for men to think, that they know, or can investigate, what ends he propos'd to himself in his actings about his creatures. The ground on which the Epicureans have rejected final causes, has been disallow'd by the philosophers of almost all other sects; and some have written sufficient confutations of it, which therefore I shall here forbear to insist on; though somethings I shall upon occasion observe, that may help, if not suffice, to discredit so unreasonable an opinion. But the Cartesian argument has been so prevalent among many learned and ingenious men, that it will be worthwhile (if it be but to excite better pens) to spend some time in the consideration of it.

A Disquisition about the Final Causes of Natural Things:
Wherein it is Inquir'd, Whether, and (if at All) with what
Cautions, a Naturalist Should Admit Them?, Robert Boyle, 1688

Robert Boyle, Anglo-Irish physicist, was born on this day in 1627. Boyle was one of the founders of the Royal Society. In 1661, Robert Boyle published *The Sceptical Chymist*, but he's best known for Boyle's Law from 1662, which states that the pressure of a gas is inversely proportional to the volume when at a fixed temperature, or $PV = k$. A portrait of Boyle hangs to this day in Kensington Palace, and Eton College has a copy from 1673 of Boyle's *Tracts ... concerning new experiments, touching the relation betwixt flame and air.*

26th – 'No More Will I My Passion Hide'

No more will I my passion hide,
Though too presuming it appear,
When long despair a heart has tried,
What other torment can I fear?
Unlov'd of her I would not live,
Nor die till she the sentence give.

Why should the fair offended be,
If virtue charm in beauty's dress?
If where so much divine I see
My open vows the Saint confess?
Amaz'd by wonders in her eyes,
My former idols I despise.

'A Song by Mr Wolseley', *A New Miscellany of Original Poems,
on Several Occasions*, 1701

27th – Moore's Sermon

For as it is not to be conceived that a man should bring himself to be
quiet and easy under an evil that presses down hard upon him, unless
it be in hopes by his patience to get rid of it, or to mend his condition.
So it is manifest that they, who believe little or nothing themselves of
a future state, cannot be stored with true arguments to prevail upon
a man to be patient under a sequestration from the happiness and
pleasures of this life.

For where will they find just motives to reduce him to a composed
mind, who by a fire or a storm has his estate swept away, or by a
malicious story his reputation blasted, or by the acute pains of a
disease his body weakened beyond hopes of recovery, if neither they
nor he are possessed with a persuasion that, being gone of this stage,
they shall live again, and receive the recompense of their virtue? And
with what conscience could the philosophers upbraid and reproach
men in distress for their grief and complaints, passions most natural
to their condition, when all they could offer to comfort them fell
short of an equivalent to their present losses and misfortunes?

I am to explain the nature of patience. By patience, in the most
comprehensive sense of it, we are to understand that Christian virtue,
whereby with a calm and even mind, we do not only bear pains,
injuries, losses, and reproaches, but perform all those duties, that are
difficult, tedious, irksome to flesh and blood, which our religion does
require, and when it is for the sake of our Lord.

Sir John Moore preached the above sermon before the Lord Mayor and
the Court of Aldermen at the Guildhall Chapel in London on 27 January
1684. John Moore was Bishop of Ely and was a chaplain to William and
Mary from 1689.

28th – Bodley's Difficult Childhood

I was born at Exeter in Devonshire, the 2nd of March, in the Year 1544; descended, both by father and mother of worshipful parentage. By my father's side, from an ancient family of Bodley, or Bodleigh, of Dunscombe by Crediton; and by my mother from Robert Hone Esq; of Offerey Saint Mary, nine miles from Exeter. My father in the time of Queen Mary, being noted and known to be an enemy to Popery, was so cruelly threatened, and so narrowly observed by those that maliced his religion, that for the safeguard of himself and my mother, who was wholly affected as my father, he knew no way so secure, as to fly into Germany; where after a while, he found means to call over my mother, with all his children and family; whom he settled for a time at Wesel in Cleveland (for there as then were many English, which had left their country, for their conscience, and with quietness enjoyed their meetings and preachings) and from thence we removed to the town of Frankford, where was in like sort another English congregation. Howbeit we made no long tarriance in either of those two towns, for that my father had resolved to fix his abode in the city of Geneva: where (as far as I remember) the English Church consisted of some hundred persons. I was at that time of 12 years of age …

*Reliquiæ Bodleianæ: or Some Genuine Remains of
Sir Thomas Bodley*, ed. T. Hearne, 1703

Sir Thomas Bodley, English courtier, was born on 2 March 1545. He is best known as the founder of the Bodleian Library at the University of Oxford. In his autobiography, from which we have taken the above excerpt, Bodley went on to say how he learned texts in Hebrew and Greek, and how he listened to passages from Homer. Although persecuted under Queen Mary, his family returned to England when she died and her half-sister Elizabeth ascended the throne. It was during the Elizabethan era that the Earl of Essex and his forces raided the wealthy Portuguese town of Faro and plundered what they could, including items from a bishop's library. This latter Essex gave to Bodley, his friend. Bodley died on 28 January 1613.

29th – A King Sentenced to Death

At the High Court of Justice for the Trying and Judging of CHARLES STUART, King of England, Jan. 29. 1648.

Whereas CHARLES STUART, King of England, is and standeth Convicted, Attainted and Condemned of High Treason, and other High Crimes, and Sentence upon Saturday last was pronounced against him by this Court, to be put to Death, by the severing of his Head from his Body, of which Sentence Execution yet remaineth to be done; These are therefore to Will and Require you to see the said Sentence Executed in the open Street before Whitehall, upon the Morrow being the Thirtieth Day of this Instant Month of January, between the Hours of Ten in the Morning, and Five in the Afternoon of the same Day, with full Effect. And for so doing, this shall be your sufficient Warrant. And these are to require all Officers, Soldiers and others, the Good People of this Nation of England, to be assisting unto you in this Service.

The Lord Clarendon's History of the Grand Rebellion, 1717

So read the Death Warrant of Charles I. On 27 January, the High Court of Justice had found the king guilty and sentenced him to death. General Thomas Fairfax famously refused to sign the warrant; as he was one of the most influential men on the Parliamentary side, he would have come under pressure to sign it. He did not attend the king's execution the following day, but remained at prayer. It was on this day that King Charles had his last meeting with two of his children, Elizabeth and Henry. It was a moving and tearful parting.

30th – Charles I's Execution

King Charles I of England was executed on 30 January 1649, constituting one of the most important events in British history, let alone Stuart history. Kings had certainly been killed, but never before had one been found guilty – albeit by a sort of kangaroo court – and publicly executed. Several days after Charles I had been executed on that bitterly cold January morning in 1649, a Royalist work was printed. *Eikon Basilike* was an extremely popular piece, and the deceased king became seen by some as a martyr. This work, however, was countered by Parliamentarian propaganda from the very able hand of John Milton in the form of *Eikonoklastes*.

Three decades later, in 1680, Elkanah Settle's treatise entitled *The Character of a Popish Successor, and What England may Expect from such a One* described the executed king as 'that Royal Martyr Charles the First, a Prince so truly pious, that his very enemies dare not asperse his Memory of Life with the least blemish of Irreligion; a prince that seal'd the Protestant Faith with his blood, who in his deplorable fate and ignominious death, bore so near a resemblance to that of the Saviour's of the World, that his suffering can do no less than seat him at the right hand of heaven'.

On 30 January 1692, Richard Bynns preached a sermon before the House of Commons. In this he said many things with references to Charles I's execution:

The 30th of January stands in our calendar a memorial, and as much a witness against those factious anti-monarchical men as that other of the 5th of November against that daring Popish impiety. They both aim'd at the public ruin, though the one happily miscarried in the attempt, the other as unhappily took effect, and it was then their power of darkness.

George Smalridge mentioned in his speech 'that black treason, which hath made this day unto us a day of shame and reproach, a day of mourning and lamentation'.

31st – Gilbert Burnet to the House of Commons

On this day in 1689, Gilbert Burnet preached a sermon before the House of Commons.

There is no instinct that is stronger and more universal, than the desire of Happiness: there is a charm in the sound of the word, which overcomes every one as soon as it is heard. If some noble minds have a largeness of soul which carries them beyond all narrow and partial regards, yet these do most passionately desire to see the happiness of the country. And it must be confessed, that to see one's country happy, and to feel one's self happy, are provocations to joy, which few men can possibly resist.

But there are perhaps very few that have the notion of Happiness, which the psalmist here sets forth. For, having considered all those blessings which are apt to make the greatest impressions on human nature, such as goodly sons, and beautiful daughters, full granaries of all sorts, fruitful flocks of sheep, and cattle fit to cultivate the ground; and the enjoying of all this so securely, that no enemy from without should break upon them, and that no disorder within should drive any away, or give so much as occasion to discontent or complaining in any part of their country or fields, rendered here streets. Upon all this he pronounces, that the people was indeed happy that in such a case; but that, after all this catalogue of blessings summed up and set together, there was a Happiness that far exceeded it. It is true, this opposition is set forth with these words: A People that is in such a case has been esteemed or called happy; but happy is the people whose God is the Lord; as if all other happiness was only imaginary, this being the only real one. And it is certain, that if we can find a nation that has both these, we must esteem it happy, without diminution or comparison.

FEBRUARY

1st – Settle and the Empress of Morocco

Condemn'd to fetters, and to sceptres born!
'Tis in this garb unhappy princes mourn.
Yet Fortune to great Courage is kind;
'Tis he wants Liberty whose soul's confin'd.
My thoughts out-fly that mightly conqueror,
Who having one world vanquish'd, wept for more:
Fetter'd in empires, he enlargement crav'd
To the short walk of one poor globe enslav'd.
My soul mounts higher, and Fate's pow'r disdains,
And makes me reign a monarch in my chains.
But 'tis my Father has decreed my fate;
Yet he shows his greatness in his hate.

Act I: Scene I, *The Empress of Morocco*, Elkanah Settle

Elkanah Settle, an English playwright, political pamphleteer and poet, was born on this day in 1648 to Josias and Sarah Settle. Baptised a few days later on 9 February, Elkanah's early life was largely uneventful until he became a King's Scholar at Westminster at the age of fifteen. 1666, the year which saw the horrors of the Great Fire of London, was a comparatively good year for Settle. He wrote his first play, *Cambyses: King of Persia*, which he was fortunate to have had performed by William Davenant's company – and to great success. Most notable among his works were *The Ambitious Slave: Or, A Generous Revenge* (1694), *The Conquest of China, by the Tartars* (1676), and the *Empress of Morocco* (1673). According to Settle's early twentieth-century biographer F. C. Brown, Settle managed to offend not only Poet Laureate John Dryden but the admired writers Thomas Shadwell and John Crowne, who, envious of the young upstart's increasing popularity, ganged up and slandered him. In terms of political allegiance, Settle is known for switching from the Whigs to the Tories, and his political pamphlets – particularly during the Late Stuart era – show how much he advocated a Protestant succession. The only play of Settle's that has survived is his *Love and Revenge: A Tragedy* from 1674, and perhaps it is this scarcity – and the fact his work was rather lacklustre in comparison with some of his peers – that accounts for him being so largely forgotten today.

2nd – Lister's Journey to Paris

I happily arrived at Paris after a tedious journey in very bad weather; for we set out of London on the 10th of December, and I did not reach Paris till the first of January; for I fell sick upon the road, and stayed five days in Bologne, behind the company, till my fever abated. Yet notwithstanding so rude a journey, I recovered, and was perfectly cured of my cough in ten days; which was the chiefest reason of my leaving London at that time of the year, and never had the least return of it all the Winter, thought it was as fierce there as ever I felt it in England. This great benefit of the French air I had experiences three times before, and had therefore longed for a passage many years; but the continuance of the War was an insuperable obstacle to my desires.

A Journey to Paris in the Year 1698,
Dr Martin Lister, 1699

Martin Lister (1639–1712), an English physician, died on this day in 1712, during the reign of Queen Anne. *A Journey to Paris in the Year 1698*, quoted above, is a truly fascinating work. It clearly shows what an English gentleman thought of Paris in the late seventeenth century! For the Stuart-era devotee, it is a must-read. Lister's entry gives a clear example of how a nasty illness can wreck one's travel plans. The war mentioned was the Nine Years' War between the French, ruled by King Louis XIV, and the Grand Alliance of Spain, the Holy Roman Empire, and the Anglo-Dutch alliance under King William III. The tentative peace that came with the Treaty of Rijswijk in 1697 was all but temporary – a few years later, the Spanish King Carlos II died and France decided to claim Spanish territory, which then began the War of the Spanish Succession (1701–14).

3rd – 'Of Love'

Anger, in hasty words or blows,
Itself discharges on our foes;

And sorrow, too, finds some relief
In tears, which wait upon our grief;
So every passion, but fond love,
Unto its own redress does move;
But that alone the wretch inclines
To what prevents his own designs;
Makes him lament, and sigh, and weep,
Disorder'd, tremble, fawn, and creep;
Postures which render him despised,
Where he endeavours to be prized.

For women (born to be controll'd)
Stoop to the forward and the bold;
Affect the haughty and the proud,
The gay, the frolic, and the loud.
Who first the gen'rous steed oppress'd,
Not kneeling did salute the beast;
But with high courage, life, and force,
Approaching, tamed th'unruly horse.

Unwisely we the wiser East
Pity, supposing them oppress'd
With tyrants' force, whose law is will,
By which they govern, spoil and kill:
Each nymph, but moderately fair,
Commands with no less rigour here.
Should some brave Turk, that walks among
His twenty lasses, bright and young,
And beckons to the willing dame,
Preferr'd to quench his present flame,
Behold as many gallants here,
With modest guise and silent fear,
All to one female idol bend,
While her high pride does scarce descend
To mark their follies, he would swear
That these her guard of eunuchs were,
And that a more majestic queen,
Or humbler slaves, he had not seen.

All this with indignation spoke,
In vain I struggled with the yoke
Of mighty Love; that conqu'ring look,
When next beheld, like lightning strook
My blasted soul, and made me bow
Lower than those I pitied now.

So the tall stag, upon the brink
Of some smooth stream about to drink,
Surveying there his armed head,
With shame remembers that he fled
The scorned dogs, resolves to try
The combat next; but if their cry
Invades again his trembling ear,
He straight resumes his wonted care,
Leaves the untasted spring behind,
And, wing'd with fear, outflies the wind.

'Of Love', Edmund Waller

Edmund Waller, an English poet and politician, was born on this day in 1606, during the early part of King James I's reign. Waller was educated at Eton College and then the University of Cambridge. Waller died in 1687, during the reign of King James II.

4th – Bellingham's Sore Toe

A moist morning. I was with Dr Roe and some of the officers at ale. My toe pains me very much. I received a note to be assisting to a friend, which I answered and composed the difference.

Thomas Bellingham, as found in his Diary for 4 February 1689

Thomas Bellingham's previous entry for 3 February stated he had a sore toe, and it clearly got worse for him. What could it have been? An ingrown toenail? Gout? The amusing thing about this entry is that it makes him more real somehow. Sometimes historical texts – including diaries – don't have that special human touch, which Bellingham certainly has.

5th – A Good Match

Dear Mother,
Since my coming to town I met with Sir John Bourchier, who hath propounded a good match for my cousin M----, if you and her father shall approve it. The gentleman is Sir William Strickland of Yorkshire, a widower of 32 years of age, having 4 daughters very young and a fair estate between 1500 per annum and 2000 after his father's death, aged between 60ty and 80ty years, and during his father's life but 300 per annum for his present maintenance. My cousin gives a

very good report of the gentleman, who desires to have a sight of her privately, without any notice till approbation, and therefore you shall do well to keep this very private and to acquaint Sir William Mewis with this proposition forthwith, that upon his answer you may take some resolution. The main discouragement is the far distance from Sir William, yet other things may make amends. I pray let me know your mind by the next, and I shall be ready to do you or yours any service, best respects to all my friends with you, I commit you to God and rest yours obliged.

> Letter dated 5 February 1631, from *Barrington Family Letters*
> *1628–1632*, Sir William Masham

Sir William Masham, 1st Baronet, was born around 1592 and became a politician in the 1620s. He sat in the House of Commons.

6th – Charles II's Death

On Monday last in the Morning, our late Gracious Sovereign, King Charles II, was seized with a violent fit by which his speech and senses were for some a time taken from him; but upon the immediate application of fitting remedies, he returned to a such a condition as gave some hopes of his recovery, till Wednesday night; at which time the Disease returning upon him with greater Violence, he Expired this Day about Noon ... In King Charles's Case, there appeared no visible Cause, either near or remote, to which, with any certainty of reason, his disease could be ascribed; and the Forerunners of it were rather to be found in the Stomach and Bowels, than in the Head. For after he was a-Bed, he was overheard to Groan most part of the night; And both then, and next Morning, before he fell into the Fit, he complained first of a heavy oppression in his Stomach, and about his Heart, and afterwards of a sharp pain in those Parts; all which Symptoms had but little relation to an apoplexy.

> *A Complete History Of England: With The Lives Of All The Kings*
> *and Queens Thereof: From The Earliest Account of Time, to the*
> *Death of His Late Majesty King William III*, 1706

King Charles II died on this day in 1685, following a stroke and an array of treatments from his physicians. The 'Merry Monarch' died in conditions that can only be described as the opposite of 'merry' – they were downright ghastly.

7th – A Fearful Fire

Monday, 1633, began by God's just hand a fearful fire in the house of one Mr. John Brigges, near ten of the clock at night; it burnt down his house with all the goods that were in it; and as I hear, that Brigges, his wife, his child, and maid escaped with their lives very hardly, having on their bodies but their shirts and smocks; and the fire burnt so fiercely that it could not be quenched till it had burnt down all the houses on both sides of the way, from St. Magnus Church to the first open place. And although there was water enough very near, yet they could not safely come at it. But all the conduits near were opened, and the pipes that carried water through the streets were cut open, and the water swept down with brooms, with help enough; but it was the will of God it should not prevail. And the hand of God was more seen in this, in as much as no means could prosper. For the three engines, which are such excellent things, yet none of these did prosper, they were broken, and the tide was very low, that they could get no water, and the pipes that were cut yielded but little water. Some ladders were broke to the hurt of many, for some had their legs broke, some their arms; some their ribs were broke, and some lost their lives. This fire burnt fiercely all night, and part of the next day (for my man was there about twelve o'clock, and said he did see the furthest house on fire), till all was burnt and pulled down to the ground; yet the timber, wood and coals in the cellars could not be quenched all that week, till Tuesday following in the afternoon, the 19th of February, for I was there then myself, and had a live coal of a fire in my hand.

Historical Notices of Events Occurring Chiefly in the Reign of
Charles I,
Nehemiah Wallington, 1869

8th – Mary and Bothwell

With a difficulty not to be imagined, not to be expressed, do I get the opportunity of writing this. My bodily indisposition, joined to the troubles of my mind, render me incapable of invention. I suffer my self to endure the eternal presence of the persons I most hate, rather than be at the pains of making an excuse to be alone. That spirit, that courage, which was used to bear me through the greatest fatigues, is now evaporated and extinct. A laziness of soul possesses me, I cannot think, cannot resolve on any thing – assist me in this perplexity, my dear Bothwell, advise me, comfort me, find some way for my relief. I have no friend but you, and sure, if you are such, you will not suffer me long to endure these insults. But what is it I am asking? 'Tis dangerous to be loyal. Poor Rizzio, only because he loved his queen, fell a sacrifice to the tyranny of this injurious husband. My life is next, nor am I spared, but for the sake of the unborn heir of empire; delivered once of that dear burden, my business in this world is done, and Darnley will reign alone.

I know my death alone can gratify the ambition of that ungrateful man, or the unceasing malice of the English Queen.

Mary Queen of Scots to the Earl of Bothwell, from *The Genuine Letters of Mary Queen of Scots to James Earl of Bothwell*, 1726

The matriarch of the Stuart family in England, Mary Queen of Scots, was executed in Fotheringhay Castle in Northamptonshire, England, on this day in 1587. What had led to such a violent end? It's a long and tragic story. Mary was born to King James V of Scotland, the son of Margaret Tudor, and his French queen, Marie of Guise. Mary became Queen of Scotland when she was only a few days old because of her father's premature death. Aged five, the young queen was betrothed to Francis, the Dauphin of France, whom she married a decade later. Mary lived in France for most of her formative years and teens, and was therefore more French than Scottish in manner. Francis died – aged just sixteen – in 1560, and the widowed teenager Mary returned to Scotland. It was in this same year that Mary lost her mother, Marie of Guise, as well.

Mary unwisely chose to marry the handsome but lecherous Henry Stuart, Lord Darnley. In 1566, Mary gave birth to a son, James – who would become King James VI of Scotland, and later King James I of England. Early in 1567 a large explosion rocked Kirk O'Field, where Darnley was staying, and he was murdered. Although many plotters were involved, Mary and the Earl of Bothwell were chiefly blamed. In April of that same year, Bothwell took Mary to Dunbar Castle where she either consented to have sex with him or was raped – this remains unclear – but she did end up marrying him. Because of the fact that Mary descended from Henry VII, she was a claimant to the throne of England, and this made her a dangerous rival for Elizabeth; she was put under house arrest in various places. It was during her long imprisonment that Mary became involved in a plot to assassinate Queen Elizabeth in order to take the throne herself. It took several blows to sever her head from her body; notoriously, when the executioner picked up her head to display to the onlookers, her head fell down because she had been wearing a wig. Those who wish to visit modern-day Fotheringhay Castle should be advised that only a tiny bit of the castle remains.

*

It was also on this day in 1693 that King William III and Mary II issued a charter to create the College of William and Mary in the colony of Virginia. The college is the second-oldest educational institution in America. The Wren Building is the oldest building at the College of William & Mary and is named after Sir Christopher Wren. Several Presidents of the United States have attended the College of William & Mary, including the third president Thomas Jefferson. After his time as the first president, George Washington became the college Chancellor. The College of William & Mary remains a thriving and respected university.

9th – The Murder of an Illegitimate Child

At the coal delivery for Newgate, my Lord Bridgeman, myself, and my brother Wylde, Recorder of London, being present: Ann Davis was indicted for murdering her male bastard child, and the indictment was not special as the Statute is for concealing it. But the Indictment was *quod Infantem masculum vivum parturiit qui quidem infans masculus adtunc & ibid. vivus existens natus per legem hujus regni Angli'spurius fuit*, Anglice, a bastard, and then goeth on in the ordinary form, that she murdered it, and doth not conclude *Cotra formam Statut* ...

The evidence it appeared, that the Prisoner lived in a chamber by herself, and went to bed on Thursday night well, without any pain, and in the middle of the same night waked full of pain, and knocked for some body to come to her, and one woman heard her knock, but came not to her, and the same night she was delivered of a child, and after, she put the child in a trunk, and did not discover it till Friday night following, and all this was found specially to have the advice of all the judges, whether that knocking for help at the time of her travail (although she conceal'd it after one day) exempts her from that Statute.

A Report of Divers Cases in Pleas of the Crown. Adjudged and Determined; in the Reign of the Late King Charles II. [1662-1669] With Directions for Justices of the Peace and Others. Collected by Sir John Kelyng, Knt ... From the Original Manuscript, Under His Own Hand. To which are Added, the Reports of Three Modern Cases, Viz. Armstrong and Lisle; the King and Plumer; the Queen and Mawgridge, 1732.

10th – Suckling's Cavalier Poetry

This one request I make to him that sits the clouds above,
That I were freely out of Debt, as I am out of Love;

Then for to dance, to drink and sing, I should be very willing;
I should not owe one lass a kiss, nor ne'er a knave a shilling.
'Tis only being in Love and Debt, that breaks us of our rest;
And he that is quite out of both, of all the World is blest:
He fees the golden Age wherein all Things were free and common;
He eats, he drinks, he takes his rest, he fears no man or woman.
Tho' Crœsus compassed great Wealth, yet he still craved more,
He was as needy a beggar still, as goes from door to door.
Tho' Ovid was a merry Man, Love ever kept him sad;
He was as far from Happiness, as one that is stark mad.
Our Merchant he in Goods is rich, and full of Gold and Treasure;
But when he thinks upon his debts, that Thought destroys his Pleasure.
Our Courtier thinks that he's preferr'd, whom every Man envies;
When Love so rumbles in his Pate, no Sleep comes in his Eyes.
Our Gallant's Cafe is worst of all; he lies so just betwixt them;
For he's in love, and he's in debt, and knows not which most vex him.
But he that can eat beef, and feed on bread which is so brown,
May satisfy his appetite, and owe no Man a Crown:
And he that is content with lasses clothed in plain woollen,
May cool his heat in every Place, he need not to be sullen,
Nor Sigh for love of lady fair; for this each wife Man knows,
As good Stuff under Flannel lies, as under silken clothes.

'Love and Debt: Alike Troublesome', *The Works of
Sir John Suckling: Containing His Poems, Letters, and Plays*,
John Suckling, 1766

Sir John Suckling was a Cavalier poet who is probably best known for his lightly erotic poem *Upon My Lady Carlisle's Walking in Hampton Court Garden*, about Lucy Hay, Countess of Carlisle. According to John Aubrey in his entry for Suckling in *Brief Lives*, Suckling invented the game of cribbage – which became a popular traditional English game and is played to this day. Suckling wasn't just a poet and a good game-player, he was an active participant in the Cavalier cause. His support included personally financing one hundred or so ostentatiously well-dressed troops for the king's Scottish expedition; their attire and subsequent military failure was ridiculed. He was also involved in the Army Plot of 1641. The idea behind this plot was to break into the Tower of London and free the Earl of Strafford. Unfortunately, the plot was uncovered and Pym finally had the excuse he needed to get rid of Strafford; the Act of Attainder was passed and Strafford was promptly executed. Suckling and the other plotters, now in mortal danger, were forced to flee abroad. In Paris, sometime in May of 1641, the exiled Suckling died – the cause of which John Aubrey attributed to suicide via poison.

11th – Carstares' Interrogation and Torture

All his objections and remonstrances being over-ruled by the majority of the privy council, the public executioner was called upon to perform his inhuman office. A thumb-screw had been prepared on purpose, of a particular construction; upon its being applied, Mr Carstares maintained such a command of himself, that, while the sweat streamed over his brow, and down his cheeks, with the agony he endured, he never betrayed the smallest inclination to depart from his first resolutions. The Earl of Queensberry was so affected, that, after telling the chancellor that he saw the poor man would rather die than confess, he stepped out of the council, along with the Duke of Hamilton, into another room, both of them being unable longer to witness the scene; while the inhuman Perth sat to the very last, without discovering the least symptom of compassion for the sufferer. On the contrary, when the executioner, by his express order, was turning the screw with such violence, that Mr Carstares, in the extremity of his pain, cried out, that now he had squeezed the bones in pieces, the chancellor, in great indignation, told him, that, if he continued longer obstinate, he hoped to see every bone of his body squeezed to pieces. At last, finding all their efforts, by means of this machinery, fruitless, after he had continued no less than an hour and an half under this painful operation, they found it necessary to have recourse to a still more intimidating species of torture. The executioner was ordered to produce the iron boots, and apply them to his legs ...

'The interrogation of William Carstares', *State Papers and Letters, Addressed to W. Carstares*, 1774

William Carstares, Church of Scotland minister and secretary to William III, was born on this day in 1649. During his incarceration his wife Elizabeth unsuccessfully petitioned the council for his release. According to the *Calendar of State Papers Domestic: Charles II, 1683 July–September*, Carstares was committed to the Gatehouse three days later on 17 February for high treason. The rather grisly excerpt above relates to the time in 1684 when Carstares was imprisoned and tortured (if you're wondering what happened to him with the iron boots, they were mercifully not used). During his ordeal, he named Robert Baillie of Jerviswood, who was later hanged, drawn, and quartered. Carstares survived this period and eventually became chaplain not only William III, but to his successors, Queen Anne and then briefly for George I. Carstares died in 1715.

12th – The Duchess of Malfi

The misery of us that are born great!
We are forc'd to woo, because none dare woo us;
And as a tyrant doubles with his words,
And fearfully equivocates, so we
Are forc'd to express our violent passions
In riddles, and in dreams, and leave the path
Of simple virtue, which was never made
To seem the thing it is not. Go, go brag
You have left me heartless; mine is in your bosom:
I hope 'twill multiply love there. You do tremble:
Make not your heart so dead a piece of flesh,
To fear, more than to love me. Sir, be confident:
What is't distracts you? This is flesh and blood, sir;
'Tis not the figure cut in alabaster,
Kneels at my husband's tomb. Awake, awake, man!
I do here put off all vain ceremony,
And only do appear to you a young widow
That claims you for her husband, and like a widow,
I use but half a blush in't.

Act I: Scene II, *The Duchess of Malfi*, from *The Dramatic Works of John Webster, Vol. I*, John Webster, 1857

John Webster (c. 1580–1634) was a dramatist of the Jacobean period, and his life spanned from around 1580 to 1634. There is no known date of birth nor date of death for him, but he certainly deserves an entry for Stuart Britain. *The Famous History of Thomas Wyatt* was co-written by Webster and Thomas Dekker and published in 1607. The monologue which is quoted above from *The Duchess of Malfi* is spoken by the Duchess, and is a popular monologue for actresses.

13th – The Glencoe Massacre

But, on the 13th day of February, being Saturday, about four or five in the morning, Lieutenant Lindsay, with a party of the foresaid soldiers, came to old Glencoe's house, where having called in a friendly manner, and got in, they shot his father dead, with several mots, as he was rising out of his bed; and the mother having got up and put on her clothes, the soldiers stripped her naked, and drew the rings off her fingers with their teeth; as likewise they killed one man more, and wounded another grievously at the same place: And this relation they say they had from their mother; and is confirmed by the deposition of Archibald MacDonald indweller in Glencoe, who farther depones, That Glencoe was shot behind his back with two shots, one through the head and an other through the body; and two "more were killed with him in that place, and a third wounded, and left for dead : And this he knows, because he came that same day to Glencoe's house, and saw his dead body lying before the door, with the other two that were killed, and spoke with the third that was wounded, whose name was Duncan Don, who came there occasionally with letters from the Brae of Marr ...

> *State Papers and Letters, Addressed to W. Carstares,*
> Joseph MacCormack, 1774

The Massacre of Glencoe (sometimes spelled Glen Coe) in Scotland occurred on 13 February 1692, during the reign of William and Mary. The orders were clear: to put everyone under seventy to the sword. Glencoe is in the Scottish Highlands, and more people died from exposure in the harsh wintry conditions than were outright murdered. In his 1966 book *William III*, historian Stephen Baxter put forth the view that King William III was constantly given batches of paperwork, and his signature on the letter was done hurriedly and without having read the contents. The Scottish Parliament condemned the event as an atrocity, and to this day the Glencoe Massacre remains a stain upon William III's reign.

14th – A Royal Wedding on Valentine's Day

The marriage between Elizabeth Stuart and Frederick, Elector Palatine, took place on this most romantic of dates in 1613. Only a few months before, Elizabeth's brother Prince Henry died, leaving the whole family devastated. The marriage, which had been so agreeable to Henry, finally took place on Valentine's Day the following year in 1613. Anne of Denmark, the bride's mother, found the whole match unworthy of her daughter's status and did not attend the ceremony, claiming she had an attack of gout. Some historians believe that the masque in Shakespeare's *The Tempest* (1611) was written and intended to be performed in honour of the wedding. After they were wed, Frederick took his new bride back home to Heidelberg. Happily, the political match turned into a romantic one as Frederick and Elizabeth fell in love. Their union would produce several children, including Rupert of the Rhine and Sophia, who later became the Electress of Hanover.

In the autumn of 1632, Elizabeth's world fell apart with the death of her beloved Frederick. He had been not only her lover and companion but also her best friend. The still-exiled widow remained in the Dutch Republic and grew fond of her eldest niece, Mary, Princess Royal and Princess of Orange. Thirty years after Frederick's death, Elizabeth died on 13 February 1662, on the eve of what would have been their forty-ninth wedding anniversary. There have been several very good biographies of Elizabeth published, Rosalind K. Marshall's *The Winter Queen: The Life of Elizabeth of Bohemia 1596–1662* and Carola Oman's *The Winter Queen* being among the best.

15th – Peter the Great's Visit to London

When the Czar left England, King William gave him leave to take any of his Subjects into his Service that he should have Occasion for; and made him a Present of a fine Yacht, called the Royal Transport, the best then in England, it carried twenty four Guns, and was contrived by the Marquis of Carmarthen, for the King to pass between England and Holland, during the Time of the War. He took with him one Mr. Fergharra, an ingenious Mathematician, bred in the University of Aberdeen, and two young Mathematicians out of Christ-Church Hospital, who, with the Ship Builders and several other Artificers were sent to Arch-Angel, the greatest Part of them in the fine Yacht.

The Life of Peter the Great, Emperor of All Russia, John Mottley, Esq., 1755

From 11 January to 21 April 1698, London had a very special visitor – Tsar Peter the Great of Russia (1672–1725). Peter's ship docked at St Katherine's Docks, near the Tower of London, and he visited many places during his stay, including the Royal Mint at the Tower of London, the Royal Society, and the Royal Observatory at Greenwich. There were a couple of reasons why Peter had been making his excursion around western Europe since 1697. The young tsar, although a Russian Orthodox Catholic, was interested in forming a coalition of Christian nations to fight against the Ottoman Empire, which was militantly Islamic. The other reason was that western European nations possessed a technological advantage over his own nation, and with his admiration of English ships, he was keen to learn more about the art of shipbuilding. This is why he ended up staying in John Evelyn's house, Sayes Court in Deptford, because that was where he would see shipbuilding in action. During his time in London, King William III and the aristocracy feted him. He also took an interest in British culture – he had noticed quite a lot during his travels – and Evelyn returned home to Sayes Court to find it had been utterly wrecked. Peter had been a party animal. Evelyn was not just an enthusiastic diarist but a keen gardener as well, and his house was renowned for its beautiful gardens. These gardens, and especially Evelyn's precious holly bushes, were quite badly damaged during Peter the Great's stay – a peccadillo worth reading about in itself! Near the end of his visit, William III had Godfrey Kneller paint Peter's full-length portrait; and so Peter the Great's visit to Stuart Britain came to an end, and thus began the long journey home to Russia, where he then began creating the Russian navy.

16th – Religion and Virtue

Religion and virtue appear in many respects so nearly related, that they are generally presumed inseparable companions. And so willing we are to believe well of their union, that we hardly allow it just to speak, or even think of 'em apart. It may however be questioned, whether the practice of the world, in this respect, be answerable to our speculation. 'Tis certain that we sometimes meet with instances which seem to make against this general supposition. We have known people, who having the appearance of great zeal in religion, have yet wanted even the common affections of humanity, and shown themselves extremely degenerate and corrupt. Others, again, who have paid little regard to religion, and been considered as mere atheists, have this given occasion to enquire, 'What honesty or virtue is, considered by itself; and in what manner it is influenced by religion. How far religion necessarily implies virtue; and whether it be a true saying, that is it impossible for an atheist to be virtuous, or share any real degree of honesty, or merit.'

And here it cannot justly be wondered at, if the method explaining things should appear somewhat unusual; since the subject-matter has been so little examined, and is of so nice and dangerous speculation. For so much is the religious part of mankind alarmed by the freedom of some late pens; and so great a jealousy is raised everywhere on this account, that whatever an author may suggest in favour of religion, he will fain little credit in the cause ...

Characteristicks of men, manners, opinions, times,
Anthony Ashley-Cooper, 1732

Anthony Ashley-Cooper, 3rd Earl of Shaftesbury, died on this day in 1713, during the reign of Queen Anne. The son of the 2nd Earl of Shaftesbury (1652–1699), Ashley-Cooper was also a politician, although nowhere as influential as his grandfather the 1st Earl of Shaftesbury had been (the first earl had been instrumental in the Exclusion Bill during Charles II's reign).

17th – Denzil Holles and Necessity

Wisdom saith, 'There is as well a time to speak, as a time to be silent'; And though wise men are often hardly put to it, to know the proper seasons of the one or the other. Yet where necessity hath left no choice, but absolutely imposeth one upon us, there can be no state upon the judgement. And would to God it could not be made most demonstrable that such a necessity we are under at this time. For no less than the laws, and with them the lives, liberties, and properties of every English-man is at stake; and we, with all other our fellow English-men, are under the highest obligation to break our guilty silence, or with our tongues in our mouths, see all our ancient rights raped from us and our posterity for ever; and our living child of liberty and property, slyly stolen from our sides, and a dead one of vassalage and misery laid in its room.

The Long Parliament Dissolved, Denzil Holles, 1676

Denzil Holles, 1st Baron Holles, died on 17 February 1680, during the reign of Charles II. Holles, born in 1598, was one of the Five Members whom King Charles I had attempted to arrest in the House of Commons in 1642.

18th – Clarendon's History of the Rebellion

All this time the King (who had been with great solemnity invited by the City of London, and desired to make his residence nearer to them than Hampton-Court) was at White-Hall, where, besides his ordinary retinue, and menial servants, many officers of the late disbanded Army, who solicited Their remainder of pay from the two Houses, which was secured to them by Act of Parliament, and expected some farther employment in the War with Ireland, upon observation, and view of the Insolence of the tumults, and the danger, that they might possibly bring to the Court, offer'd themselves for a Guard to his Majesty's Person; and were with more formality and ceremony entertained by him, than upon a just computation of all distempers, was by many conceived Seasonable. And from these Officers, warm with indignation at the Insolences of that vile rabble, which every day passed by the court, first Words of great contempt, and then, those words commonly finding a return of equal scorn, blows were fastened upon some of the most Pragmatical of the crew. This was looked upon by the House of Commons like a Levying War by the King, and much pity expressed by them, that the poor People should be so used, who came to them with Petitions (for some few of them had received some cuts, and slashes, that had drawn Blood) and that made a great argument for reinforcing their Numbers.

The History of the Rebellion and Civil Wars in England, begun in the year 1641, Edward, Earl of Clarendon, 1720

Edward Hyde was born on this day in 1609, during the reign of King James I. He would later become the 1st Earl of Clarendon. At the height of his power in the 1660s the town mansion of Clarendon House was built for him in Piccadilly, but this was demolished in the 1680s. In 1667, the unpopular Earl of Clarendon fled to France, where he wrote the *History of the Rebellion*, for which he is best known. Two of Hyde's granddaughters through his daughter Anne went on to become queens: Queen Mary II and Queen Anne.

19th – A Thief Caught in the Act

At the Lent Assizes at Cambridge, Clement Simson was indicted for breaking an house in the day-time, no body being in the house, and stealing plate to the value of 10*l*. And upon the evidence it appeared, that he had taken the plate out of a trunk in which it was, and laid it on the floor; but before he carried it away, he was surprised by people coming into the house. And the Chief Justice Hyde caused this to be found specially, because he doubted upon the Stat. of 39 Eliz. cap. 15. that enacts, that if any one be found guilty of the felonious taking away any good &c. out of any house in the day-time, above the value of 5*s*. he should not have the benefit of his clergy.

A Report of Divers Cases in Pleas of the Crown, Adjudged and Determined in the Reign of the Late King Charles II [1662–1669], London, 1732

20th – Osborne and 'a Notorious Falsehood'

Sir Robert does likewise show how he detests such scurrilous language, as the Examiner is full of for in my Answer; I have but once called a certain untruth, a notorious Falsehood, and Sr. Robert 'kerns to be much offended at the Expression'. He shows himself also far more ingenuous than the Examiner was, for he confesses many Errors in the Examiners Book, although the Examiner be very positive in the defense of them; viz. in his absolute affirming that my salary was never included in secret service; in his double charging of 200,000*l*. on the

one fifth of the excise; and in saying that the whole tax upon the first
Act for Disbanding the Army was some into the Exchequer in my
time &c. which Sir Robert is so much my friend as to acknowledge,
he believes to be otherwise, although he confesses that he has not given
himself the trouble to examine it.

The Earl of Danby's Answer to Sr. Robert Howard's book,
entitled An account of the state of his majesties revenue,
as it was left by the earl of Danby: Vol. 29, London, 1680

Thomas Osborne, 1st Duke of Leeds, was born on this day in 1633. Best
known as Lord Danby, he was a major figure in the marriage negotiations
between William III, Prince of Orange-Nassau, and Mary Stuart of York.

21st – Lady Chudleigh 'on the Vanities of this Life'

What makes fond Man the trifle Life desire,
And with such Ardor court his Pain?
Tis Madness, worse than Madness, to admire
What brings Ten thousand Miseries in its Train:
To each soft moment, Hours of Care succeed,
And for the Pleasures of a Day,
With Years of Grief we pay
So much our lasting Sorrows, our fleeting Joys exceed
In vain, in vain, we Happiness pursue,
That mighty Blessing is not here
That, like the false misguiding Fire,
Is farthest off, when we believe it near:
Yet still we follow till we tire,
Arid in the fatal Chase Expire:
Each gaudy nothing which we view,
We fancy is the wish'd for Prize,
Its painted Glories captivate our Eyes
Blinded by Pride, we hug our own Mistake,
And foolishly adore that Idol which we make.

'On the Vanities of this Life: A Pindarick Ode', from *Poems on*
Several Occasions: Together with The Song of the Three Children
Paraphras'd, Mary Clifford, Lady Chudleigh, 1703

Mary Clifford, Lady Chudleigh, was born in Devon in 1656. She married
Sir George Chudleigh, with whom she had several children. Chudleigh's
work tends to come across as overwhelmingly negative, something that is

probably evident from the above sample; her writing gives the impression that she did not like marriage in particular. To her credit, she was largely self-taught in a time when women were less likely or even able to do so. Two years before she published *Poems on Several Occasions* she published *The Ladies' Defence, Or, The Bride-Woman's Counsellor Answer'd: A Poem in a Dialogue Between Sir John Brute, Sir William Loveall, Melissa, and a Parson* (1701). Lady Chudleigh died in 1710.

22nd – Shadwell's 'The Libertine'

Nature gave us our senses, which we please:
Nor does our reason war against our sense.
By Nature's order sense should guide our reason,
Since to the mind all objects Sense conveys.
But fools for shadows lose substantial pleasures,
For idle tales abandon true delight,
And solid joys of day, for empty dreams at night.
Away, thou foolish thing, thou colic of the mind,
Thou Worm by ill-digesting stomachs bred:
In spight of thee, we'll surfeit in delights,
And never think ought can be ill that's pleasant.

The Libertine: A Tragedy,
Thomas Shadwell, 1676

Thomas Shadwell, an English playwright and poet, married Anne Gibbs sometime between February 1663 and January 1664. Shadwell was born around 1640 in Norfolk and studied at Cambridge University. Shadwell became rather political, and in the 1680s began writing pro-Whig propaganda, which rubbed Poet Laureate John Dryden up the wrong way – Dryden being a Tory. Two years after coming under attack from him, Shadwell stepped into John Dryden's shoes in 1689 when he became the second Poet Laureate. Following Shadwell's sudden death from an opium overdose – he had been using it on account of his gout – in November of 1692, Nahum Tate was appointed to Poet Laureate.

23rd – George Frideric Handel

George Frideric Handel (also spelled Haendel and Händel), one of the greatest Baroque composers, was born on 23 February 1685, in Halle, Germany. Handel grew up and ultimately became the Kapellmeister for Georg, the Elector of Hanover. From the portraits we have of him, Handel comes across as a rather pudgy, white-wigged chap. What the devil is

Handel, who is so associated with the Georgian court, doing featuring in a book dedicated to the Stuart era at all? The fact is he certainly has something to do with the Late Stuarts, as you will soon discover.

It is generally believed that the Duke of Manchester first invited Handel to London, though Handel biographer Jonathan Keates states that this is not supported by evidence. Regardless, the sequence of events that led to Handel's initiation into Stuart society is well known. Following the death of Queen Anne's oldest surviving son, William Henry, in 1700, there was more of a bond between the Stuart court and Sophia's court in Hanover. Everyone by then knew that the Hanoverians would ascend the throne once Anne died, and so a period of fashionable cultural interchange begun, introducing some aspects of German culture into Britain. Music, of course, was a part of that cultural heritage, and according to Handel's first biographer, John Mainwaring, Handel moved to England in 1710.

On 6 February 1711, Handel wrote music in honour of the queen's birthday – and both the national newspapers and the Russian diplomat Prince Boris Ivanovich Kurakin commented upon this event favourably. It was later that same month in 1711 that Handel's opera *Rinaldo* premiered at the Queen's Theatre in Haymarket. Any Baroque opera buff will immediately recognize the heavenly aria, *Lascia ch'io Pianga* from Act Two of this opera. Needless to say, *Rinaldo* proved a success and *Lascia ch'io Pianga* has remained incredibly popular even to this day. Queen Anne died in August 1714, and Handel received a £200 pension, which, again according to Keates, was a surprising gesture, considering he was a foreigner.

However, it was during the Georgian period that Handel achieved his greatest triumphs. In 1717, Handel composed his *Water Music* for King George I to enjoy by the River Thames; *Zadok the Priest*, composed by Handel for King George II in 1727, has been performed at every coronation since that time. Handel resided at 25 Brook Street, London.

In short, although he went on to create some of his greatest work during the later Georgian period, he nevertheless accomplished some of his early feats during the Late Stuart era.

24th – The Howards of Castle Howard

A noble terrace lies before the Front,
By which into a Paradise you mount.
Not greater Beauty boasts th'Idalian Grove,
Tho' that is sacred to the Queen of Love.
Such stately Trees encircle ev'ry View,
As never in Dodonas Forest grew.
Here the smooth Beach and rev'rend Oak entwine,
And form a Temple for the Pow'rs Divine:
So Ages past from ancient Bards we've heard,

When Men the Deity in Groves rever'd,
A Tow'ring Wood superior in its Kind,
Was to the Worship of the God's assign'd:
While Plebian Trees, which lowly Shade produce,
Were held unworthy of this sacred use.

*Castle Howard: The Seat of the Right
Honourable Charles Earl of Carlisle*, E. Owen, 1732

Charles Howard, 1st Earl of Carlisle, died on this day in 1685, during the reign of King James II. Howard's grandson, Charles Howard, 3rd Earl of Carlisle, began to move and ascend in political circles in the 1690s when he became a Member of Parliament for Morpeth. During the reign of William III he was Governor of Carlisle, beginning in 1693, and Lord Lieutenant of Cumberland, Lord Lieutenant of Westmorland, and a Gentleman of the Bedchamber. Born in 1669, the third earl became so successful that he commissioned the building of Castle Howard in Yorkshire in 1699. Designed by Sir John Vanbrugh (who was a Kit-Cat Club member as Howard was) and Nicholas Hawksmoor, Castle Howard remains one of the most splendid examples of English Baroque architecture in the country. Howard died in 1738, and his descendants have lived in Castle Howard ever since.

25th – Molière

Though pious, I am none the less a man;
And when a man beholds your heavenly charms,
The heart surrenders, and can think no more.
I know such words seem strange, coming from me;
But, madam, I'm no angel, after all;
If you condemn my frankly made avowal
You only have your charming self to blame.
Soon as I saw your more than human beauty,
You were thenceforth the sovereign of my soul;
Sweetness ineffable was in your eyes,
That took by storm my still resisting heart,
And conquered everything, fasts, prayers, and tears,
And turned my worship wholly to yourself.
My looks, my sighs, have spoke a thousand times;
Now, to express it all, my voice must speak.
If but you will look down with gracious favour
Upon the sorrows of your worthless slave,
If in your goodness you will give me comfort
And condescend unto my nothingness,

I'll ever pay you, O sweet miracle,
An unexampled worship and devotion.
Then too, with me your honour runs no risk;
With me you need not fear a public scandal.
These court gallants, that women are so fond of,
Are boastful of their acts, and vain in speech;
They always brag in public of their progress;
Soon as a favour's granted, they'll divulge it;
Their tattling tongues, if you but trust to them,
Will foul the altar where their hearts have worshipped.
But men like me are so discreet in love,
That you may trust their lasting secrecy.
The care we take to guard our own good name
May fully guarantee the one we love;
So you may find, with hearts like ours sincere,
Love without scandal, pleasure without fear.

Act III: Scene III, *Tartuffe, Or, The Hypocrite*, Molière

By this day in 1673 the great French playwright Molière had been dead for over a week; he had died on 17 February. He was born in Paris in 1622, with the name of Jean Baptiste Poquelin – Molière is simply his stage name. Many of his plays became popular, such as *L'École des femmes* (1662), *Le Médecin malgré lui* (1666), *Le Bourgeois gentilhomme* (1670), *Les Femmes savants* (1672), and *Le Malade imaginaire* (1673). Molière's work was adapted for the Restoration stage across the Channel in Stuart Britain. As Bruce King covers in the *Macmillan History of Literature: Seventeenth-Century English Literature* (1982), this importation invariably meant that his work took on a cruder tone. Molière's plays are a lot of fun, and you can see performances of his plays today on YouTube.

26th – Durfey's Don Quixote

We are now in pursuit of valorous adventures, entered into the pleasant fields of Mamiel, the Air is fragrant and delightful, and the Valley, near yonder tussle of verdant trees, cool and shady; therefore let us alight— And prithee take the bridle from Rosinant's Head, that he may the better taste the refreshment of this flowery pasture-, and when thou hast done so, show the same courtesy to thy own friend Dapple, for they have born us this day-with fortitude and patience, that exact from us an answerable Return of Civility.

Act I: Scene I, *The Comical History of Don Quixote*, Thomas
D'Urfey, 1694

Thomas d'Urfey (sometimes spelled Durfey), English writer and composer, died on this day in 1723, during the reign of King George. Born in 1653, D'Urfey is best known for his plays *The Banditti: Or, A Ladies Distress* (1686), *Bussy D'Ambois: Or, The Husband's Revenge* (1690), and *Love for Money: Or, The Boarding School* (1691).

27th – John Evelyn's Parents

I was born at Wotton, in the County of Surrey, about twenty minutes past two in the morning, being on Tuesday the 31st and last of October, 1620, after my father had been married about seven years, and that my mother had borne him three children; viz, two daughters and one son, about the 33d year of his age, and the 23d of my mother's.

My father, named Richard, was of a sanguine complexion, mixed with a dash of choler: his hair inclining to light, which, though exceedingly thick, became hoary by the time he had attained to thirty years of age; it was somewhat curled toward the extremities; his beard, which he wore a little peaked, as the mode was, of a brownish colour, and so continued to the last, save that it was somewhat mingled with grey hairs about his cheeks, which, with his countenance, were clear and fresh-coloured; his eyes extraordinary quick and piercing; an ample forehead,—in sum, a very well-composed visage and manly aspect: for the rest, he was but low of stature, yet very strong. He was, for his life, so exact and temperate, that I have heard he had never been surprised by excess, being ascetic and sparing. His wisdom was great, and his judgment most acute; of solid discourse, affable, humble, and in nothing affected; of a thriving, neat, silent, and methodical genius, discreetly severe, yet liberal upon all just occasions, both to his children, to strangers, and servants; a lover of hospitality; and, in brief, of a singular and Christian moderation in all his actions.

My mother's name was Eleanor, sole daughter and heiress of John Standsfield, Esq., of an ancient and honourable family (though now extinct) in Shropshire, by his wife Eleanor Comber, of a good and well-known house in Sussex. She was of proper personage; of a brown complexion; her eyes and hair of a lovely black; of constitution more inclined to a religious melancholy, or pious sadness; of a rare memory, and most exemplary life; for economy and prudence, esteemed one of the most conspicuous in her country: which rendered her loss much deplored, both by those who knew, and such as only heard of her.

The Diary of John Evelyn, 1818

John Evelyn (1620–1706), diarist and courtier, died on 27 February 1706, during the reign of Queen Anne. Next to Samuel Pepys, his friend Evelyn is the second most well-known diarist of the Stuart era. Although Evelyn and Pepys moved in the same circles, they were different. Evelyn's *Diary* remains one of the most informative accounts of major historical events in the Stuart age, but he wrote many other works as well, including: *Sculptura: Or, the History and Art of Chalcography, and Engraving in Copper: with an Ample Enumeration of the Most Renowned Masters and Their Works* (1662), *Fumifugium; Or, the Inconvenience of the Aer and Smoake of London* (1661), *Sylva, Or A Discourse of Forest Trees and the Propagation of Timber In His Majesty's Dominions* (1664), *Terra: A Philosophical Essay of Earth* (1679), and of course, *Acetaria: A Discourse of Sallats* (1669). Evelyn lived to the ripe old age of eighty-five.

28th – Two Countesses of Oxford

Aubrey de Vere, 20th Earl of Oxford, was born on this day in 1627. De Vere was colonel of the Royal Regiment of Horse Guards as well as a privy counsellor. In 1647, de Vere married Anne Bayning. In 1662, he went through a mock marriage ceremony with the actress Hester Davenport, popularly known as 'Roxalana', who bore him a son two years later. Roxalana had left her career, which evidently displeased Samuel Pepys, who wrote:

Sir W. Pen and I did a little business at the office, and so home again. Then comes Dean Fuller after we had dined, but I got something for him, and very merry we were for an hour or two, and I am most pleased with his company and goodness. At last parted, and my wife and I by coach to the Opera, and there saw the 2nd part of 'The Siege of Rhodes', but it is not so well done as when Roxalana was there, who, it is said, is now owned by my Lord of Oxford.

Roxalana, though she would call herself the Countess of Oxford until her death, was sidelined in 1673 when Aubrey de Vere legally married Diana Kirke. Diana was a court beauty and was immortalised in a portrait by Peter Lely in 1665, a mischievous glint in her eyes and one snowy breast exposed. As Diana was born sometime after 1646, that means she was well over twenty years Aubrey's junior. The couple had several children, including Lady Diana de Vere, who married one of Charles II's illegitimate sons, Charles Beauclerk, and became the Duchess of St Albans.

De Vere died in March 1703 and was buried in St John the Evangelist's chapel at Westminster Abbey. Two of his daughters – who died unmarried – were also buried in the same place. His wife, Diana, died some sixteen years later in 1719.

29th (Leap Year Only) – The Deerfield Massacre

On Tuesday, the 29th of February, 1703-4, not long before break of day, the enemy came in like a flood upon us; our watch being unfaithful; — an evil, the awful effects of which, in the surprisal of our fort, should bespeak all watchmen to avoid, as they would not bring the charge of blood upon themselves. They came to my house in the beginning of the onset, and by their violent endeavours to break open doors and windows, with axes and hatchets, awaked me out of sleep; on which I leaped out of bed, and, running to wards the door, perceived the enemy making their entrance into the house. I called to awaken two soldiers in the chamber, and returning toward my bedside for my arms, the enemy immediately broke into the room, I judge to the number of twenty, with painted faces, and hideous acclamations. I reached up my hands to the bed-tester for my pistol, uttering a short petition to God, for everlasting mercies for me and mine, on account of the merits of our glorified Redeemer; expecting a present passage through the valley of the shadow of death; saying in myself, as Isa. xxxviii. 10, 11, I said, 'In the cutting off of my days, I shall go to the gates of the grave: I am deprived of the residue of my years. I said, I shall not see the Lord, even the Lord, in the land of the living: I shall behold man no more with the inhabitants of the world.' Taking down my pistol, I cocked it, and put it to the breast of the first Indian that came up; but my pistol missing fire, I was seized by three Indians, who disarmed me, and bound me naked, as I was in my shirt, and so I stood for near the space of an hour. Binding me, they told me they would carry me to Quebec. My pistol missing fire was an occasion of my life's being preserved; since which I have also found it profitable to be crossed in my own will. The judgment of God did not long slumber against one of the three which took me, who was a captain, for by sunrising he received a mortal shot from my next neighbour's house; who opposed so great a number of French and Indians as three hundred, and yet were no more than seven men in an un-garrisoned house.

The Redeemed Captive Returning to Zion: Or, A Faithful History of Remarkable Occurrences in the Captivity and Deliverance of Mr. John Williams, Minister of the Gospel in Deerfield, who in the Desolation which Befel that Plantation by an Incursion of the French and Indians, was by Them Carried Away, with His Family and His Neighborhood, Into Canada, John Williams, 1853

The Deerfield Massacre occurred on this day in 1704 in the Province of Massachusetts Bay during Queen Anne's War.

MARCH

1st – Zouch and 'The Dove'

Take wing my Muse, and like that silver Dove,
Which o'er the world new-bath'd, did hov'ring fly
The low-couch'd Seas, and high-plac'd Land above,
Discern with faithful, though with fearful eye,
    That what both Land and Sea resounding ring
    We may to this All-makers praises sing.

He who directs the Sparrows tender flight,
And sees him safely reach the hurtlesse ground,
Guide thee in all thy Passages aright,
And grant thy Course be sure, thy Resting sound,
    From Mount of Olives, as from Hill of Bayes,
    Blest with the Branch of Peace, though not of Praise.

And you whose Care our Floating House yet saves
From sinking in the Deluge of Despair,
Whil'st with poor feather'd oars she pass the waves
Of this all-vulgar-breath'd, storm-threatning Ayre:
    Dear Lord vouchsafe with patient look t' attend
    Her flights both trembling rise, and humble end.

'The Dove', Richard Zouch, 1613

Richard Zouch (c. 1590–1661), English Member of Parliament and author, died on this day in 1661, during the reign of King Charles II. Zouch was born in Wiltshire around 1590/1, and became a Doctor of Civil Law in 1619. He is also believed to have been the author of the 1639 comedy *The Sophister*.

*

Also on this day, in 1683 Caroline of Ansbach, who would eventually become Queen consort of Great Britain as the wife of the Hanoverian King George II, was born on this day in Ansbach (in modern-day Germany). She died in 1737 at Kensington Palace from complications arising from an umbilical hernia.

2nd – Plans and Gossip

I am glad to find that your nephew growth in your opinion. He is now at the true age of forming himself, and with your assistance and encouragement, I think in the best place for doing it. Therefore, I hope he will intend it, and think it worth his pains to go about it. I am sure he hath a great belief of your kindness, and that will give you the power of persuading when there is occasion for it; so that I rely very much upon you in all that concerneth him. This is somewhat a greater trust than that of leaving it to you to make my compliments wherever you think it necessary, as indeed it was to Mr. Colbert upon such an occasion.

I have proposed your demoiselle to my wife, and I find her not averse to taking her, only she, having no exceptions to the servants she hath, cannot put away without a fault, only to make room, a method, though often used in courts, not so allowable in private families. Upon the first change I will put my wife in mind again, and if your woman is not otherwise disposed she may come; if she is, there is no hurt done.

In the meantime my credit with the French Protestants I owe wholly to you; your zeal being so notorious that it throweth a lustre upon all your poor relations. It is enough to be akin to a man that goeth twice a day to Charenton. Heaven reward you for giving such countenance to the Gospel! Sure when you come home and find my Lady Scroope return'd from hearing four masses in a morning at Notre Dame you are both very merry; for I take it to be an equal laughing match between you about your respective devotions. Pray make her my compliments, and let this be one of them.

We watch here to know how poisoning goeth on at Paris, thinking it may concern us in time, since we are likely to receive hereafter that with other fashions. Methinks you should not lose this opportunity of retrenching your table, you being a man of too much importance to be out of the danger of ratsbane. These things maketh our forest brains turn round; we are apt to think some new evil spirits are broke loose into the world to confound it. Our hope is that Mr. Savile, being a Nottinghamshire man, and once burgess of Newark, will by his influence secure us from the calamities that threaten the rest of mankind; if you do we shall be bound to pray for your worship, and so I leave you.

Letter from the Earl of Halifax to H. Savile, 1679–80

3rd – Hooke and a Flea

Though this little Creature is almost universally known to be a tall brown skipping animal, very few are acquainted with its real shape and figure, with the structure, strength, and beauty of its limbs and parts, or with the manner of its generation and increase – circumstances which could never have been discovered but by the assistance of the microscope.

The body of this creature is of an oval form, composed of several shelly scales or division most curiously jointed, and folding over one another those that cover the back meeting those that cover the belly on each side of the body, and lying, alternately, over one and under another of them. Its neck is finely arched, and resembles a lobster's tail in shape; moving too like that, very nimbly, by means of the jointing and folding over of the scales that cover it. The head is small, having on each side a quick, round, and beautiful black eye – in the middle whereof may be seen a round blackish spot, which is the pupil of the eye encompassed with a greenish glittering circle as bright and vivid as the eye of a cat. Behind each eye a small cavity appears wherein a certain thin film beset with many small transparent hairs may be observed moving to and fro, which our Author imagines may probably be the ear.

From the snout-part proceed the two forelegs, and between them are two long small feelers (or smellers, as our Author supposes). Each of them has four joints and abundance of little hairs. Just below and almost between these horns, lies the proboscis or piercer consisting of a tube, and a tongue or sucker, which can be put out or drawn in at pleasure. It has also two chaps or biters, shaped somewhat like the blades of a pair of round-topped scissors, and seeming to open and shut after the same manner. The flea with these instruments penetrates the skin of living creatures, and leaves a round red spot behind it, which we commonly term a fleabite.

Micrographia, Robert Hooke, 1665

Robert Hooke, English polymath, died on 3 March 1703, during the reign of Queen Anne. Hooke, like so many men of his class at that point in history, was very adept at many things. Along with Christopher Wren he designed the Monument to the Great Fire of London, which remains one of the greatest extant sites in the capital from the Stuart age. In his *Micrographia*, Hooke described in detail his analysis of various objects under his microscope. The most well known of his examinations was the flea. Robert Hooke's personal life is perhaps the most controversial aspect of his existence. In her biography of Hooke, Lisa Jardine stated that he had his niece stay with him as a ward, but when she was a teenager, he began having sexual intercourse with her.

4th – Pennsylvania

Another was, The Sufficiency of Truth-speaking, according to Christ's own Form of sound Words, of Yea, Yea, and Nay, Nay, among Christians, without swearing; both from Christ's express Prohibition to swear at all, Matthew. V. and for that, they being under the Tie and Bond of Truth in themselves, there was no Necessity for an Oath; and it would be a Reproach to their Christian Veracity to assure their Truth by such an extraordinary Way of speaking; simple and un- compounded Answers, as Yea and Nay, without Asseveration, Attestation, or supernatural Vouchers, being most suitable to Evangelical Righteousness. But offering at the same Time to be punish'd to the full, for false-speaking, as others for Perjury, if ever guilty of it: And here by they exclude with all true, all false and profane swearing; for which the Land did and doth mourn, and the great God was, and is not a little offended with it.

A brief account of the rise and progress of the people called
Quakers, William Penn, 1769

On 4 March 1681 King Charles II granted a charter to the Quaker William Penn for the land that would later become Pennsylvania. The most well-known seventeenth-century Quaker was one William Penn, Jr, son of Admiral William Penn. William Penn famously refused to take off his hat in front of King Charles II, and so the king light-heartedly removed his own instead. Penn gave his namesake to various tracts of land in the colonies – among them Pennsylvania, meaning 'Penn's Woods'.

5th – The Man Who Came Up with x

Sir, this is the effect of all I am able to answer to your desire, unless I more fully knew the manner of your way. I speak this the rather, and am induced to a better confidence of your performance, by reason of a geometric-analytical art or practice found out by one Cavalieri, an Italian, of which about three years since I received information by a letter from Paris, wherein was prelibated only a small taste thereof, yet so that I divine great enlargement of the bounds of the mathematical empire will ensue. I was then very desirous to see the author's own book while my spirits were more free and lightsome, but I could not get it in France. Since, being more stepped into years, daunted and broken with the sufferings of these disastrous times, I must content myself to keep home, and not put out to any foreign discoveries. Thus, with thankful acknowledgment of your so noble favour to design me worthy the communication of such a secret, I rest ready to do you all service, which may be within the power of

Your humblest servant, the true honourer of your worth, W. O.

A letter by William Oughtred to Robert Keylway, *Correspondence of Scientific Men of the Seventeenth Century: Including Letters of Barrow, Flamsteed, Wallis, and Newton, Printed from the Originals in the Collection of the Right Honourable the Earl of Macclesfield,* Vol. 1, 1841

William Oughtred, English Anglican minister and mathematician, was born on this day in 1574, during the reign of Queen Elizabeth I. Oughtred was not only one of the greatest mathematicians of the Early Modern period, but he was a highly influential one, too. He not only came up with the multiplication sign (×), which most of us have used, but he also had some important students, including Christopher Wren. According to John Aubrey's *Brief Lives*, Oughtred had the reputation of being a far better mathematician than minister, and that his preaching was 'pitiful'. Oughtred died in 1660.

6th – Francis Atterbury

Francis Atterbury, an English clergyman and Bishop of Rochester from 1713 to 23, was born on this day in 1663. His suspected Tory and Jacobite sympathies eventually landed him in very hot water during the Georgian period, when he was found to have been secretly communicating with James III, the Old Pretender. But was he really guilty?

There's an especially fine copy of *Memoirs of the Life, Character, Conduct, and Writings of Dr. Francis Atterbury, Late Bishop of Rochester from His Birth to his Banishment* (1727) by Thomas Stackhouse, A.M. at the British Library. According to this text, he preached before Queen Mary II on 29 May 1692, while he was still a student. She was so impressed by his eloquence that he became a royal chaplain to William and Mary, an appointment which continued after Mary's death in 1694 and through William III's time as sole monarch.

In 1700, Atterbury published *Vindication of the Rights, Powers, and Privileges, of that Venerable Body*. Following William III's death in 1702, the new Queen Anne made Atterbury her chaplain, thus continuing his role in the Late Stuart courts. But with the demise of the Stuarts and the rise of the Georgians, Atterbury wasn't successful in negotiating the transition of power.

It is in the Appendix of the aforementioned *Memoirs* that we learn, that on the 15 May 1723 there was some protest in the House of Lords in relation to a bill against Atterbury: 'The Evidence produced that the Lord Bishop of Rochester is guilty of the Matter … is in our Opinions, greatly defective and insufficient.' It continues, 'We are, on the whole, of Opinion, that the Proof and Probability of the Lord Bishop of Rochester's Innocence in the matter he stood charged with, were much stronger than those of his guilt.'

7th – Rob Roy

Rob Roy was among the last remains of the genuine Highlanders of the old stock, who wished to support the ancient privileges, and independence of the race. His clan had suffered great cruelties, which were attributed with much truth to their envious neighbours: and besides, when we consider the measures directed against Rob Roy as an individual, we cease to wonder at the opposition he gave to the families of Montrose and Athol; and although in his partial warfare he might not always have acted in conformity to nice principles of justice, yet it may be said, that the greater number of his errors were venial, and such as in his time, must have appeared no more than the fair and justifiable retaliation for injuries, which he himself, or others connected with him, had sustained.

> *Historical Memoirs of Rob Roy and the Clan Macgregor:*
> *Including Original Notices of Lady Grange: with an*
> *Introductory Sketch Illustrative of the Condition of the*
> *Highlands, Prior to the Year 1745*, Kenneth MacLeay, 1819

Rob Roy MacGregor was born on this day in 1671, during the reign of King Charles II. Rob was in the cattle business, and probably possessed Jacobite sympathies. He became an outlaw – and quickly, as a result, a folk hero. In popular culture, MacGregor is best known from the novel *Rob Roy* by Sir Walter Scott and the 1995 film adaptation starring Liam Neeson, Tim Roth, and Jessica Lange.

*

It was also on this day in 1639 that Charles Stewart, 3rd Duke of Richmond, was born. He lived only thirty-three short years, but married thrice – the last lady to become his wife was the celebrated Restoration beauty Frances Teresa Stuart.

8th – The Death of William III

King William III, having expired at Kensington, on Sunday, the Eighth of March, 1701/2, about Eight a-Clock in the Morning; and both Houses of Parliament being immediately assembled on this extraordinary Occasion, a Message was by the Lords sent to the Commons, to acquaint them with his late Majesty's Death: Whereupon they came to an unanimous Vote, to address the Queen, to condole with her upon this fad Occasion, and to congratulate the happy Accession of her Majesty to the Throne. Then the Lords in a Conference acquainted the Commons, That it having pleased Almighty God to take to himself the late King William III of Glorious Memory, and the Princess Anne being the only Rightful and Lawful Queen of theft the Lords had thought fit to acquaint the Commons, that Orders were given for Proclaiming her Majesty that Afternoon.

The History of Queen Anne, Abel Boyer. 1722

William III died on this day in 1702, whereafter his sister-in-law and first cousin, Anne, ascended the throne – becoming the last of the Stuart monarchs. The cause of William's death is often misattributed to a fall from his horse, and while he did indeed suffer a fall when he was riding near Hampton Court Palace one cold morning in February, that was not the cause of his death. After the accident, his physician promptly set his broken collarbone. William declared he would go to Kensington Palace, much against the wishes of those around him, who believed it best for him to stay and recuperate. But William was not the type to let a fall stop him from doing his job. After all, this was a man who had been shot at several times and led armies into battle, so he wasn't likely to start relaxing now because of a mere riding accident. He arrived at Kensington Palace where his collarbone had to be set again, and there, over the following days, he caught a chill which led to pneumonia. When his body was being inspected following his death, a locket was found hanging from his neck by a ribbon, in which were Mary's ring and a lock of her hair – proof that the man everyone had assumed to be frigid was anything but.

9th – Henry Rich's Resolve

... and so I am commanded to deliver to you, that as we have long kept together with resolutions to defend our privileges, our religion, our liberties, and laws, so we will continue in the same resolution, and the same purpose to do so, nothing shall deter us from it. If we can find peace from his Majesty upon these conditions, that religion, and laws, and our liberties, and all, may be happily secured to the kingdom, and to you all, we shall be glad of it, and it will be a blessing to us, and to you all. If it cannot be done, we are resolved, (and so I am commanded to let you know) nothing shall discourage us, neither danger, nor power, nor any thing; but if we cannot maintain our religion, our laws, and our liberties, we will perish and die for it.

Henry Rich, 1st Earl of Holland's speech, from *Two speeches delivered by the earl of Holland, and Mr. John Pym concerning a petition to His Majestie for peace, spoken in Guild-hall on the 10th of November, 1642*

Henry Rich, 1st Earl of Holland, was executed on this day in 1649. It was a grisly end for a courtier who had been so charming, and so very much a favourite of both King James I and his son Charles I. Rich had been the one entrusted by Charles I to begin showing the monarch's interest in marrying the French princess Henrietta Maria. Rich performed so well in this task that Charles sent over James Hay, Earl of Carlisle, to officially ask for the princess's hand in marriage. Things began to go wrong for Rich in 1642, however, when he didn't accompany the move of the king's court from London to Oxford. Rich was keen on bringing a rapprochement between both sides in the English Civil War in order to bring the bloodshed to an end. In 1648, he and the 2nd Duke of Buckingham made a disastrous attempt to raise troops in support of King Charles, and he was soon captured by the Parliamentarians. Despite pleas from General Fairfax, Rich and several others were condemned to death. He was executed in New Palace Yard in Westminster and buried the next day on 10 March.

10th – Cooper's Hill

Sure there are poets which did never dream
Upon Parnassus, nor did taste the stream
Of Helicon; we therefore may suppose
Those made not poets, but the poets those.
And as Courts make not Kings, but Kings the Court,
So where the muses and their train resort,

Parnassus stands; if I can be to thee
A poet, thou Parnassus art to me.
Nor wonder, if (advantag'd in my flight)
By taking wing from thy auspicious height)
Through untrac'd ways and airy paths I fly,
More boundless in my fancy than my eye:
My eye, which swift as thought contracts the space
That lies between, and first salutes the place
Crown'd with that sacred pile, so vast, so high,
That whether 'tis a part of Earth, or Sky,
Uncertain seems, and may be though a proud
Aspiring mountain, or descending cloud.

'Cooper's Hill', *Poems and Translations:
With The Sophy, a Tragedy*, John Denham, 1719

Sir John Denham (1615–1669), an Irish poet, died in London on this day in 1669, during the reign of King Charles II. 'Cooper's Hill' was a poem published by Denham in 1642.

✻

It was also on this day in 1629 that King Charles I dissolved Parliament, beginning what is known as Personal Rule, or the Eleven Years' Tyranny.

11th – Cotton's Saucy Spin on a Myth

He will not buy a pig a pike in;
But wisely will bring all things out,
And see within doors and without;
And I will show thee such a sight,
That if thou hast an appetite,
And art indeed a true-bred Cock,
When I pull of my cambric smock,
Shall make thee glory in thy being,
And bless Jove for thy sense of seeing.
Thou'lt then see I not only have
Eyes, cheeks, and lips that can enslave,
And outward beauties (or else some lie)
As captivating and as comely,
As either Juno's here, or Her's,
Who stand my fair competitors;
But such a skin, so smooth and supple,

Of legs so white a parting couple.
Such knees, such thighs, and such a bum
And such a, such a modicum,
Shall make thy melting mouth to water
Perhaps by fits, for sev'n years after.

The Judgment of Paris: a Dialogue, Charles Cotton

Charles Cotton (1630–87) was an English poet, writer, and translator. In the previous excerpt, Venus (or Aphrodite, the Goddess of Love) is using everything at her disposal to get Paris to choose her. According to the myth, the youth Paris was asked to decide which of the three goddesses Athena, Aphrodite, and Hera was the most beautiful. All three were exceptionally and equally beautiful, so they resorted to bribery. Out of the three offers the goddesses made, Paris most desired Aphrodite's offer, which was the love of Helen of Sparta, the most beautiful woman in the world. His decision, as the story goes, led to the Trojan War. Cotton in his version does a fine job of updating it for the saucy Stuart era.

12th – 'Urania to the Queen'

O, You, who like a fruitful vine
To this our royal cedar join,
Since it were impious to divide,
In such a present, hearts so tied;
Urania your chaste ears invite
To these her more sublime delights.
Then, with your zealous lover, deign
To enter David's num'rous fane.
Pure thoughts his sacrifices are,
Sabaean incense, fervent pray'r;
This holy fire fell from the skies,
The holy water from his eyes.
O should you with your voice infuse
Perfection, and create a Muse!
Though mean our verse, such excellence
At once would ravish soul and sense;
Delight in heav'nly dwellers move,
And, since they cannot envy, love,
When they from this our earthly sphere
Their own celestial music hear.

'Urania to the Queen', George Sandys, 1632

George Sandys, an English poet and colonist, died in the month of March in 1644, having been born in 1578. Sandys travelled extensively to such places as the new colony of Virginia and the Middle East. His journal about the latter trip was published as *Relation of a Journey* in 1615, which proved very popular throughout the rest of the Stuart period. Sandys translated Ovid's *Metamorphosis* in 1621, and this was considered very accomplished. Other writers such as John Dryden and Alexander Pope followed in his literary footsteps.

13th – Cinderella

Her sisters burst out a-laughing, and began to banter her. The gentleman who was sent to try the slipper, looked earnestly at Cinderella, and finding her very handsome, said it was but just that she should try, and that he had orders to let every one make tryal. He invited Cinderella to sit down, and putting the slipper to her foot, he found it went on very easily, and fitted her, as if it had been made of wax. The astonishment her two sisters were in was excessively great, but still abundantly greater, when Cinderella pulled out of her pocket the other slipper, and put it on her foot. Thereupon, in came her godmother, who having touched, with her wand, Cinderella's clothes, made them richer and more magnificent than any of those she had before.

And now her two sisters found her to be that fine beautiful lady whom they had seen at the ball. They threw themselves at her feet, to beg pardon for all the ill treatment they had made her undergo. Cinderella took them up, and as she embraced them, cried that she forgave them with all her heart, and desired them always to love her.

She was conducted to the young Prince, dressed as she was; he thought her more charming than ever, and, a few days after, married her.

Cinderella, who was no less good than beautiful, gave her two sisters lodgings in the palace, and that very same day matched them with two great lords of the court.

Cinderella, Charles Perrault, 1697

The fairy tales of Charles Perrault (1628–1703) are some of the most cherished stories in the world. He penned *The Sleeping Beauty*, *Bluebeard*, and *Puss in Boots*. There have been many versions of Cinderella, for example, but his seventeenth-century tale – with the magic pumpkin and Cinderella's fairy godmother – remains the most popular, especially when one considers that Disney's classic animated film from 1950 was based on his version of the tale. Perrault was born in Paris, France in 1628, the fifth son and youngest of seven siblings. Later on he became a member of the celebrated Académie Française. Perrault died in Paris in 1703.

14th – Ferdinando's Death by Gangrene

I am now about to procure the billet for 13 days, of the inhabitants of the towns where I quarter, and to engage for the payment as soon as the money comes to me. All which I beseech you represent to that honourable Assembly, whose care I doubt not, but will supply all our wants now represented, especially hasting down the forces of the southern parts, with the money intended for our supplies. It is advised by the commanders here not to fall upon any of the enemy's quarters at this time until we be stronger, or have certain intelligence of their weakness; In the meantime, we lie still waiting for opportunities, which shall not be neglected if one offered unto,
     Your most affectionate friend and servant, Fer. Fairfax.

> Letter from Ferdinando Fairfax dated Selby, 29 December 1642, from *A Second Letter from ... Lord Fairfax ... Presented to the Parliament 4 Jan. 1642 With an order of the Lords and Commons,* 1642

Ferdinando Fairfax, 2nd Lord Fairfax of Cameron and Parliamentarian army officer, died on this day in 1648. The cause of death is attributed to a fever that had set in after his foot had developed gangrene. Upon Ferdinando's death, his son Thomas Fairfax (1612–71) became 3rd Lord Fairfax of Cameron and one of the most important Parliamentarians.

15th – A Journey to London in the Year 1698

The cellar windows of most houses are grated with strong bars of iron, to keep thieves out, and Newgate is gated up to the top to keep them in. Which must be of vast expense!
     As the houses are magnificent without, so they furnish them within accordingly. But I could not find, that they had any bureaus of ivory.
     Upon viewing the braziers and turner's shops, I found it true what my countryman Monsieur Justell formerly told me, that according to his catalogue, there were near threescore utensils, and conveniences of life more in England than in France. But then the English, since the breach of their commerce with France, lie under great necessities

of several commodities fitting for the ease and support of human life, as counterfeit pearl necklaces, fans, toothpicks, and toothpick cases, and especially prunes, the calamity of which has been so great for ten years past, that they have no had enough to lay round their plum porridge at Christmas.

I must give a faithful account descend even to the kennels. The gutters are deep, and laid with rough edges, which make the coaches not to glide easily over them, but occasion an employment for an industrious sort of people call'd Kennel-Rakers.

The Squares in London are many and very beautiful, as St. James, Soho, Bloomsbury, Red Lion. Devonshire, none of the largest, and Hogsdon not yet finish'd. But that which makes the dwelling in this City very diverting, is the facility of going out into the fields, as to Knightsbridge, where is an excellent spring garden, to Marylebone, where is a very good bowling-green, Islington as famous for cakes, as Stepney is for buns.

A Journey to London, in the year, 1698. After the ingenuous method of that made by M. Lyster to Paris, Samuel de Sorbière, 1698

A Journey to London in the Year 1698 is as interesting as the piece by Lister on which it was based. It's fascinating to see how much London and its environs have changed in the past three centuries. For example, the author mentions how enjoyable it was to go into the 'fields' of Knightsbridge. For those who have not visited London, Knightsbridge is very central, and is where famous British shops such as Harrods are now situated; it is very close to Kensington – just another village outside of London in the Stuart period.

16th – A King, and No King

If there be any thing in which I may
Do good to any creature, here speak out;
For I must leave you: and it troubles me,
That my occasions for the good of you,
Are such as call me from you: else, my joy
Would be to spend my days among you all.
You shew your loves in these large multitudes
That come to meet me, I will pray for you,
Heaven prosper you, that you may know old years,
And live to see your childrens children sit
At your boards with plenty: when there is
A want of any thing, let it be known

To me, and I will be a Father to you:
God keep you all.

'A King, And No King', Francis Beaumont and
John Fletcher, 1619

Francis Beaumont was an English playwright and one of the most renowned writers of the Jacobean period. Collaboration between playwrights during this period was quite common and Beaumont was no exception, working with the likes of John Fletcher. Beaumont worked alone on a masque in honour of the marriage between Princess Elizabeth Stuart and Frederick V, Elector Palatine, but this was not performed due to the untimely death of Elizabeth's brother, Henry, Prince of Wales. Beaumont died in March 1616, and was buried in Westminster Abbey.

17th – Massinger's Death

A brave discovery beyond my hope,
A plot even offer'd to my hand to work on!
If I am dull now, may I live and die
The scorn of worms and slaves! Let me consider;
My lady and her mother first committed,
In the favour of the duchess, and I whipped!
That, with an iron pen, is writ in brass
On my tough heart, now grown a harder metal.
And all his bribed approaches to the duchess
To be conceal'd! Good, good. This to my lady
Deliver'd, as I'll order it, runs her mad.
But this may prove but courtship; let it be,
I care not, so it feed her jealousy.

Act III: Scene II, *The Duke of Milan,* Philip Massinger, 1623

Philip Massinger, English dramatist, died on 17 March 1640, during the reign of King Charles I. Massinger, born in 1583, was one of the main names associated with Jacobean and Caroline theatre. As with his contemporaries, he collaborated often – especially with Francis Beaumont and John Fletcher.

18th – The Princess of Cleves

The Duke de Nemours' passion for Madame de Cleves was at first so violent, that he had no relish left for any of the ladies he paid his addresses to before, and with whom he kept a correspondence during his absence; he even lost all remembrance of his engagements with them, and not only made it his business to find out excuses to break with them, but had not the patience to hear their complaints, or make any answer to the reproaches they laid upon him. The Queen-Dauphin herself, for whom his regards had been very tender, could no longer preserve a place in that heart which was now devoted to the Princess of Cleves. His impatience of making a tour to England began to abate, and he showed no earnestness in hastening his equipage. He frequently went to the Queen-Dauphin's Court, because the Princess of Cleves was often there, and he was very easy in leaving people in the opinion they had of his passion for that Queen; he put so great a value on Madame de Cleves, that he resolved to be rather wanting in giving proofs of his love, than to hazard its being publicly known; he did not so much as speak of it to the Viscount de Chartres, who was his intimate friend, and from whom he concealed nothing; the truth is, he conducted this affair with so much discretion, that nobody suspected he was in love with Madame de Cleves, except the Chevalier de Guise; and she would scarcely have perceived it herself, if the inclination she had for him had not led her into a particular attention to all his actions, but which she was convinced of it.

The Princess of Cleves, Madame de La Fayette, 1678

Madame de La Fayette, a French countess and authoress, was baptised on 18 March 1634. Her first novel was *The Princess of Montpensier*, which she published anonymously in 1662. *The Princess of Cleves*, her most popular work, is generally considered to be the first French novel. She was friends – perhaps more – with another major French author, François de La Rochefoucauld (1613–1680), the author of *Maximes*. Madame de La Fayette died in 1693.

19th – Cicilia and Clorinda

Prithee peace, and learn to love, and then thou wilt cease to wonder at my silence. Dost thou think the first sight of the objects we love can so little possess our souls, that there should be room for workd; what has Manlius seen in Otho, till this minute, that could call him dull or vain; if not, sure Clorinda's eyes and reason must beget both amazement and wonder, and let not the excellent Clorinda, because I am silent, doubt her power; for know, by busy soul was full of surprising joys, and inexpressible wonder ...

Act II: Scene II, *Cicilia and Clorinda, Or, Love in Arms*,
Thomas Killigrew, 1664

Thomas Killigrew, English dramatist, died on this day in 1683, during the reign of King Charles II. *Cicilia & Clorinda, or, Love in Arms, A tragic-comedy* (1663), from which the above excerpt was taken, was dedicated to Lady Anne Villiers.

20th – I Think, Therefore I Am

Perception is another attribute of the soul; but perception too is impossible without the body: besides, I have frequently, during sleep, believed that I perceived objects which I afterwards observed I did not in reality perceive. Thinking is another attribute of the soul; and here I discover what properly belongs to myself. This alone is inseparable from me. I am – I exist: this is certain; but how often? As often as I think; for perhaps it would even happen, if I should wholly cease to be. I now admit nothing that is not necessarily true: I am therefore, precisely speaking, only a thinking thing, that is, a mind (mens sive animus), understanding, or reason, - terms whose signification was before unknown to me. I am, however, a real thing, and really existent; but what thing? The answer was, a thinking thing.

Discourse on the Method,
René Descartes, 1637

Cogito ergo sum: I think, therefore, I am. René Descartes was one of the most influential philosophers in history, let alone during the Stuart period. Born in March 1596, Descartes had an interesting life, for he woke daily at noon – keep that in mind – and largely did what he wanted. He published *La Géométrie* (1637) with his *Discourse on Method,* and then, in 1641, he published *Meditations on First Philosophy, in Which Is Proved the Existence of God and the Immortality of the Soul.* Descartes never married, but had one known intimate relationship with a servant woman, Helena Jans van der Strom, with whom he had a daughter, whom they named Francine. Alas, Francine died aged five from scarlet fever. Helena married someone else, and Descartes continued doing what he was best at – mathematics and philosophy. By the end of his life, he was so well respected that Queen Christina of Sweden decided she wanted to meet him, so she invited him to her country. Unfortunately, Descartes did not fare well in the brutally cold Swedish climate, nor the early hours in which he was expected to attend to the queen (from 5 a.m.), and soon he became ill and contracted pneumonia. Descartes died in Stockholm, Sweden, in February 1650.

21st – Ussher, Archbishop of Armagh

The Primacy of Ireland: This was 1624, making up exactly the number of one hundred Archbishops of that See, from the first, supposed to be Patricius; of whom we read much, and much to his credit, in diverse ancient writers. Being thus promoted to the highest dignity his profession was capable of in his native country, he was so far from being elated or puffed up with such an high advancement, so far from ceasing to preach the Gospel, that he became so exceeding lowly, as to put pride out of countenance wheresoever he met with it; and so laborious in the ministry, as to over-toil himself, even to the wasting of his spirits, (by constant Lord's day and weekday labours) till a Quartain ague seized upon him, and afflicted him for three quarters of a year together. The grandeur of this place rather invited him to most lowly converses with the meanest of the ministry under his government, than to any the least appearance of domineering over them; though they might be such men as others in his office would rather have bestowed frowns than smiles upon: but he was satisfied these men were of honest intentions and lives, and so he carried to them as Brethren, a name he loved to call the lowest by.

The Life of Dr. James Ussher, Archbishop of Armagh, 1702

James Ussher, Irish Archbishop of Armagh, died from an internal haemhorrage on 21 March 1656, during the Interregnum. Oliver Cromwell ordered and paid for Ussher's funeral to take place in Westminster Abbey.

22nd – Ancient Person of My Heart

Ancient Person, for whom I
All the flattering Youth defy;
Long be it ere thou grow
Old, Aching, shaking, crazy, cold.
But still continue as thou art,
Ancient Person of my Heart,

On thy withered Lips and dry,
Which like barren Furrows lie,
Brooding Kisses I will pour,
Shall thy youthful Heat restore.
Such kind Show'rs in Autumn fall,
And a second Spring recall;

Nor from thee will ever part,
Ancient Person of my Heart.

Thy Nobler Parts, which but to name,
In our Sex would be counted shame,
By Age's frozen grasp possess'd.
And, sooth'd by my reviving hand,
In former warmth and vigour stand.
All a lover's wish can reach,
For thy joy my love shall teach:
And for thy pleasure shall improve
All that Art can add to Love.
Yet still I love thee without Art,
Ancient Person of My Heart.

'Of a Young Lady to her Ancient Lover',
John Wilmot, 2nd Earl of Rochester, 1714

23rd – The Doctor Militant

Bold Whigs and fanatics now strive to pull down
The true Church of England, both mitre and crown;
To introduce Anarchy into the nation,
As they did Oliver's late usurpation.
In Queen Ann's happy reign
They attempt it again,
Who burn the text, and the preacher arraign.
Sachev'rell, Sachev'rell, thou art a brave man,
To stand for the Church, and our gracious Q. Ann.
In James's Reign, when the Church had a Fall,
The Peers and the Prelates King William did call,
That he might recover what then did decline,
And settle the Crown in the Protestant Line;
For that pious End
He did recommend
The late Toleration, that Whigs did befriend.

'The Doctor Militant: Or, Church Triumphant',
from *Whig and Tory: Or, Wit on both Sides:
Being a Collection of State Poems*. London, 1713

By the Late Stuart era, the main two, newly emerged political groups, the Whigs and the Tories, were often at each other's throats.

24th – The Death of a Tudor Queen

And when she could not pray with her tongue, with her hands and eyes she directed her pious lifting of her heart to God, and herein she prayed, in that she grieved inwardly that she could not pray, as was plainly to be gathered by her signs.

The 24th of March, which was the Eve of the Annunciation of the Blessed Virgin, she (which was born on the Eve of the Nativity of the same blessed Virgin) was called out of the prison of her body unto an everlasting country in Heaven, most quietly departing this life by that manner of death which Augustus wished; in the 44th year of her reign, and of her age the 70. Unto which no King of England ever attained before.

The most sorrowful miss of her, which she left to the English, was assuaged by the great hope conceived of the virtues of King James her successor: who after a few hours was proclaimed King with the most joyful shouts and acclamations of all men. No oblivion shall smother her glory, for her most happy memory liveth, and so shall live in men's minds to all posterity. As who (to use no other than her successor's words) in wisdom and felicity of government, surpassed, (without envy be it spoken) all the princes since the days of Augustus.

Annals, Or, The History of the Most Renowned and Victorious Princess Elizabeth, Late Queen of England, William Camden, 1635

Elizabeth Tudor, the last of the Tudor dynasty, died on this day in 1603, at her residence in Richmond Palace. With her death the Tudor line came to an end, and the Scottish Stuarts' line in England began. Elizabeth had had a long and successful reign of nearly forty-five years. Elizabeth was the daughter and only child between King Henry VIII and his second wife and consort, Anne Boleyn. Indeed, it was circumstances such as these that have maintained such a hold upon popular imagination to this day – in countless books, films, and songs. Even by the end of the seventeenth century, she was still widely admired:

A professed regard to the Common-weal of the People of England steadily pursued did raise the English Monarchy under the Administration of Q. Elizabeth (of blessed memory) to as high a degree of Glory as it did ever attain to when it stood upon its natural Foundation.

Anonymous, from A Letter Humbly Addressed to the Most Excellent Father of His Country King William III, by a Dutiful and Well-meaning Subject, 1698

25th – Happy New Year!

Happy New Year! That's right, according to the Julian calendar – which most of Stuart Britain used (except for Scotland, which had been using that newfangled Gregorian calendar since 1600!) – today is the start of the New Year. It makes sense, doesn't it? We've gone through winter and spring will soon be here. This day is also known as Lady Day.

*

On this day in 1625 Anne Harrison, the English memoirist known by her married name Lady Fanshawe, was born.

Endeavour to be innocent as a dove, but as wise as a serpent; and let this lesson direct you most in the greatest extremes of fortune. Hate idleness, and curb all passions; be true in all words and actions; unnecessarily deliver not your opinion; but when you do, let it be just, well-charitable, and plain. Be charitable in all thought, word, and deed, and every ready to forgive injuries done to yourself, and be more pleased to do good than to receive good.

Be civil and obliging to all, dutiful where God and nature command you; but friend to one, and that friendship keep sacred, as the greatest tie upon the earth, and be sure to ground it upon virtue; for no other is either happy or lasting.

Endeavour always to be content in that estate of life which it hath pleased God to call you to, and think it a great fault not to employ your time, either for the good of your soul, or improvement of your understanding, health, or estate; and as these are the most pleasant pastimes, so it will make you a cheerful old age, which is as necessary for you to design, as to make provision to support the infirmities which decay of strength brings.

The Memoirs of Lady Fanshawe, Lady Anne Harrison
Fanshawe, 1830

Aged seventeen, Anne Harrison was married to her second cousin, the thirty-five-year-old Richard Fanshawe, in 1644. Their marriage proved to be very happy, and the couple went on to have some fourteen children. Sadly, however, most of these children died. The historian Antonia Fraser suggested in her book *The Weaker Vessel: Woman's Lot in Seventeenth-Century England* that this more than likely had something to do with the family's constant travelling abroad. She died in February 1680 and was buried next to her beloved husband Richard at St Mary's Church, Ware.

26th – Vanbrugh's Provok'd Wife

What cloying meat is love – when matrimony's the sauce to it? Two years marriage has debauch'd my five senses. Every thing I see, every thing I hear, every thing I smell, and every thing I taste – methinks has wife in't.

No boy was ever so weary of his tutor, no girl of her bib, no nun of doing penance, or old maid of being chaste, as I am of being married.

Sure there's a secret curse entail'd upon the very name of wife. My lady is a young lady, a fine lady, a witty lady, a virtuous lady – and yet I hate her. There is but one thing on Earth I loathe beyond her: that's fighting. Would my courage come up to a fourth part of my ill nature, I'd stand buff to her relations, and thrust her out of doors.

But marriage has sunk me down to such an ebb of resolution, I dare not draw my sword, tho' even to get rid of my wife. But here she comes ...

Act I: Scene I, *The Provok'd Wife: A Comedy,*
Sir John Vanbrugh, 1753

Sir John Vanbrugh, architect and dramatist, died on 26 March 1726, during the reign of King George I. Vanbrugh was also a member of the rather notorious Whig drinking club the Kit-Kat Club. The most memorable portrait of Vanbrugh comes from Kneller's Kit-Kat series, and Vanbrugh comes across as a plump, ruddy-faced man with a very impressive periwig. On 19 April 1705 Vanbrugh's Queen's Theatre was opened; the location today is where the current Her Majesty's Theatre stands, famed for its long-running Andrew Lloyd Webber musicals.

27th – The End of the Jacobean Era

King James I/VI died on this day in 1625, leaving his son, Charles, the new king. The transition from Tudor to Stuart rule went surprisingly well given the hotbed of religious troubles facing Britain at that time. James was an ideal choice – he was raised Protestant, but his mother had been a well-known Catholic. As a result, Catholics thought he would be kinder to them than Elizabeth had been; this proved to be incorrect. James has often been criticised, not only by his contemporaries but by historians over the centuries. According to the nineteenth-century historian Kenneth MacLeay, 'King James' was 'a man of puerile parts and degenerate mind'. But others disagree:

James has been hardly and not very fairly dealt with by various writers, and latterly Sir Walter Scott has contributed the aid of his able pen in turning him into ridicule for failings that belonged to the ignorance or superstitions of the times, and did not attach to him individually. If lie was in dread of witchcraft, how should the blame attach to him, when the most enlightened civilians and the most learned divines of his day gave credence to it not merely in Scotland but in Europe?

Preface, *Letters to King James the Sixth from the Queen [and others]*, from the originals in the Library of the Faculty of Advocates, University of Edinburgh

28th – The Spanish and Raleigh

His Majesty perceiveth, by a letter he hath received from the Spanish ambassador, that you have not been yet with him, to acquaint him with the order taken by His Majesty about Sir Walter Ralegh's voyage; and therefore would have you go to him, as soon as you can possibly, to relate until him particularly His Majesty's care of that business, and the course he hath taken therein.

Letter dated 28 March 1617, from George Villiers, Earl of Buckingham, to Secretary Winwood

29th – Specious, Positive Narration

Yet, notwithstanding that all this appear'd; and that this was all that did appear (besides a Discourse of a Petition, sor the Petition it self they would not produce, sign'd with C. R. which is before set down in terms) the Specious, Positive Narration of the whole, by Mr Pym, before the Evi dence was read; the Denying what was Now proved, and confess'd by themselves, by Mr Wilmot, Ashburnham, and Pollard, upon the Former Examination; the Flight of Mr Jermyn, and Mr Piercy, and some others; the mention of some clauses in the Petition sign'd with C. R; and some envious, dark glances, both in Mr Goring's Examination, and Mr Piercy Letter, at the King and Queen, as if They knew more than was express'd, so transported the Hearers (who made themselves Judges too) that taking all that was said, to be proved, they quickly voted, That there was a design to bring up the Army to force the Parliament; resolv'd to accuse Mr Jirmyn and Mr Piercy of High Treason; committed the three Members of the House of Commons to several Prisons, and put them from being Members, that in their rooms they might bring in three more sit for their service, as they shortly did; gave Colonel Goring publick thanks, for preserving the Kingdom, and the Liberties of Parliament; and fill'd the People with Jealousy for their

Security, and with universal Acclamations of their great wisdom and vigilancy.

The History of the Rebellion and Civil Wars in England:
Begun in the Year 1641, Edward Hyde, Earl of Clarendon, 1702–04

*

It was also on this day in 1628 that Tobias Matthew, Archbishop of York, died, during the reign of King Charles I.

30th – A Scottish Nobleman

James Stewart, 1st Duke of Richmond, 4th Duke of Lennox, and Royalist during the English Civil Wars, died on 30 March 1655. Born in 1612, Stewart was a Scottish nobleman who held various important governmental roles, including the Lord Warden of the Cinque Ports and, from 1641, Lord Steward of the King's Household. He was in attendance to Charles I during the latter's trial and execution in 1649. Before the horrors of war, however, he took delight in a spot of acting. There are two rather handsome portraits of James Stewart by Anthony van Dyck, one from around 1636 (now found in the English Heritage at Kenwood House) and one from 1637 (now at the Metropolitan Museum of Art in New York City).

31st – Donne's 'The Flea'

John Donne, the great English metaphysical poet and clergyman, died on this day in 1631, during the reign of King Charles I. Luckily for Donne, he died before the civil wars broke out during the following decade. When he was still alive, he had his image carved. This can still be seen today in St Paul's Cathedral, London; the tell-tale signs of intervening fire damage are still visible. One of his greatest – and most erotic – poems is unquestionably 'The Flea', which was published after Donne's death in 1633:

> Mark but this flea, and mark in this,
> How little that which thou deniest me is;
> It sucked me first, and now sucks thee,
> And in this flea our two bloods mingled be;
> Thou know'st that this cannot be said
> A sin, nor shame, nor loss of maidenhead,
>   Yet this enjoys before it woo,
>   And pampered swells with one blood made of two,
>   And this, alas, is more than we would do.

Oh stay, three lives in one flea spare,
Where we almost, nay more than married are.
This flea is you and I, and this
Our marriage bed, and marriage temple is;
Though parents grudge, and you, w'are met,
And cloistered in these living walls of jet.
    Though use make you apt to kill me,
    Let not to that, self-murder added be,
    And sacrilege, three sins in killing three.

Cruel and sudden, hast thou since
Purpled thy nail, in blood of innocence?
Wherein could this flea guilty be,
Except in that drop which it sucked from thee?
Yet thou triumph'st, and say'st that thou
Find'st not thy self, nor me the weaker now;
    'Tis true; then learn how false, fears be:
    Just so much honor, when thou yield'st to me,
    Will waste, as this flea's death took life from thee.

APRIL

1st – A Satire Against Marriage

Marriage! 'Tis but a licens'd Way to sin;
A Noose to catch religious Woodcocks in:
Or the Nick-Name of Love's malicious Fiend,
Begot in Hell to persecute Mankind:
'Tis the Destroyer of our Peace and Health,
Mispender of our Time, our Strength and Wealth;
The Enemy of Valour, Wit, Mirth, all
That we can virtuous, good, or pleasant call:
By Day 'tis nothing but an endless Noise,
By Night the Eccho of forgotten Joys:
Abroad the Sport and Wonder of the Crowd,
At Home the hourly Breach of what they vow'd:
In Youth it's Opium to our lustful Rage,
Which sleeps awhile, but wakes again in Age:
It heaps on all Men much, but useless Care;
For with more Trouble they less happy are.
Ye Gods! that Man, by his own Slavish Law,
Should on himself such Inconvenience draw.
If he would wiser Nature's Laws obey,
Those chalk him out a far more pleasant Way,
When lusty Youth and fragrant Wine conspire
To fan the Blood into a gen'rous Fire.
We must not think the Gallant will endure
The puissant Issue of his Calenture,
Nor always in his single Pleasures burn,
Tho' Nature's Handmaid sometimes serves the Turn:
No: He must have a sprightly, youthful Wench,

In equal Floods of Love his Flames to quench:
One that will hold him in her clasping Arms,
And in that Circle all his Spirits charms;
That with new Motion and unpractis'd Art,
Can raise his Soul, and reinsnare his Heart.
Hence spring the Noble, Fortunate, and Great,
Always begot in Passion and in Heat:
But the dull Offspring of the Marriage-Bed,
What is it! But a human Piece of Lead;
A sottish Lump engender'd of all Ills;
Begot like Cats against their Fathers Wills.
If it be bastardis'd, 'tis doubly spoil'd,
The Mother's Fear's entail'd upon the Child.
Thus whether illegitimate, or not,
Cowards and Fools in Wedlock are begot.
Let no enabled Soul himself debase
By lawful Means to bastardise his Race;
But if he must pay Nature's Debt in Kind,
To check his eager Passion, let him find
Some willing Female out, who, tho' she be
The very Dregs and Scum of Infamy:
Tho' she be Linsey-Woolsey, Bawd, and Whore,
Close-stool to Venus, Nature's Common-Shore,
Impudent, Foolish, Bawdy, and Disease,
The Sunday Crack of Suburb-Prentices;
What then! She's better than a Wife by half;
And if thour't still unmarried, thou art safe.
With Whores thou canst but venture; what thou'st lost,
May be redeem'd again with Care and Cost;
But a damn'd Wife, by inevitable Fate,
Destroys Soul, Body, Credit, and Estate.

A Satyr Against Marriage, John Wilmot, 1680

John Wilmot, the notorious 2nd Earl of Rochester, was born on this day amidst the troubled times of the English Civil Wars. Wilmot was often in trouble himself; he was incarcerated in the Tower of London at one point for abducting an heiress, Elizabeth Malet, who became his wife. This kind of behaviour was frowned upon, and incarceration was a light sentence compared to death, the more typical punishment meted out in the period. But if he hadn't abandoned himself utterly to pleasure, what other poems would we now be able to enjoy?

2nd – 'There's Nothing in Him'

I've tried him drunk and I've tried him sober and there's nothing in him.

King Charles II speaking of Prince George of Denmark

Prince George of Denmark was born on 28 October 1653. George was devoted to his wife, but has retained a somewhat boorish reputation; although he was a faithful husband to Queen Anne. Anne herself followed George to the grave some six years later. George was disappointed that William III chose not to give him an important position in the latter's military campaigns. The Windsor Guildhall in Windsor, Berkshire, England, has a statue of George on the outer portion of the building, opposite a statue of his wife.

3rd – Markham's Masterpiece

If a horse chance to swallon down any hen's dung with his hay, it will fret his guts, and make him to void much filthy matter at his fundament. The cure whereof is, to take a pint of wine, half a pint of honey, and two spoonfuls of smallage feed bruised, and mixing them well together, to give it the horse to drink, and then to walk him well upon the same that he may empty his belly. But if the horse chance to lick up any other venomous thing, as Neut, or such like, which you shall know by the instant swelling of his body, and the trembling of all his members, then the cure is, first to put him into a sweat, either by clothes or exercise, then to let him blood in the palate of the mouth, and look how much he bleedeth, so much let him swallow down hot; or else give him strong wine and salt mixed together: or else, take the root, and leaves, and fruit of briony, which being burnt to ashes, give the horse a good spoonful thereof, with a pint of sweet wine to drink.

Masterpiece: containing all Knowledge touching
the curing all diseases in horses, Gervase Markham, 1710

Gervase Markham (c. 1568–1637) wrote many books designed to teach or aid – early how-to books, if you will. Of these, he is best known for his *The English Housewife, Containing the Inward and Outward Virtues Which Ought to Be in a Complete Woman* (1615), which contained information on cosmetics, and cookery, to distillations.

4th – The Spleen

While In the light and vulgar Crowd
Thy Slaves more clamorous and loud.
By laughter unprovok'd thy Influence too confess.
In the imperious Wife thou Vapours art,
Which from o'er-heated Passions rise
In clouds to the attractive Brain,
Until descending thence again
Thro' the o'er-cast and show'ring Eyes,
Upon the Husband's soft'ned Heart,
He the disputed Point must yield.
Something resign of the contested Field;
'Till Lordly Man, born to Imperial Sway,
Compounds for Peace, to make his Right away
And Woman arm'd with Spleen do's servilely obey,

The Fool, to imitate the Wits,
Complains of thy pretended Fits;
And Dullness, born with him would lay
Upon thy accidental Sway;

Because thou do'st sometimes presume
Into the ablest Heads to come,
That often Men of Thoughts refin'd,
Impatient of unequal Sense,
Such flow returns, where they so much dispense,
Retiring from the Crowd, are to thy Shades inclin'd,
O'er me alas! Thou dost too much prevail,
I feel thy force, while I against thee rail;
I feel my Verse decay, and my crampt Numbers fail.
Thro' thy black Jaundies I all Objects see,
As dark and terrible as thee
My Lines decry'd, and my employment thought
An useless Folly, or presumptuous Fault.

> *The Spleen: A Pindarique Ode*, Anne Finch,
> Countess of Winchilsea, 1709

Anne Finch, Countess of Winchilsea, an English poetess, was born in April of 1661. The poem I've selected is unquestionably her most popular work, which she published anonymously in 1701. Anne and her husband, Heneage, were Jacobites, an understandable choice when one considers how close she became to Mary of Modena as one of her maids of honour when Mary was still the Duchess of York. The Countess of Winchilsea died in 1720 in London.

5th – Pocahontas and John Rolfe

At his entrance before the King, all the people gave a great shout. The Queen of Appamatuck was appointed to bring him water to wash his hands, and another brought him a bunch of feathers, instead of a Towel to dry them: having feasted him after their best barbarous manner they could, a long consultation Was held, but the conclusion was, two great stones were brought before Powhatan: then as many as could laid hands on him, dragged him to them, and thereon laid his head, and being ready with their clubs, to beat out his brains, Pocahontas the King's dearest daughter, when no entreaty could prevail, got his head in her arms, and laid her own upon his to save him from death: whereat the Emperor was contented he should live to make him hatchets, and her bells, beads, and copper; for they thought him as well of all occupations as themselves. For the King himself will make his own robes, shoes, bows, arrows, pots; plant, hunt, or do any thing so well as the rest.

> *The True Travels, Adventures and Observations of Captaine John Smith, in Europe, Asia, Africke, and America: beginning about the year 1593, and continued to this present 1629,* John Smith, 1704

On this day in 1614, Matoaka (better known as Pocahontas), the daughter of paramount chief Wahunsenacawh (popularly known as Powhatan), married the Englishman John Rolfe. This unlikely pairing took place during the reign of King James I, when the nation was involved in the Anglo-Powhatan War (1609–14). In 1616, Pocahontas and John travelled to England where she was presented to James I. The king was so taken by her that he invited her to Ben Jonson's *The Vision of Delight* masque. In England Pocahontas took the name Rebecca, and so was known as Rebecca Rolfe. She and John had a son, Thomas Rolfe. Pocahontas is best known for her association with the English colonist John Smith, whom she saved from being executed, as mentioned in the excerpt above. In 1617 she fell sick – possibly from pneumonia – and died; she was buried in St George's Church, Gravesend.

6th – Willem van de Velde

Willem van de Velde the Younger, Dutch painter, died on this day in 1707, during the reign of Queen Anne. Willem, born in Leiden in the Dutch

Republic in 1633, came from a Dutch family full of talented artists. His father was Willem van de Velde the Elder (1611–93) and his brother was Adriaen van de Velde (1636–72). Willem van de Velde the Younger mainly painted maritime scenes involving ships, yachts, and shorelines. Following the massive upheaval which resulted from the French invasion of the Dutch Republic in 1672 (known by the Dutch as *Rampjaar*, or 'Disaster Year'), many fled – including the Van de Veldes. They were welcomed by Charles II of England; father and son Van de Velde were given a studio, where they continued to paint many such works in the Queen's House in Greenwich. Today, Van de Velde artworks can be seen in many museums throughout the world, including the Rijksmuseum in Amsterdam, the National Gallery in London, and the National Maritime Museum in Greenwich.

7th – Davenant and The Unfortunate Lovers

Where is your reason, sir? You that are wise
Enough to govern armies in their rage,
In your own fury now should be so wise
To rule your self. Though this sweet lady's truth
And virtues sacred are, and firm to our
Belief; yet in the high importance of
A wife, you should take care to match where not
A single doubt, though ne'er so weak, could be
By envy urg'd!

The Unfortunate Lovers, William Davenant, 1643

William Davenant (1606–68), English playwright and poet, died on 7 April 1668, during the reign of King Charles II. Davenant was a rather prolific playwright whose works include *The Unfortunate Lovers* (1643), *Love and Honour* (1649), *The Platonick Lovers* (1655), *The Rivals* (1668), and *The Man's the Master* (1669). In his portraits Davenant is depicted with a rather peculiarly shaped nose – this is due to the syphilis he picked up from a prostitute. According to John Aubrey, who knew him rather well, Davenant would tell his friends that his real father was William Shakespeare. Aubrey attended Davenant's funeral at Westminster Abbey.

8th April – The Earl of Romney, Libertine

The King told me that he intended to send me into Holland, and expressed a deal of kindness to me, but told me withal that he could not have made choice of me, but that the Prince of Orange had sent him word he liked me very well. The same day, Lord Sunderland, Halifax, and I walked together, and talked much to the advantage of the Prince. Upon all occasions, the King expressed great kindness to the Prince.

Diary entry dated 1 June 1679, from *Diary of the Times of Charles the Second by the Honourable Henry Sidney, (afterwards Earl of Romney) Including His Correspondence with the Countess of Sunderland, and Other Distinguished Persons at the English Court, Vol. I*, Henry Sidney, 1843

Henry Sidney, 1st Earl of Romney, an English statesman, was born on this day in 1641, during the reign of King Charles I. Sidney held various important civic roles including Warden of the Cinque Ports, Lord Lieutenant of Ireland, and Master-General of the Ordnance. The king that Sidney refers to in the above entry is King Charles II; the Prince of Orange was later to become King William III. The latter certainly liked Sidney, for he made him Viscount Sidney and Earl of Romney when he assumed power. In her book, *The Weakest Vessel: Woman's Lot in Seventeenth-Century England*, Antonia Fraser claims that the very handsome Sidney was yet another Restoration rake, but unlike some of the others, he refused to provide for his numerous illegitimate offspring. What cheek! His mistresses included Diana Kirke, who became the Countess of Oxford following her marriage to Aubrey de Vere, and Grace Worthley. He died in 1704, unmarried, possibly an alcoholic – and on his birthday, too.

9th – A Rebel's Birth

His figure and the external graces of his person were such that nature perhaps never formed anything more complete: his face was extremely handsome, and yet it was a manly face, neither inanimate nor effeminate, each feature having its peculiar beauty and delicacy. He had a wonderful genius for every sort of exercise, an engaging aspect, and an air of Grandeur: in a word, he possessed every personal advantage; but in proportion to the greatness of his personal was the deficiency of his mental accomplishments. He had no opinions, but such as he derived from others; and those who first insinuated themselves into his friendship, took care to inspire him with none, but such as were perni cious. The astonishing beauty of his outward form excited universal admiration; those who before were looked upon as handsome were now forgotten at Court, and all the gay and beautiful of the fair sex were at his devotion. He was particularly beloved by the King; but the universal terror of husbands and lovers. This did not long continue; for nature not having endowed him with qualifications to secure the possession of the heart, the fair sex soon perceived the defect.

The Count of Grammont's description of the Duke of Monmouth

James Crofts, eldest son of Charles II and his Welsh mistress Lucy Walter, was born on 9 April 1649. The birth, which made the exiled king a father for the first time, was the one joy that had come into his life following his father's execution three months previous, in January.

The man who became known as James Scott, Duke of Monmouth and Buccleuch, was born in Rotterdam. There is debate as to whether or not his parents were married; Monmouth was in all probability an illegitimate son. James Crofts, as he then was known, had a difficult upbringing in which his father eventually had him kidnapped from his mother, who died in desperate circumstances. Charles overindulged his son and the boy proved a poor student, failing to grasp basic writing and mathematics until his teens. Monmouth had some spectacularly nasty facets to his personality. He was prone to violence upon the slightest provocation or perceived slight against him or his father. In time, however, he became a talented and capable military leader.

When he was fourteen, his father married him off to the twelve-year-old Scottish heiress Lady Anna Scott, Duchess of Buccleuch, and together they had several children. The extraordinarily handsome Monmouth was a known libertine and notoriously unfaithful to his wife. His promiscuity matched his father's. From what can be gleaned from Aphra Behn's *Love-Letters Between a Gentleman and His Sister*, the Duke of Monmouth was sleeping with Lord Grey's wife, so he (Grey) thought it was okay to sleep with his aforementioned wife's sister. Monmouth's most notable mistress for a time was Eleanor Needham, with whom he had two children. In the decade that preceded his death, however, Monmouth fell in love with Lady Henrietta Wentworth; she became his last mistress and the great love of his life.

Monmouth's continual involvement in political intrigues led to his exile, and William and Mary received him at their court in the Dutch Republic. Upon hearing of his father's death in early 1685, he was persuaded by fellow exiles to take his father's throne, which had by then passed to his uncle, King James II. Monmouth's Rebellion was disastrous. Monmouth, fleeing from the Battle of Sedgemoor, was eventually caught near Ringwood and hauled to London where he was imprisoned in the Tower of London.

On 15 July 1685 he was taken from his cell in the Bell Tower and up to Tower Hill, where he ascended the scaffold and gave the executioner a bag of money. This was a standard practice in order to hopefully be killed quickly and as painlessly as possible. Unfortunately, the executioner was

Jack Ketch – the man who had badly botched the beheading of William, Lord Russell, back in 1683. The thirty-six-year-old rebel leader knelt and laid his head on the block and suffered five strikes of the axe, which still did not sever his head, forcing Ketch to finish him off with a knife. Monmouth's execution has as a result been remembered as one of the most horrific executions in Tower history.

10th – Political Intrigues

To the Earl of Jersey:

My Lord,
I have received your Lordship's of March the 25th, O.S. I shall take what care I can to know the use that person I mentioned may be of; though 'til some proposal be made him, he will be very shy, that being much his temper. I take it that his relation will be able to persuade him to do all the services he can, when he shall come to England. He must certainly know if any design is carrying on against England, who are the persons that correspond, and what encouragement they have from England and Scotland. These are my present thoughts, which I submit to your Lordship's.
I have just now received the enclosed.
Brisac was evacuated on the first instant, as it was promised. I am, &c.

Manchester, letter dated 10 April 1700

11th – A Double Coronation

Their Majesties being come from Whitehall to Westminster (the King by water in his royal barge, about a quarter past ten o'clock in the morning, and the Queen by land in her chair, a little before eleven o'clock) ... And by half an hour past eleven, their Majesties, and the whole proceeding were conducted into Westminster Hall; at the upper end whereof a throne being erected, their Majesties repaired thereunto, and took their seats under their states on the inside of the table ... Their Majesties, arrayed in their royal robes of crimson velvet furred with ermine, the king on the right hand with a crimson velvet cap on his head, and the queen on the left with a rich circlet of gold on her head; all the nobility in robes of crimson velvet, with their caps and coronets in their hands; and the rest who formed the proceeding being richly clad, or wearing their proper and peculiar robes or habits, but all uncover'd, marched on foot upon to breadths of blue cloth, spread from the steps of the throne in Westminster Hall to the steps of the theatre in the Choir of the Church of Westminster. The whole passage being railed in, and guarded with his Majesty's Horse and Foot Guards: And all the streets, windows, balconies, and scaffolds crowded with such an infinite number of spectators, as were scarce ever seen before, expressing great joy by shouts and universal acclamations.

An Account of the Ceremonies Observed in the Coronations of the Kings and Queens of England: viz. King James II and his royal consort, King William III and Queen Mary, Queen Anne, King George I, and King George II and Queen Caroline, London, 1760

William and Mary were crowned joint King and Queen of England on 11 April 1689 – William became William III and Mary became Mary II. In the lead-up to the coronation, a replica St Edward's chair was built for Mary, as she and her husband were in fact to be crowned as that extremely rare thing – a diarchy. The sumptuous ceremony took place in Westminster Abbey, but things did not go smoothly. Shortly before she was expected to head towards the abbey, Mary received an unsettling note from her father – the man whose throne she and her husband were about to assume – and she had to pull herself together to get through the ceremony undisturbed. The wooden replica chair that Mary used for her coronation is now on display in the Westminster Abbey Museum.

12th – Stone Walls Do Not a Prison Make

> Stone walls do not a prison make,
> Nor iron bars a cage;
> Minds innocent and quiet take
> That for a hermitage;
> If I have freedom in my love,
> And in my soul am free,
> Angels alone that soar above
> Enjoy such liberty.

'To Althea, From Prison', *Lucasta*, Richard Lovelace, 1642

Richard Lovelace (1617–57) was an English poet and Cavalier army officer during the English Civil Wars. Both John Aubrey and Anthony Wood described Lovelace as one of the most beautiful gentlemen. As to the identity of 'Lucasta', that still remains a mystery.

13th – Behn's *The Rover*

Beau: Forgive me; oh so very well I love, Did I not know that thou hadst been a Whore, I'd give thee the last proof of Love — and marry thee.

Will: The last indeed for there's an end of Loving; do, marry him, and be curst by all his Family: marry him, and ruin him, that he may curse thee too. But hark ye, Friend, this is not fair; 'tis drawing sharps on a man that's only arm'd with the defensive Cudgel, I'm for no such dead doing Arguments; if thou art for me, Child, it must be without the folly, for better for worse; there's a kind of Nonsense in that Vow Fools only swallow.

La Nu: But when I've worn out all my Youth and Beauty, and suffer'd every ill of poverty, I shall be compell'd to begin the World again without a Stock to set up with. No faith, I'm for a substantial Merchant in Love, who can repay the loss of Time and Beauty; with whom to make one thriving Voyage sets me up for ever, and I need never put to Sea again.

Beau: Not to be expos'd to Storms of Poverty, the Indies shall come to thee See here — this is the Merchandize my Love affords.

The Rover, Or, The Banish'd Curtizans, Aphra Behn, 1677

14th – A poet's tragic end

What uncouth roads afflicted lovers pass!
How strange, prepost'rous steps their sorrow trace!
Oh, Alcibiades, if thou art just,
Forgive th'Excess of love that bred distrust.
Driven by that, disguis'd I hither came,
Yet here and ev'ry where my griefs the same.
But kind Draxilla's friendship can dispel
The thickest clouds that on sad bosoms dwell:
That does alleviate my griefs, and give
My weary'd soul a soft and kind reprieve;
Which ever to forget, would be as hard,
And as impossible, as to reward.

Act II: Scene I, *Alcibiades*, Thomas Otway, 1675

Thomas Otway (1652–85), a Restoration playwright and poet, died in extreme poverty in Tower Hill on this day in 1685, during the reign of King James II. Accounts vary as to how he met his death; stories range from his choking on bread he had begged for, to falling down dead in a tavern. Either of these would have been a sad end for this talented playwright. Otway was born on 3 March 1651 and educated at Winchester. His first play was *Alcibiades* (1675), which was then followed by *Don Carlos, Prince of Spain* (1676), *Titus and Berenice* (1677), *The Cheats of Scapin* (1677), and his most famous play, *Venice Preserv'd* (1682). There is speculation, based on letters, that Otway fell in love with Restoration actress Elizabeth Barry, but it appears that she did not reciprocate his feelings – as a result, he enlisted in the army. There were at least two duels in which Otway appears to have been involved during his tumultuous life.

15th – 'The Storm'

I see the use; and know my blood
Is not a sea,
But a shallow, bounded flood,
Though red as he;
Yet have I flows as strong as his,
And boyling streams that rave
With the same curling force and hiss,
As doth the mountain'd wave.

But when his waters billow thus,
Dark storms and wind
Incite them to that fierce discuss,
Else not inclin'd.
Thus the enlarg'd, enraged air
Uncalms these to a flood;
But still the weather that's most fair
Breeds tempests in my blood.

Lord, round me then with weeping clouds;
And let my mind
In quick blasts sigh beneath those shrouds,
A spirit-wind:
So shall that storm purge this recluse
Which sinful ease made foul,
And wind and water to thy use
Both wash and wing my soul.

'The Storm', from *The Sacred Poems and
Private Ejaculations of Henry Vaughan*, Boston, 1856

April was a rather important month in Henry Vaughan's life, for he was born on 17 April 1621, and died on 23 April 1695. Vaughan, a talented Welsh poet and translator of religious works, was from Llansantffraed, Brecknockshire, Wales.

16th – Aphra Behn

Like it! by Heav'n, I never saw so much beauty. Oh the Charms of those sprightly black eyes, that strangely fair face, full of smiles and dimples! Those soft round melting cherry Lips! And small even white Teeth! Not to be expressed, but silently adored! Oh one Look more, and strike me dumb, or I shall repeat nothing else till I am mad.

Act III: Scene II, *The Rover*, Aphra Behn, 1677

On 16 April 1689 the Restoration playwright and poetess Aphra Behn died. Behn, who was likely born around 1640, is widely considered to be the first woman to make a living as a professional writer. She was a monarchist, a Tory, and in all probability a Jacobite sympathiser. Maureen Duffy, who conducted a massive amount of research into Behn's life for her 1977 biography *The Passionate Shepherdess: The Life of Aphra Behn 1649–1689*, explained how difficult it is to find much information about the first twenty years of Behn's life; the little we do know is sometimes enmeshed with doubt and further questions. She may have gone to the English colony of Suriname in South America, where she may have fallen in love with a man there. What Duffy was able to find was that Aphra's maiden name was probably Johnson, and Behn was her married name. Who exactly Mr Behn was remains an enigma, but Duffy believed him to be a merchant, possibly one Johan Behn. But by 1666 Aphra seems to have been widowed; she never remarried.

She wrote several plays and novels during the Restoration, including *Abdelazar: The Moor's Revenge* (1676), and *Oroonoko* (1688). These works were often set in exotic places and featured a cast of equally exotic characters, which were probably inspired by her time in Suriname, a country in the north-eastern part of South America.

But Behn wasn't only a playwright and poet; there is reason to believe that she may also have been a government spy. She was a supporter of the Stuarts and probably held Jacobite sympathies. Unfortunately, we don't know much more about her – and she remains a truly fascinating and mysterious figure of the Restoration era. She died shortly after William and Mary came to the throne, and was buried in Westminster Abbey.

17th – The Broken Heart

Forgive me now I turn to thee' thou shadow
Of my contracted lord!
Bear witness all; I put my mother's wedding ring upon
His finger; 'twas my father's last bequest.
Thus I new-marry him, whose wife I am:
Death shall not separate us. Oh, my lords,
I but deceiv'd your eyes with antic gesture,
When one news straight came huddling on another,
Of death! And death! And death! Still I danced forward!
But it struck home, and here, and in an instant.
Be such mere women, who, with shrieks and out cries,
Can vow a present end to all their sorrows,
Yet live to [court] new pleasures, and outlive them:
They are the silent griefs which cut the heart strings;
Let me die smiling.
One kiss on these cold lips, my last! crack, crack —
Argos now's Sparta's king. Command the voices
Which wait at th'altar, now to sing the song I fitted for my end.

Act V: Scene III, *The Broken Heart,* John Ford, 1633

John Ford, an English dramatist, was baptised on this day in 1586. He was the son of a wealthy family in Devon. Ford's famous works include *'Tis Pity She's a Whore* (1630) and *The Broken Heart* (1633). Ford died c. 1639.

18th – The Princess over the Water

Princess Louisa Maria Teresa Stuart, daughter of the exiled King James II and his queen, Mary of Modena, died on this day in 1712, aged only nineteen. The cause of death was small pox, that dreadful disease which had cut short many a person's life in the Stuart era, including her half-sister, Queen Mary II, in 1694. Louisa's brother, James Francis Edward Stuart, had also contracted the disease at the same time but survived. Their half-sister, Queen Anne, still had two more years to live and rule as Queen of Great Britain. Louisa Maria had been born, raised, and died in exile with her family – never so much as setting foot in Britain. She was only nine years old when her father died – his parting advice to her and her older brother James was to remain good Catholics. There are a few portraits of Louisa Maria, and the one by François de Troy, c. 1705, is perhaps the most captivating. In this painting, Louisa Maria has her dark brown hair bound up with yellow and red flowers, and she holds a little posy of flowers in her left hand. Her dress is blue satin, exquisitely embroidered with golden thread. But it is how she stares directly at the viewer with her dark eyes, so lifelike, that makes it rather striking. Earlier, in 1695, French Baroque portraitist Nicolas de Largillière painted Louisa and her brother James. The siblings were painted again four years later in 1699, this time by Alexis-Simon Belle. This last painting is now in the Royal Collection at the Palace of Holyroodhouse, in Scotland.

*

It was also on this day in 1689 that the 'Hanging Judge' George Jeffreys died. In 1681, King Charles II had made him a Baronet. Jeffreys presided over the notorious Bloody Assizes of 1685, which followed the Duke of Monmouth's failed rebellion. Around 2,500 men were brought before Jeffreys and sentenced either to death or transportation to the West Indies for a life of slavery on the plantations. Jeffreys was very good at his job, and King James II was pleased with his devoted efforts and rewarded him that autumn with the position of Lord Chancellor.

19th – A Critical Bastard

Man is a little world and bears the face,
And picture of the University:
All but resembleth God, all but his glass,
All but the picture of his majesty.
Man is the little world (so we him call)
The world the little God, God the great All.

Epigram 4, 'De *Microcosme*', from *Chrestoleros*,
Thomas Bastard, 1598

The rather unfortunately surnamed Reverend Thomas Bastard died on this day in April 1618, during the reign of King James I. Bastard was a poet as well as a clergyman. Some might have been of the opinion that Bastard lived up to his name as he was probably behind the 1591 tract *An Admonition to the City of Oxford*, in which he pointed fingers at distinguished members of the academic and clerical communities and admonished them for their alleged sexual escapades. Bastard was also an epigrammatist, as can be seen above. In 1598, 285 of his epigrams were collected and published as *Chrestoleros* – his most famous work.

*

It was also on this day in 1733 that Elizabeth Hamilton (*née* Villiers) died. Elizabeth, also known as Betty, is reputed to have been King William III's mistress. Following Mary II's death, William broke with Betty and married her off to George Hamilton, creating them the Earl and Countess of Orkney. The couple got on well and despite Elizabeth's age – she was in her forties – soon had children. They lived in Cliveden, the great estate in Buckinghamshire.

20th – My Lord General Came

My Lord General came into the House clad in plain black clothes with grey worsted stockings, and sat down, as he used to do, in an ordinary place. Then he began to speak, and presently he put on his hat, went out of his place, and walked up and down the stage or floor in the midst of the House, with his hat on his head, and chid them soundly. After this had gone on for some time, Colonel Harrison was called in to remove the Speaker, which he did; and it happened that Algernon Sydney sat next to the Speaker on the right hand. The General said to Harrison, 'Put him out!' Harrison spake to Sydney to go out, but he said he would not go out and waited still. The General said again, 'Put him out!' Then Harrison and Wortley [Worsley] put their hands upon Sydney's shoulders as if they would force him to go out. Then he rose and went towards the door.

Journal entry dated 20 April 1653 by Robert Sidney,
2nd Earl of Leicester, as found in *The Love Letters
of Dorothy Osborne to Sir William Temple, 1652–54*

21st – Law's Economics

Some think if interest were lowered by law, trade would increase, merchants being able to employ more money and trade cheaper. Such a law would have many inconveniencies, and it is much to be doubted whether it would have any good effect; indeed, if lowness of interest were the consequence of a greater quantity of money, the stock applied to trade would be greater, and merchants would trade cheaper, from the easiness of borrowing and the lower interest of money, without any inconveniencies attending it.

*Money and Trade Considered: With a Proposal for
Supplying the Nation with Money*, John Law, 1705

John Law, a Scottish economist, was baptised on 22 April 1671. In *Crime, Cash, Credit and Chaos: A Brief History of the Life and Work of John Law*, author Colin McCall recounts that Law killed Edward Wilson in a duel in 1694. Elizabeth Villiers, William III's supposed mistress, was involved in the imbroglio but the specifics are still somewhat sketchy. Law was sentenced to death by hanging for his crime, but it was probably Elizabeth's influence that saw him go free. He moved to France, where he eventually became the finance minister.

22nd – One Cervantes, Buried Twice

Now the truth of the matter concerning the helmet, the steed and the knight which Don Quixote saw, was this: there were two villages in that neighbourhood, one of them so small that it had neither shop nor barber, but the other adjoining to it had both, and the barber of the bigger served also the lesser, in which a person indisposed wanted to be let blood, and another to be trimmed; and for this purpose was the barber on the road, carrying with him his brass basin. Fortune so ordered it, that as he was upon the road, it began to rain, and that his hat might not be spoiled, for it was a new one, he clapped the basin on his head, which being well scoured, glittered half a league off. He rode on a grey ass, as Sancho said, and this was the reason why Don Quixote took the barber for a knight, his ass for a dapple-grey steed, and his basin for a golden helmet: for he very readily adapted whatever he saw to his knightly extravagancies and wild conceits. When he saw the poor cavalier approach, without staying to reason the case with him, he advanced at Rocinante's best speed, and couched his lance low, designing to run him through and through. But when he came up to him, without checking the fury of his career, he cried out: 'Defend yourself, caitiff, or surrender willingly what is so justly my due.' The barber, not suspecting or apprehending any such thing, seeing this phantom coming upon him, had no other way to avoid the thrust of the lance, but to let himself fall down from the ass: and no sooner had he touched the ground, than leaping up nimbler than a roe-buck, he began to scour over the plain with such speed, that the wind could not overtake him.

Don Quixote de la Mancha, Miguel de Cervantes, 1605

The great Spanish poet and playwright Miguel de Cervantes Saavedra died on this day in 1616. So why include him in a book about Stuart Britain? Well, Cervantes' work did not just impact the Spanish-speaking world. Thomas D'Urfey, for instance, wrote a version of *Don Quixote* in the late seventeenth century.

In 1571, Cervantes fought alongside other Catholics in the Battle of Lepanto against the Ottomans and suffered several wounds, one of which rendered his left hand unusable. Four years later, he was captured by the Barbary pirates, taken to their main port in Algiers, and sold into slavery for the next five years. Eventually enough money was gathered and Cervantes was released; it's likely that he drew from his experiences to write *Don Quixote*. A day after his death, he was buried in the Convent of las Trinitarias Descalzas in Madrid. Over time, however, the exact spot where his body had been placed was forgotten, and in the early twenty-first century a team of archaeologists decided to try to find his remains. On 11 June 2015, the probable remains of Cervantes were reinterred in a formal burial.

23rd – Shakespeare's Death

If thou survive my well-contented day,
When that churl Death my bones with dust shall cover
And shalt by fortune once more re-survey
These poor rude lines of thy deceased lover,
Compare them with the bett'ring of the time,
And though they be outstripp'd by every pen,
Reserve them for my love, not for their rhyme,
Exceeded by the height of happier men.
O! then vouchsafe me but this loving thought:
'Had my friend's Muse grown with this growing age,
A dearer birth than this his love had brought,
To march in ranks of better equipage:
But since he died and poets better prove,
Theirs for their style I'll read, his for his love'.

Sonnet 32, William Shakespeare

William Shakespeare died on 23 April 1616, during the reign of King James I. Born in Stratford-upon-Avon in Warwickshire, England, Shakespeare is arguably the greatest writer in all history, let alone British history, and has become a sort of demigod to admirers of his sonnets and plays. Born in 1564, this son of a glover eventually travelled to London and became an actor and playwright. Shakespeare had an amazing range – able to write high-spirited plays such as *A Midsummer Night's Dream* and extremely violent dark tragedies such as *Titus Andronicus*. He wrote the long poems *Venus and Adonis* and *The Rape of Lucrece*, both dedicated to his patron the Earl of Southampton. Several of Shakespeare's plays were performed before royalty, at the courts of Queen Elizabeth (who died in 1603) and her successor, King James I. Upon his gravestone reads this warning:

'Blessed be ye man who spares these stones and curst be he ye moves my bones.'

24th – A Journal of the Plague Year

Indeed the Work was not of a Nature to allow them Leisure, to take an exact Tale of the dead Bodies, which were all huddled together in the Dark into a Pit; which Pit, or Trench, no Man could come nigh, but at the utmost Peril. I observ'd of ten, that in the Parishes of Aldgate, and Crips legate. White- Chappel and Stepney, there was five, six, seven, and eight hundred in a Week, in the Bills, whereas if we may believe the Opinion of those that liv'd in the City, all the Time, as well as I, there died some times 2,000 a week in those Parishes; and I saw it under the Hand of one, that made as strict an examination into that Part as he could, that there really died an hundred thousand People of the Plague, in it that one Year, whereas the Bills, the Articles of the Plague, was but 68,590.

If I may be allowed to give my Opinion, by what I saw with my Eyes, and heard from other People what were Eye Witnesses, I do verily believe the fame, viz. that there died, at least, 100,000 of the Plague only, besides other Distempers, and besides those which died in the Fields, and Highways, and secret Places, out of the Compass of the Communication, as it was called; and who were not put down in the Bills, tho' they really belonged to the Body of the Inhabitants. It was known to us all, that abundance of poor despairing Creatures, who had the Distemper upon them, and were grown stupid, or melancholy by their Misery, as many were, wandered away into the Fields, and Woods, and into secret uncouth Places, almost any where to creep into a Bush, or Hedge, and DIE.

A Journal of the Plague Year, Daniel Defoe, 1722

Daniel Defoe, the English writer and political pamphleteer, died on 24 April 1731. He is best known for his novels *Moll Flanders* (1722), *Roxana* (1724), *A Journal of the Plague Year* (1722), and *Robinson Crusoe* (1719). *A Journal of a Plague Year* follows one man's experiences through life during the plague outbreak of 1665. *Robinson Crusoe*, a tale of a sole survivor of a shipwreck, is a well-loved children's adventure classic. *Moll Flanders* and *Roxana* were remarkable for their time as Defoe wrote from a fallen woman's perspective. Born in London and prohibited from attending a university because he was from a Dissenting family, Defoe nevertheless received a good education from Morton's Academy in the Stoke Newington area. When he was still a young man Defoe joined the Monmouth Rebellion of 1685 as a rebel. It wasn't all he thought it would be, and when King James II issued a royal pardon a few weeks later, he took advantage of it and left – thus sparing himself the horrors of the Battle of Sedgemoor and the Bloody Assizes. He must have believed there was something in Monmouth's claims of legitimacy, because later on he wrote a pamphlet on the possibility of a succession through Monmouth's line. A staunch supporter of William and Mary and the Glorious Revolution that had placed them on the throne, Defoe wasn't the type to sit idly by when other writers began attacking William because of his foreign origins. Defoe hit back at William's critics with the hugely popular *The True-Born Englishman: A Satire* of 1701. During the reign of Queen Anne, Defoe was placed in a pillory as punishment for seditious pamphleteering. There, instead of having rotten food (or worse) thrown at him, he was pelted with flowers. Defoe was also the putative writer of *A General History of Pyrates* (1724), in which the author stated that it was dangerous for 'governments to be negligent, and not take an early care in suppressing these sea bandits before they gather strength'.

25th – Temple's Love

I ask you these questions very seriously; but yet how willingly would I venture all to be with you. I know you love me still; you promised me, and that's all the security I can have in this world. 'Tis that which makes all things else seem nothing to it, so high it sets me; and so high, indeed, that should I ever fall 'twould dash me all to pieces. Methinks your very charity should make you love me more now than ever, by seeing me so much more unhappy than I used, by being so much farther from you, for that is all the measure can be taken of my good or ill condition. Justice, I am sure, will oblige you to it, since you have no other means left in the world of rewarding such a passion as mine, which, sure, is of a much richer value than anything in the world besides. Should you save my life again, should you make me absolute master of your fortune and your person too, I should accept none of all this in any part of payment, but look upon you as one behindhand with me still. 'Tis no vanity this, but a true sense of how pure and how refined a nature my passion is, which none can ever know except my own heart, unless you find it out by being there ...

For God's sake let me hear of all your motions, when and where I may hope to see you. Let us but hope this cloud, this absence that has overcast all my contentment, may pass away, and I am confident there's a clear sky attends us.

My dearest dear, adieu.

Sir William Temple to Dorothy Osborne in a letter dated
18 May 1654

Sir William Temple, 1st Baronet, an English statesman, was born on 25 April 1628, during the reign of King Charles I. The lady to whom he addressed the above love letter was Dorothy Osborne. Despite protestations from both families, the two lovers overcame the various social and societal obstacles in their way and married in 1654. Temple was an important figure when it came to bringing about the 1677 marriage between William III of Orange and Princess Mary of York. England and the Dutch Republic had been through three wars (known as the Anglo-Dutch Wars) and a political alliance between both Protestant nations proved to be more important than even Temple himself could have anticipated. Temple died in 1699 during the reign of King William III.

26th – Racked and Hanged

By one who is come lately from Oxford, it is certified that Sir Arthur Aston, the Governor of Oxford, a grand papist, doth so tyrannise over the inhabitants of Oxford, misusing the Mayor and Alderman, and all the Protestants in the town.

There was a gentleman that was in Oxford at a tavern, where he called for a pint of sack, enquiring about some in the town, to whom he came about monies due to him. The vintner asked him from whence he came, he answered from London. The said vintner gave notice thereof to Sir Arthur Aston, who caused him to be apprehended, and the next day to be racked, and examined upon the rack, he make it appear that his business was about monies due to him, and produced a note, and nothing could be suspected justly by him but fair; yet, nevertheless, such as the Governor's cruelty, that after he had racked him, he cause him the next day to be hanged upon the gallows.

From Nehemiah Wallington's Diary, 26 April 1644

Nehemiah Wallington was an English artisan and Puritan who lived from 1598 to 1658. He is best remembered for keeping journals during the English Civil Wars, which among other things contained details of Matthew Hopkins' witchfinding trials. These journals shed valuable light upon the action of the period.

27th – Shakespeare's Scottish Play

Glamis thou art, and Cawdor; and shalt be
What thou art promis'd. ── Yet do I fear thy nature:

It is too full o' the milk of human kindness,
To catch the nearest way. Thou wouldst be great;
Art not without ambition; but without
The illness should attend it: what thou wouldst highly,
That wouldst; thou holily; wouldst not play false,
And yet wouldst wrongly win: thouldst have, great Glamis,
That which cries, 'Thus thou must do, if thou have it;
And that which rather thon dost fear to do,
Than wishest should be undone.' Hie thee hither,
That I may pour my spirits in thine ear,
And chastise, with the valour of tongue,
All that impedes thee from the golden round,
Which fate and metaphysical aid doth seem
To have thee crown'd withal.

Act 1: Scene 5, *Macbeth*, William Shakespeare, 1623

Macbeth, one of Shakespeare's greatest tragedies, was written early in the seventeenth century and performed before King James I in 1611. In this excerpt, Lady Macbeth receives word from her husband, sending ambitious thoughts coursing through her head.

28th – Betterton and the Amorous Widow

But I say. Yes. Do you think you shall keep me always stifling within doors, where there's no body to be seen but your old fusty self? No, I'll to the play, where there's all sorts of company and diversion; where the actors represent all the briskness and gaiety of life and pleasure; where one is entertain'd with airy Beaux, and fine Gallants, which ogle, sigh, and talk the prettiest things in the World. Methinks 'tis rare to hear a young brisk fellow court a handsome young Lass, and she all the while making such pretty dumb Signs: first turns aside to fee who observes, then spreads her Fan before her Face, heaves up her Breasts, and sighs at which he It ill swears he loves her above all the World— and presses hard his Suit; tells her, what force her Beauty, her Wit, her Shape, her Mien, all join'd in one, are of. At which she blushing curtsies low, and to her self replies, What charming Words he speaks! His Person's Heavenly, and his Voice Divine. By your Leave, Husband, you make me stay long.

The Amorous Widow, Or, The Wanton Wife, Thomas
Betterton, 1710

Thomas Betterton, English playwright, actor, and theatre manager, died on this day in 1710, during the reign of Queen Anne. Born around 1635 in London to an under-cook to Charles I, he eventually found his way onto the stage. Betterton has the reputation of being one of the best English actors in history, and was very serious and professional about his craft. In 1681 he became the manager of United Company. Betterton was a very popular actor, so much so that Samuel Pepys's wife, Elizabeth, named her dog after him. Betterton even had his portrait painted by Sir Godfrey Kneller in the 1690s.

29th – John Cleveland, Cavalier Poet

Shall I presume
Without perfume
My Christ to meet
That is all sweet!

No, I'll make most pleasant posies.
Catch the breath of new blown roses;
Top the pretty merry flowers,
Which laugh in the fairest bowers:
Whose sweetness Heaven likes so well,
It stops each morn to take a smell:
Then I'll fetch from the Phoenix nest
The richest spices, and the best:
Precious ointments I will make,
Holy myrrh and aloes take;
Yea, costly Spikenard, in whose smell
The sweetness of all odours dwell.
I'll get a box to keep it in,
Pure as his alabaster skin ...

'Mary's Spikenard', *The Works of
Mr John Cleveland*, John Cleveland, 1687

John Cleveland, an English poet and Royalist during the English Civil War, died on this day in 1658; he was born in 1618.

30th – Mary of York

Mary Stuart, Princess of York, was born on 30 April 1662 in St James's Palace, during the reign of her uncle King Charles II. As the daughter and eldest surviving child of James, Duke of York, and his wife, Anne Hyde, Mary's birth heralded little national joy. According to Samuel Pepys, 'The Duchess of York is brought to bed of a girl, at which I find nobody pleased.' The king was only two years into his reign and expected to produce a legitimate heir to the throne. Although the king was very capable of impregnating his lovers, his wife Catherine proved unable to bear him children. Mary, as a result of this and later the so-called Glorious Revolution of 1688/89, became Queen Mary II.

MAY

1st – 'The Maypole' & Death by Viper Wine

The May-pole is up,
Now give me the cup;
I'll drink to the garlands around it;
But first unto those
Whose hands did compose
The glory of flowers that crown'd it.

A health to my girls,
Whose husbands may earls
Or lords be, granting my wishes,
And when that ye wed
To the bridal bed,
Then multiply all, like to fishes.

'The Maypole', Robert Herrick (1591–1674)

*

It was also on this day in 1633, during the reign of Charles I, that Venetia, Lady Digby, one of the great beauties of the first half of the seventeenth century, died in rather mysterious circumstances. Married to Kenelm Digby and widely admired, one can suppose she tried everything within her power to maintain her famed and esteemed beauty once the effects of age began to take their toll. One of the things she used was viper wine – a wine which had viper venom mixed into it. Sir Kenelm Digby went into her bedchamber one morning and found her dead – but in such a state as to make her seem as though she was only asleep. The distraught widower had the great

Flemish Baroque painter Anthony van Dyck paint her on her deathbed. Van Dyck also created another sumptuous posthumous portrait of Lady Digby between 1633/34.

While it has never been proven that the viper wine was responsible for killing Lady Digby, many other ladies – especially in the early part of the Stuart era and in the preceding Elizabethan age – could die from their hazardous make-up.

2nd – The Demolition of Cheapside Cross

How? Steal the lead from Cheapside-Cross (O base!)
I'll take my oath on't 'tis a heavy case:
Some fay the Devil did it, and I grant
The Devil is a mighty Puritant.
He never could endure the Crosse, because,
Man (on the Crosse) was ransom'd from his claws;
But whofoe're 'twas, Brownist, Punk or Pimp:
If not the Devil, 'twas the Devils Imp ...

... And no true Christian justly can repine,
To let a Crosse stand as a Christian sign.
Knaves may deface it, fools may worship it,
All which may be for want of grace or wit,
To those that wrong'd the Crosse this is my curse,
They never may have crosses in their purse.

From 'Verses upon the Defacing of Cheape-side Crosse,
with the Picture of Christ and Saint Peter', *Works of
John Taylor, the Water Poet: Vol. 1,* John Taylor, 1630

The Eleanor Cross that stood in Westcheap (Cheapside), London, known as the Cheapside Cross, was demolished on 2 May 1643 by order of Parliament. By the time it was pulled down, this monument had been there for well over 300 years. The story of the Eleanor Crosses is very much worth mentioning here for it is a rather romantic tale of royal love and loss.

In 1290, Eleanor of Castile, Queen consort of England and wife of King Edward I (Edward Longshanks), died in Hadby, Nottinghamshire, aged forty-nine. Her husband was by her side. Edward and Eleanor had married in 1254, in a rare love match that continued throughout their lives; the Spanish-born queen even accompanied her husband on his Crusade in 1270. The couple had fifteen children together, including the future King Edward II. After her death, the grieving widower-king had her body embalmed and commanded that every place her coffin rested overnight on its way to Westminster Abbey was to be memorialised by the erection of an exquisitely crafted stone cross, each built between 1291–94. These were made at the following sites: Lincoln, Grantham, Stamford, Geddington, Northampton, Stony Stratford, Woburn, Dunstable, St Albans, Waltham, Westcheap, and Charing. For nearly a decade, Edward held onto his grief for his beloved wife, but diplomatic pressures for peace led to his marrying Margaret of France in 1299. At his death in 1307, he was buried beside his beloved first wife in Westminster Abbey.

And as you can see, what had been erected out of love was torn down by the hatred of those who thought it popish and idolatrous. As of 2016, only three of the original twelve crosses are still standing. Although visitors to London may, as they step outside from Charing Cross station, find themselves in front of a Charing Cross, that is actually a Victorian replica.

*

It was also on this day in 1711 that Laurence Hyde, 1st Earl of Rochester, died, during the reign of his niece Queen Anne. As a son of the Earl of Clarendon and brother of Anne Hyde, Duchess of York, Hyde was well positioned for a good place in the government.

3rd – A Murder of an Archbishop

Francis Branson, commander of the ship Anne and Hester, aged 30 years or thereabouts, in the behalf of his Majesty testifieth, that William Kelso, Chirurgeon, and John Bowland, mate of the said ship, being aboard, in the great cabin at sea, the 16th day of April last, 1680, amongst other discourses that then passed between them, the said William Kelso in hearing of this Deponent, did declare in the great cabin, that he was the Chirurgeon General, in the late rebellion in Scotland, and that after the Duke of Monmouth had been there and qualified them, Kelso cut off his hair and wore a Periwig, and made his escape into the north of Ireland, and from thence transported himself to Dublin, and was there some small time, and from thence he made his escape to Bristol, and there he stayed a while, and after went up to London. He then at the same time did declare, that he knew those persons that murdered the Archbishop of St. Andrews, and that they had made their escape disguised, and could not be found; that there were six of them that set upon him, when he was in his coach, going over a plain three miles from a village, that they hauled him out of his coach and told him that he had betrayed them, and therefore nothing should satisfy them but his blood. His Daughter being in the coach with him, opened her bosom, and desired them to spare her father and kill her, but they fell upon him with their pistols, first pistoling him, and then hewed him in pieces with their swords; all which words were spoken by the said Kelso, when we were coming from England, being then bound for the Isle of May.

Sworn to in Court, the 4th January 1680, in Boston, in New England. That this is a true copy taken and compared with the original, 4th January 1680. Attest, Edward Rawson, Secretary. A copy of the Deposition of Francis Branson.

From *Letters from the English Kings and Queens, Charles II, James II, William and Mary, Anne, George II, &c: To the Governors of the Colony of Connecticut, Together with the Answers Thereto, from 1635 to 1749: and Other Original, Ancient, Literary and Curious Documents*, ed. R.R. Hinman, 1836

James Sharp, Archbishop of St Andrews, was brutally murdered by a band of Presbyterians on this day in 1679, during the reign of King Charles II. Born in May 1618 to William and Isabel Sharp, James later attended King's College in Aberdeen. A monument to James Sharp was erected in Holy Trinity Church, St Andrews, later that year.

4th – Eclipsed by the Son-in-Law

James Thornhill, English Baroque painter, died on this day in 1734, during the reign of King George II. Born in Dorset around 1675, Thornhill's work adorns some of the most beautiful stately homes in the country; from Blenheim Palace to Chatsworth.

His most famous work is undoubtedly both the great artwork that adorns the ceiling and walls of the Painted Hall in the Old Royal Naval College, Greenwich, and the eight scenes he painted in St Paul's Cathedral in London. In the former work, William and Mary are an integral focal point with Mary regally looking directly at the viewer and William outstretching his hand, offering peace and liberty to Europe. It's no surprise that William and Mary take such a dominant position on the ceiling. On the list of major benefactors, William III comes in as the second-highest benefactor with the very large sum of £19,500. Interestingly, the most generous sum came from one Robert Osbolton, Esq. Osbolton gave five hundred pounds more than the king – £20,000!

Thornhill depicted William and Mary surrounded by Virtues and trampling upon tyranny and arbitrary power; William's landing on British soil during the Glorious Revolution of 1688 is also depicted. Other notable Stuart-era persons are depicted throughout the Hall, including John Flamsteed, and Tycho Brahe. Thornhill even left a self-portrait of himself on a wall. There are the six constellation signs painted in an arch; in the upper hall is Queen Anne and her husband, Prince George of Denmark. On the back wall of the Hall, some Hanoverians are present. In a similar manner to the Divine Right of Kings propaganda inherent in Rubens' paintings, which adorn the Banqueting House of Whitehall Palace, so the Painted Hall is Thornhill's propaganda piece about the Protestant succession in Britain following the Glorious Revolution.

Thornhill's daughter, Jane, married an up-and-coming artist William Hogarth, whose fame would ultimately eclipse that of his father-in-law. Hogarth is best remembered for his *Gin Lane* and *Beer Street* depictions.

5th – A Native of Formosa

The Third Law is against Adulterers, viz. They shall for the first offence pay a fine of 100 Copans (each Copan being a piece of gold weighing a pound) and those who have not money to pay such a fine, they shall be publicly whipped by the hand of the hangman. But if any person be guilty of the same crime a second time, he of she shall be beheaded. For though, as will appear in the following chapter about religion, every many may have as many wives as his estate is able to maintain; yet if any man shall carnally know another woman besides his own wives, to some he has promised fidelity, he is guilty of Adultery. The same law obliges all these who are unmarried provided they be natives of the country. But this law does not extend to Foreigners, to whom the natives are wont to offer virgins or whores, to made use of at their pleasure, with impunity.

An Historical and Geographical Decription of Formosa, an Island Subject to the Emperor of Japan, George Psalmanazar, 1704

George Psalmanazar (born c. 1679) claimed to be a native of Formosa (Taiwan) and the first of his people to visit Europe. In his *An Historical and Geographical Description of Formosa*, published during the reign of Queen Anne, Psalmanazar went into great detail about the clothing that the 'Formosans' wore, the diseases from which they suffered, the superstitious customs of their culture, of what their traditional diet consisted, their economy, and their laws (as highlighted in the above excerpt). It all made for quite interesting reading, although it was a total fake – Psalmanazar, you see, was a conman. After many had been duped by his imaginative descriptions of Formosa, it later transpired that Psalmanazar was certainly no Formosan – he was a Frenchman!

Jonathan Swift (1667–1745) took the opportunity to ridicule Psalmanazar in his satirical essay *A Modest Proposal*, in which he wrote:

But in order to justify my friend, he confessed, that this expedient was put into his head by the famous Salmanaazor, a native of the island Formosa, who came from thence to London, above twenty years ago, and in conversation told my friend, that in his country, when any young person happened to be put to death, the executioner sold the carcass to persons of quality, as a prime dainty; and that, in his time, the body of a plump girl of fifteen, who was crucified for an attempt to poison the Emperor, was sold to his imperial majesty's prime minister of state, and other great mandarins of the court in joints from the gibbet, at four hundred crowns.

Psalmanazar died in England in early May 1763.

6th – Cotton's Advice

Most Excellent Majesty,

We your Lords Spiritual and Temporal and the Commons of your realm assembled in this your Parliament, having received out of your mere grace, your royal command, to declare unto your Highness our advise and counsel, for the further continuing, or final break between your Majesty, the Emperor, and the Spanish King touching the rendition of the Palatinate, to the due and former obedience of your illustrious son the Prince Palatine; and that of marriage, between the Lady Mary Infanta of Spain, and the most excellent Prince your son, now Prince of Wales; We conceive it not unfit to offer up to your admired wisdom and consideration these important motives and resolution.

By contemplation whereof, we assume to ourselves that your Majesty apparently seeing the infinite calamity fallen of late unto the Christian world, by means of these disguised Treaties of Amity, and marriage before time, frequently used with your progenitors, and now lately with yourself by the House of Austria, and Spain, to advance themselves to the Monarchy of Europe, will graciously be pleased to accept our humble advice ...

From 'A Remonstrance of the Treaties of Amity and Marriage, Before time, and of Late of the House of Austria and Spain, &c.', in *Cottoni Posthuma: Divers Choice Pieces of that Renowned Antiquary Sir Robert Cotton, Knight and Baronet*, Sir Robert Cotton, 1672

Sir Robert Bruce Cotton, 1st Baronet, an English antiquarian and founder of the Cotton Library, died on 6 May 1631, during the reign of King Charles

1. Reading through his speeches, it becomes clear that Cotton enjoyed history – he often mentioned the reigns of previous kings and the troubles they encountered.

7th – Us, the Happy Instrument

It having pleased Almighty God, to make us the happy instrument of rescuing these nations from imminent dangers, and to place us upon the throne of these kingdoms, we think ourselves obliged to endeavour, to the uttermost, to promote the welfare of our people: which can never be effectually secured, but by preventing the miseries that threaten them from abroad.

When we consider the many unjust methods the French kind hath, of late years, taken, to gratify his ambition, that he has not only invaded territories of the Emperor, and the Empire, now in amity with us, laying waste whole countries, and destroying the inhabitants, by his armies; but declared war against our allies, without any provocation, in manifest violation of the treaties confirm'd by the guarantee of the crown of England, we can do no less than join with our allies, in opposing the designs of the French king, as the disturber of the peace, and the common enemy of the Christian world ...

> King William III, in a speech given at Hampton Court Palace on 7 May 1689, from *The Life of John, Duke of Marlborough, Prince of the Roman Empire*, 1743

When the 'Immortal Seven' (William Cavendish, 4th Earl of Devonshire; Henry Compton, Bishop of London; Richard Lumley, Baron Lumley; Thomas Osborne, 1st Earl of Danby; Henry Sidney; Edward Russell; and Charles Talbot, 12th Earl of Shrewsbury) invited William of Orange to invade England in 1688, it was bound to be a mutually beneficial situation for both sides. William had been fighting the French for years, and he wasn't going to refuse the temptation of the English Royal Navy, among other things. For the Protestants in Britain, a Catholic succession under James II was assured, and William – conveniently married to James II's eldest daughter and former heir, Mary – was the perfect alternative. He was a staunch Protestant (a Calvinist, specifically), seen by European Protestants as a heroic figure, and he had Stuart blood in his veins – albeit from his mother, Mary Stuart, Princess Royal and Princess of Orange. William believed in God's plan, as the above excerpt from his speech shows, as well as his continued and heartened desire to stop the French from their expansionism.

8th – Tempted by the Serpent

Serpent: Not eat? Not taste? Not touch? Not cast an eye
Upon the fruit of this fair tree? And why?
Why eat'st thou not what Heav'n ordain'd for food?
Or canst thou think that bad which Heav'n call'd good?
Why was it made, if not to be enjoy'd?
Neglect of favours makes a favour void:
Blessings unus'd pervert into a waste
As well as surfeits: woman, do but taste:
See how the laden boughs make silent suit
To be enjoy'd; look how their bending fruit
Meet thee halfway: observe but how they crouch
To kiss thy hand: coy woman, do but touch:
Mark what a pure vermilion blush has died
Their swelling cheeks, and how for Shame they hide
Their palsy heads, to see themselves stand by
Neglected: woman, do but cast an eye.
What bounteous Heaven ordain'd for use, refuse not;
Come, pull and eat: y' abuse the things ye use not.

Book I: Emblems, Francis Quarles, 1634

Francis Quarles, an English poet, was born on this day in 1592, during the reign of Queen Elizabeth I. Quarles died in 1644.

*

It was also on this day in 1670 that Charles Beauclerk, 1st Duke of St Albans, was born to King Charles II and his mistress Nell Gwynn, an actress. He was created Duke of St Alban's on 10 January 1684, and married Aubrey de Vere's daughter, Diana.

9th – Blood and the Crown Jewels

Thomas 'Colonel' Blood attempted to steal the Crown Jewels from the Tower of London on this day in 1671. The self-styled 'Colonel' Blood's daring attempt to steal the Crown Jewels is one of the most often-told facts about the Stuart era. Blood struck up a friendship with the Keeper of the Jewels and on 9 May he and several of his cronies visited the Tower. They beat the Keeper hard on the head, gagged and bound him before turning their attentions to what they'd come for. They bashed down the crown, the orb, and sawed the sceptre in half and hid these precious items among their clothing. It just so happened that the Keeper's son arrived in time to see what was going on and a chase ensued, but the villains were apprehended. This hadn't even been Blood's first crime. Back in 1663, the former Irish Parliamentarian had attempted to take control of Dublin Castle, but was thwarted and was forced to flee in order to save his life. He also tried to kidnap the Duke of Ormond on a couple of occasions.

Blood went back to the Tower – this time as prisoner – but he managed to get an audience with the king, who visited him in his cell. Whatever was spoken in that private interview worked out in Blood's favour; King Charles II, instead of severely punishing Blood for his crime, ended up giving him a reward – lands in England and Ireland. On 1 August 1671, Charles's Secretary of State, Lord Arlington, noted that Thomas Blood had been given a pardon from any and all crimes from 1660 to that point. Why did Charles do this? I don't believe anyone's been able to figure that out.

The coronation regalia Blood tried to steal were actually quite new. During the Commonwealth, Parliament decided to do away with all vestiges of monarchy. Cromwell ordered all of the royal regalia to be burned and melted down, and so it was done. Only a few items were smuggled away in time and preserved, including a coronation spoon. Most of the Crown Jewels we can see in the Jewel House at the Tower of London today were made for Charles II in 1661 for his own coronation. Other items are from subsequent monarchs.

10th – Sir Fopling Flutter

Dorimant: She means insensibly to insinuate a Discourse of Me, and artificially raise her jealousy to such a height, That transported with the first Motions of her Passion, she shall fly upon me with all the Fury imaginable, as soon as ever I enter; the Quarrel being thus happily begun, I am to play my Part, confess and justify all my roguery, swear her impertinence and ill humour makes her intolerable, tax her with the next Fop that comes into my head, and in a huff march away; slight her, And leave her to be taken by whosoever thinks it worth his time to lie down before her.

Med: This vizard is a spark, and has a genius that makes her worthy of your self, Dorimant.

The Man of Mode, Or, Sir Fopling Flutter: A Comedy,
George Etherege, 1703

George Etherege, a Restoration era playwright and poet, probably died on this day in 1692.

11th – 'Strafford's Life Should Be Preserved'

The Earl of Bedford secretly undertook to his Majesty, that the Earl of Strafford's Life should be preserved; and to procure His Revenue to be settled, as amply as any of his Progenitors; the which he intended so really, that, to my knowledge, he had it in design to endeavour to obtain an Act for the setting up the Excise in England, as the only natural means to advance the King's profit. He fell sick, within a week after the Bill of Attainder was sent up to the Lords House; and Died shortly after, much afflicted with the Passion and Fury which he perceived his Party inclined to: in so much as he declared, to some of near trust to him, that He feared, 'the Rage and Madness of this Parliament, would bring more Prejudice and Mischief to the Kingdom than it had ever sustained by the long Intermission of Parliaments.' He was a wise man, and would have proposed and advised Moderate courses; but was not incapable, for want of Resolution, of being carried into violent ones, if His Advice were not submitted too. And therefore many, who knew him well, thought his Death not unseasonable, as well to his Fame, as his Fortune; and that it, rescued him as well from some possible Guilt, as from those visible Misfortunes, which men of all Conditions have Since undergone. As soon as the Earl of Bedford was dead, the Lord Say (hoping to receive the reward of the Treasurership) succeeded him in his undertaking ...

The History of the Rebellion and Civil Wars In England,
Begun in the Year 1641, Edward Hyde, Earl of Clarendon, 1798

Francis Russell, 4th Earl of Bedford, died on this day in 1641.

12th – Strafford's Execution

On the 12th of May, I beheld on Tower-hill the fatal stroke which severed the wisest head in England from the shoulders of the Earl of Strafford, whose crime coming under the cognizance of no human law or statute, a new one was made, not to be a precedent, but his destruction. With what reluctancy the King signed the execution, he has sufficiently expressed; to which he imputes his own unjust suffering—to such exorbitancy were things arrived.

The Diary of John Evelyn, 1818

Thomas Wentworth, 1st Earl of Strafford, was executed on 12 May 1641. Strafford defended himself bravely and eloquently, so much so that he won. Pym, unable to stomach this, pulled the last card he had to play – an Act of Attainder against Strafford. King Charles agonised over whether he should sign the death warrant, for Strafford had been his loyal servant. In the end the king caved in and signed it, but regretted it for the rest of his life. The earl's execution was even made the subject of poetry, as evidenced by Sir John Denham's poem 'On the Earl of Strafford's Trial and Death':

> Great Strafford! worthy of that name, though all
> Of thee could be forgotten but thy fall,
> Crush'd by imaginary treason's weight,
> Which too much merit did accumulate.

13th – A Bitter Homecoming

But to myself I posted to England to see how fortune had dealt with me for my estate there, whither when I came, to add more vexation and grief I found our house extirpated and sold out of the name, the land, and revenue in like sort dispersed and severed to many buyers, which if my wild and wandering head had had any brains or consideration as one of sixteen or seventeenth years of age might have had and so kept in England, it might have been the cause it had not come to ruin as it hath done or at least so soon.

And if I had not been reasonably well under laid, I mean with money at my coming out of Germany which journey was very chargeable to me, I might have begged, for any friendship of my own kindred, and I must confess I found great friendship from those that were mere stranger to me which was Sir L. Tresham and his Lady, in whose house I have writ these my poor labour and for whose sake I reduced them to this head, and seeing my expectation had failed me here and no employment in England in that faculty of soldiery, which I have followed from my youth. I do give a Longum Vive to my Sovereign Lord and King, King Charles and will try my fortune again where I first raised it, and where I left a great deal of dead land which, if it please God, a happy peace to be between the Emperor and his subjects I may come to such an estate there as may beseem a greater man than myself. But yet so far am I bound to fortune (if there be any such a thing as fortune but divine providence) it hath delivered me from servitude, kept me since like a gentleman, and in good respect with greater persons than myself and at last left me in another manner of estate than when I first departed my native country. And so here is an end of the peregrination of Sidnam Poynes.

The Relation of Sydnam Poyntz, Sydenham Poyntz, 1624–36

Sydenham Poyntz (born *c.* 1607) was a Parliamentarian army officer during the First English Civil War. In his *Relation of Sydnam Poyntz* (also spelled Poynts or Poynes), he describes his life and times after he had fought on the Continent during the Thirty Years War, when he returned home to England. It must have been a bitter homecoming to find that his family home, possessions, and land had been sold. And, to makes things worse, he found that he could not find employment. In all probability, he must have returned to the Continent until the civil war began back home. It is not known when he died, nor indeed is there much information about him at all after 1650.

14th – Two Louis

King Louis XIII of France died on 14 May 1643, coincidentally on the same date on which his father King Henri IV had been assassinated in 1610. This is important because Louis had been the brother of Henrietta Maria, queen of England, Scotland, and Ireland.

As a result, Louis' son became King Louis XIV – who eventually became known as 'Le Roi Soleil', the Sun King. That being said, young Louis was far too young to rule in his own right. Louis' mother, Anne of Austria, was heavily manipulated by Cardinal Mazarin, so much so there were rumours of an affair between them; she had her husband's will voided and became sole regent until 1651. The Duke D'Enghien was Louis de Bourbon, Prince of Condé – a French military general. King Louis XIII and King Louis XIV often had their first names written as 'Lewis' in English pamphlets during the Stuart period. Louis XIII was Henrietta Maria's brother, and so Louis XIV was the first cousin of King Charles II and King James II of England, Scotland, and Ireland.

15th – Tempting a Wife

I count more than ever, Madame, upon your journey to the Pyrenees. If you love me, as all your letters assure me, you should promptly take a good coach and come. We are possessed of a considerable property here, which of late years my family have much neglected. These domains require my presence, and my presence requires yours. Enough is yours of wit or of good sense to understand that.

The Court is, no doubt, a fine country – finer than ever under the present reign. The more magnificent the Court is, the more uneasy do I become. Wealth and opulence are needed there; and to your family I never figured as a Croesus. By dint of order and thrift, we shall ere long have satisfactorily settled our affairs; and I promise you that our stay in the Provinces shall last no longer than is necessary to achieve that desirable result.

Three, four, five – let us say, six years. Well, that is not an eternity! By the time we come back we shall both of us still be young. Come, then, my dearest Athenais, come, and make closer acquaintance with these imposing Pyrenees, every ravine of which is a landscape and every valley an Eden. To all these beauties, yours is missing ...

Our huge, luscious peaches are composed of sugar, violets, carnations, amber, and jessamine; strawberries and raspberries grow everywhere; and nought may vie with the excellence of the water, the vegetables, and the milk ...

Now, madame, I am really tired of coaxing and flattering you, as I have done in this letter and in preceding ones.

Do you want me, or do you not? – Montespan.

> Letter dated 15 May 1667, from the *Memoirs of Madame de Montespan*, Françoise-Athénaïs de Rochechouart de Mortemart Montespan

Louis Henri de Pardaillan de Gondrin, Marquis de Montespan, was soon disappointed – she did not want him. His extremely beautiful young wife was none other than Françoise-Athénaïs, popularly known as Madame de Montespan, who was at the time of the letter well on the road to becoming one of the most celebrated of King Louis XIV's mistresses. Athénaïs went to court as a lady-in-waiting to Henriette-Anne (Minette), the Duchess d'Orleans, and it was there that she began to attract the king's attention. While some men enjoyed the material comforts that such a position could offer, the Marquis de Montespan was not the type to allow Athénaïs to cuckold him, even if it was with the king. He became intensely jealous, made scenes in public, and it is likely that he physically attacked Athénaïs. Although the Marquis would have been well within his rights as her lawful husband to be outraged by her infidelity, King Louis was not going to tolerate his bad behaviour. In 1670, the ball got rolling to bring the marriage between the couple to an end. Athénaïs, although beautiful and entertaining, was not very nice. Indeed, from various accounts she appears to have been downright nasty to Louis' wife Queen Maria Theresa and to Louis' mistress Louise de La Vallière. During the late 1670s, she was implicated in one of the most shocking scandals in French history, known as the Affair of the Poisons. Rumours spread that Athénaïs had engaged in black magic in order to make Louis fall for her.

16th – A Rhinoceros in England

Sir Dudley North, an English economist and politician, was born on this day in 1641, during the reign of King Charles I and shortly before the troubled times of the English Civil Wars began. His personal life appears unblemished by the adultery so readily dabbled in by many of his contemporaries. He married Anne, who was the daughter of Sir Robert Cann, an MP for Bristol. He had several brothers, three of whom were interesting in their own right. It was Roger North, the lawyer and biographer, who recorded an amusing story involving his brothers – of the first recorded rhinoceros to arrive in England:

I shall give an account of the most impudent buffoon lie raised upon him, and, with brazen affirmations of truth to it, dispersed from the court one morning, that ever came into fools' heads; and Satan himself would not have owned it for his legitimate issue. It fell out thus: a merchant, of Sir Dudley North's acquaintance, had brought over an enormous rhinoceros, to be sold to showmen for profit. It is a noble beast, wonderfully armed by nature for offence; but more for defence, being covered with impenetrable shields, which no weapon would make any impression upon; and a rarity so great, that few men, in our country, have, in their whole lives, opportunity to see so singular an animal. This merchant told Sir Dudley North, that if he, with a friend or two, had a mind to see it, they might take the opportunity at his house, before it was sold. Hereupon Sir Dudley North proposed to his brother, the lord keeper, to go with him upon this expedition; which he did, and came away exceedingly satisfied with the curiosity he had seen.

17th – Black Bart Roberts

Bartholomew Roberts sailed in an honest employ from London, aboard of the Princess, Captain Plumb, commander, of which ship he was second mate. He left England November, 1719, and arrived at Guinea about February following, and being at Anamaboe, taking in slaves for the West Indies, was taken in the said ship by Captain Howel Davis. In the beginning he was very averse to this sort of life, and would certainly have escaped from them had a fair opportunity presented itself; yet afterwards he changed his principles, as many besides him have done upon another element, and perhaps for the same reason too, viz. preferment; and what he did not like as a private man he could reconcile to his conscience as a commander.

The Buccaneers and Marooners of America: Being an Account of the Famous Adventures and Daring Deeds of Certain Notorious Freebooters of the Spanish Main, Alexandre Olivier Exquemelin, 1704

Bartholomew Roberts, Welsh pirate, was born on 17 May 1682, during the reign of King Charles II.

*

It was also on this day in 1649 that the Banbury Mutiny occurred. Soldiers from the New Model Army rose up against Cromwell but failed. On Cromwell's orders, the three leaders of the mutiny, James Thompson, Corporal Perkins, and John Church, were executed by firing squad on 17 May 1649. All three were Levellers. Those who believe in the principles for which the Levellers stood commemorate the men's deaths annually on Levellers' Day.

18th – Smalridge's Sermon

Must we wait, till the apologists for rebellion and murder have brought forth their strong reasons, and till we have tried the strength of those pleas, which they have to advance, in defence of bloodshed and parricide, before we proceed to determine anything in our own thoughts about them? Might we not, in this case, safely appeal to the first judgements of those, who are so hardy as to defend this day's treason, or even those, who were so wicked as to commit it? For, although there be no crime so heinous, which may not find some advocates, none so shocking to human nature, which men, violently pushed on by the instigation of the Devil, and given over to a reprobate mind by the just judgement of God, may not bring themselves, at last, to consent unto ...

> *A Sermon Preach'd Before the Right Worshipful the Court of Aldermen: At the Cathedral Church of St Paul, London, on Monday, January 31 1708/9.* George Smalridge, 1709

George Smalridge, an English clergyman and Bishop of Bristol, was born on this day in 1662, during the reign of King Charles II.

19th – The Hind and the Panther Transversed

'Tis no matter for that, let me alone to bring my self off. I'll tell you, lately I writ a damn'd Libel on a whole Party, sheer Point and Satyr all through, Egad. Call'd 'em Rogues, Dogs, and all the Names I could think of, but with an exceeding deal of Wit that I must needs fay. Now it happen'd before I could finish this Piece, the Scheme of Affairs was altered, and those People were no longer

Beasts. Here was a Plunge now: Should I lose my labour, or libel my Friend? Tis not every Body's Talent to find a Salvo for this: But what do me I, but write a smooth delicate Preface, where in I tell them that the Satyr was not intended to them; and this did the Business.

'The Hind and the Panther Transversed', from *The Works and Life of the Right Honourable Charles: Late Earl of Halifax, Including the History of His Lordship's Times, Parts 1-2*, Charles Montagu, 1715

Charles Montagu, 1st Earl of Halifax, an English politician and poet, died on this day in 1715, during the reign of King George I.

20th – Sprat's History of the Royal Society

Thus they continued without any great Intermissions, till about the year 1658. But then being called away to several parts of the Nation, and the greatest number of them coming to London, they usually met at Gresham College, at the Wednesdays and Thursdays Lectures of Dr. Wren, and Mr. Rook: where there joined with them several eminent persons of their common acquaintance: The Lord Viscount Brouncker, the now Lord Brereton, Sir Paul Neil, Mr. John Evelyn, Mr. Henshaw, Mr. Slingsby, Dr. Timothy Clark, Dr. Ent, Mr. Ball, Mr. Hill, Dr. Crone: and divers other Gentlemen, whose inclinations lay the some way. This Custom was observed once, if not twice a week, in Term time; till they w ere scattered by the miserable distractions of that Fatal year; till the continuance of their meetings there might have made them run the hazard of the fate of Archimedes: For then the place of their meeting was made a Quarter for Soldiers. But, (to make hast through those dreadful revolutions; which cannot be beheld upon Paper, without horror; unless we remember, that they had this one happy effect, to open men's eyes to look out for the true Remedy) upon this followed the King's Return; and that, wrought by such an admirable chain of events, that if we either regard the easiness, or speed, or blessed issue of the Work; it seems of itself to contain variety, and pleasure enough, to make recompense, for the whole Twenty years Melancholy, that had gone before.

The History of the Royal Society of London, for the Improving of Natural Knowledge, Thomas Sprat, 1667

Thomas Sprat, Dean of Westminster, died on 20 May 1713, during the reign of Queen Anne. Sprat had been an Anglican bishop and an English divine.

*

It was also on this day in 1609 that publisher Thomas Thorpe published William Shakespeare's sonnets for the first time.

21st – The Birth of a Pope

First in these fields I try the sylvan strains,
Nor blush to sport on Windsor's blissful plains:
Fair Thames flow gently from thy sacred spring,
While on thy banks Sicilian Muses sing;
Let vernal airs thro' trembling osiers play,
And Albion's cliffs resound the rural lay.

You, that too wise for pride, too good for pow'r,
Enjoy the glory to be great no more,
And carrying with you all the world can boast,
To all the world illustriously are lost!
O let my Muse her slender reed inspire,
Till in your native shades you tune the lyre:
So when the Nightingale to rest removes,
The Thrush may chant to the forsaken groves,
But, charm'd to silence, listens while she lings,
And all th'aerial audience clap their wings.

Daphnis and Strephon to the shades retir'd,
Both warm'd by Love, and by the Muse inspir'd;
Fresh as the morn, and as the season fair,
In flow'ry vales they fed their fleecy care.

'Spring, The First Pastoral', Alexander Pope, 1704

Alexander Pope, major English satirist and writer, was born on this day in 1688, during the reign of King James II.

*

It was also on this day in 1662 that King Charles II of England married the Portuguese Princess Catherine of Braganza.

22nd – The King's Speech

My Lords and Gentlemen, after it pleased Almighty God to take to his
Mercy the late king, my dearest brother, and to bring me to the throne
of my ancestors, I immediately resolved to call a parliament as the best
means to settle everything upon those foundations that may make my
reign both easy and happy to you, towards which I am disposed to
contribute all that is fit for me to do. What I said to my Privy Council
at my first coming there, I am desirous to renew to you, wherein
I fully declared my opinion concerning the principles of the Church
of England, whose members have showed themselves so eminently
loyal in the worst of times, in defence of my father, and support of my
brother, or Blessed Memory, that I will always take care to defend and
support it. I will make it my endeavour to preserve this state, as it is
now by law established, and I will never depart from the just rights
and prerogatives of the Crown ...

> *His Majesties Most Gracious Speech to both Houses of
> Parliament on Friday the 22nd of May 1685*, James II, from
> The British Library Board, 515.l.18.(34)

**In the above excerpt from King James II's speech, the king was only in the
third month of his reign.**

23rd – 'Go Pay Your whore'

Mirabel: Welcome to Paris once more, my dear Captain, we have
  eat heartily, drank roudly, paid plentifully, and let it go for once.
  I liked every thing but our women, they looked so lean and
  tawdy, poor creatures! 'Tis a sure sign the Army is not paid. Give
  me the plump Venetian, brisk and sanguine, that smiles upon me
  like the glowing Sun, and meets my lips like sparkling wine, her
  person shining as the glass, and spirit like the foaming liquour.
Dugard: Ah, Mirabel, Italy I grant you; but for our women here
  in France, they are such thin brawn fallen jades, a man may as
  well make a bedfellow of a cane-chair.
Mirabel: France! A light unseasoned country, nothing but
  feathers, foppery, and fashions; we're fine indeed so are our
  coach-horses; men say we're courtiers, men abuse us; that we
  are wise and politick, non credo seigneur. That our women
  have wit; parrots, mere parrots, assurance, and a good
  memory sets them up; There's nothing on this side the Alps
  worth my humble service t'ye. Ha, Roma la Santa! Italy for my
  money; their customs, gardens, buildings, paintings, policies,

wine and women! The paradise of the world; not pester'd with a parcel of precise old gouty fellows, that would debar their children of every pleasure that they themselves are the sense of. Commend me to the Italian familiarity: Here, son, there's fifty crowns, go pay your whore her week's allowance.

Act I: Scene I, *The Inconstant: Or, the Way to Win Him. A Comedy*, George Farquhar, 1751

George Farquhar, Londonderry-born actor and then dramatist, was buried in May 1707, having died on 29 April. Farquhar's theatrical career began on the stage in several secondary character roles. It was during his stint in John Dryden's play *The Indian Emperor* that he forgot to change his real sword for a foil and nearly killed the man he was stage-fighting with. This was enough to put an end to his acting career, but it was apparently no great loss for he wasn't a gifted actor. His talent truly lay in playwriting – the most popular of which was *The Beaux' Stratagem* from 1707.

*

Also on this day in 1701 Captain William Kidd, having been convicted of piracy, was executed by hanging, during the reign of King William III. In an Act published 14 June 1705 (under Queen Anne) the money and goods that were taken when Kidd was arrested were donated to the Royal Hospital for Seamen in Greenwich.

24th – Cecil's Trouble

Sir George,

The Queen again invested in their portions, you know very well that all of them can allege that the Queen sailed in diverse conditions which were obligatory in common, as the liberty they should have in transporting grain, with some other conditions to have horse in pay, and such like, with which they will plead as matter of right, besides the voice of their common calamity, which may seem to deserve dispensation, though in strict construction they lie open to her Mjesty's justice. Thus do you see that I sail between two rocks, wherein I must desire you pilotage, which is the principal motive of this letter, having tired myself with many other dispatches; and so I leave you to God his protection.

Your loving and assured friend, Ro. Cecyll.

Letter dated Whitehall 28 January 1600, from *Letters of Sir Robert Cecil to Sir George Carew*, Robert Cecil, 1838

Robert Cecil, 1st Earl of Salisbury, Lord Privy Seal under both Elizabeth I and James I, and Lord High Treasurer under James I, died on 24 May 1612. In 1603, it was in Cecil's home, Theobalds House, that the newly ascended James stayed for a few days, where he gave out many knighthoods to his loyal followers in attendance.

25th – Tumbledown Dick

And therefore now he [Oliver Cromwell] thought it time to show his son Richard to the world, whom to avoid the suspicion of designing the sovereignty to be hereditary in his family ... They in Council concluded, he could scare survive another Paroxysm; at which the Privy Council being astonished, they immediately repaired to him about his settling a successor, whom by the Petition he was to declare in his lifetime; but was then scare himself, which they perceiving, interrogated him, if he appointed not his son Richard? Whereunto he answered in the affirmative.

Flagellum, or, The Life and Death, Birth and Burial of Oliver Cromwell, the Late Usurper, faithfully described, James Heath, 1669

Richard Cromwell, Lord Protector, resigned from his position on this day in 1659. Richard has been given a hard time over the years, both during his lifetime and posthumously, being nicknamed 'Tumbledown Dick'. Richard Cromwell died during the reign of Queen Anne in 1712.

26th – Pepys's End

Up: and to the Office, where all the morning, and then home, and put a mouthful of victuals in my mouth; and by a hackney-coach followed my wife and the girls, who are gone by eleven o'clock, thinking to have seen a new play at the Duke of York's house. But I do find them staying at my tailor's, the play not being to-day, and therefore I now took them to Westminster Abbey, and there did show them all the tombs very finely, having one with us alone, there being other company this day to see the tombs, it being Shrove Tuesday; and here we did see, by particular favour, the body of Queen Katherine of Valois; and I had the upper part of her body in my hands, and I did kiss her mouth, reflecting upon it that I did kiss a Queen, and that this was my birth-day, thirty-six years old, that I did first kiss a Queen. But here this man, who seems to understand well, tells me that the saying is not true that says she was never buried, for she was buried;

only, when Henry the Seventh built his chapel, it was taken up and laid in this wooden coffin; but I did there see that, in it, the body was buried in a leaden one, which remains under the body to this day. Thence to the Duke of York's playhouse, and there, finding the play begun, we homeward to the Glass-House, and there showed my cousins the making of glass, and had several things made with great content; and, among others, I had one or two singing-glasses made, which make an echo to the voice, the first that ever I saw; but so thin, that the very breath broke one or two of them. So home, and thence to Mr. Batelier's, where we supped, and had a good supper, and here was Mr. Gumbleton; and after supper some fiddles, and so to dance; but my eyes were so out of order, that I had little pleasure this night at all, though I was glad to see the rest merry, and so about midnight home and to bed.

Entry dated 23 February 1669, *The Diary of Samuel Pepys*

Samuel Pepys, naval administrator famed posthumously for his diary, died on 26 May 1703, during the reign of Queen Anne. While his *Diary* is by far the work with which we most associate with Samuel Pepys, it was not published during his lifetime. Of course, being a diary it was intensely private – so much so it was written in what at first appears to be undecipherable code. In reality, this code was actually shorthand created by Thomas Shelton in the early 1600s. Shorthand was useful because it not only kept things private but also made writing faster – once you got the hang of how to use it. What Pepys did publish, however, was what we know as the *Memoires Relating to the State of the Royal Navy of England,* a defense against accusations of negligence in relation to ships during his time as secretary of the Admiralty. The *Memoires,* published in 1690 during the reign of William and Mary, was Pepys' way of fighting back against his accusers. Samuel married Elizabeth, a teenager, and together they lived on Seething Lane near the Tower of London.

27th – A Disgusted Liselotte

Le monde est pire encore que vous ne l'imaginez, et one ne peut faire une idée de tous les vices qui dominent; je connais un homme tellement dépravé, que ses exces s'étendaient jusque sur des animaux. Depuis que je le sais, je ne puis le voir sans horreur; il était au service de Monsieur: il était un vrai miserable et tout a fait dépourvu de raison. (The world is worse than you can imagine, and one can not get an idea of all vices that dominate; I know a man so depraved, that his excesses extended onto animals. After I learned of this, I could not look at him without horror; he was in the service of Monsieur. He was a real wretch and quite devoid of reason).

Letter dated 3 Decembre 1705, found in *Correspondance complète de madame duchesse d'Orléans née Princesse Palatine, mère du régent; traduction entièrement nouvelle par G. Brunet, accompagnée d'uné annotation historique, biographique et littéraire du traducteur,* Charlotte-Elisabeth, Duchesse d'Orléans, 1855

And so you have a taste of the frankness for which Charlotte-Elisabeth, Duchesse d'Orléans, was known; this lady was born on this day in 1652. Charlotte-Elisabeth was the second wife of Monsieur, Philippe duc d'Orléans – his first wife being Minette (also known as Henrietta-Anne, daughter of King Charles I of England and Henrietta Maria). Charlotte-Elizabeth is best remembered by her nickname, Liselotte; she was a notorious gossip, tomboy, and generally comes across as being larger-than-life character at the court. Originally from Germany, Liselotte used to be a playmate of William III of Orange and was a potential wife for him. Her father, however, decided that a match with France was more attractive, and Liselotte moved to France to wed Philippe – at which time she was also obliged to convert from Calvinism to Roman Catholicism. For anyone remotely interested in the Stuart era, which largely coincided with the reign of Louis XIV of France, Liselotte's *Memoirs* are a must-read. Liselotte's descendants include her great-granddaughter, the ill-fated Marie Antoinette, Queen of France.

28th – The Battle of Solebay

The Battle of Solebay was fought on this day in 1672, as part of the Third Anglo-Dutch War. It was the first naval battle of the war. The ship *Royal James* was burned during the fight; this event is commemorated in *The Burning of the Royal James at the Battle of Solebay* by Willem van de Velde, the Younger.

✻

Also on this day in 1644 occurred the Bolton Massacre during the English Civil War. The strongly Parliamentarian town of Bolton, Lancashire, was stormed by a Royalist force led by Prince Rupert of the Rhine. According to Michael Braddick in *God's Fury, England's Fire*, the Parliamentarians hanged one of their Royalist prisoners in front of his fellow Cavaliers, and so when Rupert's forces successfully took Bolton, the resulting carnage was an act of retaliation – which, of course, was later used heavily in turn by Parliamentarian propaganda.

29th – The Return of the King

This day, his Majesty, Charles II. came to London, after a sad and long exile and calamitous suffering both of the King and Church, being seventeen years. This was also his birthday, and with a triumph of above 20,000 horse and foot, brandishing their swords, and shouting with inexpressible joy; the ways strewn with flowers, the bells ringing, the streets hung with tapestry, fountains running with wine; the Mayor, Aldermen, and all the companies, in their liveries, chains of gold, and banners; Lords and Nobles, clad in cloth of silver, gold, and velvet; the windows and balconies, all set with ladies; trumpets, music, and myriads of people flocking, even so far as from Rochester, so as they were seven hours in passing the city, even from two in the afternoon till nine at night.

I stood in the Strand and beheld it, and blessed God. And all this was done without one drop of blood shed, and by that very army which rebelled against him: but it was the Lord's doing, for such a restoration was never mentioned in any history, ancient or modern, since the return of the Jews from their Babylonish captivity; nor so joyful a day and so bright ever seen in this nation, this happening when to expect or effect it was past all human policy.

Entry dated 29 May 1660, *The Diary of John Evelyn*

John Evelyn, a Royalist during the English Civil Wars, had good cause to be excited. Charles II's birthday fell on this day, which was also the day he entered London in triumph because the Republic had come to an end and the Stuart monarchy been restored. To commemorate this event, every 29 May since 1660 was celebrated as Oak Apple Day (or Royal Oak Day). It was named after the oak tree in which Charles had hid following his defeat at the Battle of Worcester in 1651. Monarchists in the United Kingdom continue to celebrate Oak Apple Day to this very day, even though it was abolished as a public holiday back in the nineteenth century.

30th – Dido, Queen of Carthage

These words are poison to poor Dido's soul,
O speak like my Æneas, like my love:
Why look'st thou toward the sea? The time hath been
When Dido's beauty changed thine eyes to her;
Am I less fair then when thou sawest me first?
O then Æneas, tis for grief of thee:
Say thou wilt stay in Carthage with my Queen,

And Dido's beauty will return again:
Æneas, say, how canst thou take thy leave?
Wilt thou kiss Dido? O thy lips have sworn
To stay with Dido: canst thou take her hand?
Thy Hand and mine have plighted mutual faith,
Therefore unkind Æneas, must thou say,
Then let me go, and never say farewell.

Act V, *The Tragedy of Dido Queen of Carthage*, Christopher
Marlowe and Thomas Nash, 1594

Christopher Marlowe (b. 1564) was stabbed to death on 30 May 1593. His violent end has usually been attributed to a tavern brawl and argument over a bill. Marlowe was stabbed above the right eye with a dagger; the man who did this, Ingram Frizer, was pardoned a month after this fatal incident. Although he died a decade before the Stuart era began in 1603, Marlowe's literary impact, with works such as *The Tragical History of Doctor Faustus* and *Hero and Leander*, was important to the playwrights who came after him. The story of the tragic Queen of Carthage not only inspired Marlowe but others who followed him in the next century such as Nahum Tate, and Baroque composer Henry Purcell, who wrote the music for *Dido and Aeneas* during the reign of William and Mary.

31st – Habernfeld's Plot

Most Illustrious and most Reverend Lord,

All my senses are shaken together as often as I revolve the present business, neither doth my understanding suffice, to conceive what Wind hath brought such horrid things, that they should see the Sunshine by me: for unexpectedly this good Man became known unto me, who when he had heard me discoursing of these Scotch stirs, said, that I knew not the Nerve of the business, that those things which are commonly scattered abroad are superficial. From that hour he every day became more familiar to me, who acknowledging my dexterity herein, with a full breast poured forth the burdens of his heart into my bosom, supposing that he had discharged a burden of Conscience wherewith he was pressed. Hence he related to me the Factions of the Jesuits, with which the whole earthly World was assaulted; and showed, that I might behold how through their Poison, Bohemia and Germany were devoured, and both of them maimed with an irreparable wound; that the same Plague did creep through the Realms of England and Scotland, the matter whereof, revealed in the adjacent writing, he discovered to me: Which things having heard, my Bowels were contracted together, my Loins trembled with horror, that a pernicious Gulf should be prepared for so many thousands of Souls: With words moving the conscience, I inflamed the mind of the Man; he had scarce one hour concocted my admonitions, but he disclosed all the secrets, and he gave free liberty that I should treat with those whom it concerned, that they might be informed hereof. I thought no delay was to be made about the things: The same hour I went to Sir William Boswell, the King's Leiger, at the Hague, who being tied with an Oath of Secrecy to me, I communicated the business to him, I admonished him to weigh these things by the balance, neither to deser, but act, that those who were in danger might be speedily succoured.

Andreas ab Habernfeld's Letter to the Archbishop, 1640

This was the letter which uncovered the Popish Plot that came to be known as Habernfeld's Plot after the discoverer, Andreas ab Habernfeld. In *A Critical Review of the State Trials*, published almost a century later in 1735, 'As to Habernfeld's Plot, his Grace showed, he sent the Papers to the King, immediately after his receiving them: And by those it appeared, There was a Conspiracy against own Life: He wondered therefore with what colour they could produce those Papers against him.' In Roger L'Estrange's *A Brief History of the Times* from 1687, several questions are posed, two of which are as follows: 'Was the pretended Popish Plot of 1678 only a copy drawn from Habernfeld's original of 1640? And was Habernfeld's model itself an historical truth, or a fiction?' J. P. Kenyon mentioned Habernfeld's Plot in his book, *The Popish Plot*, in which he stated Oates's plot of the 1670s was one of a handful of 'venerable antecedents'.

JUNE

1st – The Compleat Angler

Give me your hand: from this time forward I will be your Master, and teach you as much of this art as I am able; and will, as you desire me, tell you somewhat of the nature of some of the fish which we are to angle for; and I am sure I shall tell you more than every Angler yet knows.

And first I will tell you how you shall catch such a Chub as this was and then how to cook him as this was. I could not have begun to teach you to catch any fish more easily than this fish is caught; but then it must be this particular way, and this you must do:

Go to the same hole, where in most hot days you will find floating near the top of the water, at least a dozen or twenty Chubs; get a grasshopper or two as you go, and get secretly behind the tree, put it then upon your hook, and let your hook hang a quarter of a yard short of the top of the water, and 'tis very likely that the shadow of your rod, which you must rest on the tree, will cause the Chubs to sink down to the bottom with fear; for they be a very fearful fish, and the shadow of a bird flying over them will make them do so; but they will presently rise up the top again, and there lie soaring till some shadow affrights them again. When they lie upon the water, look out the best Chub, which you setting yourself in a fit place, may very easily do, and move your rod as softly as a snail moves, to that Chub you intend to catch; let your bait fail gently upon the water three or four inches before him, and he will infallibly take the bait, and you will be as sure to catch him; for he is one of the leather-mouth'd fishes, of which a hook does scarce ever lose his hold: and therefore give him play enough before you offer to take him out of the water. Go your way presently, take my rod, and do as I bid you, and I will sit down and mend my tackling till you return back.

The Compleat Angler: Or The Contemplative Man's Recreation,
Izaak Walton, 1653

Izaak Walton's *The Compleat Angler: Or The Contemplative Man's Recreation* was a very popular and fashionable book in Stuart Britain.

*

It was also on this day in 1648 that the Battle of Maidstone was fought, as part of the English Civil Wars.

2nd – The Loss of a Son

My sweet boy Rab, on Tuesday May 25th, was removed to my very sore and just grief. All who knew him bore witness of his piety, wisdom, learning, above many fellows. He had two of three year a flu, and when it went away, there remained for other two years a great rumbling of wind in his belly; which within these two months did weaken him sore, and made him keep in. Both he and I did still expect a recovery till the last fortnight, when he belly and legs began to swell … In that morning, after a potion which he (the physician) said to me, in my ear, he thought occasioned his greatest pain, he some shots of wind in his belly which tormented him fearfully, to a great crying of as great a pain as ever woman had at her last shower: they were indeed the passion of death. One of these, was in the morning at nine, lasted above an hour, another, at six at night, greater and longer. In both, always crying to God in great devotion and patience, beseeching a hastening of removal. When the height of these fits was over, he craved all pardon for clamour, rested on God, blessed him, exhorted all to the love and fear of God, recommended me the care of his brother and sisters, exhorted me to a spiritual walk and diligence to make use of my gift; and then, about ten o'clock, composed himself for rest. He most quietly, without pain or motion, breathed out his spirit …
  Your sorrowful cousin,

Robert Baillie, Glasgow, 1658

Such family tragedies were a common part of life in Stuart Britain. You may have noticed that 'June 2nd' was not listed at the heading of this letter. Sometimes letters from the Stuart era – as with any other time period – were undated, which can be problematic for researchers of any period. Such was the case with the excerpt from above, which was dated only June 1658.

3rd – The Chick in the Egg

What Aristotle says on the subject of the reproduction of the chick in ovo is perfectly correct. Nevertheless, as if he had not himself seen the things he describes, but received them at second hand from another expert observer, he does not give the periods rightly; and then he is grievously mistaken in respect of the place in which the first rudiments of the egg are fashioned, stating this to be the sharp end, for which he is fairly challenged by Fabricius. Neither does he appear to have observed the commencement of the chick in the egg; nor could he have found the things which he says are necessary to all generation in the place which he assigns them. He will, for instance, have it that the white is the constituent matter (since nothing naturally can by possibility be produced from nothing.) And he did not sufficiently understand how the efficient cause (the seminal fluid of the cock,) acted without contact; nor how the egg could, of its own accord, without any inherent generative matter of the male, produce a chick.

Aldrovandus, adopting an error akin to that of Aristotle, says besides, that the yolk rises during the first days of the incubation into the sharp end of the egg, a proposition which no eyes but those of the blind would assent to; he thinks also that the chalazae are the semen of the cock, and that the chick arises from them, though it is nourished both by the yolk and the white. In this he is obviously in opposition to Aristotle, who held that the chalazae contributed nothing to the reproductive powers of the egg.

Animal Generation, from *The Works of William Harvey*,
William Harvey, 1847

William Harvey, English physician, died on this day in 1657, during the Commonwealth. The Kentish physician made the monumental discovery that blood circulates throughout the body. Born in the Elizabethan age in 1578, he was both financially privileged and naturally intelligent enough to warrant going to university. He even studied abroad at the much-respected University of Padua, where he studied under Hieronymus Fabricius, who in turn had studied under Andreas Vesalius. The latter was a highly influential anatomist in the sixteenth century, notable chiefly because he found fault with certain aspects of Galen's work, as made evident in his 1543 work entitled, *On the Fabric of the Human Body.* Galenic medicine, although an ancient system, had gone largely unchallenged for centuries. William Harvey was going to turn the medical world upside down. In contrast to Galen's beliefs, Harvey theorised that it was the heart and not the liver which was the source from which the veins emanated. In 1628, Harvey published his findings in *Exercitatio Anatomica de Motu Cordis et Sanguinis in Animalibus.*

4th – The Last Duties of Love and Respect

The body of the king being embalmed, under the orders of Herbert and Bishop Juxon, was removed to St. James's. The usurpers of the government refused permission to bury it in Henry the Seventh's Chapel, from a dread of the indignation of the crowds who would assemble on so solemn and interesting an occasion; but at last, after some deliberation, the council allowed it to be privately interred in St. George's Chapel at Windsor, provided the expenses of the funeral should not exceed five hundred pounds. The last duties of love and respect were (according to Charles's express desire) paid to their sovereign's corpse by the Duke of Richmond, the Marquis of Hertford, Lord Southampton, Lord Lindsey, the Bishop of London (Juxon), Herbert, and Mildmay, who, on producing a vote of the Commons, were admitted by Whichcote, the governor of Windsor Castle, to the chapel. When the body was carried out of St. George's Hall, the sky was serene and clear; but presently a storm of snow fell so fast, that before it reached the chapel the pall and the mourners were entirely whitened. When the bishop (Juxon) proposed to read the burial service of the Church of England, the fanatical governor roughly refused, saying, 'that the Common Prayer Book was put down, and he would not suffer it to be used in that garrison where he commanded.'

Memoirs of Archbishop Juxon and His Times, William Juxon, 1869

William Juxon, an English clergyman and Archbishop of Canterbury, died on 4 July 1663, during the reign of King Charles II. Juxon was also in attendance at the execution of King Charles I outside Whitehall Palace in 1649.

5th – A Duchess's Conduct

The first time that my favour with the princess Anne of Denmark became an object of public attention, was upon the quarrel between her sister queen Mary and her, which happen'd a few years after the Revolution: Here therefore your lordship might naturally expect that I might begin my relation: But as I have been blamed for some memorable parts of the princess's conduct before that quarrel, it will be necessary to my present purpose to go back a little farther; and, perhaps, it may not be improper to say something even of the birth and first growth of that favour, which has given occasion to all the calumnies with which I have been aspersed. The beginning of the princess's kindness for me had a much earlier date than my entrance into her service. My promotion to this honour was wholly owing to impressions she had before received to my advantage; we had used to play together when she was a child, and she even then expressed a particular fondness for me. This inclination increased with our years. I was often at court, and the princess always distinguished me by the pleasure she took to honour me, preferably to others, with her conversation and confidence. In all her parties for amusement, I was sure, by her choice, to be one; and so desirous she became of having me always near her, that, upon her marriage with the prince of Denmark in 1683, it was, at her own earnest request to her father, I was made one of the ladies of her bed-chamber.

> *An Account of the Conduct of the Dowager Duchess*
> *of Marlborough: From Her First Coming to Court,*
> *to the Year 1710*, Sarah, 1st Duchess of Marlborough, 1742

Sarah Churchill (*née* Jennings), 1st Duchess of Marlborough, a favourite of Queen Anne and wife of military leader John Churchill, was born on this day in 1660. According to her husband's early biographer Thomas Lediard, Sarah's father was Richard Jennings and his wife, Frances. Sarah, as described by historian Hester W. Chapman in *Queen Anne's Son*, had a 'fiendish temper' and a 'maniacal arrogance' that would eventually lead to her falling out with not only the queen, but with members of her own family. She was so domineering a character that this is probably the reason why John Closterman painted her as the central figure in the Churchill family portrait.

6th – The Ashmolean Museum

The collection was originally begun in the time of Elizabeth, or James I., by John Tradescant. According to one account, he was a Dutch merchant settled in London, who had been originally one of the refugees expelled from Holland by the bigots of those days on religious grounds, like so many others who helped to augment the wealth of England at that period. Whether this account is correct or not, he was a man of great acquirements on various subjects, especially in botany and horticulture. He was employed by the Lords Salisbury and Wotton. He bore the title of the King's Gardener, was sent in the fleet to Algeria, and collected plants in Barbary and the Mediterranean Islands. He was also selected by Lord Danby to take charge of the Botanical Garden, but died about that time. He was assisted and succeeded by his son, who kept the then celebrated Tradescant's Ark until the time of Charles II. It was the earliest collection of the kind formed in England, and chiefly consisted of what are called curiosities, without regard to whether they were objects of Natural History — the works of God, or Antiquities — the works of Man, in the olden time. The collection, with the additions of Ashmole, included Birds, Beasts, and Fishes, especially the productions of distant countries, all that was comprised under the general name of 'Rarities.' Such was the general character of a Museum down to our own time ...

Ashmole added his large collection of books and manuscripts; no books were named in Tradescant's Catalogue. He proposed to present this valuable collection to the University of Oxford, who accepted the offer, and to show their sense of the value of it, erected the present building for it.

> *The Ashmolean Museum: Its History, Present State and Prospects:*
> *a Lecture Delivered to the Oxford Architectural and Historical*
> *Society, November 2, 1870, Vol. 19,* John Henry Parker, 1870

The Ashmolean Museum opened its doors for the first time on 6 June 1683, in Oxford. Princess Anne of Denmark, later Queen Anne, was in attendance, and the gloves which she wore to this event are now on display at the museum. As stated in the excerpt above, the Ashmolean, though it was named after its founder Elias Ashmole, owes a great deal of its early collection to the Tradescants – John Tradescant the Elder and John Tradescant the Younger.

7th – Banstead Village

Bansted is a small village, and a vicarage in the Deanery of Ewell; stands on the Downs, to which it gives a name, famous for its wholesome air, and formerly much prescribed by the London physicians to their patients, as the *ultimum refugium*, and is famous for its small, sweet mutton. The earth is whitish, a kind of chalk, mixed with flints and sand. Junipers flourish here; and where the land hath been ploughed, grows plenty of wild tansy, thyme, and a flower much like a marigold, but larger. In this parish is a house called Canons, which, with a parsonage, is said to have been appropriated to the Priory of St Mary-Overies in Southwark, from whence some canons were removed; within its precincts is a well of threescore fathoms deep. About half a quarter of a mile distant is a gate, called Can-Hatch. In this parish stands a seat belonging to the family of Buckles (which is in the manor of Great-Borough) where is standing a chapel. From this place is a stately prospect into Kent, Hertfordshire, Middlesex, Buckinghamshire, part of Oxfordshire beyond Henley upon Thames, Hampshire, Berkshire, part of Surrey, and a full view of the City of London, from the Tower to Westminster.

Natural History and Antiquities of the County of Surrey: Begun in the Year 1673, John Aubrey, 1718

John Aubrey, an English biographer and antiquary, was buried at St Mary Magdalene Church in Oxford on this day in 1697. Aubrey suffered from ill health and left many works uncompleted, including his most famous work, *Brief Lives*, which is a collection of mini biographies of historical figures both contemporary and historical. Aubrey wasn't just interested in people, but in diverse subjects such as economics – he wrote about the improvement in clothing manufacturing under Charles II – and natural history and antiquities. In *The Natural History of Antiquities of the County of Surrey*, which was excerpted above, we can see how different things are now. 'Bansted' is present-day Banstead in Surrey. Aubrey was friends with several notable persons, including the dramatist William Davenant and the antiquarian Anthony à Wood. Aubrey's other works were also unfinished and needed helping hands to sort them out for publication. *Miscellanies Upon Various Subjects* was begun by Aubrey in 1652 and he kept working on it, on and off, until the 1690s. At that point he sent it to James, Earl of Abingdon and wrote, 'It was my intention to have finished my Description of Wiltshire (half finished already) ... but my age is now far too spent for such undertakings.' And so he passed the task of completing it to Thomas Tanner.

*

Also on this day, in 1662 Celia Fiennes was born, in Wiltshire, shortly after the Restoration of the Stuarts to the throne. Fiennes is important because she travelled extensively throughout England between 1682 and 1712, noting her thoughts as she went along. The most surprising element of her travels is that she was neither married nor escorted properly for the time – she usually only had servants with her. In her writings, Fiennes describes her travels to English towns and cities such as Bath, Yeovil, and Daventry, among others. She visited several stately homes, including Woburn Abbey, and palaces, including her visit to Hampton Court Palace where she had a look around Queen Mary II's temporary apartments in the old Tudor Water

Gallery. She also explored various northern cities and towns and visited the stunning Lake District.

8th – The Winter Princess

Sophia of Hanover died on 8 June 1714. Sophia was the daughter of Elizabeth Stuart and so was the heir to Queen Anne's throne. When Anne died less than two months after Sophia, the thrones of England, Scotland, and Ireland passed to Sophia's son, Georg Ludwig – King George I. Stuart Britain might well have had a Queen Sophia! It is often asked why the British throne went to the Germans, and this is largely down to a matter of religion. Many of those closest to the throne by blood were Roman Catholics, including the legitimate heir – James Francis Edward Stuart – but it was decided in the Act of Settlement of 1701 during the reign of King William III that the throne would only go to those of the Protestant faith. As a result, a great many people who were more closely linked to throne by blood were excluded in favour of the Hanoverians. The reason for this was quite simple. Electress Sophia of Hanover, sister of Rupert of the Rhine, was the daughter of the Stuart Princess Elizabeth, who was in turn the daughter of King James I. As this line was predominantly Protestant, they became the heirs to the Protestant Stuarts' throne.

9th – These Distracted Times

Thomas Tomkins, a Welsh composer, died on this day in 1656, during the time of the Commonwealth. Tomkins's *These Distracted Times* is quite possibly the most perfect music to convey the extremely tumultuous period of the English Civil Wars. There is an inherent sadness to the music that encompasses feelings of suffering and loss. Tompkins composed music to go with the lines from II Samuel, 18:33 (KJV): 'When David heard that Absalom was slain he went up into his chamber over the gate and wept, my son, my son, O Absalom my son, would God I had died for thee!' When one considers how many sons were killed during the Civil War, this piece is even more moving.

10th – A Warming-Pan Baby

James Francis Edward Stuart was born to Mary of Modena and James II in St James's Palace on this day, 10 June 1688. This birth was surrounded by rumour, including the oft-repeated tale that Mary's baby had died and a newborn child was smuggled into the chamber in a warming pan. This ludicrous story was even believed by baby James's older half-sisters Mary and Anne. The less intriguing historical reality is that there were dozens of courtiers in attendance at the birth, including Charles II's widow, Catherine of Braganza.

Upon his father's death in 1701, James Francis was proclaimed James III by his Jacobite supporters. In 1715, James landed in Scotland as part of the Jacobite invasion of 1715, but this proved a disaster, not helped by his falling severely ill upon his (late) arrival. By 1719, both his parents and his sister Louisa Maria were dead, and he married the Polish noblewoman Maria Clementina Sobieski, who was a granddaughter of the Polish hero Jan Sobieski III (of Battle of Vienna fame). The couple had two sons, Charles Edward and Henry Benedict. The latter became a Cardinal in the Roman Catholic Church, but the former became the leader of the Jacobite rebellion of 1745 and was known as 'The Young Pretender' and, more famously, Bonnie Prince Charlie. The Jacobites fought against King George II's army and were defeated at the Battle of Culloden on 16 April 1746.

James Francis died in 1766 and was buried in St Peter's Basilica in the Vatican City. And so, the Prince of Wales was denied his birthright because of his parents' religion.

11th – Kenelm Digby on Honey

The honey of dry open countries, where there is much wild thyme, rosemary, and flowers, is best. It is of three sorts, Virgin-honey, Life-honey, and Stock-honey. The first is the best. The Life-honey next. The Virgin-honey is of bees that swarmed the spring before, and are taken up in autumn; and is made best by choosing the whitest combs of the hive, and then letting the honey run out of them lying upon a sieve without pressing it, or breaking off the combs. The Life-honey is of the same combs broken after the Virgin-honey is run from it; the merchants of honey do use to mingle all sorts together. The first of a swarm is called Virgin-honey. That of the next year, after the swarm was hatched, is Life-honey. And ever after, it is honey of Old-stocks. Honey that is forced out of combs will always taste of wax. Hampshire honey is most esteemed at London. About Bisleter there is excellent good. Some account Norfolk honey the best.

The Closet of Sir Kenelm Digby Knight Opened, Kenelm Digby, 1669

Sir Kenelm Digby, English courtier and diplomat, died on this day in 1665, during the reign of Charles II. According to Anne MacDonell in the introduction to the 1910 publication of *The Closet of Sir Kenelm Digby Knight*

Opened, 'But if Sir Kenelm consorted only with the great, it was with the great of all social ranks ... Digby was too great a gentleman to be above exchanging receipts with the professors of the "mystery ... he had an eye for all".'

12th – The Raid on the Medway

Up very betimes to our business at the office, there hiring of more fire-ships; and at it close all the morning. At noon home, and Sir W. Pen dined with us. By and by, after dinner, my wife out by coach to see her mother; and I in another, being afraid, at this busy time, to be seen with a woman in a coach, as if I were idle, towards Turner's; but met Sir W. Coventry's boy; and there in his letter find that the Dutch had made no motion since their taking Sheerness; and the Duke of Albemarle writes that all is safe as to the great ships against any assault, the boom and chain being so fortified; which put my heart into great joy.

When I come to Sir W: Coventry's chamber, I find him abroad; but his clerk, Powell, do tell me that ill news is come to Court of the Dutch breaking the Chain at Chatham; which struck me to the heart. And to White Hall to hear the truth of it; and there, going up the back-stairs, I did hear some lackeys speaking of sad news come to Court, saying, that hardly anybody in the Court but do look as if he cried, and would not go into the house for fear of being seen, but slunk out and got into a coach ... my mind is so sad and head full of this ill news that I cannot now set it down ... and so home, where all our hearts do now ache; for the news is true, that the Dutch have broke the chain and burned our ships, and particularly 'The Royal Charles'.

Entry for 12 June 1667, *The Diary of Samuel Pepys*

On this day in 1667, the Dutch delivered a major (and embarrassing!) blow to the English when they captured the *Royal Charles* (previously named *Naseby*) and sailed it into Dutch waters. The Duke of Albemarle's assurance that the fleet was secure on the Medway (Chatham) proved exceptionally – and even dangerously – optimistic. A Dutch offensive led by Michiel de Ruyter, Willem Joseph van Ghent, and Cornelius de Witt made its way from the Dutch Republic (the Netherlands) up to the River Medway in Kent. (The River Medway is the major river to the south of the River Thames.) One of the major naval anchorages was located in Chatham Dockyard, and after they had attacked and taken Sheerness, the Dutch sailed on Chatham. Albermarle was forced to order ships sunk so the Dutch couldn't take them away; all in all, thirteen English ships were lost, resulting in the Royal Navy's loss of approximately £200,000.

A story quickly spread that while the Dutch were successfully attacking English ships, the king was occupied with his mistress Castlemaine in running around a room after a moth, thus inadvertently indicating where his priorities lay. In the face of such unmitigated disaster, Commissioner Peter Pett (whose model ships and plans were taken as well) was scapegoated and sacked from his position. In his entry for 13 June, Pepys went so far as to write that Pett deserved to be hanged.

This event was immortalised in several works of art, including Ludolf Backhuysen's 1667 oil painting, *Dutch attack on the Medway, the* Royal Charles *carried into Dutch water, 12 June 1667.* The depiction encapsulates the political defeat, for in the centre of the image, the ship bears not only Charles II's royal standard, but also the Dutch colours.

The ship was scrapped but its stern carving was retained and is now displayed in the collection of the Rijksmuseum in Amsterdam. Ultimately, the Raid on the Medway forced King Charles II to settle on a peace with the Dutch in the Treaty of Breda (1667).

June 13th – From a Wife to Her Husband, the King.

My dear heart,

You must tell me, if you please, whether in case it be not at Yarmouth, it shall be at Boston, one of the two, assuredly; therefore, give orders. I dread the sea so much, that the very thought of it frightens me, not on account of the fleet of the rebels; though that is a beast that I hate, but I fear it not.

I am very glad you have shown your people that you have always desired an accommodation, but since the factious men in the Parliament have answered you with so much insolence, after you sent with such gentleness, I doubt not but your courage and resolution will prevail over their rashness and rebellion; and, although I have always much wished an accommodation, yet, seeing their insolence, I am satisfied that it has not depended on you, and that you should pursue your plans with firmness.

God help you, your cause being so just. He never was a protector of rebellion. You have acted the part of a good and just king in desiring the paths of mildness, which being those of justice, you were bound to follow. Protect your servants; that will acquire you others, and punish those who offend you, the Parliament has set you the example of it, but theirs is left-handed and ours right.

I received yesterday a letter from Pym, by which he sends me word that he fears I am offended with him, because he has not had a letter from me for a long time. I beg you tell him that that is not the case, and that I am as much his friend as ever, but I have so much business, that I have not been able to write by expresses, and by the post it is not safe. Remember me also to Prince Rupert, and tell him from me, that he must not hazard himself, as I understand he does. Remember me to Charles, James, and Prince Maurice, and believe truly, my dear heart, that had I not already loved you as much as I do, the courage you have shown against all the accidents which have happened, would make me do it, and will make me live and die.

Entirely yours.

> Letter dated 16 October 1642 from Henrietta Maria,
> queen consort, to her husband, King Charles I

King Charles I married Henrietta Maria in person on 13 June 1625, having already been married by proxy. Their early marriage was a rocky one, but in time – and especially after the Duke of Buckingham's assassination – they came to be deeply devoted to each other. In 1629, Henrietta Maria went through the trauma of a miscarriage, and the personal tragedy brought the young couple even closer together. Charles and Henrietta Maria were truly committed to each other, although that didn't prevent rumours from circulating – in particular, those involving Henrietta Maria and the courtier, Henry Jermyn. Charles and Henrietta weathered many storms, but their relationship was cut short when he was executed in 1649.

June 14th – The Battle of Naseby

The Battle of Naseby was fought on this day in 1645 in Northamptonshire, England, and resulted in a decisive Parliamentary victory. This three-hour-long confrontation was one of the most important and decisive battles in British history. According to the eighteenth-century Scottish historian and philosopher David Hume in his *History of Great Britain* (1789), 'At Naseby was fought, with forces nearly equal, this decisive and well-disputed actions, between king and parliament. The main body of the Royalists was commanded by the king himself, the right wing by Prince Rupert, the left by Sir Marmaduke Langdale. Fairfax, seconded by Skippon, placed himself in the main body of the opposite army. Cromwell in the right wing: Ireton, Cromwell's son-in-law, in the left. The charge was begun, with his usual celerity and usual success, by Prince Rupert.'

Parliament's New Model Army under Fairfax and Cromwell were more organised, disciplined, and were greater in numbers than the Royalist army under Prince Rupert of the Rhine and King Charles I. After an initial good start for the Royalists, things ended badly for them.

Prince Rupert, again according to Hume, 'sensible too late of his error, left the fruitless attack on the enemy's artillery, and joined the king, whose infantry was now totally discomfited. Charles exhorted this body of cavalry not to despair, and cried aloud to them, one charge more, and we recover the day. But the disadvantages under which they laboured, were too evident; and they could by no means be induced to renew the combat. Charles was obliged to quit the field, and leave the victory to the enemy.'

The Royalists suffered around 1,000 casualties and about 5,000 others were taken prisoner. The victorious Parliamentarian troops turned their attentions to the camp followers, which were largely comprised of Welsh women. Believed by their attackers to be Irish, these 'whores' as they were called, were subjected to facial disfigurements – for example, some had their noses slit – and others were killed.

The Battlefield Trust's website has some exceptionally good information available to download, especially for Civil War enthusiasts who wish to visit the sites associated the Battle of Naseby. This site contains a clear battlefield trail, which takes visitors to all key sites of action. There are several viewpoints, including Prince Rupert's, and Fairfax's, and the site helpfully indicates which roads are single track only, and which footpaths are open.

15th – Marital Relations

The lady told him again, that rather than any, other than King James should ever reign in this place, she would rather eat their hearts in salt, though she were brought to the gallows instantly. He told her, that the Secretary had too much wit ever to live under a man that had a foreign stock, having been so fortunate under a woman, that was tractable, and to be counsel led. The lady told him, that he need not long triumph upon her poor brother's mishap, for if he kept in this mind, she could expect no better end of him than the same, or a worse destiny. Thus being newly reconciled *usque ad conjugalem copulam* (up until marital relations) which was not in more two years before, they departed in passion, not according to the rule of the philosopher, that *omne animal post coitum triste* (every animal is sad after intercourse), but by the distemper of an atheist, that, besides Raleigh's Alcoran, admits no principles. Within ten days after, he came again, but without any other affection, than a Flemish jade comes to a courser-mare, desiring only an heir-male, to prevent the brothers that are next, whom he hates damnably, and protesteth to some of his friends, that, next to his wise, he abhorreth them above any ...

Letter dated December 1601, 'Lord Henry Howard to Mr E. Bruce',
The Secret Correspondence of Sir Robert Cecil with James VI,
King of Scotland, ed. Sir D. Dalrymple, 1766

Henry Howard, 1st Earl of Northampton, died on 15 June 1614, during the reign of King James I. In the above letter, Howard writes about Dorothy Devereux (c. 1564–1619), who was the daughter of Lettice Knollys and Walter Devereux, and so sister to the ultimately doomed favourite of Queen Elizabeth, Robert Devereux, 2nd Earl of Essex. Dorothy became a widow after the death of her first husband, Sir Thomas Perrot (1553–94). She later married Percy, Earl of Northumberland (1564–1632), who is the husband to whom Howard refers in the exchange. It may seem strange to us that Lord Henry Howard would talk about Dorothy and Percy's sexual relations, but, then again, aristocratic marriages were often heavily involved in politics. Howard relates that Percy had relations with his wife with more regularity than was expected because he hated his brothers so much that he wanted Dorothy to bear him heirs as soon as possible, to exclude them from the line.

*

It was also on this day in 1707 that the renowned Baroque painter Antonio Verrio died. Verrio's exquisite work can be seen in some of the most amazing historical places in the country, including Hampton Court Palace's William III State Apartments. His work adorns the King's Staircase and the King's Little Bedchamber.

16th – A Great Churchill

John Churchill, 1st Duke of Marlborough, died on this day in 1722, having led one of the most extraordinary lives of the Late Stuart era. From an impoverished aristocratic background he worked his way up from lowly page to soldier to become one of the greatest military leaders in British history.

17th – Addison to Pope

To Alexander Pope:

I was extremely glad to receive a letter from you, but more so upon reading the contents of it. The work you mention will, I dare say, very sufficiently recommend itself when your name appears with the proposals: and if you think I can any way contribute to the forwarding of them, you cannot lay a greater obligation upon me, than by employing me in such an office. As I have an ambition of having it known that you are my friend, I shall be very proud of showing it by this or any other instance. I question not but your translation will enrich our tongue, and do honour to our country; for I conclude of it already from those performances with which you have obliged the public. I would only have you consider how it may most turn to your advantage. Excuse my impertinence in this particular, which proceeds from my zeal for your ease and happiness. The work would cost you a great deal of time, and, unless you undertake it, will, I am afraid, never be executed by any other; at least I know none of this age that is equal to it besides yourself.

I am at present wholly immersed in country business, and begin to take a delight in it. I wish I might hope to see you here some time, and will not despair of it, when you engage in a work that will require solitude and retirement.

Letter dated 26 October 1713, Joseph Addison

Joseph Addison, an English writer and one of the founders of the *Spectator* magazine, died on this day in 1719. Born in 1672, Addison grew to fortune and power under the reign of William III.

18th – Of Counterpoint

Before notes of different measure were in use, their way of composing was, to let pricks or points one against another, to denote the concords; the length or measure of which points, was sung according to the quantity of the words of syllables which were applied to them. And because, in composing our descant, we set note against note, as they did point against point, from thence it still retains the name of Counterpoint.

In reference to composition in Counterpoint, I must propose unto you the bass, as the groundwork or foundation upon which all musical composition is to be erected. And from this bass we are to measure or compute all those distances or intervals which are requisite for the joining of other parts thereto.

A Compendium of Practical Musick in Five Parts, Christopher Simpson, 1667

Christopher Simpson (c. 1602–69) was an English composer and viola da gamba musician who often worked for wealthy Catholic families. Simpson dedicated the above work to William Cavendish, the Duke of Newcastle, and in this dedication, Simpson states that 'it is but a compendium (my Lord) yet contains all that is requisite to the knowledge of practical musick'.

Simpson's music remains popular with lovers of Early Music and is readily available to listen to, unlike some of the most obscure composers of the Stuart period.

19th – The Trial of Edward Coleman

May it please you my Lord, and you Gentlemen of the jury; Mr. Edward Coleman, now the prisoner at the Bar, stands indicted for High Treason, and the Indictment sets forth, that the said Edward Coleman, endeavouring to subvert the Protestant religion, and to charge and alter the same; And likewise to stir up Rebellion and Sedition amongst the King's liege people, and also to kill the king; did on the 29th of September in the twenty seventh year of the reign of our Sovereign Lord the King, at the Parish of St. Margaret's Westminster in this county, compose and write two several letter to one Monsieur Le Chese, that was then servant and confessor to the French King, and this was to procure the French King's aid and assistance to him and other traitors, to alter the religion practiced, and by Law established here in England, to the Romish superstition. The indictment sets forth likewise, that on the same day, he did write and compose two other letters to the same gentleman, that was servant and confessor to the said king, to prevail with him to procure the French king's assistance to alter the religion in this kingdom established to the Romish religion.

The *Tryal of Edward Coleman, Gent. For Conspiring the Death of the King*. London, 1678

Edward Coleman (1636–78) was an English Catholic who was employed as Mary of Modena's secretary for some years in the 1670s until 1676. The 1670s and early 1680s witnessed a massive anti-Catholic wave which became known as the Popish Plot. This, concocted by Titus Oates and Israel Tonge, accused many – including those in the royal sphere – of conspiracy to kill Charles II in order to place his Catholic brother James upon the throne. Coleman was one of the accused, and due to his interactions with Frenchmen such as François de la Chaise (Monsieur Le Chese) and Barillion, the French ambassador, it was enough to condemn him. At Tyburn, on 3 December 1678, Coleman was subjected to a traitor's death of hanging, drawing, and quartering. The above excerpt comes from his trial, and this was published in the year of his execution. In 1929, Coleman was beatified by the Roman Catholic Church under Pope Pius XI.

20th – The Fair Penitent

Away, I think not of him. My sad Soul
Has form'd a dismal melancholy scene.
Such a retreat as I would wish to find;
And unfrequented vale, o'ergrown with trees
Mossy and old, within whose lonesome shade,
Ravens, and birds ill omen'd, but a brook
That bubbling, winds among the weeds: no mark
Of any human shape that had been there,
Unless a skeleton of some poor wretch,
Who had long since, like me, by Love undone,
Sought that sad place out to despair and die in.
There I fain would hide me,
From the base world, from malice, and from shame.

Act II: Scene I, *The Fair Penitent*, Nicholas Rowe, 1703

Nicholas Rowe, an English dramatist, died on this day in 1718. The multilingual Rowe was born in Bedfordshire, England, in 1673. He became Poet Laureate of the United Kingdom in 1715 during the reign of King George I.

21st – Inigo Jones on Stonehenge

Being naturally inclined in my younger years to study the arts of design, I passed into foreign parts to converse with the great masters thereof in Italy; where I applied myself to search out the ruins of those ancient buildings, which in despite of time itself, and violence of barbarians, are yet remaining. Having satisfied myself in these, and returning to my native country, I applied my mind more particularly to the study of architecture. Among the ancient monuments whereof, found here, I deemed none more worthy the searching after, than this of Stone-Heng; not only in regard of the founders thereof, the time when built, the work itself, but also for the rarity of its invention, being different in form from all I had seen before; likewise, of as beautiful proportions, as elegant in order, and as stately in aspect, as any.

King James, in his progress the year One Thousand Six Hundred and Twenty, being at Wilton, and discoursing of this antiquity, I was sent for by the Right Honourable William, then Earl of Pembroke, and received there his Majesty's Commands to produce, out of mine own practice in architecture, and experience in antiquities abroad, what possibly I could discover concerning this of Stone-Heng ...

1. Mid-seventeenth-century card players, as depicted by Flemish Baroque artist Josse van Craesbeeck. Card games were very popular during the Stuart period. (Courtesy of the Getty's Open Content Program)

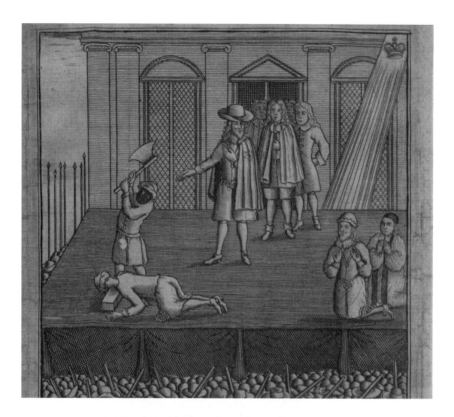

Above: 2. The execution of King Charles I on 30 January 1649, outside the Banqueting House of Whitehall Palace, sent shockwaves throughout both the kingdoms of Stuart Britain and Europe. (Courtesy of the British Library Flickr)

Left: 3. After the Restoration of the Stuart monarchy in 1660, King Charles II's reign was troubled by plague, fire, and a love life that overshadowed the politics of his government. The 'Merry Monarch' died in 1685. (Courtesy of the British Library Flickr)

3. *A Tale of a Tub*, written and published in the Late Stuart era, was one of Jonathan Swift's (1667–1745) most renowned satirical works. (Courtesy of the British Library Flickr)

4. Alexander Pope (1688–1744) was a major satirical writer, poet, and translator during the eighteenth century, but began writing and publishing during the Late Stuart era. (Courtesy of the British Library Flickr)

5. Abraham Cowley (1618–67) was an English Royalist poet famed for his poems during the English Civil War. (Courtesy of the British Library Flickr)

6. John Milton (1608–74) was not only one of the most important figures during the Republic, he remains one of the most admired English writers in history. (Courtesy of the British Library Flickr)

7. Louis XIV, whose reign (1643–1715) spanned the reigns of six Stuart monarchs from Charles I to Anne and into the Georgian era. (Courtesy of the Getty's Open Content Program)

JAMES, DUKE OF MONMOUTH.

8. The dashing but doomed James Scott, Duke of Monmouth – eldest son of King Charles II and Lucy Walter. Involved in plots and a rebellion, his botched execution at the hand of Jack Ketch in July 1685 has become infamous. (Author's collection)

Above 9. This monument marks the site of the Battle of Sedgemoor, which decisively ended Monmouth's Rebellion in 1685. (Author's collection)

Below: 10. 'The Protestants Martyrs: or, the Bloody Assizes.' The trials of the Monmouth rebels were presided over by Judge Jeffreys, who became notorious as the 'Hanging Judge'. (Courtesy of the British Library)

LONDON: Printed by *F. Bradford*, at the *Bible* in *Fetter-Lane*.

11. In this painting by Peter Lely we have Diana Kirke, a famed court beauty, who married Aubrey de Vere, 20th Earl of Oxford. Their daughter, Diana, married Charles Beauclerk, an illegitimate son of Charles II and Nell Gwynn, and became the Duchess of St Albans. (Courtesy of the Mellon Collection, Yale Center for British Art)

12. Louise de Keroualle, Duchess of Portsmouth, was the French Catholic mistress of King Charles II. She outlived her royal lover by many years, dying in 1734, aged eighty-five. (Courtesy of the Getty's Open Content Program)

Left: 13. A portrait of James Hay, 1st Earl of Carlisle, by an unknown artist, *c.* 1660s. The style is typical of the English School of the late seventeenth century. (Courtesy of the Getty's Open Content Program)

Below: 14. Castle Howard, one of the great examples of English Baroque architecture, was commissioned in 1699 for the Howard family and earls of Carlisle, who reside there to this day. (© Gavin Orland)

15. Out of the catastrophic destruction of the Great Fire of London (1666), Sir Christopher Wren's English Baroque cathedral took the place of the former medieval building. (Author's collection)

Above: 16. The Queen's House, Greenwich, was designed by Inigo Jones for Anne of Denmark and completed in 1636 for her daughter-in-law, Henrietta Maria. It is now part of the National Maritime Museum. (Author's collection)

Below: 17. An exterior view of the part of Kensington Palace in which the King's State Apartments are located. Originally Nottingham House, it was purchased by William and Mary in 1689 and enlarged to designs by Sir Christopher Wren. (With kind permission of Historic Royal Palaces)

Above: 18. Abington Hall, Northampton, Stuart-era home of William Shakespeare's granddaughter, Elizabeth Barnard. (Author's collection)

Below: 19. Aston Hall is a Jacobean stately home built for the Holte family and located in Birmingham. King Charles I spent the night here shortly before the Battle of Edgehill. (Courtesy of Birmingham Museums Trust)

Above: 20. Het Loo Palace in the Netherlands, built for William and Mary in the late seventeenth century. (Author's collection)

Below: 21. Blenheim Palace, a gift from a grateful nation to John Churchill, 1st Duke of Marlborough following his victory over the French at the Battle of Blenheim in 1704. (Courtesy of the British Library)

Published June 6.1806. by Cadell & Davies, Strand.

North View of Blenheim, in Oxfordshire, the Seat of the Duke of Marlborough.

Right: 22. Robert Hooke and Christopher Wren designed the Monument to the Great Fire of London, which was constructed from 1671 to 1677 near the area in Pudding Lane where the inferno began in 1666. It has 311 steps and is 202 feet tall. (Author's collection)

Below: 23. Plaque on Tower Hill in memory of those who were executed there, including William Laud, Archbishop of Canterbury, and James Scott, Duke of Monmouth. (Author's collection)

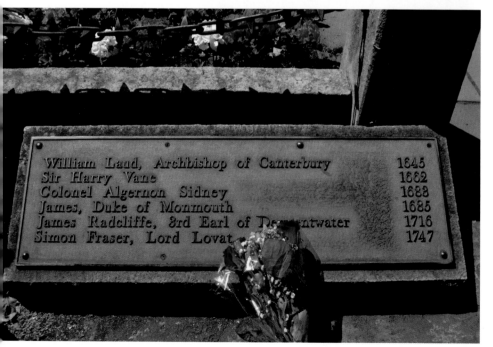

Left: 24. John Locke (1632–1704) was a highly influential philosopher whose allegiance lay with William and Mary during the Glorious Revolution. Locke's political theories later heavily influenced the American Declaration of Independence. (Courtesy of the British Library Flickr)

Below: 25. *Calm Sea* (1665/6). Willem van de Velde and his father (also Willem van de Velde) were influential Dutch marine (seascape) painters. At one point, they had a studio in the Queen's House, Greenwich. (Courtesy of the Getty's Open Content Program)

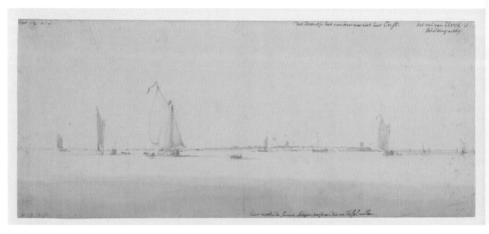

Right: 26. A scene from John Crowne's 1685 play *Sir Courtly Nice: Or, It Cannot Be*. A decade before, Crowne's *Calisto: Or, The Chaste Nymph* was performed by the future Queen Mary II, the future Queen Anne, and notable courtiers such as Sarah Jennings, the Duke of Monmouth, and Nell Gwynn. (Courtesy of the British Library Flickr)

Below: 27. Frans Snyders and Jan Boeckhorst's vibrant depiction of a mid-seventeenth-century kitchen. (Courtesy of the Getty's Open Content Program)

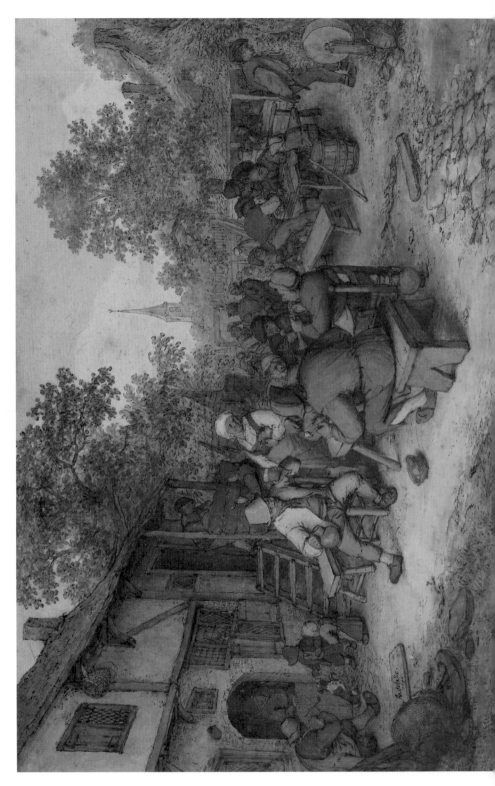

28. Adriaen van Ostade's *Peasant Festival on a Town Street* (1674). (Courtesy of the Getty's Open Content Program)

As far nevertheless, as from History, ancient or modern, may be gathered, there is little Likelihood of any such Matter, considering especially what the Druids were; also, what small Experience the Britains, anciently inhabiting this Isle, had, in Knowledge of what ever Arts, much less of Building, with like Elegancy and Proportion, such goodly Works as Stone-Heng.

The Most Notable Antiquity of Great Britain: Vulgarly Called Stone-Heng, on Salisbury Plain, Restored, Inigo Jones, 1725

Inigo Jones, an English architect known for the English Palladian style, died on 21 June 1652. Jones was a talented man, not only renowned for his architecture, but also his theatrical design, working on many court masques.

22nd – Earthquakes and Astronomy

The account you have sent your friends of the late dreadful Siciilan concussions, are, like those of an historian, large and particular enough as to the damages done by them to that at present unhappy island. I would wish they had been accompanied by particulars of the state of the air before, at, and immediately after them; or such other circumstances, as by the sequel of this letter you find remarkable earthquakes.

For, not many years since, discoursing with some ingenious merchants who had liv'd long at Smyrna (where they happen more frequently than with us) they acquainted me with several circumstances attending them; which seemed also to intimate, that the Earth itself was not at all moved, excepting near those places where noises were hard under ground, and eruptions happened, such as we hear of now from Siciliy, and lately bad accounts of from Jamaica where a like dreadful earthquake happened the first of June last. A sea captain, my neighbour Captain Guy, was ashore in that island when it began; and his relations confirm all that was told me by our Smyrna merchants. September 8th last, we had a small earthquake here, and I have since met with a book of Keckerman's, concerning such another that happened just 91 years before, September the 8th, 1601 at two o'clock in the morning.

A Letter Concerning the Natural Causes of Earthquakes,
John Flamsteed, 1693

John Flamsteed was given the position of Astronomer Royal on this day in 1675. This was the first time anyone had been given this position, and while

Flamsteed was paid £100 per annum, the twenty-nine-year-old apparently had to pay for many instruments himself. Christopher Wren designed the Flamsteed House, and Robert Hooke was involved in the construction. Flamsteed had a rather antagonistic relationship with Isaac Newton, who by some accounts was not a very nice fellow. Flamsteed was a chronically ill man and was touched by King Charles II in an effort to cure him. A king's touch was believed to cure scrofula, among other things, and Charles touched tens of thousands of his subjects during his life. In the above excerpt, we see another interest of Flamsteed's, earthquakes and natural phenomena.

*

It was also on this day in 1679 that the Battle of Bothwell Bridge was fought. Charles II's son, the Duke of Monmouth, crushed the rebellion of the Scottish Covenanters. It was Monmouth's handling of this insurrection that helped cement his position as a capable leader.

23rd – The Glutton's Fever

For as a vernal lark, but lately dress'd
In her first down, abandoning her nest,
Stretcheth her pinions, her small force assays
Flutters, and falls before her flight she raise,
Fears every blast, that scarce commit she dare
A walnut's weight to the light wafting air:
So fares my muse, yet scarcely got on wing,
Now in the region high enough to sing:
Such be the musters of her fears, so much
She doubts her strength, and blasting envy's touch.
But the chaste bay not every songster wears,
Nor of Apollo's sons prove all his heirs:
'Tis not for all to reach at Shakespeare's height,
Or think to grow to solid Jonson's weight,
To bid so fair as Chapman for a fame,
Or match (your family) the Beaumont's name.

The Glutton's Fever, Thomas Bancroft, 1633

Thomas Bancroft (c. 1596–1658) was an English poet who mainly wrote poems and epigrams. Not too much is known about Bancroft, except that he was born in Derbyshire, attended St Catherine's College, Cambridge, and authored *The Glutton's Fever* (1633) as his first publication. He also published *Two Books of Epigrammes and Epitaphs* (1639), *The Heroical Lover* (1658), and *Times out of Tune* (1658).

24th – Monmouth's Declaration

As Government was originally instituted by God, and this or that form of it chosen and submitted to by Men, for the Peace, Happiness, and Security of the Governed, and not for the private interest, and personal greatness of those that rule ...

Now, therefore, we do hereby solemnly declare and proclaim War against J. D. of Y. as a Murderer, and an Assassin of innocent Men, a Traitor to the Nation, and a Tyrant over the people. And we would have none that appear under his banner to flatter themselves with expectation of forgiveness, it being our firm resolution to prosecute him, and his adherents, without giving way to treaties and accommodations, until we have brought him and them to undergo what rules of the constitution, and the statutes of the realm, as well as the Laws of Nature, Scripture, and Nations, adjudge to be punishment due to the enemies of God, Mankind, their Country, and all things that are Honourable, Virtuous, and Good.

'The Declaration of James Duke of Monmouth', *An account of the proceedings against the rebels, and other prisoners, tried before the lord chief justice Jeffries, and other judges in the West of England, in 1685, for taking arms under the duke of Monmouth*, 1716

The 'J.D. of Y' was James, Duke of York, whom the author of the above referred to by his previous title and not that of King James II. This piece also accuses the king of murder and treason – damning accusations against a sovereign. There were those who believed that James had poisoned his brother Charles II, but this is very unlikely. By 24 June 1685, the Duke of Monmouth and his followers were embroiled in the uprising known as Monmouth's Rebellion.

June 25th – Racine's Britannicus

True; He begins there where Augustus ended.
But much I sear, that, devious in his Course,
Nero will end as t' other did begin.
In vain he counterfeits: the thin Disguise
Lets in a piercing Eye: His Brow betrays him:
His Composition's Cruelty and Pride,

Th'inherent Vices of the Blood he sprung from.
First Fruits of Tyranny are always fair.
So Caius for a time was Rome's Delight,
But his feign'd Goodness turning into Fury,
He that was Rome's Delight became her Horror.
But after all, what is't to me, if Nero
Should chance to persevere in Virtue's track?
Did I to him commit the Helm of State
To be conducted as the Senate listed?
If he affects The Father of his Country,
And hugs himself in gew-gaw titles, let him:
But is not Agrippina still his Mother?
And yet what Term, what Name are we to give
Th' Attempt which this Day's rising Sun reveal'd?
He knows (nor can their Passion be unknown)
That Junia by Britannicus is lov'd:
And yet the tender Maid, by this same Nero,
This virtuous Nero, is in dead of Night
Forc'd from her own Apartment:
Was it Hatred Or Love inspir'd his Mind?

Act I: Scene I, *Britannicus*, Jean Racine, 1669

Jean Racine (1639–1699) was one of the three great French dramatists of the seventeenth century, along with Corneille and Molière.

26th – Moral Good and Evil

Since there are so many, both Philosophers and Theologians, that seemingly and verbally acknowledge such things as Moral Good and Evil, Just and Unjust, that contend notwithstanding that these are not by Nature, but Institution, and that these is nothing Naturally or Immutably Just or Unjust; I shall from hence fetch the Rise of this Ethical Discourse or Inquiry concerning things Good and Evil, Just and Unjust, Laudable and Shameful: (For so l find these Words frequently used as synonymous in Plato, and other Ancient Authors) demonstrating in the first place, that if there be any thing at all Good or Evil, Just or Unjust, there must of necessity be something Naturally and Immutably Good and Just. And from thence I shall proceed afterward to show what this Natural, Immutable, and Eternal Justice is, with the branches and species of it.

A Treatise Concerning Eternal and Immutable Morality,
Ralph Cudworth, 1731

Ralph Cudworth, an English philosopher, died on 26 June 1688, during the reign of King James II.

27th – Two Undeniable Maxims

It appearing therefore by what hath been said, the reformation of this church to have been built on these two undeniable maxims, as ancient, for aught I know, as Christianity itself in the island — (1) that the king, as supreme governor, had a right of calling his clergy together, and by their advice causing the liturgy, or any thing else juris positivi in the church, defaced by the rust of antiquity, to be reformed; and they, under him, of declaring the articles of faith agreeable to the holy scriptures, and ever taught for such by the ancient primitive fathers and doctors in it — (2) that neither the pope, nor other from him, had any right of meddling in the English church, but by his permission and allowance; which is manifest by his sending no legate, but on the king's desire, and, when he did, he was treated with, or he came into the land, when he should have exercise of his power, and how much should be put in execution] — and that the statute, under Henry VIII, that saith in effect as much, is no other than a declaration of the common law, that is the custom of the realm — the next enquiry will be, for acquitting the church of England in point of schism, how this separation from Rome was made.

An Historical Vindication of the Church of England in Point of Schism, Roger Twysden, 1847

Sir Roger Twysden, 2nd Baronet, an English politician and historian, died on this day in 1672, during the reign of King Charles II.

28th – A Collection of Antiques

Most Excellent Sir,

Having heard from many person of the rarity of the antiques which Y.E. has collected together, I longed to come to see them, in company with your countryman, Mr. George Gage, but on account of the departure of that gentleman towards Spain, and in consequence of the pressuse of my business, this idea has been given up…I will also send you a list of those works that I have at home; or, should they be done on purpose, such pictures as would be more to Y.E.'s taste. In short, one could begin to form some negotiation that would be well for both parties. This gentleman is called Francis Pieterssen de Grebbel, a native and an inhabitant of Haarlem – and honourable and respectable person, on whose sincerity we may place the greatest confidence.

Letter from Peter Paul Rubens to Sir Dudley Cartleton, March 1617/8

Peter Paul Rubens, a Flemish Baroque painter, was born on 28 June 1577. Rubens (1577–1620) was quite possibly the most influential painter of his time. A few of his most popular works include *Samson and Delilah* (1609/10), *Le Chapeau de Paille* (1622–5), and *The Garden of Love* (1633/4). Rubens' human figures were often very plump and this is where the term 'Rubenesque' comes from. Rubens also painted landscapes with charming bucolic scenes that undoubtedly influenced the subsequent rococo art movement in Britain. In King Charles I Rubens found a patron who did not merely collect art because he could, but because he had a genuine appreciation for it. As a result, he painted many portraits of King Charles, including the equestrian portraits that are so synonymous with that ill-fated king. Rubens is best known for the sumptuous and symbolically rich paintings that adorn the impressive ceiling in the Banqueting House, Whitehall.

*

It was also on this day in 1613 that the Globe Theatre in Southwark burned down, after one of the cannons used during a production of *Henry VIII* managed to set the wooden building alight. This was the same Globe with which William Shakespeare is so often connected.

29th – Camel Face

James Hay, Scottish courtier and diplomat, was given an English baronetcy on this day in 1615. As a result, he became Baron Hay of Sawley, Yorkshire; he continued to be a competent and well-respected courtier under James I. Princess Elizabeth Stuart, later Queen of Bohemia, often referred to Hay affectionately as 'camel face' because of his facial features. Hay was involved in the marriage negotiations between Charles I and Henrietta Maria.

In 1622, Hay became 1st Earl of Carlisle (his portrait is in the image section of this book), which title his son from his first marriage to Honora Denny, James, inherited in 1636 when Hay died following a stroke.

Hay's second wife, the beauteous Lucy Hay, survived him and became one of the most well-known women of the English Civil War period. Lucy had an affair with George Villiers, 1st Duke of Buckingham, and was later rumoured to be the mistress of both the Earl of Strafford and John Pym. It is believed that Lucy was the inspiration for Milady de Winter in *The Three Musketeers* by Alexandre Dumas.

*

It was also on this day in 1644 that the Battle of Cropredy Bridge was fought as part of the English Civil Wars. The Royalists (Cavaliers) were commanded by King Charles I, while the Parliamentarians (Roundheads) were commanded by Sir William Waller. This battle, which lasted all day in Oxfordshire, had no decisive outcome.

30th – A Poisoned Princess?

Henrietta Anne of England, best known affectionately as Minette, died on 30 June 1670, during the reign of her brother, King Charles II. Her death was both unexpected and tragic, for she was only twenty-six years old. As the youngest child of King Charles I of England and Henrietta Maria, she was born in the midst of the chaos of the English Civil Wars, in Exeter; the young princess's childhood had little stability. Two years later she was smuggled out of the country and brought up at the French court, where she eventually married Philippe, Duc d'Orléans – the younger brother of King Louis XIV. Philippe was what we would today define as homosexual. Unfortunately, his behaviour left much to be desired; he was intensely jealous, petulant and arrogant. 'Monsieur', as he was known, cruelly carried on his affair with the Chevalier de Lorraine right in front of his wife, who was known as 'Madame'. Minette was an ebullient and attractive young woman, and her great popularity simultaneously made Monsieur jealous and envious. Minette appears to have had a brief fling with her brother-in-law, Louis XIV, but that died down quickly and he was soon enageged in an affair with her lady-in-waiting Louise de La Vallière.

'Madame' was the means by which her brother Charles II agreed to the secret Treaty of Dover with Louis XIV. While she was in England with her family she had a largely happy time of it and Louis even allowed her to stay longer in spite of his brother's demands she return home. Shortly after returning home to France, however, the twenty-six-year-old Minette suddenly became violently ill and died at the Château de Saint-Cloud. Rumours swept the courts that she had been poisoned on order of her husband or his lover. For a while, even Charles appears to have believed this to be the case – Monsieur and his close associates had treated Minette appallingly – so it sadly wouldn't have been much of a surprise if they had indeed poisoned her. Most historians, however, believe that Minette may have suffered from anorexia and that her death was probably due to acute peritonitis.

JULY

1st – Our Misfortune at Chatham

Sir,

I have received yours of the 5th wherein you complain of our staunchness in delivering over to you our news. The truth is, it has been so bad of late, that I took no pleasure in sending it. But I am deceived, if I did not give you a particular relation of what passed in our misfortune at Chatham, and the disorder it put men's minds into. God be thanked we are since very quiet. And, though the affront was very sensible to us, it hath not been attended with any ill accidents, to endanger our quiet at home. Many have murmured much at it; but, it going no further than talk, we have been content to dissemble the hearing of it.

Since my last, the enemy return'd into the river again, where, having spent some days, without making any kind of attempt upon us, they yesterday put to sea again, and will continue, as we suppose, their bravadoes upon the coasts; and at least alarm us with offering at the doing us some new mischief. To be the readier for which they have divided their fleet, as we are assured from Holland, into three squadrons ...

All our letters from Holland persuade us the peace will be quickly made; God grant it be so. After which, I tell the Baron de Isola, in my enclosed letter to him, that he will be most welcome here. And, whatsoever his opinion is, we cannot hinder ourselves from believing that as soon as France perceives the States will agree with us, they will lose no time in joining it. And thus it behoves us to proceed, how ill soever our neighbours take it of us.

The Right Honourable the Earl of Arlington's Letters to Sir William Temple, from July 1665 to September 1670, London, 1701

The above refers to the humiliating Dutch attack on the English navy at Chatham.

*

It was also on this day in 1622 that William Parker, 13th Baron Morley, 4th Baron Monteagle, died, during the reign of King James I. Monteagle is best known in history for being the person who uncovered the Gunpowder Plot of 1605 when he was sent an anonymous letter warning him not to attend the opening of the Houses of Parliament. His brother-in-law, Francis Tresham, one of the plotters, was probably the one who sent this to him.

2nd – The Miner's Friend

I am very sensible a great many among you do as yet look on my invention of raising water by the impellent force of fire, a useless sort of a project, that never can answer my designs or pretensions; and that it is altogether impossible that such an engine as this can be wrought under ground, and succeed in the raising of water, and draining your mines, so as to deserve any encouragement from you. I am not very fond of lying under the scandal of a bare projector; and, therefore, present you here with a draught of my machine, and lay before you the uses of it, and leave it to your consideration whether it be worth your while to make use of it or no. I can easily give grains of allowance for your suspicions, because I know very well what miscarriages there have been by people ignorant of what they pretend to ... I have often lamented the want of understanding the true powers of nature, which misfortune has, of late, put some on making such vast engines and machines, both troublesome and expensive, yet of no manner of use, inasmuch as the old engines, used many ages past, far exceeded them; and I fear, whoever, by the old causes of motion, pretends to improvements within this last century, does betray his knowledge and judgment; for more than an hundred years since, men and horses would raise by engines, then made, as much water as they have ever since done, or I believe ever will, or according to the law of nature ever can do; and though my thoughts have been long employed about water works, I should never have pretended to any invention of that kind, had I not happily found out this new, but yet a much stronger and cheaper force or cause of motion, than any before made use of.

The Miner's Friend, Thomas Savery, 1702

Thomas Savery (c. 1650–1715) was an English inventor whose steam engine was patented on this day in 1698. A year later, Savery presented a small model of this engine before the members of the Royal Society. He also demonstrated his invention in front of King William III, who was, according to Savery, full of encouragement.

*

It was also on this day in 1644 that the Battle of Marston Moor was fought. This major battle of the First English Civil War is reputed to have been the largest battle ever fought on English soil. Some 4,000 Cavaliers (Royalists) were slaughtered, considerably more than the 300 Roundheads (Parliamentarians) who were slain. Over 1,000 Cavaliers were captured. Even Prince Rupert's beloved poodle, Boye, was killed during the encounter.

3rd – A Protuberance of Stone

As for what Dr. Plot produces out of Camden and Childrey, in confirmation of his fourth argument, viz. that the Ophiomorphites of Cainesham have some of them heads. I doubt not but it is a mistake, proceeding from their credulity. For Mr. Willughby and my self enquiring diligently there after such stones, and the common people affirmed, thath there were such found, we not satisfied with their assertion, but desirous ourselves to see them, were at last directed to a man's house, who was said to have one; to whom when we came, he showed us the stone, which indeed at the upper extreme had some kind of knop or protuberance of stone, but not at all resembling the head of any animal.

> Letter from Mr Ray to Dr Robinson, from *Philosophical Letters Between the Late John Ray and Several of His Correspondents, Natives and Foreigners. To which are Added Those of Francis Willughby*, 1718

Francis Willughby, an English ichthyologist and ornithologist, died on 3 July 1672, during the reign of King Charles II.

4th – A Geometrical Solution

Though I am a stranger to your person, yet I am well acquainted with the fame of your singular skill in the mathematics, and thereupon have so far pre sumed, as to intreat your assistance for the geometrical solution of the inclosed diagram, which, to you that have attained the perfection of the analytical art, perhaps will not appear difficult. But, whether all that may be performed by algebraical equations may like wise be wrought geometrically according to a lineary operation, I am not able to resolve, and therefore in treat to be instructed from you. The present proposition will haply conduce to the invention of that so much desired and long sought for problem, for the finding of two mean proportionals between two extremes given, which having hitherto exercised the wit and endeavours of the most famous geometricians, I presume would not prove unworthy your pains, who, by the general suffrages of all men, are deservedly reported the ablest mathematician that our age knows. Sir, I have been beholding to Mr. Elias Allen for the conveyance of this letter; and if you will vouchsafe me the favour, at your best leisure, to return me two or three lines in answer, and cause it to be left with Mr. Allen for me, I shall rest very thankful for the courtesy; and ever remain, Yours to be commanded, in what I am able,

Letter dated London, 2 June 1642, from *Correspondence of Scientific Men of the Seventeenth Century: Including Letters of Barrow, Flamsteed, Wallis, and Newton, Printed from the Originals in the Collection of the Right Honourable the Earl of Macclesfield Vol. 1*, Will Price, 1841

5th – Newton's *Opticks* and *Principia*

The Cause of Reflection is not the impinging of light on the solid or impervious parts of bodies, as is commonly believed. This will appear by the following considerations. First, that in the passage of light out of glass into air there is a reflection as strong as in its passage out of air into glass, or rather a little stronger, and by many degrees stronger than in its passage out of glass into water. And it seems not probable that air should have more strongly reflecting parts than water or glass. But if that should possible be supposed, yet it will avail nothing; for the reflection is as strong or stronger when the air is drawn away from the glass (suppose by the Air-Pump invented by Otto Gueriet, and improved and made useful by Mr. Boyle) as when it is adjacent to it.

Opticks, Isaac Newton, 1704

Isaac Newton's *Philosophae Naturalis Principia Mathematica* was published on 5 July 1687, during the reign of King James II. Isaac Newton, English genius, was born on 25 December 1642. A Fellow of the Royal Society, he is best remembered in history as one of the greatest scientists who ever lived. The genius behind the theory of gravity, Newton was a Cambridge professor who thrived on intellectual discussion and alchemical experimentation. Although he had an inauspicious birth in Lincolnshire in 1642, he did very well in his studies and became a major early figure in the Enlightenment due to his many scientific achievements. He was known for his exacting temperament and was often getting into arguments with fellow scientists such as Robert Hooke and John Flamsteed, among others.

In 1696, Newton became a Warden at the Royal Mint, then based in the Tower of London, where he oversaw the production of new, state-of-the-art coins. In 1698, Newton oversaw the Great Recoinage, wherein coin money was created in such a way as to prevent the widespread practice of currency clipping.

6th – The Battle of Sedgemoor

The Battle of Sedgemoor during the Monmouth Rebellion was fought on 6 July 1685. Widely considered to be the last battle fought on English soil, it was the last chance also in an increasingly futile endeavour. Within months of James II's accession to the throne in early 1685, his nephew James Scott, Duke of Monmouth, left his exile on the Continent and sailed to England. Thus began the ill-fated Monmouth Rebellion, in which the popular Protestant Duke of Monmouth invaded England in order to take the throne away from his uncle, the Catholic King James II. On board his ship were eighty-odd followers, a truly pitiful number for a rebellion of its kind, but Monmouth was certain that all Englishmen would rise up and join him against his uncle. The rebellion lasted a little over a month, but with his poorly trained and armed rebels Sedgemoor was the place in which Charles II's eldest illegitimate son, the Duke of Monmouth, led one last attempt to beat the king's army.

Outnumbered by the better-trained and better-equipped royalist soldiers, Monmouth's ragtag army had little chance. Monmouth, a seasoned general, knew the limitations of his rebel army well enough and so had few options open to him. He and Lord Grey climbed the Church of St Mary, Bridgwater and surveyed the enemy encampment; the tower that these men climbed is now known as Monmouth's Tower. As an experienced military leader, Monmouth knew that his cause only had one last chance – a night attack. They muffled their horses' hooves and made their way to the encampment, narrowly missing patrolling dragoons. Suddenly shots were fired and their cover was blown; the Battle of Sedgemoor had just begun. What followed was little less than carnage. Although there have been many wars since 1685, the Battle of Sedgemoor remains one of the last pitched battles to take place on English soil.

Monmouth and several other rebel leaders fled the bloody field, but with a £5,000 reward on his head Monmouth was soon caught and punished. Forde, Lord Grey, Monmouth's friend, got off lightly after he penned a full confession. Those who weren't killed on the battlefield were rounded up and marched into a nearby church in Westonzoyland. Some were summarily executed. Some died of their wounds inside the church. The rest faced trial at the Bloody Assizes, presided over by the notorious 'Hanging Judge' Jeffreys. Some were executed, some 'transported' – sent over to New World colonies effectively as slaves – while others were severely fined. Monmouth, even though he was King James's nephew, met with a very bad end on Tower Hill. He had one of the grisliest botched executions in history.

7th – The Enemy Approaches

The seventh of July in the forenoon we had a hot alarm, at the arrival here of the Count of Stirum, who desired his Imperial Majesty to send a speedy supply of men to the army, as being much inferior to the enemies in number, and upon that account, unable to stop their progress. But our fears were exceedingly increased by the afternoon, when the Count of Caprara came hither to inform the Emperor of the near approach of the Turks, and to desire him, without any further delay, to remove from thence with the Archduke, the enemy being not only stronger than was at first reported, but reinforc'd by a considerable number of rebels and Tartars; and accordingly in the evening the Emperor departed from Vienna for Clooster Newburg, intending to go from thence to Lintz. The same day the Boors came hither in great numbers, flying from all parts, be reason of the cruelties of the Turkish Army, against all such as they met with in their passage.

An Impartial and true Accounts of all the most considerable Passages and Actions relating to the Siege of the Imperial City Vienna being the Memoirs of a considerable Officer of that Garrison who was actually in Service there till the Siege was rais'd, 1683

*

Henry Compton, Bishop of London, also died on this day in 1703, during the reign of Queen Anne.

8th – La Belle Stuart

Frances Teresa Stewart, the model for Britannia, was born on 8 July 1647. Often referred to as 'La Belle Stuart' because of her great beauty, she inspired artists, poets, and royals alike. King Charles II was one of many who grew besotted by Frances, but she famously refused to become his mistress. Indeed, she eloped with the Duke of Richmond, instead! In a gown of golden yellow fabric and holding a bow in her left hand, with pearls adorning her ears and neck, Frances' allure is unmistakable in Peter Lely's portrait of her from 1662–5.

*

It was also on this day in 1663 that John Clarke's draft of the Rhode Island Royal Charter was approved and sealed by King Charles II.

9th – Marlborough's Noble Action

London.
To ye Duke of Marlborough.

My Lord,
   Remembering how great a trouble your Grace thought fit to give yourself in honouring me with an answer, when I sent you my thanks for a most particular piece of service your goodness had done me with ye Queen (which, as ye motto I've chosen says, *Je n'oublieray jamais*) made me once resolve (though on this great occasion finding myself one of those whose consciousness of thorough good will and wishes towards your Grace could easily have let me dare to dispense with forms) not to venture a second opportunity whereby your time, so precious to ye public, might be diverted to less important uses that it is and ought to be employed in. By really, my Lord, as ye news of your Grace's late noble action on ye Danube was too full of wonder to let one speak at all upon't at first hearing, so no sooner could our thought get vent, but that they represent too many great and good consequences, too much glory to her Majesty and her arms, too many universal advantages to all her allies, too much security to ye future liberty and peace of Europe, and too much immortal fame to yourself (from ye essential share your personal example and conduct had in gaining ye victory) to be possibly past over in admiring silence only by your zealous and faithful friends, at a time too when even ye tepid ones of your prosperity, nay, ye very prejudiced themselves, are forced to mention it with just applause ...

Letter from John Hervey, 1st
Earl of Bristol, 9 July 1704

10th – An English Pirate

All fair content dwell here, and may our strains
Give you that choice delight which crowns our pains.
Our subject's low, yet to your eyes presents

Deeds high in blood, in blood of Innocents:
Transcends them low, and your invention calls
To name the sin beyond this black deed falls.
What heretofore set others' pens a-work,
Was Ward turn'd Pirate, our is War turn'd Turk.
Their trivial scenes might best afford to show
The baseness of his birth, how from below
Ambition oft takes root, makes men forsake
The good, thee enjoy, yet know not. Our Muse doth doth take
A higher pitch, leaving his Piracy
To reach the heart itself of villainy.

> 'Prologue', *A Christian turn'd Turk: Or, The Tragical Lives
> and Deaths of the two Famous Pirates, Ward and Dansiker,*
> Robert Daborne, 1612

**Jack Ward was an English pirate who lived from around 1553
to 1622. Originally from Faversham in Kent, in 1610 he converted
to Islam in keeping with other Barbary pirates.**

11th – Peace Treaty Negotiations

I am very glad to learn that the ambassadors of France have said
that they sincerely desire peace, and that they wish to terminate the
negotiations speedily. With respect to the last article, I do not at all
believe it; but it is always desirable to see so clearly that they fear to
break off the negotiations, which is the only ground that remains for
us to hope they may soon be brought to a conclusion. It is the more
necessary for that purpose to press the negotiations. The best means of
attaining that object is, to negotiate secretly through the ambassador
of the state; for, as for the mediator, we see clearly that he seeks only
to delay. It is indeed inconceivable that we should be agreed with
France on all essential points, and yet unable to conclude a peace; and
that only because each of the two parties suspects the intentions of the
other. It seems to me that this is not difficult to be cleared up, and that
we might then come to a conclusion in some way or other. The Earl
of Portland has informed you of what passed between him and the
Marshal Boufflers: I do not expect much from it. It is probable that
he will receive only an answer in general terms. Thus every thing will
have to be done at The Hague, as I always thought it would.

> Letter dated 11 July 1697, from King William III of England,
> Scotland, and Ireland to Antony Heinsius,
> Grand Pensionary of Holland

The above describes how negotiations were underway between France and the Anglo-Dutch alliance under William III.

12th – The Battle of the Boyne

The Battle of the Boyne, part of the Glorious Revolution, was fought on 12 July 1690, by the River Boyne in Ireland. James II, who had fled Britain in 1688 when his nephew and son-in-law William of Orange had invaded, organised his supporters (the Jacobites) in Ireland to fight William's supporters (the Williamites).

Over a thousand people died. This battle is often claimed to have been the one that won the war for the Williamites, and that's both true and false. The battle that definitely ensured things were in William's favour was the Battle of Aughrim in 1691, which usually gets ignored but is no less strategically important. When Richard Talbot, 1st Earl of Tyrconnell, learned the news of this defeat, he suffered a stroke and died a few days later.

13th – Suicide or Murder?

He replied, that my lord Devonshire had received too many marks of his fidelity, to distrust it, and that Mr. Ferguson and others in Holland knew very well that he had been employed by some in London to disperse those books which gave an account of my Lord Essex's death; and that several gentlemen had been so industrious to detect that hard murder, that they had done it beyond all contradiction, having received a full account of it from one who was present at the time of its being committed, and was now safely disposed of: that he had been often with my Lord Devonshire from those gentlemen about that affair, and that my lord was fully acquainted with all the particulars of that assassination, and if his late Majesty had lived but a little longer, did resolve to say it openly before him in council, but now reserved it for the approaching parliament, and would then bring it before the house of lords. He added farther, that my Lord Devonshire's friends were in great apprehension that his lordship would be assassinated; for that it was known at White-hall, that his lordship had fully discovered the murder of my Lord Essex, and was master of all the parts of that affair, both as to the contrivance and execution; and there fore they advised my lord to keep within, or retire into the country till the Parliament's sitting.

The Secret History of the Rye-House Plot,
Ford Grey, 1754

The Rye House Plot proved fatal to many of those associated with it. This is no less true for Arthur Capell, 1st Earl of Essex, whose death on this day in 1683 remains a source of mystery and speculation. According to Robert Bruce, 1st Earl of Ailesbury, Capell slit his own throat with a penknife. In 1684, in a tract entitled *Upon the Execrable Murther of the Right Honourable Arthur Earl of Essex*, the author puts forward the theory that Cappell was murdered and did not commit suicide, just as the extract above relates. The reasoning was that self-murder was completely against Capell's nature and sense of morality. This is one of those events in history that will probably remain a mystery.

14th – Goring's Debauchery

George Goring, Lord Goring, was born on 14 July 1608. Goring, a staunch Royalist during the English Civil Wars, fought at the Battle of Marston Moor where he decked the Scottish infantry before getting hammered by Cromwell.

Writing about her time in Spain in the 1650s, diarist Ann, Lady Fanshawe, described Goring thus:

At that time had a command under Philip the Fourth of Spain, against the Portuguese: he was generally esteemed a good and great commander ... he was exceeding facetious and pleasant company, and in conversation, where good manners were due, the civillest person imaginable, so that he would blush like a girl. He was very tall, and very handsome: he had been married to a daughter of the Earl of Cork, but never had a child by her. His debauchery beyond all precedents, which at last lost him that love the Spaniards had for him.

The old Royalist Goring died in Madrid in 1657.

15th – Monmouth's Botched Execution

The execution of James Scott, Duke of Monmouth and Buccleuch, took place on this day in 1685, on Tower Hill. James, affectionately known as Jemmy, was the eldest illegitimate son of the 'Merry Monarch' King Charles II and the beautiful Welsh royalist exile, Lucy Walter. Scott led the disastrous Monmouth Rebellion of 1685. His uncle, King James II/VII, showed his brother's favourite son no mercy. At Tower Hill the executioner Jack Ketch awaited him; Monmouth was subjected to one of most notoriously botched executions in British history. It took between five to seven blows plus further sawing with a knife to sever the doomed duke's head from his shoulders.

Following his death, his mutilated corpse was taken back into the Tower and he was interred in the Chapel of St Peter ad Vincula, by the wall behind the altar. Those buried near him include Anne Boleyn and Katherine Howard – Henry VIII's beheaded wives. The Duke of Monmouth, who had been declared a Companion of the Order in 1663, had this honour formally revoked as a result of his rebellion in 1685.

16th – A Theologian from Great Snoring

As I am assured that there is an infinite and independent Being, which we call a God, 'and that it is impossible there should be more Infinities than one, so I assure myself that this one God is the Father Of all things, especially of all Men and Angels, so far as the mere act of Creation may be styled Generation; that he is Father yet, and in a more peculiar manner, the Father of all those whom he regenerateth by his Spirit, whom he adopteth in his Son, as Heirs and Co-heirs with him, Rom.8, whom he crowneth with the reward of an eternal Inheritance in the Heavens. But beyond, and far above all this, besides his general offspring and peculiar people, to whom he hath given power to become the sons of God, Rom. 8. 14. I believe him the Father, in a more eminent and transcendent manner, of one singular and proper son, his own, his beloved, his only begotten Son; whom he hath not only begotten of the blessed Virgin, by the coming of the Holy Ghost, and the over-shadowing of his power; not only sent with special authority as the King of Israel; not only raised from the dead, and made Heir of all things in his House, but antecedently to all this, hath begotten him by way of eternal generation in the same deity and majesty of himself.

An Exposition of the Apostle's Creed, from the Holy Scriptures and Bishop Pearson, John Pearson, 1704

John Pearson, an English theologian, died on this day in 1686, in the amusingly named village of Great Snoring, in Norfolk.

17th – The Princes in the Tower

In July 1674, in consequence of an order to clear the White Tower from all contiguous buildings, as the workmen were digging down the stairs which led from the king's lodgings to the chapel in the said

Tower, about ten feet in the ground, were found the bones of two striplings in (as it seemed) a wooden chest, which upon the survey were found proportionable to the ages of the two brothers, viz., about thirteen and eleven years. On inquiry it was concluded that they were the bones of the murdered princes, and in consequence, after they had been sifted from the rubbish, they were honourably interred in the chapel of Henry VII in Westminster.

A civil and ecclesiastical history of England, to 1829: Vol. 1, Dr. C. St. George, 1830

It was on 17 July 1674 that workmen demolishing a crumbling turret in the White Tower came across a chest containing the skeletons of two children, one taller than the other. The remains were and are believed to be those of the two princes in the tower, who had suddenly disappeared without a trace in 1483 while they were residing at the Tower of London. The tradition was that monarchs stayed at the royal apartments there before their coronation ceremony, so this wasn't particularly strange. The boys, the twelve-year-old uncrowned King Edward V and his younger brother, nine-year-old Richard of Shrewsbury, Duke of York, were the sons of King Edward IV and Queen Elizabeth Woodville. Sometime during their residence at the Tower, however, they suddenly and inexplicably disappeared. This mystery has been the stuff of legend for over 500 years. Their uncle, Richard, Duke of Gloucester, was widely suspected of ordering their deaths, or at least thought guilty of not protecting them; he was crowned King Richard III on 3 July 1483. Until the bodies are exhumed and undergo more in-depth forensic analysis, there is no solid proof that these are the princes – though given the circumstantial evidence, it's highly likely. In her book *The Princes in the Tower,* historian Alison Weir stated that the skeletons were found with remnants of velvet fabric – a resource that could only have been affordable to the wealthiest people in society, and furthermore only available as a material from the fifteenth century – which, once again, only further supports the probability that these skeletons belonged to the lost princes in the Tower. King Charles II had the remains buried in Westminster Abbey, with a memorial to them designed by Sir Christopher Wren.

*

It was also on this day in 1645 that Robert Carr (also spelled Kerr), an English politician and courtier, died. Carr is most well known for being the favourite of King James I, with whom he probably had an affair. Everything was going smoothly for Robert until his and his wife's involvement in the Overbury Poisoning Scandal. Carr was replaced in the king's heart by George Villiers, later 1st Duke of Buckingham.

18th – The Roaring Girl

Dearest no.
Though wildly in a labyrinth I go,
My end is to meet thee: with a side wind
Must I now sail, else I no haven can find
But both must sink for ever. There's a wench
Called Moll, mad Moll, or merry Moll, a creature
So strange in quality, a whole city takes
Note of her name and person, all that affection
I owe to thee, on her in counterfeit passion,
I spend to mad my father: he believes
I dote upon this Roaring Girl, and grieves
As it becomes a father for a son,
That could be so bewitch'd: yet I'll go on
This crooked way, sigh still for her, feign dreams,
In which I'll talk only of her, these streams
Shall, I hope, force my father to consent
That here I anchor rather then be rent
Upon a rock so dangerous, Art thou pleased,
Because thou seest we are way-laid, that I take
A path that's safe, though it be far about.

Act I: Scene I, *The Roaring Girl*,
Thomas Middleton and Thomas Dekker, 1607–10

Thomas Middleton, an English poet and dramatist, died in July of 1627, though the precise date is unknown.

19th – The Salem Witch Trials: Reversal of Attainder

Province of the Massachusetts Bay: Anno Regni Anna Regina Decimo. An Act to reverse the attainders of George Bur roughs and others for Witchcraft Forasmuch as in the year of our Lord one Thousand six hundred ninety two several Towns within this Province were infested with a horrible Witchcraft or possession of devils: And at a Special Court of Oyer and Termina holden at Salem in the County of Essex in the same year 1692. George Burroughs of Wells, John Procter, George Jacobs, John Willard, Giles Core, and Martha his wife, Rebecca Nurse and Sarah Good all of Salem aforesaid Elizabeth How of Ipswich, Mary Bailey, Sarah Wild and Abigail Hobbs all of Topsfield, Samuel Wardell, Mary Parker, Martha Carrier, Abigail Falkner, Anne Foster, Rebecca Fames, Mary Post and Mary Lacey all of Andover, Mary

Bradbury of Salisbury, and Dorcas Hoar of Beverley were severally Indicted convicted and attainted of Witchcraft, and some of them put to death, others lying still under the like sentence of the said Court, and liable to have the same Executed upon them.

The Influence and Energy of the Evil Spirits so great at that time acting in and upon those who were the principal accusers and witnesses proceeding so far as to cause a prosecution to be had of persons of known and good reputation, which caused a great dissatisfaction and a stop to be put thereunto until their Majesty's pleasure should be known therein: And upon a Representation thereof accordingly made her late Majesty Queen Mary the Second of blessed memory by Her Royal Letter given at her Court at Whitehall the fifteenth of April 1693 was Graciously pleased to approve the care and Circumspection therein; and to Will and require that in all proceedings agile persons accused for Witchcraft, or being possessed by the devil, the greatest Moderation and all due Circumspection be used, so far as the same may be without Impediment to the Ordinary Course of Justice.

And some of the principal Accusers and Witnesses in those dark and severe prosecutions have since discovered themselves to be persons of profligate and vicious conversation.

Reversal of Attainder 17 October 1711, *Records of Salem Witchcraft: Copied from the Original Documents*, Vol. 2, Roxbury, 1864

Sarah Good and Susannah Martin – both accused and found guilty of witchcraft in the Salem Witch Trials – were both executed by hanging on this day in 1692.

20th – Lord Grey's Colourful History

Some short time after the Bill of Exclusion had met with the fate it deserved, in the house of lords, the Duke of Monmouth, my Lord Shaftesbury, my Lord Russell, and myself, being together at Thanet house (as we often were about that time) there began a discourse amongst us upon the rejecting that bill; and though it be impossible for me to repeat what each man said, yet I well remember it was the opinion of all, that the king would never suffer that bill to pass the house of lords, unless compelled to it; and that all those, who had appeared for it in the two houses of parliament, were marked out for destruction, if ever your majesty came to the crown. After some discourse of that kind I remember my Lord Shaftesbury expressed himself to this purpose: That it was our own faults, if we did not obtain that bill, and several other things, of the king, which the people of England had set their hearts upon; for there was a great ferment in the kingdom, occasioned by the many prorogations, and dissolutions of parliaments, and other artifices used to stifle the popish plot, and prevent the execution of justice on those concerned in it and by the lords throwing out the bill of exclusion; which all thinking men looked upon as the king's act, and did believe him to be in all parts of the popish plot except the murder of himself, which he did not think was intended, knowing the papists were well assured of his zeal to their religion.

> *The Secret History of the Rye-House Plot:*
> *and of Monmouth's Rebellion*, Ford Grey, 1685

Ford Grey, 1st Earl of Tankerville, was born on 20 July 1655, during the Commonwealth. He proved to be a man who could talk his way out of trouble. This was crucial, especially given the fact that Grey managed to get himself into trouble on a number of occasions, not least at home. Hold on to your periwigs! This is going to be like an episode of *Jeremy Kyle*, Stuart-era style! Grey first married Lady Mary Berkeley, before he then seduced, ran off with, and impregnated her sister, Henrietta! The *London Gazette* posted a plea to find the missing young woman. In the Stuart era, as in other periods in history, one's in-laws were considered siblings, and any sexual relations between the two were considered incestuous. The whole case was so sensational and scandalous that even the celebrated playwright Aphra Behn took to her quill to write volumes based on Ford and Henrietta's relationship – *Love Letters from a Noble Man to his Sister, Mixed with the History of their Adventures*, which was printed in London in 1685, and *The Amours of Philander and Silvia: Being the Third and Last Part of the Love-Letters between a Noble Man and his Sister*, printed in London in 1687. In these rather flowery, romantic fictional letters, Behn cheekily turned the four key figures in the scandal into her fictional characters. Grey became Philander, Henrietta became Sylvia, Mary became Myrtilla, and it is probable that the character of Cesario was based on Grey's best friend, James, Duke of Monmouth. In this, Behn states that Myrtilla was in love with Cesario, but then turned her flippant affections to his friend Philander before they then eloped. Upon returning to England, Myrtilla resumed her now-adulterous affair with Cesario, and Philander finds himself hopelessly in lust and love with Myrtilla's sister, Henrietta.

As if that wasn't bad enough, Grey was involved in some of the most well-known plots and rebellions of the Late Stuart era. Grey, whom James Scott, Duke of Monmouth, considered to be a good friend, was implicated in the Rye House Plot of 1683 with the duke. The Monmouth Rebellion was a disaster to say the least, and Monmouth and Grey were captured. Monmouth lost his head on Tower Hill, and Grey very nearly came to that himself but he wrote a full confession about everything, now known as *The Secret History of the Rye-House Plot and of Monmouth's Rebellion.* Grey died in 1701, during William III's reign.

21st – Upon the Model of the Nut-Brown Maid

Thou, to whose eyes I bend, at whose Command
Tho' low my Voice, tho' artless be my Hand,
I take the sprightly reed; and sing, and play;
Careless of what the censuring World may say;
Bright Chloe, Object of my constant Vow;
Wilt thou awhile unbend thy serious Brow?
Wilt thou with pleasure hear thy Lover's strains,
And with one Heav'nly Smile o'erpay his Pains?
No longer shall the Nut-brown Maid be old,
Tho' since her Youth three hundred Years have roll'd;
At thy Desire she shall again be raised,
And her reviving Charms in lasting Verse be prais'd.

'A Poem, Upon the Model of The Nut-brown Maid',
Matthew Prior, 1709

Matthew Prior, an English poet and diplomat, was born on this day in 1664, during the reign of King Charles II.

22nd – Colonel Rainsborow's Prisoner

Right Honourable, My duty enjoineth me to render you an account of our affairs here. I formerly received an order of the honourable House of Commons that Mr. Fountayne, whom I received as Colonel Rainsborowe's prisoner, should be sent in safeguard to Bristol castle; but by whom this service should be performed the order did not specify ...

Sir, I humbly pray that the honourable House of Commons maybe acquainted with the truth of these our present affairs. That I may receive their order how to dispose of Mr. Fountayne; how the regiment shall be disposed of; whether it be their pleasure that I forthwith draw off from Wallingford and disband, or whether we shall continue in that service till that garrison be reduced, and then immediately disband. All my officers being resolved unanimously, that whatsoever the parliament commandeth us, that we will observe and do; and whither they command us to go, thither we will go. Only we desire, that, while we continue in their service, a settled course may be taken, that my soldiers, who carry their lives in their hands, may receive their pay, which is the life of their lives.

In expectation of order in these particulars, I rest Sir, your most humble servant, Thomas Bulstrode.

Letter dated 22 July 1646, *Memorials of the Great Civil War in England from 1646 to 1652*, ed. Henry Cary, 1842

Colonel Thomas Bulstrode was a Parliamentarian during the English Civil Wars. Unfortunately, not much more is known about him. The Mr Fountayne that is mentioned in the letter was, according to the Earl of Clarendon, a lawyer who had been imprisoned for his loyalty to Charles I. Notice the request to receive pay? That was a problem for both Cavalier and Roundhead alike, and soldiers usually lived with their pay in arrears.

23rd – Wenceslaus Hollar's Travels

He travelled to several great Cities in Germany, through Frankfort to Cologne and Antwerp; and return'd again to Cologne, where he resided some Time with difficulty enough to subsist. Thus passing some Time or Years in drawing Views and Plans of Cities, which are printed from the Plates he has done, he also etch'd a Book of small Heads from Henzelman and Biler; at Cologne he published a View of Herbipolis or Wurtzburg, where under is writ, *Hollar delineavit in Legatione Arundeliana ad Imperatorem*. And he made a large Drawing, a Prospect of the City of Prague, which being curiously and exactly done with the Pen and Pencil (no doubt) gave great Pleasure and Satisfaction to the noble Earl of Arundel, who then was there on the Spot, Anno 1635; which drawing is of the same Magnitude with the Print engraved after it, on two long Plates. He did many Drawings with the Pen in all Countries and Places where he resided, in England, in Germany and Flanders; though few of them are entirely finished, and fewer preserved, though certainly, he drew most Part of all the Designs for his Plates that he engraved. Thus it happened that the Earl of Arundel passing through Germany to the Imperial Court, as Hollar was recommended to him at Collen, being pleas'd with his Drawings and Representation of those Towns he had an Intention to visit in his Embassy, he took him along with him: By this Opportunity Hollar had the Patronage of the greatest Collector and Lover of Arts then living, besides a Prospect of being recommended in England to the Favour of his Majesty King Charles the First, then known to be the Royal Encourager of all curious Arts and ingenious Men, which drew many excellent Artists into this Nation.

> *A Description of the Works of the Ingenious Delineator and Engraver Wenceslaus Hollar, Disposed Into Classes of Different Sorts: With Some Account of His Life*, George Vertue, 1745

Wenceslaus Hollar, a Bohemian etcher, was born in Prague on 23 July 1607, during the reign of King James I. Hollar's etchings have been a gift to those of us interested in how places looked back in the seventeenth century. He went back and forth from London to Antwerp throughout a period dating from the 1630s to the early 1650s, and his first etchings in England were, according to Arthur M. Hind's *Wenceslaus Hollar and his Views of London and Windsor in the Seventeenth Century*, made in 1637, and include the *View of Greenwich*. Among his work includes a bird's-eye view of Windsor Castle, c. 1670; St. George's Chapel in Windsor Castle, c. 1671; and a depiction of what the regalia of the Order of the Garter looked like c. 1672. According to John Aubrey, Hollar married a lady-in-waiting by the name of Mrs Tracy, with whom he had a son and a daughter. In George Vertue's 1745 book *A Description of the Works of the Ingenious Delineator and Engraver Wenceslaus Hollar*, many of Hollar's works were listed in categories: Religious subjects, Histories and Fables, Maps and Plans, Ships, Italian designs, Dutch landscapes, Portraits, and more – and it becomes obvious how much work Hollar did during his career.

*

It was also on this day in 1727 that Simon Harcourt, 1st Viscount Harcourt, Lord Chancellor of Great Britain, died. He was born in 1660.

24th – The Founding of the Bank of England

On 24 July 1694, William and Mary founded the Bank of England. By the time they had ascended to the throne, the currency was having serious problems with counterfeiting. Another problem was that William wanted war with France, and this required money that Parliament was ill-inclined to give him. A variety of financial schemes were offered in order to solve this situation, and King William approved of one in particular. Scottish entrepreneur William Paterson concocted a system in which a large loan would be made to the government at a rate of 8 per cent interest. Charles Montagu, 1st Earl of Halifax, William and Mary's Chancellor of the Exchequer, was a major proponent of this scheme. All that was left was to attain official royal approval; and on 24 July 1694 William and Mary founded the Bank of England.

The creation of the Bank of England was not only a matter of economics but of politics. After the Glorious Revolution of 1688, two distinct political groups came to the forefront of British political life: the Tories and the Whigs. If there is anything about the political spectrum of the Late Stuart courts you need to know, it's that these two groups did not get on well together. An overwhelming majority of those involved in the creation of the Bank of England were Whigs. Montagu, importantly, was a Whig. Robert Harley, who later became the Chancellor of the Exchequer under Queen Anne, became a notable critic of the Bank of England, and created the rival Tory Land Bank (I did mention that these two parties didn't get along). Nineteenth-century historian G. M. Trevelyan stated that the Bank of England was established 'against the opposition of the Tories, who were jealous of the monied interest'. The first Governor of the Bank of England from 1694 to 1697 was John Houblon; he was also a director in the New East India Company. This company was very much a Whig-heavy company – once again adding to the politicised nature of the entire financial system.

*

Also on this day in 1689, Prince William, Duke of Gloucester, the longest-living child of Princess Anne, was born, during the reign of William and Mary. This sickly boy ultimately lived only eleven years, dying shortly after his birthday party at Windsor Castle in 1700.

25th – Getting Away with Murder

Archibald Campbell, 1st Duke of Argyll, was born on this day in 1658 – the son of Archibald Campbell, 9th Earl of Argyll (he who was executed on the maiden following the disastrous Monmouth Rebellion of 1685). A controversial figure in British history in his own right, largely because of his involvement in the Glencoe Massacre of 1692, Campbell was given the dukedom by King William III in 1701, some nine years after the massacre. This lead to the not unreasonable opinion that he had been rewarded instead of punished!

26th – Brilliana Harley

Dear Ned,

I hear Mr Moore is come down. I long to hear from him, how your father and you do. I pray God I may hear well of you, and that I may see your father and you with comfort ... I hope your father will come down for a little time. I thank God I was yesterday at church, in the morning, but the afternoon was so wet I durst not go, and I thank God I find myself reasonably well today. Your brothers are well at Clanver, and your sisters are well. I pray God bless you, as I desire my own soul should be blessed. So I rest,

Your most affectionate mother,
Brilliana Harley

Letter dated 26 July 1641, *Letters of the Lady Brilliana Harley*, 1854

Brilliana Harley (*née* Conway) was one of the many remarkable figures of the Stuart era. In her article 'Lady Brilliana Harley and the Siege of Brampton Castle', Alison Stuart, a researcher of the Stuart period, wrote, 'At his insistence Brilliana and her daughters were left at Brampton Bryan, an island of Parliamentary sympathy in a sea of Royalists. Being a practical woman, she turned her mind to what she would need in the event of hostilities and added powder, match and flintlocks to her housewifely shopping list.' Indeed, she successfully defended her home in a three-month siege. And yet, her excellent and copious letters are what she's best remembered for now. It was in one her letters to her son that she reminded him that she had sent him cake and he should eat it – motherly instincts were the same then as now.

*

It was also around this time that Mary Frith, popularly known as 'Cutpurse Moll', was active as a pickpocket. Her unusual lifestyle and dress made her a popular curiosity. She even inspired *The Roaring Girl* (1607–10) by Thomas Middleton and Thomas Dekker.

27th – Bonnie Dundee

May it please your Grace,

The coming of a herald and trumpeter to summon a man to lay down arms, that is leving in peace at home, seems to me a very extraordinary thing, and, I suppose, will do so to all that hears of it. While I attended the Convention at Edinburgh, I complained often of many people's being in arms under the pain of treason being given them, I thought it unsafe for me to remain longer among them. And because some few of my friends did me the favour to convey me out of the reach of these murderers, and that my Lord Levingston and several other officers took occasion to come away at the same time, this must be called being in arms ... Besides, tho' it were necessary for me to go and attend the meeting, I cannot come with freedom and safety, because I am informed there are men of war, and foreign troops in the passage; and, till I know what they are, and what are their orders, the meeting cannot blame me for not coming. Then, my Lord, seeing the summons has proceeded on a groundless story, I hope the Meeting of States will think it unreasonable, I should leave my wife in the condition she is in.

Letter dated 27 March 1689 from John Graham, Viscount Dundee, to the Duke of Hamilton, *Letters of John Grahame of Claverhouse, Viscount of Dundee,* 1826

The first Jacobite Uprising was in full swing, and the Battle of Killiecrankie was fought on this day in 1689, ending in a Pyrrhic victory for the Jacobites. The great Jacobite leader, John Graham of Claverhouse, 1st Viscount Dundee, affectionately known as 'Bonnie Dundee', was shot and killed during this battle. His death was a huge blow to the Jacobites, and it greatly impacted morale.

*

Also on this day in 1625, Edward Montagu, 1st Earl of Sandwich, was born. Montagu's power and influence helped his kinsman, Samuel Pepys, obtain his position with the Naval administration. Montagu was a major figure during the Protectorate – he even signed the document that proclaimed Oliver Cromwell the Lord Protector of the Commonwealth. Following Cromwell's death and the poor substitute of his son Richard Cromwell in the position of Lord Protector, Montagu, like many others, realised that the Stuart line would probably be restored, and made the necessary steps to switch allegiances. Edward Montagu died during the Battle of Solebay in 1672; his charred body washed up on shore.

28th – The Despair

Beneath this gloomy shade,
By Nature only for my sorrows made,
I'll spend this voice in cries,
In tears I'll waste these eyes,
By love so vainly fed;
So lust of old the deluge punished.
Ah, wretched youth, said I;
Ah, wretched youth! twice did I sadly cry;
Ah, wretched youth! the fields and floods reply.

When thoughts of love I entertain, I meet no words but
Never, and, In vain:
Never, alas! that dreadful name
Which fuels the infernal flame:
Never! My time to come must waste;
In vain! torments the present and the past:
In vain, in vain! said I,
In vain, in vain! twice did I sadly cry;
In vain, in vain! the fields and floods reply.

No more shall fields or floods do so,
For I to shades more dark and silent go ...

'The Despair', Abraham Cowley

Abraham Cowley, an English poet, died on 28 July 1667, during the reign of King Charles II. Cowley was born in London in 1618, and his love for poetry stems from reading Edmund Spenser's *Faerie Queene* (and I can't say I blame him). His works included *A Poem on the Late Civil War* (1679) and the piece for which is arguably best remembered, *The Mistress* (1647). During the English Civil Wars, he was a Royalist and followed Queen Henrietta Maria into exile in France.

*

Also on this day in 1675, Bulstrode Whitelock, a Parliamentarian during the English Civil Wars and Lord Keeper of the Great Seal of England, died.

29th – The Chaste Nymph

From what a horrid dream do I awake?
I am afraid my sense does yet mistake.
From these celestial tyrants I am freed;
But still the thought does horror in me breed.
I cannot yet compose my restless soul,
The storm is ended, but the billows roll.
But oh! which tears my soul, a shame remains;
My rising blood does almost break my veins:
A fiery blushing flame's around my face;
I'm all on fire with rage at my disgrace:
For I'm enough dishonour'd, and asham'd
To breathe, but in the air, where love is nam'd.

But be disgrac'd with an attempt so foul,
I hate this place, the world, the gods, my soul.

Act III, *Calisto*, from *The Dramatic Works of
John Crowne*, John Crown, 1873

This masque was first performed in front of King Charles II and his queen, Catherine of Braganza, and their court. What's interesting is how many famous historical persons were not only in attendance, but were actually taking a performing part. Princess Mary (later Queen Mary II) performed the lead of Calisto; she was accompanied by others, including her younger sister, Anne (later Queen Anne), Sarah Jennings (later the 1st Duchess of Marlborough), the Duke of Monmouth, Nell Gwynn, and Henrietta Wentworth, among others. As for the playwright, John Crowne, he lived from around 1641 to 1712, and was buried in St Giles-in-the-Fields on 27 April 1712.

30th – Maria Theresa

Notre reine était de la plus grande ignorance, mais la meilleure femme et la plus vertueuse du monde, qui avait de la grandeur et savait bien tenir une cour. Elle croyait tout ce que le roi lui disait, le bon et le mauvais. Elle avait de vilaines dents noires et gâtées. On prétend que cela venait de ce qu'elle prenait toujours du chocolat; souvent elle mangeait aussi beaucoup d'ail. Elle était grosse et petite, et avait une belle peau blanche. Quand elle ne marchait ni ne dansait elle paraissait plus grande. Elle mangeait fréquemment et long-temps, mais c'étaient de petits morceaux, comme si c'eût été pour un petit serin. Elle ne pouvait renier son pays; elle avait beaucoup de manières espagnoles. Elle aimait extraordinairement le jeu; elle jouait la bassette, le reversis et l'ombre, et quelquefois la petite prime; mais jamais elle ne gagnait, parce qu'elle ne savait pas bien jouer.

Mémoires sur la cour de Louis XIV et de la Régence,
Charlotte-Elisabeth Orléans

Maria Theresa, Louis XIV's queen consort and wife, died on this day in 1683. In the excerpt above, Liselotte recalls her impression of the late Queen of France, Maria Theresa. For those who do not read French, she stated that, although she was quite ignorant, the queen was nevertheless one of the best and most virtuous women in the world. She was quite fat and liked to play card games – but wasn't very good at them. Maria Theresa was Louis' first cousin and she had to put up with both his philandering and the cruelty of some of his mistresses, especially the aforementioned Madame de Montespan.

31st – The Wedding

Is not the bridegroom come yet? Sure he has overslept himself; there is nothing but wondering within; all the maids are in uproar, one says he is a slow thing, another says, she knows not what to say, but they all conclude, if ever they marry, they'll make it in their bargain to be sure of all things before matrimony. Fie upon him! If I were to be his wife, I'd show him a trick for't ere a year came about, or it should cost me a fall, I warrant him.

Act II: Scene III, *The Wedding*, James Shirley

Shirley was born in London in 1596, and Shirley's substantial works were a fabulous blend of tragedy, romance, wit, and comedy. According to Anthony Wood, Shirley and his wife died shortly after the Great Fire of London in 1666, having lost a great deal in the inferno.

AUGUST

1st – Sunset for the Stuarts

But, greatest Anna! While thy Arms pursue
Paths of renown, and climb ascents of fame
Which nor Augustus nor Eliza knew;
What poet shall be found to sing thy name?
What Numbers shall Record? What Tongue shall say
Thy wars on land, Thy Triumphs on the Main?
Oh fairest model of imperial sway!
What equal pen shall write Thy wond'rous Reign?
Who shall attempts and victories rehearse
By Story yet untold, unparallell'd by verse?

An Ode, Humbly Inscrib'd to the Queen: On the
Late Glorious Success of Her Majesty's Arms,
Matthew Prior, 1706

The Stuart dynasty ended on 1 August 1714, with the death of Queen Anne. As the second surviving child of James, the Duke of York's marriage with his first wife, Anne Hyde, it would have been thought impossible that she would one day inherit the throne. 'It is reported of her late Majesty Queen Anne, that she learned to speak properly of the famous Tragedian Mrs. Barry, and from hence was enabled to deliver her speeches to the Parliament in so graceful a manner, that they lost much their beauty and energy when they were afterwards read,' stated the editor Anne Deanes Devenish in the preface to *The Works of Nicholas Rowe* in 1753. Anne had gradually suffered more and more from health problems as she grew older, including gout.

2nd – Campbell and the Glencoe Massacre

And another witness of the same declares that, upon the same 13th
of February, Glenlyon, and Lieutenant Lindsay, and their soldiers, did,
in the morning before day, fall upon the people of Glencoe, when they
were secure in their beds, and killed them; and he being at Innerrigen,
fled with the first, but heard shots; and had two brothers killed there,
with three men more, and a woman; who were all buried before he
came back. And all these five witnesses concur, That the foresaid
slaughter was made by Glenlyon and his soldiers, after they had been
quartered, and lived peaceably and friendly with the men of Glencoe,
about 13 days; and that the number of those whom they knew to be
slain were about 25: And that the soldiers, after the slaughter, did burn
the houses, barns, and goods; and carried away a great spoil of horse,
colt, and sheep, above a thousand.

> *State Papers and Letters, Addressed to W. Carstares,* ed.
> Joseph MacCormack, 1774

Robert Campbell of Glenlyon, 5th Laird of Glenlyon, died on this day in
1696, during the reign of King William III. His rather dark reputation stems
from his role as a commanding officer during the Glencoe Massacre of
1692. Glenlyon is in Perthshire, a county in central Scotland, and Campbell's
home Meggernie Castle lies close by the River Lyon.

3rd – Evelyn's Discovery of Grinling Gibbons

This day I first acquainted his Majesty with that incomparable young
man Gibbon, whom I had lately met with in an obscure place by
mere accident as I was walking near a poor solitary thatched house,
in a field in our parish, near Sayes Court. I found him shut in; but
looking in at the window I perceiv'd him carving that large cartoon
or crucifix of Tintoret, a copy of which I had my selfe brought from
Venice, where the original painting remaines. I asked if I might enter;
he open'd the door civilly to me, and I saw him about such a work as
for ye curiosity of handling, drawing, and studious exactnesse, I never
had before seene in all my travells. I questioned him why he worked
he told me it was that he might apply himselfe to his profession
without interruption, and wondred not a little how I had found him
out. I asked if he was un willing to be made knowne to some greate
man, for that I believed it might turn to his profit; he an swer'd he
was yet but a beginner, but would not be sorry to sell off that piece;
on demanding the price he said £100. In good earnest the very frame

was worth the money, there being nothing in nature so tender and delicate as the flowers and festoons about it, and yet the worke was very strong; in the piece was more than 100 figures of men, &c. I found he was likewise musical, and very civil, sober, and discreet in his discourse. There was onely an old woman in the house. So desiring leave to visit him sometimes, I went away.

Of this young artist, together with my manner of finding him out, I acquainted the King, and begg'd that he would give me leave to bring him and his worke to Whitehall, for that I would adventure my reputation with his Majesty that he had never seen anything approch it, and that he would be exceedingly pleased, and employ him. The King said he would himselfe go see him. This was the first notice his Majestie ever had of Mr. Gibbon.

Entry dated 18 January 1671, *The Diary of John Evelyn*

Grinling Gibbons, top Baroque woodcarver, died on 3 August 1721. Gibbons was born to James and Elizabeth Gibbons in Rotterdam, the Dutch Republic, on 4 April 1648. As you can see, his work adorns some of the most important buildings in the land – Hampton Court Palace, Windsor Castle, Kensington Palace, and many more. That being said, Gibbons did not only work with limewood, but also later worked on stone. His stone carvings adorn parts of Blenheim Palace, which was built to honour John Churchill, 1st Duke of Marlborough's victory at the Battle of Blenheim.

4th – A Meaner Opinion of Love

I can't tell whether what he said was from Inspection, or whether the Stone which had tormented Epicurus, almost during the whole course of his life, had not afforded him leisure to be amorous But this is most certain, that never any man had a meaner opinion of Love than he.

In his opinion, it was a sort of fever, destructive to the body in fine, a short Epilepsy. He look'd upon it as a shortner of the days of the most vigorous; and judg'd that the Gout the Weakness of the eyes the trembling of the nerves, were all caused by the commerce with women and that they who desired to live in Health, or at least be free from Infirmity and Pain, ought to practice this Precept that he had frequently in his Mouth, to eat moderately, use much exercise, and to have nothing to do with women.

Now although he allow'd his wise man to marry upon certain considerations, yet he always was against the illegal use of women. There was nothing he had more in abomination, than those common prostitutes, who may be properly styl'd, The sinks of luxury and lasciviousness, and who may be said to be carried away with the torrent of their passion. There are (notwithstanding the depredation of Time) sufficient testimonials in his writings of his aversion to such practices, and the Severity with whicn he forbid all his followers, entertaining any commerce with persons of that character; but above all, the living after the manner of the cynics. All which sufficiently shows his chastity and modesty.

Epicurus's *Morals*, trans. John Digby, 1712

5th – A Masque and a Murder

Move now with measur'd sound,
You charmed grove of gold;
Trace forth the sacred ground
That shall your forms unfold.
Diana and the starry Night for your Apollo's sake
Endue your Sylvan shapes with pow'r this strange delight to make.
Much joy must needs the place betide where trees for gladness move:
A fairer sight was ne'er beheld or more expressing love.

Yet nearer Phoebus' throne
Meet on your winding ways,
Your bridal mirth make known
In your high-graced Hayes.
Let Hymen lead your sliding rounds, and guide them with his light,
While we do Io Hymen sing in honour of this night:
Join three by three, for so the Night by triple spell decrees,
Now to release Apollo's knights from these enchanted trees.

Masque in Honour of the Marriage of Lord Hayes, Thomas
Campion, 1607

Thomas Campion (1567–1620) was an English writer, poet, and physician. The *Masque in Honour of the Marriage of Lord Hayes* was performed for Lord Hayes (later 1st Earl of Carlisle) and his bride, Honora Denny, the daughter of the Earl of Norwich. Sadly, the bride died seven years later from complications resulting from a miscarriage. The *Somerset Masque* Campion later wrote was in honour of the infamous 1613 marriage between King James I's favourite, Robert Carr, Earl of Somerset, and Frances Howard, recently divorced from the Earl of Essex. In 1615, these newlyweds would become implicated in a scandal that rocked the Jacobean court – the murder by poison of Thomas Overbury – who was a prisoner in the Tower of London. According to G. E. P. Arkwright's biographical memoir in the 1889 publication of the *Masque in Honour of the Marriage of Lord Hayes*, Overbury was one of Campion's patients during the former's incarceration in the Tower. Campion died on 1 March 1620.

6th – *The Alchemist*

Not always necessary:
The children of perdition are oft-times
Made instruments even of the greatest works:
Beside, we should give somewhat to man's nature,
The place he lives in, still about the fire,
And fume of metals, that intoxicate
The brain of man, and make him prone to passion.
Where have you greater atheists than your cooks?
Or more profane, or choleric, than your glass-men?
More antichristian than your bell-founders?
What makes the devil so devilish, I would ask you,
Satan, our common enemy, but his being
Perpetually about the fire, and boiling
Brimstone and arsenic? We must give, I say,
Unto the motives, and the stirrers up
Of humours in the blood. It may be so,
When as the work is done, the stone is made,
This heat of his may turn into a zeal,
And stand up for the beauteous discipline,
Against the menstruous cloth and rag of Rome.
We must await his calling, and the coming
Of the good spirit. You did fault, t'upbraid him
With the brethren's blessing of Heidelberg, weighing
What need we have to hasten on the work,
For the restoring of the silenced saints,
Which ne'er will be, but by the philosopher's stone.
And so a learned elder, one of Scotland,
Assured me; aurum potabile being
The only med'cine, for the civil magistrate,
T' incline him to a feeling of the cause;
And must be daily used in the disease.

The Alchemist, Ben Jonson, 1610

Ben Jonson, English dramatist, died on 6 August 1637, during the reign of King Charles I. Jonson was a contemporary of the likes of Shakespeare and Kyd during a great boom in English drama.

7th – Satyrs upon the Jesuits

The Rage of Poets damn'd, of Women's Pride
Condemn'd, and scorn'd, or proffer'd Lust deni'd;
The malice of Religions angry Zeal,
And all, cashier'd resenting States-men feel:
What prompts dire hags in their own blood to write
And fell their very Souls to Hell for spite:
All this urge on my rank envenom'd spleen,
And with keen Satyr edge my stabbing Pen:
That its each home-set Thrust their blood may draw,
Each drop of Ink like Aquafortis gnaw.
Red hot with Vengeance thus, I'll brand disgrace
So deep, no time shall e'er the marks deface:
Till my severe and exemplary doom
Spread wider than their guilt, till it become
More dreaded than the Bar, and frighten worse
Than damning Pope's Anathema's and Curse.

'Prologue', *Satyrs upon the Jesuits*,
John Oldham, 1681

John Oldham (1653–83), an English poet and translator, was born in early August 1653 in Shipton Moyne, Gloucestershire.

8th – Syrup of Turnips

Syrup of Turnips is a very celebrated remedy here in England, and no where else; which after it had been used by many in proportionable quantities, at seasonable times for three months successively, they have notwithstanding all its praises, gone off, without the least abatement of their coughs, or improvement in their habit of body. Neither can I any ways discover, whence those pretended virtues should precede, or in what part of the Turnip its wonderful strength doth lie. It's apparent enough, that the expressed boiled juice is waterish and windy, not nourishing, nor abstersive, neither hath it such a cooling quality, as to have the least prevalence in abating the Hectic Fever; so that I do look upon it to be a foolish vain medicine. True it is, that the sugar in it may seem to allay the saline slime, smooth, and lenify the gullet, which upon this occasion is ever very rough, and so in some measure seem to ease that part for a little time; but after it hath been some little time in the stomach, turns into a very sour, piercing, and almost corroding moisture, which allowing after some considerable time it doth arrive to the lungs and windpipe, must under those qualification render the said parts more rough, and rather provoke, than in the least abate the cough.

The Vanities of Philosophy and Physick, Gideon Harvey, 1700

Gideon Harvey (1636–1702) was a Dutch physician who studied at the University of Oxford and then the University of Leiden back in the Dutch Republic. His negative view about the use of syrup of turnips is very much in keeping with his views about modern medicine. During the reign of King William III, a fellow Dutchman, he was given the position of physician at the Tower of London. Harvey died in Middlesex, England, in 1702.

9th – *Astraea Redux*

Now with a general peace the world was blest,
While ours, a world divided from the rest,
A dreadful quiet felt, and worser far
Than arms, a sullen interval of war:
Thus when black clouds draw down the labouring skies,
Ere yet abroad the winged thunder flies,
An horrid stillness first invades the ear,
And in that silence we the tempest fear.
The ambitious Swede, like restless billows toss'd,
On this hand gaining what on that he lost,
Though in his life he blood and ruin breathed,
To his now guideless kingdom peace bequeath'd.
And Heaven, that seem'd regardless of our fate,
For France and Spain did miracles create;
Such mortal quarrels to compose in peace,
As nature bred, and interest did increase.

Astraea Redux: A Poem on the happy Restoration and
return of His Sacred Majesty Charles II,
John Dryden, 1660

John Dryden, the great English poet, was born on this day in 1631 in the small village of Aldwinckle in Northamptonshire. Dryden eventually went up to Cambridge University, and became one of the most talented poets and playwrights of the seventeenth century. Although he found work as a poet during the Interregnum, Dryden was really a Royalist, and his true nature was revealed in the panegyric *Astraea Redux*, in honour of the Restoration in 1660. *Absalom and Achitophel* (1681), arguably Dryden's best-remembered poem, controversially satirised various members of Charles II's court, skilfully turning Charles into King David, Charles's illegitimate son the Duke of Monmouth into Absalom, and Shaftesbury into Achitophel. Dryden composed the poem *Annus Mirabilis: The Year of Wonders* (1666), in which he wrote about the 'prodigious fire'.

Dryden was also a prolific translator of classical literature, including Homer's *Iliad*, Virgil's *The Georgics* and *Aeneid*, Horace's *Odes*, Ovid's *Metamorphoses*, and works from later writers Boccaccio and Chaucer. As for his plays, Dryden wrote several, including *All For Love* of 1678, based on Shakespeare's *Antony and Cleopatra*. In this play, Dryden's Cleopatra states, 'My love's a noble madness ... But I have loved with such transcendent passion, I soared, at first, quite out of reason's view, and now am lost above it.' Dryden's position under Charles II and then Charles's successor James II was generally pleasant enough, but that changed in 1688.

Seventeenth-century Britain was not hospitable to Catholics, and especially after the revolution of 1688, Dryden – as a Catholic – soon found himself in an uncomfortable situation. He was ultimately given the boot when he refused to pledge loyalty to the new Protestant sovereigns, William and Mary. Dryden worked with the English composer Henry Purcell, who didn't seem to mind that Dryden was no longer in the good books of high society. When Dryden died in 1700, William III was still on the throne, although by that time he ruled alone.

10th – Maarten Tromp

Upon the way we met fifteen ships and frigates of the Parliament, among whom one was an Admiral, whom I intended to view, taking in all my sails, except both my Marsh Sails, whom we did avail until the midst of the stangs. Being within a canon-shot, he shot a ball over our ship, we answered not, he shot another, to which we answered with one; presently he gives me a broad side, being within a musket-shot, and shot all his side through our ship and sails: Diverse were wounded, some with the loss of their arms, some other wise; thereupon we presently gave him our broadside, not knowing what they intended, which for as yet I know not, because they did not speak a word to us, neither we to them, and we fell thereupon to a general fight. In mean while came the Commander Bourn out the Downs, with twelve of such like ships and frigates mounted, as he told himself to the said Commander John Thyssen, and Captain Peter Alders, being aboard of him with sixty to seventy, and the frigates with thirty eight to fifty pieces of Ordnance, who in the fame while assaulted our Fleet from behind; and we fought thus from half an hour past four till nine of the clock, the darkness departing us from another; when both the Admirals a little beyond the reach of their Ordnance cast their Sails towards the Lee for to gather their Fleets, and to mend what was shot to pieces, we floated the whole night with a light on every Ship. The thirtieth in the morning, we saw the English Fleet driven windward from us, who made sail and went towards Dover.

Letter dated 30 May 1652, Maarten Harpertszoon Tromp

A sharpshooter from William Penn's ship killed Maarten Harpertszoon Tromp on this day in August 1653.

*

It was also on this day in 1675 that King Charles II placed the foundation stone for the Royal Observatory in Greenwich.

11th – His Last Mistress

Lady Henrietta Wentworth, an English baroness and royal mistress, was born on 11 August 1660. Her mother, Philadelphia, and she lived at their ancestral home, Toddington Manor, in Bedfordshire, England. Henrietta's father had been a Royalist during the English Civil Wars and died during the time of strife. Henrietta took part in John Crowne's 1675 masque, *Calisto: Or, The Chaste Nymph*, along with the Princesses of York, Mary and Anne, Sarah Jennings (later Sarah Churchill, 1st Duchess of Marlborough), and finally, James Scott, Duke of Monmouth. Around 1680, Monmouth and Henrietta embarked upon a romantic affair – he being married at the time – and they lived together at Toddington Manor before fleeing abroad when Monmouth was later exiled. Monmouth's execution in 1685 affected Henrietta greatly, and she died less than a year later on 23 April 1686. And, much to his discredit, Henry Savile regurgitated the malicious court gossip about the cause of Henrietta's premature death in a letter to the Marquess of Halifax dated 24 April 1686:

My Lady Henrietta Wentworth is dead, having sacrificed her life to her beauty, by painting so beyond all measure that the mercury got into her nerves and killed her. She has left her land to her mother for life; afterwards it goes to my Lady Lovelace.

Tuberculosis, following severe depression after Monmouth's death, was the probable cause of her death – not poisoning by make-up. In the letter, Savile correctly stated that Henrietta's estate went to her mother, Philadelphia, and afterwards to Lady Lovelace.

12th – The Witchfinder-General

'The Discoverer never travelled far for it, but in March 1644 he had some seven or eight of that horrible sect of Witches living in the town where he lived, a town in Essex called Maningtree, with diverse other adjacent witches of other towns, who every six weeks in the night (being always on the Friday night) had their meeting close by his house and had their several solemn sacrifices there offered to the Devil, and bid them go to another witch who was thereupon apprehended, and searched, by women who had for many years known the Devil's marks, and found to have three teats about her, which honest women have not. So upon the command from the Justice they were to keep her from sleep two or three nights, expecting in that time to see her familiars, which the fourth night she called in by their several names, and told them what shapes, a quarter of an hour before they came in, there being ten of us in the room, the first she called was

1. Holt, who came in like a white kitten.
2. Jarmara, who came in like a fat spaniel without any legs at all, she said she kept him fat, for she clapped her hand on her belly and said he sucked good blood from her body.
3. Vinegar Tom, who was like a long-legg'd Greyhound, with a head like an ox, with a long tail and broad eyes, who when this discoverer spoke to, and bade him go to the place provided for him and his angels, immediately transformed himself into the shape of a child of four years old without a head, and gave half a dozen turns about the house, and vanished at the door.
4. Sack and Sugar, like a black rabbit.
5. Newes, like a polcat.

The Discovery of Witches, Matthew Hopkins, 1647

Matthew Hopkins, self-proclaimed 'Witchfinder-General' died on this day in 1647. Throughout the chaos of the English Civil Wars in the 1640s, Matthew Hopkins terrorised East Anglia with the cruel methods he employeed to 'find' witches. By the 1620s, witchcraft trials had decreased substantially compared with earlier periods, mainly due to judges thinking that they couldn't really prove guilt in such cases. Between 1645 and 1647, upon his death, Hopkins was most active in his search to find, interrogate, and convict 'witches'. Many of those who were accused were executed. Hopkins's story makes for the perfect horror, which is why it was made into a film in 1968 starring Vincent Price, aptly titled *The Witchfinder General*.

13th – The Battle of Blenheim

The Conquering Genius of our Isle returns,
Inspired by Anne the Godlike Hero burns.
Retrieves the Fame our ill lead Troops had lost
And spreads reviving Virtue through the Host.
In distant Climes the wondering Foe alarms,
And with new Thunder Austria's Eagle arms;
The Danube's banks forgetting Caesar's name
Shall echo to the sound of Marlb'rough's Fame.
The Shepherds pipes rejoice o're Gallick blood
And with Eternal purple stain the Flood.

'On the Duke of Marlborough's Victory', *The Second Volume of
Miscellaneous Works*, London, 1705

The Battle of Blenheim was fought on 13 August 1704, as part of the ongoing War of the Spanish Succession. It was a major victory for Stuart Britain and her allies. As a result of his glorious victory, John Churchill was rewarded with the former royal park and the ruin of Woodstock Manor (where King Henry II housed his mistress, Fair Rosamund), as well as the sum of £240,000 – a very generous amount of money. Woodstock Manor became the site upon which the Churchills built their famous Baroque residence, Blenheim Palace.

14th – A House Fire

In silent night when rest I took,
For sorrow neer I did not look,
I waken'd was with thundring noise
And Piteous shreiks of dreadful voice.
That fearful sound of fire and fire,
Let no man know is my Desire.
I, starting up, the light did spy,
And to my God my heart did cry
To strengthen me in my Distresse
And not to leave me succourless.
Then coming out beheld a space,
The flames consume my dwelling place.
And, when I could no longer look,
I blest his Name that gave and took,
That layd my goods now in the dust:
Yea so it was, and so 'twas just.

It was his own: it was not mine;
far be it that I should repine.
He might of All justly bereft,
But yet sufficient for us left.
When by the Ruines oft I past,
My sorrowing eyes aside did cast,
And here and there the places spye
Where oft I sate, and long did lie.
Here stood that Trunk, and there that chest;
There lay that store I covnted best:
My pleasant things in ashes lye,
And them behold no more shall I.
Under thy roof no guest shall sitt,
Nor at thy Table eat a bit.
No pleasant tale shall 'ere be told,
Nor things recounted done of old.
No Candle 'ere shall shine in Thee,
Nor bridegroom's voice ere heard shall bee.
In silence ever shalt thou lye;
Adieu, Adieu; All's vanity.

'On the Burning of Our House', *The Works of
Anne Bradstreet in Prose and Verse*,
Anne Bradstreet, 1666

Anne Bradstreet (c. 1612–72) was an English poetess, possibly from Northampton, who became a colonist in New England. The poem from which we have taken our excerpt is quite moving. Bradstreet relates the devastation caused by a house fire and she consoles herself with the reminder that they were only material possessions.

15th – To the Playhouse

To the Privy Seal and Whitehall, up and down, and at noon Sir W. Pen carried me to Paul's, and so I walked to the Wardrobe and dined with my Lady, and there told her, of my Lord's sickness (of which though it hath been the town-talk this fortnight, she had heard nothing) and recovery, of which she was glad, though hardly persuaded of the latter. I found my Lord Hinchingbroke better and better, and the worst past. Thence to the Opera, which begins again to-day with "The Witts," never acted yet with scenes; and the King and Duke and Duchess were there (who dined to-day with Sir H. Finch, reader at the Temple, in great state); and indeed it is a most excellent play, and admirable scenes. So home and was overtaken by Sir W. Pen in his coach, who has been this afternoon with my Lady Batten, &c., at the Theatre. So I followed him to the Dolphin, where Sir W. Batten was, and there we sat awhile, and so home after we had made shift to fuddle Mr. Falconer of Woolwich. So home.

Entry dated 15 August 1661, *The Diary of Samuel Pepys*

16th – 'The Definition of Love'

My Love is of a birth as rare
As 'tis, for object, strange and high;
It was begotten by despair,
Upon impossibility.

Magnanimous despair alone
Could show me so divine a thing,
Where feeble hope could ne'er have flown,
But vainly flapped its tinsel wing.

And yet I quickly might arrive
Where my extended soul is fixed;
But fate does iron wedges drive,
And always crowds itself betwixt.

For fate with jealous eye does see
Two perfect loves, nor lets them close;
Their union would her ruin be,
And her tyrannic power depose.

And therefore her decrees of steel
Us as the distant poles have placed,
(Though Love's whole world on us doth wheel)
Not by themselves to be embraced,

Unless the giddy heaven fall,
And earth some new convulsion tear,
And, us to join, the world should all
Be cramped into a planisphere.

As lines, so loves oblique may well
Themselves in every angle greet:
But ours, so truly parallel,
Though infinite, can never meet.

Therefore the love which us doth bind,
But fate so enviously debars,
Is the conjunction of the mind,
And opposition of the stars.

'The Definition of Love', Andrew Marvell, 1681

This day, 16 August 1678, saw the death of Andrew Marvell, one of the great English metaphysical poets. Marvell, born in November of 1620, grew up to become a Republican during the time of the Protectorate.

17th – Admiral Blake's Corpse

The day of his death the corpse was left un touched in its cabin, as something sacred; but next morning skilful embalmers were employed to open it; and, in presence of all the great officers of the fleet and port, the bowels were taken out and placed in an urn, to be buried in the great church in Plymouth. The body, embalmed and wrapped in lead, was then put on board again and carried round by sea to Greenwich, where it lay in state several days, on the spot since consecrated to the noblest hospital for seamen in the world. On the 4th of September a solemn procession was formed on the river. The corpse was placed on a state barge, covered with black velvet, and adorned with pencils and escutcheons. Trumpeters in state barges, which bore his pennons, and other barges, carrying the great banners of the Admiralty and the Commonwealth others again bearing the sword and target, the mantle, crest and helmet, preceded the body.

Robert Blake, Admiral and General at Sea: Admiral and General at Sea, William Hepworth Dixon, 1852

Robert Blake (1598–1657), one of the greatest naval admirals in British history, died on this day in 1657. Blake was baptised in the church of St Mary the Virgin in Bridgwater, Somerset, and educated in Bridgwater and then at the University of Oxford. Despite the great funeral service in Westminster Abbey on 4 September 1657 (as detailed above) his remains were exhumed during the Restoration and – along with other Parliamentarians like him – reburied nearby in St Margaret's churchyard. The Blake Museum in his hometown of Bridgwater in Somerset is a fine museum for Blake and Stuart-era fans alike, especially those interested in Monmouth's Rebellion of 1685.

18th – The Pendle Witches

Though public justice hath passed at these Assises upon the Capitall offenders, and after the Arraignement & trial of them, judgement being given, due and timely Execution succeeded; which doth import and give the greatest satisfaction that can be, to all men; yet because upon the carriage, and event of this business, the Eyes of all the parts of Lancashire, and other Counties in the North parts thereunto adjoining were bent: And so infinite a multitude came to the Arraignement & trial of these Witches at Lancaster, the number of them being known to exceed all others at any time heretofore, at one time to be indicted, arraigned, and receive their trial, especially for so many Murders, Conspiracies, Charmes, Meetings, hellish and damnable practises, so apparant upon their own examinations & confessions. These my honourable & worthy Lords, the judges of Assize, upon great consideration, thought it necessary & profitable, to publish to the whole world, their most barbarous and damnable practises, with the direct proceedings of the Court against them, as well for that there doe pass diverse uncertain reportes and relations of such Evidences, as was publicly given against them at their Arraignment. As for that diverse came to prosecute against many of them that were not found guilty, and so rest very discontented, and not satisfied. As also for that it is necessary for men to know and understande the means whereby they work their mischief, the hidden mysteries of their devilish and wicked Enchantments, Charmes, and Sorceries, the better to prevent and avoid the danger that may ensue. And lastly, who were the principal authors and actors in this late woeful and lamentable Tragedy, wherein so much Blood was spilt.

The Wonderfull Discoverie of Witches in the Countie of
Lancaster, Thomas Potts, 1612

The trials of the Pendle Witches began on this day in 1612 in Lancaster, during the reign of King James I. It is a tragedy that these trials are often overlooked, especially considering the better-known Salem Witch Trials later in the period, but these were nevertheless very important. Exodus 22:18 (KJV): 'Thou shalt not suffer a witch to live' – and they didn't.

19th – Master Nicholas's Letter

Master Nicholas,

I have received your letter, and that you sent me from the king, which writes me word, he has been very well received in Scotland,

and that both the army and the people have showed a great joy to see the king, and such that they say was never seen before: pray God it may continue. For the letter that I wrote to you concerning the commissioners, it is that they are to dispatch business in the king's absence. I thank you for your giving me advice of what passes in London, and so I rest

Your friend,

Henrietta Maria R.

Letter dated 19 August 1641, *Letters of Queen Henrietta Maria: including her private correspondence with Charles the First: collected from the public archives and private libraries of France and England,* ed. Mary Anne Everett, London, 1857

20th – The Murder of the De Witt Brothers

A groundless report was in the mean time spread, that the mob of the neighbouring villages and towns had taken arms, and were coming to plunder the Hague. This in creased the tumult, and some of the burghers cried out, We stay here to guard a couple of rogues, who will certainly be rescued before to morrow, by force or fraud; and if they escape ', the town will be next day all in blood and con fusion, and our houses plundered. Upon which many requested, that the de Witts might be carried to the town-house, where they would be kept securely, without any trouble. Others cried out, let us tie them to the gibbet and shoot them. Upon which one of the mob bid them follow him, and he would be their leader j and then with their muskets and smith's hammers they broke up the doors, and came to the chamber, where they found the pen sionary sitting upon the foot of the bed, read ing his bible, and his brother laid down in his night gown. The pensionary aik'd them what they would have, and why all that violence? One of them answer'd, You must walk down, for we will have your lives'; Cornelius rising from the bed, spoke roughly to the fellow, and bid him go down; but the pensionary seeing that no reason would do, he took his brother by the hand to go downstairs, where he was wounded by a pike over the eye; upon which he held up his hands 'and eyes to heaven, recommending his soul to God; and as he went out, was forc'd by the mob to the very place where he had been assassinated two months before, and barbarously murder'd, covering his face with his cloak, as Cæsar did; and his last words were, well, men! Well, citizens! And soon after his brother underwent the same fate. Upon this, the companies retired under their respective colours in good order, while the barbarous mob carried their dead bodies to the gallows, where they hung the pensionary a foot higher than his brother, and afterwards mangling their corps, cut their clothes in a thousand pieces and sent them about the country, as if they had been trophies of a conquest; and some of them cut out large pieces of their flesh, which they broil'd and ate. Thus fell these two great men by popular fury; Cornelius de Witt in the 49th, and the pensionary in the 47th year of his age, both equally zealous for the glory and liberty of their native country, and formerly as much belov'd, as now they were hated by the people, who look'd upon them to be the causes of all the calamities with which their country was at that time overwhelm'd.

The True Interest and Political Maxims of the
Republic of Holland, Pieter de la Court, 1746

The De Witt brothers, Jan and Cornelius de Witt, were horrifically murdered and mutilated on 20 August 1672. Jan de Witt, Grand Pensionary of Holland, was a controversial figure in his time because he was looking for ways to reduce the power of the House of Orange and increase that of the States-General. And so a ruse was set wherein Cornelius was arrested and taken into jail. Jan promptly went to remove his brother from jail and it was then that a mob descended upon them. The brothers were beaten and killed, and bits of their bodies were cut away as macabre trophies. The Rijksmuseum in Amsterdam usually displays Jan de Baen's painting of this event. In this rather disturbing piece of art, a man with a torch shines light upon the grisly scene of the brothers strung up by their feet, their bodies mutilated and their faces and sexual organs having been hacked off. To this day, this event is seen as a shocking part of the history of the Netherlands.

21st – A Royal Bastard

Arabella Churchill, James, Duke of York's mistress, gave birth to their son James FitzJames on 21 August 1670. Born in Devonshire in 1648, Arabella was the eldest daughter of Sir William Churchill and thus the sister of John Churchill, who would go on to become one of the greatest military leaders in British history. Arabella was not considered beautiful by the standards of the day; indeed, she was very slim – the opposite of the voluptuous figure that was then considered ideal. According to Thomas Lediard, Arabella gave birth to four of James's children: two daughters and two sons, one of which was the aforementioned James FitzJames.

*

Also on this day in 1693, Patrick Sarsfield, 1st Earl of Lucan, died.

22nd – Ship Money and Piracy

Our good King in his piety and pity to those poor Captives, had formerly, (with that Ship-money so grudgingly paid,) built and sent out diverse ships to the same purpose; and (God assisting a work so Religious, and becoming a Christian Prince) he provailed therewith against the pirates of Salé, freed many of his Subjects, from barbarous slavery in that place: whereupon he made preparation also against those of Algiers, intending the like mercy for the Christians there, but was prevented in his design by the Scottish insurrection, which forced him Northward. And before his intentions could return to motion, for that Southern Expedition, this unhappy Parliament (by his authority) met at Westminster, where (that it might be conceived some others had Bowels as well as He) a Bill was preferred, and disputed upon, concerning a fleet to the fore-mentioned end; for the maintenance of which, though it might easily have been concluded, by settling of Ship-money in a Parliamentary way, with an Order for the manner or levying the same, to the Subjects liking, (which had been a more safe and sensible kind of payment, then many disbursments extorted since, and might have been a mean to continue God's national blessing upon the whole Kingdom, by increasing (in that sort) all men's hearts and hands, in so charitable and Christian a work) yet because it was a path wherein the King had trod, and they had no purpose to deal either with or for him, in any such friendly or loyal way, as might shadow his apprehended haltings from his people's eyes by making that clearly Legal, which had formerly appeared somewhat Parting.

A Vindication of King Charles: Whereunto is Added A True Parallel Betwixt the Sufferings of Our Saviour and Our Sovereign, Edward Symmons, 1648

The excerpt above refers to the Ship Money tax that Charles I levied in 1634, in order to raise funds without Parliament's approval. Charles had every right to levy this tax, as other monarchs had done in the past, but he didn't only impose it on coastal towns but on inland ones as well. This, along with the fact that the nation was not at war, was met with great hostility. Ship Money, and the resulting outrage it provoked, was one of the major grievances that laid the foundations for civil war. Indeed, the First English Civil War began on 22 August 1642, when King Charles I raised his standard in Nottingham.

23rd – Buckingham's Murder

George Villiers, 1st Duke of Buckingham, was stabbed to death by John Felton on this day in 1628, at the Greyhound Inn in Portsmouth. Buckingham's assassination was met with widespread approval, as he had been almost universally despised for some time. Many had come to see him not only as completely incompetent in both the political and military arenas, but also plain wicked. Charles gave his dear friend a splendid state funeral, but the route was lined with hostile persons who spat towards the coffin as it went by. Felton was convicted of the duke's assassination on 27 November, and paid for his (rather popular) crime by hanging from the Tyburn tree later that month in 1628. Even Henrietta Maria, who for much of her early marriage was in Buckingham's shadow, was pleased with one notable outcome of his demise; the husband and wife grew closer and they embarked upon a much happier relationship.

It was a horrible death for a man who had had it all – incredibly good looks, intelligence, charisma, and the most powerful benefactor in the country, the king. James I (VI of Scotland) was a rather odd fellow whose court was considered debauched in comparison with that of his predecessor. While very learned, the king had a proclivity for being quite coarse and vulgar at times. He had several male favourites – who were rumoured to have been his lovers – including Robert Carr (or Kerr), Earl of Somerset, and George Villiers. It was the latter, Villiers, who has become considered the most important of James's favourites.

George Villiers, 1st Duke of Buckingham's legacy has been assured thanks to the historical fiction of the nineteenth century – he is best known now as a key figure in Alexandre Dumas's *The Three Musketeers*.

24th – 'The Cruel Maid'

> And, cruel maid, because I see
> You scornful of my love, and me,
> I'll trouble you no more, but go
> My way, where you shall never know
> What is become of me; there I
> Will find me out a path to die,
> Or learn some way how to forget
> You and your name for ever; yet
> Ere I go hence, know this from me,
> What will in time your fortune be;
> This to your coyness I will tell;
> And having spoke it once,
> Farewell.

The lily will not long endure,
Nor the snow continue pure;
The rose, the violet, one day
See both these lady-flowers decay;
And you must fade as well as they.
And it may chance that love may turn,
And, like to mine, make your heart burn.

And weep to see't; yet this thing do,
That my last vow commends to you;
When you shall see that I am dead,
For pity let a tear be shed;
And, with your mantle o'er me cast,
Give my cold lips a kiss at last;
If twice you kiss, you need not fear
That I shall stir or live more here.

Next hollow out a tomb to cover
Me, me, the most despised lover;
And write thereon, this,
Reader, know,
Love kill'd this man.
No more, but so.

'The Cruel Maid', Robert Herrick

Robert Herrick, an English poet and Cavalier, was probably baptised on this day in 1591, during the reign of Queen Elizabeth I. In the 1879 introduction to *Chyromela: A Selection from the Lyrical Poems of Robert Herrick*, Francis Turner Palgrave wrote that 'for the men of the Restoration period he was too natural, too purely poetical, he had not the learned polish, the political allusion, the tone of the city, the didactic turn, which were then and onwards demanded from poetry'. His most famous poem is 'To the Virgins, to Make Much of Time', from which comes the phrase 'gather ye rosebuds'. Often referred to as a *carpe diem*, or 'seize the day' poem, it has been very influential upon subsequent centuries' poetry, music, and visual art – most notably 'Gather Ye Rosebuds While Ye May' (1909) from John William Waterhouse, one of the great artists of the Pre-Raphaelite movement of the late nineteenth century. Herrick died in 1674, having lived through some of the period's major events – the end of the Tudor dynasty, the beginning of the Stuart one, the English Civil Wars, the Interregnum and Commonwealth, and the Restoration. One can only wonder what he made of it all.

25th – A Lusty Imposter

We have an account from the Assizes of Horsham in Sussex that on Munday se'nnight last a fellow was indicted and tried there, for personating and pretending himself to be the late Duke of Monmouth, and by that means drawing considerable sums of money out of the zealots of that country. It appeared that he lodged at the house of one Widow Wickard (tho' with seeming privacy) where his true friends visited him and were admitted to kiss his hand upon their knees, he said he was the true legitimate son of K. Charles the 2*d*. and that his Uncle K. James had that honor for him as to execute a common criminal in his stead... Upon his trial he declared himself to be the son of him that keeps the Swan Inn in Leicester, adding that he could not help it if the people would call him the Duke of Monmouth, he never bid them do so, but told 2 Justices of the Peace before, who had sent for him, his true name and made so cunning a defence, and none of his zealots coming in against him (being prosecuted only by Major Brewer) that he was cleared of the indictment, only the Lord Chief Justice after wards bound him to good behaviour, for which he soon found bail, amongst his party, who maintained him like a prince in prison, and 3 or 4 of the chief of them attended him to the Bar at his Trial and believe him still to be the true The Gaoler got the first day he was committed 40*s*. of people that came to see this impostor at 2*d*. a piece.

Letter dated 25 August 1698 from Mr Humfrey Wanley

There can be no doubt that the Duke of Monmouth was very much dead by the time this pretender was out and about. There were plenty of witnesses to the very badly botched execution of that doomed duke on 15 July 1685, but that didn't prevent rumours from circulating. Some people spread the tale that he – the king's nephew – was replaced at the last minute with some other criminal in his stead (as is clearly stated in the excerpt). Some later believed Monmouth was the true identity of the French Man in the Iron Mask – for why else would his face have been hidden away? Imposters and conmen are sprinkled throughout history, and From the excerpt above, we can glean that the Stuart era was certainly no exception. Monmouth was considered extremely handsome and was very successful with women. This same letter relates that this imposter – who must have also been quite aesthetically pleasing – managed to have sex with about fifty women in the town!

26th – Love's Representation

Lionel: I am undone! Ruined! I have lost the sight of this pretty creature, and shall never find her more! Which way shall I go? Whom shall I enquire of? What shall I do, to have a glimpse of her? I have only this comfort; where e'er she is, she is too beautiful to be long conceal'd. From henceforth, I blot all former faces out of my heart. I am tir'd with these daily beauties of the town, whom we see painted and patch'd in the afternoon in the play-house, in the evening at the park, and at night in the drawing room; so that we have half enjoy'd 'em before we speak to 'em.

Merry: Lost! Undone! Beautiful! I am sure I heard these words plain. He is in love, and after the manner of that sort of madman is talking to himself, of his mistress. If he be we shall have fine work: There are ten Keepwells in that Lionel: he'll commit rapes, burglaries, fire houses, or any thing, but he'll have her; and for money, he'll throw it away like dirt. I pity his poor father; but he grudg'd his money for honest terse, and so he's right enough serv'd.

Act II: Scene I, *Bellamira, or The Mistress*, Charles Sedley, 1687

Sir Charles Sedley, one of the most notorious of the Restoration rakes, was buried at Southfleet Church in Kent on this day in 1701. Although he is best remembered for his outrageous antics, he was also an accomplished writer, as we can see from the excerpt above.

*

It was also on this day in 1676 that Robert Walpole, 1st Earl of Orford and the first Prime Minister of Great Britain, was born, during the reign of King Charles II.

27th – Bellamira

Leaning her Hand upon my Breast,
There on Love's Bed she lay to rest;
My panting Heart rock'd her asleep,
My heedful Eyes the Watch did keep;
Then Love by me being harbour'd there,
Chose Hope to be his Harbinger;

Desire, his Rival, kept the Door;
For this of him I begg'd no more,
But that, our Mistress t'entertain,
Some pretty Fancy he wou'd frame,
And represent it in a Dream,
Of which myself should give the Theme.
Then first these Thoughts I bid him show,
Which only he and I did know.

'Love's Representation',
Sir John Suckling (1609–1641)

28th – A Hostile Encounter

We embarked in October of 1697, and passed the sea that separated California from New Mexico. As soon as we set foot on land, the people, being ignorant of our design, (as not understanding our language, or we theirs) imagining that we came to take from them their pearl fishery, as had been attempted several times before by others, came in great multitudes against us, who had but an inconsiderable number of Spaniards to defend us. The violence with which they attack'd us, and multitude of darts and stones they threw at us, our soldiers sustained so vigorously, that they beat 'em back with success, and soon put them to flight.

An extract from a Memoir, concerning the Discovery of a Passage by Land to California, Francis Maria Picolo, 1702

29th – Lilburne's Troubles

I the penman hereof, have abundantly tasted of God's tossing and tumbling dealings with me in this world, which to me as a mere man hath been nothing but a vale of tears, yea a pilgrimage, full of sorrows and afflictions to my earthly house of clay. I was about twenty years old, in the year 1637, by the Bishops, I was forced to flee out of England into these parts for shelter, the usual and most noble receptacle among all the parts of the earth of many a brave and gallant Christian sprit. And at my going back into England, in the same year, I was apprehended there and imprisoned by them; and after that I was imprisoned by the Lords of the King's council; after which I was imprisoned by the judges of the Star Chamber, by whom for three years together I suffered the execution of one of the most cruel sentences, that I think any of you in any history whatsoever hath read to be inflicted upon a man that lived after the undergoing it.

Apologetical Narration, Relating to his Illegal & Unjust Sentence,
John Lilburne, 1652

John Lilburne, a Leveller, died on 29 August 1657. Lilburne's radical political and religious views had caused him a great deal of hardship during his life. In the above excerpt, Lilburne describes his numerous imprisonments during Charles I's reign. Indeed, he appears to have spent a large amount of his adulthood in prison. Unfortunately, things didn't get better for him when the monarchy was abolished and the Republic came into being. Lilburne then found himself increasingly at odds with the new republic, too, and again he found himself in a cycle of imprisonment and exile. By the end of his life, however, he had left the Leveller movement and converted to Quakerism.

30th – A Bigamist or a Divorcee?

At the same sessions, Thomas Middleton, Tooth-drawer on Ludgate Hill, was indicted for marrying two wives, and upon his trial, he produced a sentence of Divorce from his first wife under Seal Causa, Adultery on her part.

A Report of Divers Cases in Pleas of the Crown: Adjudged and Determined; in the Reign of the Late King Charles II, London, 1739

Bigamy could certainly land a person in a lot of trouble in Stuart Britain. That being said, it looks like Thomas Middleton was able to show the court enough evidence to prove that he was only married to one woman. He was probably able to get back to Ludgate Hill to continue extracting teeth shortly thereafter, which certainly beats time in a prison cell. Then again, perhaps a cell would be preferable to two bickering wives?

31st – The Pilgrim's Progress

By this river-side, in the meadows, there were cotes and folds for sheep, a house built for the nourishing and bringing up of those lambs, the babes of those women that go on pilgrimage. Also there was here one that was intrusted with them, who could have compassion; and that could gather these lambs with his arm, and carry them in his bosom, and gently lead those that were with young.

The Pilgrim's Progress, John Bunyan, 1678

John Bunyan, an English Christian writer, died on 31 August 1688. *The Pilgrim's Progress* was one of the most successful books of the seventeenth century, if not *the* most. Bunyan was born in 1628, fought in the New Model Army during the English Civil Wars, and suffered bouts of depression throughout his life.

SEPTEMBER

1st – Grief A-La-Mode

Now I remember 'em: Lady Wrinkle, Oh, that smug old woman! There's no enduring her affectation of youth, but I plague her; I always ask whether her daughter in Wiltshire has a grandchild yet or not. Lady Worthy – I can't bear her company, she has so much of that virtue in her heart, which I have in my mouth only. Mrs. After-Day, Oh, that's she that was the great beauty – the mighty toast about town, that's just come out of the small-pox, she's horribly pitted they say; I long to see her and plague her with my condolence.

The Funeral: Or, Grief A-La-Mode, Richard Steele, 1701

Richard Steele, an Irish playwright, writer, and politician, died on 1 September 1729. Steele is probably best known for being one of the founders of the 1709 journal *The Tatler*, which has ended up as the modern *Tatler*. *The Funeral: Or, Grief A-La-Mode*, from 1701, was dedicated to Geertruida Johanna Quirina van der Duijn, the Countess of Albemarle, better known as the wife of Arnold Joost van Keppel – a favourite of King William III.

*

Also on this day in 1644, the Battle of Tippermuir was fought during the First English Civil War. Led by James Graham, 1st Marquis of Montrose, the Royalists were victorious over the Covenanters.

2nd – The Great Fire of London

About seven rose again to dress myself, and there looked out at the
window, and saw the fire not so much as it was and further off. So
to my closet to set things to rights after yesterday's cleaning. By and
by Jane comes and tells me that she hears that above 300 houses
have been burned down tonight by the fire we saw, and that it is now
burning down all Fish-street, by London Bridge. So I made myself
ready presently, and walked to the Tower, and there got up upon one
of the high places, Sir J. Robinson's little son going up with me; and
there I did see the houses at that end of the bridge all on fire, and
an infinite great fire on this and the other side the end of the bridge;
which, among other people, did trouble me for poor little Michell and
our Sarah on the bridge. So down, with my heart full of trouble, to
the Lieutenant of the Tower, who tells me that it begun this morning
in the King's baker's' house in Pudding Lane, and that it hath burned
St. Magnus's Church and most part of Fish-street already. So I down
to the water-side, and there got a boat and through bridge, and there
saw a lamentable fire. Poor Michell's house, as far as the Old Swan,
already burned that way, and the fire running further, that in a very
little time it got as far as the Steeleyard, while I was there. Everybody
endeavouring to remove their goods, and flinging into the river or
bringing them into lighters that layoff; poor people staying in their
houses as long as till the very fire touched them, and then running
into boats, or clambering from one pair of stairs by the water-side
to another. And among other things, the poor pigeons, I perceive,
were loth to leave their houses, but hovered about the windows and
balconys till they were, some of them burned, their wings, and fell
down. Having staid, and in an hour's time seen the fire: rage every
way, and nobody, to my sight, endeavouring to quench it, but to
remove their goods, and leave all to the fire, and having seen it get as
far as the Steele-yard, and the wind mighty high and driving it into
the City.

Entry for 2 September 1666, *The Diary of Samuel Pepys*

The Great Fire of London began on this fateful day in 1666, beginning in a
baker's shop on Pudding Lane. It is often claimed that the Lord Mayor, upon
hearing about the fire, exclaimed, 'Pish! A woman could piss it out!' The
veracity of this story cannot be proven, and so may well be apocryphal. At
any rate, it's quite amusing. Modern-day Pudding Lane bears a plaque which
indicates that the Great Fire began there, and there is also the fabulous
Monument to the Great Fire of London, designed by Robert Hooke and Sir
Christopher Wren. At the time of writing this, I have climbed the Monument

twice, and thoroughly recommend it to anyone visiting London (getting up and down that flight of stairs will ensure you get your daily exercise!).

3rd – Oliver Cromwell's Death

He died on Friday the said 3 of September at 3 of the clock in the afternoon, though diverse rumours were spread, that he was carried away in the tempest the day before: his body being opened and embalmed, his milt was found full of corruption and filth, which was so strong and stinking, that after the corpse were embalmed and filled with aromatic odours, and wrapped in cerecloth, six double, in an inner sheet of lead, and a strong wooded coffin, yet the filth broke through them all, and raised such a noisome stink, that they were forced to bury him out of hand but his name and memory stinks worse.

Flagellum, or, The Life and Death, Birth and Burial of Oliver Cromwel, the Late Usurper, faithfully described, James Heath, 1669

Ah, the smell of propaganda. Oliver Cromwell, Lord Protector, died on 3 September 1658, following an illness, probably malarial fever. Cromwell became Lord Protector on 16 December 1653. As a man who had been so very much against the powers of the Crown, he quite comfortably allowed himself the splendours of a sovereign once in power. Where did this Cromwell come from? A descendant of Thomas Cromwell's sister, Oliver Cromwell lived in Ely, Cambridgeshire.

4th – James I's Declaration

Those petitions being sent from the House of Commons by a select number unto Us then being at Newmarket for Our health, the House forbare to proceed in any business of important, purposing, as was apparently discerned, and as the even proved, so to continue until the return of their messengers with Our Answer, which we understanding, and being desirous to have the time better disbanded, as was fit (the shortness thereof, by reason of the approach of Christmas being respected) required Our Secretary to deliver a message unto them for this purpose, which he did, first by word of mouth, and after by appointment of the House.

His Majesties Declaration, touching his proceedings in the late assemblie and convention of Parliament, London, 1621

5th – Letter from the Sun King

My Cousin, I have received the letter which you wrote to me on the 17th of this month, in which you inform me that M. de Bentinck has applied to you for a third conference, but that, as I had intimated to you, in one of my letters, that I wished you not to have any more interviews with him, you had thought best, after taking counsel with Marshal Villeroy, not to accept it, without, however, an absolute refusal. I cannot but commend your regularity; but, as you must now have received my orders by the letter, which I wrote to you the day before yesterday, I have only to refer you to what you have therein seen of my intentions.

Letter dated 19 July 1697, King Louis XIV to Marshal Boufflers, from *Letters of William III, and Louis XIV, and Their Ministers: Illustrative of the Domestic and Foreign Politics of England, from the Peace of Ryswick to the Accession of Philip V. of Spain. 1699–1700, Vol. 1, 1848*

King Louis XIV of France was born on 5 September 1638, during the reign of King Charles I of England. Charles I and baby Louis were related by the fact that Charles's wife, Henrietta Maria, was Louis' paternal aunt. As a youth, Louis had a passion for ballet, and Italian-born Baroque composer Jean-Baptiste Lully composed many works during the Sun King's reign. 'L'etat c'est moi' or 'I am the state' is probably the most famous thing Louis XIV said, and it was with good reason – he was an absolute monarch.

6th – The Catholic Whore

I was casually shown the Duchess of Portsmouth's splendid apartment at Whitehall, luxuriously furnished, and with ten times the richness and glory beyond the Queen's; such massy pieces of plate, whole tables, and stands of incredible value.

Entry dated 10 September 1675, *The Diary of John Evelyn*

Louise Renée de Penancoët de Kérouaille, Duchess of Portsmouth and former mistress of King Charles II, died on this day in 1649. As she was a potent combination of French and Catholic, she was one of the least popular of Charles's many mistresses.

From the portraits we have of her, she was indeed a beautiful lady. With her almond eyes, porcelain skin and dark hair, it is not difficult to see what appealed to Charles. Due to the fact that Louise was rather chubby, Charles affectionately nicknamed her 'Fubbs' (although he spelled this 'Fubs'). From her rivals, namely Nell Gwynn, Louise was given less kindly nicknames, such as 'Squintabella'. Louise's famous and aristocratic descendants include the Lennox sisters (in the eighteenth century), and Diana, Princess of Wales.

*

It was also on this day in 1708 that Sir John Morden, 1st Baronet, an English merchant and founder of Morden College, died, during the reign of Queen Anne.

7th – The Great Plague

Plague is one of the most lethal diseases in human history. Symptoms of plague include fever, buboes (painful swellings of the lymph nodes), vomiting, and finally death – and all transpiring over a period of lethal illness spanning three to five days, or perhaps up to two weeks at most. The plague epidemic that swept through London in 1665 was the worst outbreak the city had faced since the Black Death of 1348. Plague spread from fleas on black rats (although new research suggests gerbils), which would carry the bacterium *Yersinia pestis*. Plague had been an intermittent problem throughout the Stuart age, cropping up from time to time, but this outbreak was different.

The Turks and the Dutch had already had bad outbreaks of plague earlier in the 1660s, and with the increase in trading routes it's no surprise that the disease turned up in Britain. In London, the insalubrious slums of St Giles-in-the-Fields were the first place where the dreadful contagion began to show up. Those who could leave London did; the royal court moved out of the city and Queen Catherine and her ladies travelled to Tunbridge. Infected houses were marked with a red cross on the door, and the words 'Lord have mercy on us' would also be placed here. Sick people were taken to the pest houses. On Monday 26 June 1665, Pepys recorded in his diary that 'the plague increases mightily', followed the next day by, 'In my way to Westminster Hall, I observed several plague houses in King's street.'

The common belief at this time was that plague was spread by foul smells, and so fumigation was considered the best deterrent. Fumigation involved burning strong-smelling things such as brimstone, amber, and saltpetre. Those who were plague doctors wore beak-shaped masks, the beak filled with sweet-smelling herbs – again with the belief that this would prevent contagion. With this idea in mind, many people, including children, took up smoking tobacco, believing again that this would halt the disease from entering their lungs. Fumigation and smoking weren't the only preventative measures that were used; stray dogs and cats were slaughtered as well. This last measure backfired spectacularly because once these animals were taken out of the equation, black rats had no predators and were thus able to thrive and the plague became worse.

While the mortality rate was pretty bad, not everyone who contracted the plague died. Prince Rupert's younger brother Maurice contracted it during the English Civil War and survived. Some even survived in the pest houses and were given a certificate that they were cleared of the plague. At its peak, 7,000 people died from plague a week. It is estimated that over 100,000 people may have died from this episode of plague. The Great Fire of London ultimately destroyed the foul dwellings that had been so perfect for the harbouring of disease in 1666.

8th – An Unfortunate Princess

Elizabeth Stuart, daughter of King Charles I of England, Scotland, and Ireland, died on 8 September 1650, during her imprisonment in Carisbrooke Castle on the Isle of Wight. Elizabeth was buried in St Thomas's Church in the town of Newport on the island. It was only during the Victorian period that Elizabeth emerged from this forgotten part of history. Her remains were analysed, and her bones revealed that she had suffered in her life from rickets – a disease which affected both her father, Charles, and her paternal grandfather, James. She was only fourteen years old.

*

It was also on this day in 1664 that the Dutch surrendered New Amsterdam to the British, who changed the name to New York in honour of James Stuart, Duke of York (later King James II).

9th – A Hedonist

I have known considerable Men sometimes pass for the Ornaments of the Court, and immediately be thought ridiculous; to be liked again, then sall into Contempt, without any alteration, either in their Persons, or their Conduct.

A Man retires with the Applause of the whole World, who, the next Day finds himself the Subject of our Raillery, without knowing how he came to forfeit the good Opinion we had of him so lately. The true Reason is, be cause we rarely judge of Men by solid Advantages, which good Sense uses to discover; but by the Fashion, whose Applause ends, as soon as the Fancy which produced it. The Works of Authors are subject to the same Inequality of our Judgment. When I was young Theophile was admired, in spite of his Irregularities and

Negligence, which made a shift to escape through want of Judgment, or Attention in the Courtiers of that time. I have seen him since universally cried down by all the Versifiers, without any respect to his fine Imagination, and the happy Graces of his Genius.

The Works of Monsieur de Saint-Évremont, Charles de Marguetel de
Saint-Denis de Saint-Évremond, 1700

Charles de Marguetel de Saint-Denis de Saint-Évremond (sometimes spelled Évremont), a French soldier and writer, died on this day in 1703, in London. There are several portraits of Saint-Évremond, who is easily identifiable because of the very large wen, or cyst, that protrudes between his eyebrows. Despite his appearance, Saint-Évremond nevertheless managed to be quite a ladies' man and became a known hedonist.

*

It was also on this day in 1585 that Armand Jean du Plessis, better known as Cardinal Richelieu, was born. As a French statesman and Cardinal of the Roman Catholic Church, it would appear that he had nothing whatever to do with Stuart Britain. In fact, he was a major political figure in European affairs during the reign of King Louis XIII, a contemporary of King Charles I of England. As Louis XIII was the brother of Charles's wife, Henrietta Maria, it follows that Richelieu was involved:

In those days affairs were not managed in France as at present: Louis XIII then sat upon the throne, but the Cardinal de Richelieu governed the kingdom; great men commanded small armies, and small armies did great things: the fortune of great men de pended solely upon ministerial favour, and blind devotion to the will of the minister was the only sure method of advancement.

Memoirs of Count Grammont: Vol. 1, Anthony Hamilton,
Count of Grammont, 1809

10th – Henrietta Maria's Death

Henrietta Maria, queen consort, died on this day in 1669 from a possible overdose. As the youngest daughter of King Henri IV of France and his second wife Marie de Medici, she was always destined to become the wife of some European noble or other. After attempts at a Spanish marriage failed miserably, Charles I of England, Scotland, and Ireland turned his attentions to a French alliance. Henrietta and Charles were married by proxy, and subsequently again in person. She was a small woman, with very long arms and quite bad teeth. Charles soon found out that Henrietta Maria was feisty, argumentative, and rather aggressively Catholic. Quarrelling rocked the early part of their marriage, and at one point Charles became so fed up with her French staff that he sent them packing. It was only after the assassination of Charles's favourite, the Duke of Buckingham, that things improved for the royal couple. Henrietta Maria gave birth to nine children: Charles James (stillborn), Charles II, Mary, James II, Elizabeth, Anne, Catherine (stillborn), Henry, and Henrietta Anne. Henrietta Maria, Queen of England was buried in the Basilique Royale de Saint-Denis along with her youngest daughter, Princess Henrietta (Minette).

11th – The Battle of Malplaquet

As soon as I had dispatched my Letter to you on Saturday from Havre, we were alarmed with the Enemy's marching to attack the Prince of Hess, upon which the whole Army was immediately put in Motion, but it was next day at noon before all the Troops could come up. In the Morning they sent out a detachment of four hundred Horse to observe our March, which the Head of the Prince of Hess's Troops attacked, and took the Colonel who commanded them, with the Lieutenant-Colonel and several other Officers, and about fifty Prisoners. Upon Notice of our Army's lying on this Side the Haye, the Enemy stretched out their Line from Quievrain to the Right, which they continued to do the next Day, and yesterday they possessed themselves of the Wood of D---r and Blaregnies, where they immediately began to entrench. This Motion of the Enemy kept our Army for two nights under their Arms; and in the Evening, as soon as the twenty-one battalions and four Squadrons we were expecting from Tournay were come within reach, it was resolved to attack them, and the necessary Dispositions being made, we accordingly began at eight this Morning. The fight was maintained with great obstinacy till near twelve o-clock, before we could force their entrenchments and drive them out of the wood into the plain, where their horse was all drawn up, and ours advancing upon them, the whole Army engaged and fought with great fury till past thre in the afternoon, when the enemy's horse began to give way, and to retire to Maubeuge and Valenciennes, and part of them towards Conde. We pursued them to the Defilee of Bavay with great slaughter, all our troops behaving themselves with the greatest courage.

Letter from The Duke of Marlborough, from *The Military History of the Late Prince Eugene of Savoy, and of the Late John Duke of Marlborough*, London, 1737

The Battle of Malplaquet was fought on 11 September 1709, as part of the Wars of the Spanish Succession. John Churchill and Prince Eugene of Savoy had already successfully teamed up and won at the Battle of Blenheim a few years earlier. Their winning combination was rewarded with yet another big victory at Malplaquet, but it was won at a high cost. Malplaquet was a very brutal and bloody encounter for both sides; the Allies lost between 21,000 and 24,000 troops.

12 – The Battle of Vienna

Yet should the Turk prevail, what would be the end, but in time an establishment of Mahometanism instead of Christianity which is the consequence wherever the Turks become absolute masters; neither can the Papists pretend to a more infallible resolution to the contrary, then the Protestants. But why do I dwell so long upon this supposition, for no man that knows the difference will elect the former (viz. Mahometanism) and nothing but a local necessity can force the latter (meaning Romanism). But to return to what hath been said, to wit, that wherever the Turks are absolute masters Mahometanism will take footing, which we see has happened in all the eastern countries, for though there be as yet a handful of Christians in Asia, Anatolia, Grecia, Romania, &c. it's a thing worth observation, that in less than 200 years the Christian religion has almost ceased in all the Eastern countries, notwithstanding it had for more than a thousand years before been present in these parts ...

The Present State of the German and Turkish Empires,
David Abercrombie, 1686

The two-day siege known as the Battle of Vienna came to an end on this day in 1683. Although British troops were not directly involved, the outcome would probably have affected Britain had the allies been defeated, and so it remains of key historical importance. The Ottoman Empire was very much engaged in a religious war, and sought to reconquer Europe and convert the Christian kingdoms of Europe to Islam. The Qu'ran 33:25–36 states: 'Allah repulsed the disbelievers in their wrath; they gained no good. Allah averted their attack from the believers. Allah is ever Strong, Mighty. And He brought those of the People of the Scripture who supported them down from their strongholds, and cast panic into their hearts. Some ye slew, and ye made captive some.' The 'People of the Scripture' refers to Jews (whose holy book is the Torah) and Christians (whose holy book is the Bible). Being *Kafir*, or unbelievers, a term which can be applied to anyone who isn't Muslim, Christians and Jews were either to be converted to Islam or killed. With so dangerous a threat to Christendom looming, the armies of a Christian Europe joined together. The Ottomans began their advance in March 1683, led by Sultan Mohammed IV at the head of some 200,000 troops. Along with Naseby and Blenheim; the Battle of Vienna was without question one of the most important battles of the Stuart Age.

13th – A Life Cut Short

But the joy of seeing her (Mary, Princess of Orange's) eldest brother peaceably enthroned was much allayed and in a manner prevented, by her sorrow for the loss of her youngest brother, Henry of Oatlands, Duke of Gloucester, who just before her landing died of the small-pox on September 13, in the twentieth year of his age, much lamented by the king, and much beloved by all that knew him, as a prince excellently qualified, religious, learned, valiant, and wise above his years, an affectionate brother, a good master, and a true friend.

A Complete History Of England: With The Lives Of All The Kings and Queens Thereof: From The Earliest Account of Time, to the Death of His Late Majesty King William III, London, 1706

Henry Stuart, Duke of Gloucester, died on this day in 1660, shortly after the Restoration. He had just turned twenty. Henry was the youngest son of King Charles I and his wife Henrietta Maria and was born in Oatlands Palace in 1640, shortly before the Civil War kicked off. It was Henry who, along with his elder sister Elizabeth, had been the last of their family members to see and speak with Charles I before his execution in 1649. Charles had taken his child in his arms and tenderly told them to be wary of those who were going to look after them. Henry and Elizabeth were taken to Carisbrooke Castle on the Isle of Wight, where the fragile Elizabeth died on 8 October 1650.

Oliver Cromwell had Henry released in 1652, whence he journeyed to his mother in Paris. Unfortunately, the relationship between mother and child was evidently fractious – largely due to religious differences. Growing up in a staunchly Protestant atmosphere impacted young Henry's religious views, and his mother's attempt to convert him to Catholicism was met with obstinacy and irritation. Henry was an excellent tennis player; Pepys and Evelyn wrote about him in their respective diaries. The young man was buried eight days after his death in Westminster Abbey. Henry's sister, Mary, would follow him to the grave just three months later and from the same dreadful disease.

*

Also on this day in 1645 the Battle of Philiphaugh was fought in Philliphaugh (near Selkirk, Scotland), during the English Civil Wars. The Royalist army, led by the Marquis of Montrose, was attacked and destroyed by a Covenanter army led by Sir David Leslie. Robert Spottiswood, a Scottish lawyer, was taken prisoner after the battle and was executed in St Andrews. He is best remembered for his great dignity upon the scaffold. According to Revd. George Whishart's *Memoirs of the most renowned James Graham, marquis of Montrose,* 'Scotland was then in a reasonable posture of quiet; for the old grudges were raked up for a while, by removing the principal heads of the opposite parties, whereof some had suffered at Philiphaugh, and others were detained prisoners in England, or banished.'

14th – Reflections upon Learning

Languages being the Channels by which most of our Learning is conveyed, it is necessary to the attaining of Knowledge, that these should be kept clear and open; if the Streams in these run muddy, or are corrupted, all the Knowledge that is convey 'd by them must be obscure. Words at the best are no very certain signs of things; they are liable to ambiguity, and under that ambiguity are often subject to very different meanings; and though this, as far as it is the common condition of speech must be submitted to, and is no objection in plain laws and easy precepts, that are intelligible enough in any language; yet in matters of science, it is much otherwise; these are nice things; the strict meaning is to be observed in them; nor can we mistake a word without losing the notion.

Reflections Upon Learning: Wherein is Shown the Insufficiency Thereof, in Its Several Particulars: in Order to Evince the Usefulness of Necessity of Revelation, Thomas Baker, 1708

Thomas Baker, an English antiquarian, was born on 14 September 1656, during the Protectorate. Baker's love of history is evident in the way he sought to make his work as accurate as possible by using original documents, also known as primary sources. Baker died from a stroke in 1740, just two months shy of his eighty-fourth birthday.

15th – A Liar and a Malcontent

In September 1678, Oates and Tonge, together, made a composition of a damnable, hellish story, that they called the Popish Plot. And, as such as it was, it was sworn before Sir E.B.G and presented, with wondrous formalities of zeal, and caution, to his Late Majesty himself. There were Jesuits' letters, forsooth, to be seized at the post-house, to patch up the credit of a broken business ...

The history of the interval betwixt Oates' damnable discovery, and (if the conceit be not too trivial) the discovery of damnable Oats, has been the entertainment of all peoples tongues, and thoughts, and the amazement of Christendom, no less then the horror of all good men: to see the foundations of Three Kingdoms, shaken with the breath of four or five prostitute, mean, and stigmatized varlets. An imperial monarchy well-nigh sunk into a Common-Wealth, upon the credit of notorious imposters, and common cheats.

> *Brief History of the Times Etc. in a Preface to the*
> *Third Volume of Observators*, Roger L'Estrange, 1687

Titus Oates, the malicious fabricator of the Popish Plot, was born on this day in 1649. It wouldn't be an exaggeration to say that his whole life was a series of failures and poor judgment. Oates failed to earn a degree, he failed to keep jobs – the list goes on and on. He took on several pseudonyms, including 'Friar Ambrose'. In his book *The Popish Plot*, J. P. Kenyon describes Oates as a very dodgy man with psychopathic tendencies. In 1676, Oates was sacked from the Navy as chaplain of the ship *Adventurer* because of sodomy – a serious offense in Stuart Britain. In 1678, he teamed up with Israel Tonge and concocted a story that Catholics were plotting to assassinate King Charles II and to replace him with his Catholic brother, James, Duke of York (later James II). The 'Sir E.B.G.' who is referred to in the above excerpt was Sir Edmund Berry Godfrey, a magistrate, who was later murdered and found in a ditch. The unmitigated hysteria that arose as a result of Oates and Tonge's fearmongering soon became fatal and several people lost their lives. In 1696, Oates was at it again, when he wrote *A Tragedy, Called the Popish Plot, Reviv'd: Detecting the Secret League Between the Late King James and the French King: the Popish Conspiracy to Murder His Present Majesty King William*. Oates died in 1705 in obscurity. His legacy remains one of ridicule and infamy.

16th – William Penn, Admiral of the Royal Navy

Cromwell sent an expedition to seize the Spanish West Indies. He put Penn in charge of the fleet, and made Venables General of the Army. The two commanders, without conference one with the other, sent secret word to Charles II, then in exile on the Continent, and offered him their ships and soldiers. This transaction, though it seemed for the moment to be of none effect, resulted years afterward in the erection of the Colony of Pennsylvania. Charles declined the offer; 'he wished them to reserve their affections for his Majesty till a more proper season to discover them'; but he never forgot it. It was the beginning of a friendship between the House of Stuart and the family of Penn, which William Penn inherited.

The expedition captured Jamaica, and made it a British colony; but in its other undertakings it failed miserably; and the admiral, on his return, was dismissed from the navy and committed to the Tower.

William Penn, George Hodges, 1901

William Penn, Admiral of the Royal Navy, died on this day in 1670, during the reign of King Charles II. Not to be confused with his son, who was also called William Penn, the Quaker who founded Pennsylvania, this William Penn was a well-respected naval officer who was born in Bristol in 1621. During the tumultuous time of the English Civil Wars, Penn was a Parliamentarian who became vice-admiral to Admiral Blake. He and his wife lived in Tower Hill, where they raised a family. In the above excerpt, early twentieth-century historian George Hodges relates how, on 10 May 1655, Admiral William Penn and General Robert Venables took over Jamaica from Spain. That was all well and good, but their main mission was to attack La Hispaniola. For their lack of success, both were sent to the Tower of London. Sir William Penn had his portrait done by Sir Peter Lely around 1665. He died five years later in 1670.

*

It was also on this day in 1701 that the exiled King of England, James II, died at the Château de Saint-Germain-en-Laye, France. He died following a stroke, with his second family all around him, having been betrayed in his eyes by his first. In *A Brief History of the Kings of England, Particularly those of the Royal House of Stuart, of Blessed Memory* (1766), Anthony Weldon wrote, 'James II, of blessed Memory, had the Courage of his grandfathers, and the religion of his mother; the malice and inveteracy of his father, and was altogether ruled by Priests and Jesuits.'

17th – Carlos II of Spain

'My worthy friends' quoth Lewis, 'henceforth let us live neighbourly, of my own temper, but it has been my misfortune to live among quarrelsome neighbours. There is but one thing can make us fall out, and that is the inheritance of Lord Strutt's estate. I am content, for Peace's sake, to waive my right, and submit to any expedient to prevent a law-suit; I think an equal division will be the fairest way.'

John Bull Still in His Senses: Being the Third Part of Law is a
Bottomless-pit, John Arthbuthnot, 1712

King Carlos II of Spain, the last Hapsburg monarch of Spain, became king on 17 September 1665. Carlos's whole life was a tragic affair from the beginning; he was an unfortunate product of generations of close inbreeding. The king's calamitous lineage produced in him a vast array of debilitating physical and mental disabilities, which made it difficult for him to perform such basic tasks as talking and eating. King Carlos II was married to Marie Louise, and although Carlos loved his wife, who seemed to have returned his affections, they were unable to have children – he was in all likelihood impotent. Marie Louise, depressed and lonely, died under mysterious circumstances, leading to rumours that she had been poisoned. Like mother, like daughter.

When Carlos died childless in 1701, he named Philippe of Anjou as his successor. The prospect of a massive empire of French and Spanish territories, including New World land and trade, was hugely disconcerting. Louis claimed no such thing would happen, and King William III warned everyone not to trust Louis's word. No one believed him and Louis invaded the Spanish Netherlands. The War of the Spanish Succession had broken out; it would last until 1714. Churchill teamed up with Prince Eugene of Savoy and the Dutch Republic to form the Great Alliance. Churchill's name would go down in history for the Grand Alliance's victories at the aforementioned Battle of Blenheim in 1704 (an utterly horrific outcome with over 20,000 deaths), and the Battle of Ramillies in 1706. In the above excerpt, Arbuthnot satirizes the whole situation, casting Louis XIV as Lewis Babboon (for Louis' House of Bourbon) who wants Lord Strutt's estate (Strutt being Carlos II).

18th – Revolution in the Air

I went to London: where I found the Court in the utmost consternation upon report of the Prince of Orange's landing, which put Whitehall into so panic a fear, that I could hardly believe it possible to find such a change. Writs issued now in order to the Parliament and a declaration to back the good order of Elections, with great professions of maintaining the Church of England: but without giving any sort of satisfaction to the people, who now began to show their high discontent at several things in the Government: how this will end, God only knows.

Entry dated 18 September 1688, The Diary of John Evelyn

1688 proved to be one of the most important years in British history, let alone the history of Stuart Britain. When King James II and his second wife, Mary of Modena, were delivered of a healthy son, James Francis Edward Stuart, this proved to be the straw that broke the camel's back. Immediately after this birth there were rumours that the baby was a changeling; it became known as the 'Warming-Pan Baby'. These unfounded rumours spread along with the fears of a Catholic succession. The latter was of great concern, especially to some of the most influential men of the day. Seven of these men – William Cavendish, 4th Earl of Devonshire; Henry Compton, Bishop of London; Richard Lumley, Baron Lumley; Thomas Osborne, 1st Earl of Danby; Edward Russell; Henry Sidney; and Charles Talbot, 12th Earl of Shrewsbury – were thereafter known as the 'Immortal Seven' because they sent a letter inviting James II's nephew (and son-in-law) William III of Orange to come and take the throne.

19th – An Essay upon Reason and Religion

There is nothing that gives men a greater dissatisfaction, than to find themselves disappointed in their Expectations, especially of those things, in the having or not having, of which they themselves are most concern'd And therefore, all that go about to give demonstrations in matters of religion, and fail in the attempt, do not only leave men less devout, than they were before, but also with great pains aud Industry lay in their minds the grounds and foundation of Atheism; for the generality of mankind, either out of laziness or diffidence of their being able to Judge aright, in points that are not very clear, are apt rather to take things upon trust, than to give themselves the trouble to examine whether they be true or no; but when they find what a man under takes to give them for a demonstration is really none at all, they do not only conclude that they are deceived by him, but begin to him, but begin to suspect, they have been ill used by thole who first imposed upon them a notion, for which perhaps no demonstration can be given, and from this suspicion they ran to another of a more dangerous consequence, that what is not demonstrable, may also not be true.

An Essay upon Reason and Religion, George Villiers, 2nd Duke of
Buckingham, 1705

George Villiers, 2nd Duke of Buckingham, was created a Knight of the Garter on this day in 1649. Villiers was one of the most debauched of the Restoration rakes. As the son of the murdered 1st Duke of Buckingham and the rich heiress Katherine Manners, he was born into privilege and an elite social rank. This was to be, however, of short duration, for the

English Civil Wars thrust him and his younger brother, Francis, into combat. Francis was killed in battle, and eventually George and other Royalists like him had no choice but to flee the country and go into exile. As soon as the Restoration began, Villiers married Mary Fairfax – the daughter of the major Parliamentarian leader, Sir Thomas Fairfax. Villiers was not a faithful husband, one of his liaisons taking place with a married woman: Countess Anna Maria, wife of Francis Talbot, 11th Earl of Shrewsbury. Anna Maria's husband couldn't stomach being made a cuckold – especially in so public a manner. Understandably enraged and dishonoured, the Earl of Shaftesbury demanded a duel with the Duke of Buckingham in 1668. George ended up killing Francis in the duel, and Anna Maria moved in with George and his wife, who protested to no avail. And so they lived in a *ménage à trois*, during which time Anna Maria gave birth to Buckingham's son (who died soon after); she then went into a convent but then married again. No duels or scandals plagued this marriage, and she died in 1702. The notorious Villiers met his end in a grubby room, with none of his former ebullience left to him. Can some moral be found in this? I leave that to you, gentle reader.

20th – The Treaty of Ryswick

That there be an universal perpetual peace, and a true and sincere friendship between the Most Serene and Mighty Prince William the Third, King of Great Britain, and the most Serene and Mighty Prince Lewis the Fourteenth the most Christian King, Their Heirs and successors, and between the kingdoms, states, and subjects of both, and that the same be so sincerely and inviolably observed and kept, that the one shall promote the interest, honour, and advantage of the other, and that on both sides a faithful neighbourhood and true observation of peace and friendship, may daily flourish and increase.

The Acts and Negotiations: Together with the Particular Articles at Large, of the General Peace, Concluded at Ryswick, by the Most Illustrious Confederates with the French King. To which is Premised, the Negotiations and Articles of the Peace, Concluded at Turin, Between the Same Prince and the Duke of Savoy, London, 1698

So begins the Treaty of Ryswick, which was signed on 20 September 1697. This treaty ended the War of the Grand Alliance (also known as the Nine Years' War), which pitted England, Spain, and the Dutch Republic against France. As part of this treaty Louis XIV officially recognised William III as King of England, Scotland, and Ireland, although Louis had aided the exiled James II and housed him in one of his chateaus. The peace would be only temporary, for major warfare would start up again with the death of Spain's King Carlos II and the subsequent War of the Spanish Succession.

*

Also on this day in 1643, the Battle of Newbury, part of the English Civil Wars, was fought in Newbury, Berkshire. Among the dead was Lucius Cary, 2nd Viscount Falkland. According to historian Blair Worden, the Battle of Newbury might have ended the war in the king's favour, but for the lack of gunpowder.

21st – Cessations

For the Rt. Honourable the Earl of Lauderdale, Lord Secretary of Scotland.

My Lord,
   I doubt not but you have heard of McEntosh going to Lochaber, to possess himself of that lands of Glenluy and Locharchaig, which Lochyall keeps from him by strong hand. The Earl of Murray endeavoured to agree them, but could not, and returned home not pleased; yet McEntosh having granted Lochyall a cessation, the Earl of Murray write to me, and offered to meet me at the place of treaty in Lochaber, to see if we could agree, but have no command from my L. Com. I would not meddle, so neither did my L. Murray. McEntosh had no assistance but his own friends and tenants, and some few of my L. Huntley's, so that when Lochyall and he met, they were very near a like number. They have treated long, and have had many renewed cessations, and at last are towards a settlement, for young Glenurchy, who is a tryster, and upon the place with 200 men, writes to me that on Sunday last they were within two thousand five hundredth marks of the prize, and were next to treat of the terms of payment and security; so that is like all will end peaceably. McCoull hath sent to desire to speak with me, and I have yielded to it. These agreements, I hope, will break all the broken men. My wife mends slowly, yet I hope, God willing, is in the way of recovery. Adieu.

Letter dated 21 September 1665 Archibald, Earl of Argyll,
to John, Duke of Lauderdale, *Letters from Archibald,*
Earl of Argyll, to John, Duke of Lauderdale, 1829

22nd – Executed for Witchcraft

Martha Corey was executed by hanging on this day in 1692. Why? Corey was a woman accused of witchcraft during the infamous Salem Witch Trials. Her husband, Giles Corey, had also been accused and found guilty of witchcraft and had been executed. The method for killing Giles Corey was not hanging, but he was instead pressed. This means he was laid on the ground and heavy stones were placed upon him until his body was crushed. Martha's execution is believed to be the last time a person was executed for witchcraft in the colonies.

23rd – Van Leeuwenhoek and Emana

Honourable Gentlemen, I now take the liberty of communicating to you these my following observations. A certain ancient surgeon, that is a great collector of foreign curiosities, had entreated another surgeon, for whom he had an esteem, that when he was in the East Indies, and discover'd in the plants or seeds of those parts any particular operation or effect, that he would impart some of 'em to him, with an account of their said operation; whereupon he had received from the East Indies the seed of a tree called Emana, of which the description and operation is as follows 'tis a tree much about the bigness of an Elder Tree, and the flower, the scent and figure of it is not very different, but the branches are armed with thorns 'tis used inwardly by nobody, excepting some Women, that, disagreeing with their Husbands, make use of it in order to kill themselves; it being consequently a certain poison. When these Women have made such a heathenish and impious resolution, they take half a handful of those leaves, boiling them in water and rubbing in a certain oil which they call Sinselen, and so drink or eat it up. Half an hour after, they perceive a kind of convulsion in their head, and vomit or retch four or five times. Lastly, they lost their senses, and, foaming at the mouth, they gret and speak like fools or madmen till they die.

Philosophical Transactions, Giving Some Accoupt of the Present Undertakings, Studies, and Labours of the Ingenious in Many Considerable Parts of the World, London, 1708

Anthonie van Leeuwenhoek (1632–1723), a major Dutch scientist during the seventeenth century, wrote the above. In the Dutch Republic (present-day Netherlands) Anton van Leeuwenhoek made some great advances in the field of microscopy. He greatly improved the design of the microscope; some of the things he studied under his revised scope included bacteria and even his own semen (when he observed spermatozoa, he concluded that each sperm contained a mini person, which conformed with a view known as Preformationism – a popular theory during the Stuart era). Van Leeuwenhoek is often called 'the Father of Microscopy'.

24th – Colonel Popham's State Funeral

Yet the earl of Warwick, who had served them so faithfully, and with such success, was removed from the command of the fleet, which was put into the hands of land officers, such as Blake and Popham, who, notwithstanding, behaved well, quickly gained the love of the sailors, and grew in a short time knowing seamen themselves. As for prince Rupert, he continued cruising and making prizes, throughout the greatest part of the year 1649, while the war continued hot in Ireland; but things taking a new turn there, entirely in the parliament's favour, orders were given by the parliament to their admirals Blake and Popham, to block up the prince's squadron in the port of Kinsale, which they accordingly did, and reduced them to such extremities, that his men began to defect in great numbers; so that finding his cafe desperate, the whole kingdom of Ireland in a manner conquered, all hopes of succor lost, and very indifferent terms to be hoped for from the conquerors.

Lives of the Admirals and Other Eminent British Seamen, Vol. 1,
John Campbell, 1750

Colonel Edward Popham, a naval and army officer, was given a splendid state funeral in Westminster Abbey on this day in 1651. Born around 1610, Popham was one of the three 'generals at sea' during the Interregnum, the others being Admiral William Blake and Richard Deane. It was this triumvirate that destroyed Prince Rupert of the Rhine's fleet in 1650. As with most of the other Parliamentarians who were interred in Westminster Abbey, Popham's remains were removed following the Stuart Restoration.

*

It was also on this day in 1645 that the Battle of Rowton Heath was fought. The Roundheads (commanded by Sydenham Poyntz) and Cavaliers (commanded by King Charles I) clashed in various sites around Rowton, Cheshire, all of which resulted in a victory for the Parliamentarians. In recognition of his achievement, Parliament awarded Poyntz £500.

25th – Arbella Stuart

'On the 25th of September, 1615,' says Nichols, 'that ill-fated and persecuted lady, Arabella Seymour, daughter of Charles, Earl of Lennox, cousin-german of Henry Darnley, father of King James, died in the Tower of London.'

The Life and Letters of Lady Arabella Stuart, ed. Elizabeth Cooper, 1866

Arbella Stuart, a potential successor to the throne of England, died on 25 September 1615. Arbella was the daughter of Elizabeth Cavendish, Countess of Lenox, and Charles Stuart – the brother of Henry Stuart, Lord Darnley (second husband of Mary Queen of Scots). This meant that she was a descendant of King Henry VII via his daughter Margaret Tudor. As such she was certainly in line to the throne, and she could have potentially ascended the throne after her cousin Queen Elizabeth I died in 1603. By 1610, Arbella was unmarried, and with any marriage requiring consent from her cousin, King James I, marriage was unlikely. But that all changed when she fell in love with William Seymour, 2nd Duke of Somerset. He was twelve years her junior, and they were secretly wed. An issue presented itself in that William was also from a very important family – his ancestors also went back to Henry VI, but via that king's daughter Mary. As a result, the match between Arbella and William was a nightmare for James I, as it would have been for Elizabeth I. When the news of their marriage was uncovered, James promptly had both imprisoned. William was placed in the Tower of London, and Arbella was placed under house arrest.

A plan, however, was concocted in which the two, who weren't expected to escape, would flee to France where they could live in peace. The saying 'the best laid plans of mice and men often go awry' is certainly relevant here. She could have reached France, but she wanted to wait for her husband (who was running late) and she was captured near Calais; her husband had taken a ship to Flanders. Arbella was incarcerated in the Tower of London, where she refused to eat, leading to her death – aged only about forty – on this day. Her body was embalmed, the bill for which totaled £6 13s 4d. King James I had her coffin placed in the same vault in which his mother rests in Westminster Abbey. She was buried there on 29 September 1615.

26th – Considerable Sums

To Mr. Richbell and Mr. Stanyan.

Gentlemen,

I received your letter of the 24th of September by Mr Deane, and although the paper you gave in to my Lord Treasurer of the state of your account, which his Lordship transmitted to me, is very perplexed, and in some points unintelligible; yet I have at last attained to the understanding of your whole affair. I have formed a state of your account in a plain method, beginning with the balance charged upon you at the foot of your account declared before the Barons of the Exchequer to the last of April 1682, by which you must be bound. That is, there can be no looking back or raveling into what was then done by the Barons. I have taken the discharge from Mr Stone, and I have (as my opinion) allowed of every sum, for which he could five me a reasonable or equitable voucher. For I must tell you, there are very many vouchers wanting for considerable sums ... I will own that you have much improved the revenue, which has been expensive to you; but you must remember likewise, that your enjoyment of those improvements did recompense the charges you were at: and this particular, for which you crave £10,000, being perfect matter of bounty, it is not fit for me to say more than represent it as such. The king knows best how to dispense his favours; and I wish you may taste of them. I am, Gentlemen, your very affectionate servant, Clarendon, C.P.S.

> Letter of 1686, *The correspondence of Henry Hyde,*
> *Earl of Clarendon, and his brother Laurence Hyde,*
> *Earl of Rochester; with the diary of Lord Clarendon from 1687*
> *to 1690, containing minute particulars of the events attending the*
> *revolution and the diary of Lord Rochester during his embassy to*
> *Poland in 1676*

27th – My Dearest Life

My dearest life

But in great extremity I would not put you to any trouble. You know while there was any tolerable freedom of any other means of converse, I never urged this. Now in your closer imprisonment I most humbly beg of you that by such faithful messengers as these your condition may sometime be reported to which I am otherwise like to be a most unhappy stranger. God keep you in good health, and me in my right wits, and then I dare (if it be your pleasure) I fear nothing, or what is more, for your sake can be afraid of anything.

> Letter dated 27 September 1652, Thomas Hervey to Isabella May,
> *Letter-books of John Hervey*

28th – A Death at Althorp

Of the patriots who fought, sword carefully in scabbard, in this glorious cause, Robert Spencer, second Earl of Sunderland, was one of the most illustrious. His father, Henry Spencer, the first Earl, had fallen in the King's army at Newbury in 1643, held on that side it seems from a feeling of personal honour. His mother was Dorothy Sidney, the beautiful and witty 'Sacharissa', whom van Dyck and Edmund Waller combined to immortalise. In September 1702, at his country seat at Althorpe, which had been so magnificently adorned out of the public purse, the Earl was taken dangerously ill. On the 28th he quitted for ever the intrigues and factions of the world.

> *Tarnished Coronets, Studies in the History of the British Peerage,*
> Muriel Nelson D'Auvergne, 1911

Robert Spencer, 2nd Earl of Sunderland, died at his estate at Althorp on 28 September 1702, during the reign of Queen Anne. Spencer was a big gambler, which gave his family some financial difficulties.

29th – Doing Good to Posterity

Dr Thomas Tenison, Archbishop of Canterbury during the reign of William and Mary, was born on this day in 1636, during the reign of King Charles I. It was in his position as Chaplain in Ordinary to William and Mary that Tenison preached *A Sermon Concerning Doing Good to Posterity*, at Whitehall Palace on 16 February 1690:

This is the Common Rule concerning good, not only that it is to be done, but that we are to do what, upon the whole matter, is the greatest good which we are capable of doing in our sphere and condition ... If the good be equal in other respects, he that does the charity that lasts but a day, does well; but he that does the good that does some years, does still better. He who is of good will, gives a cup of cold water to a thirsty man, performs a charitable office, but that person is, by much, the greater benefactor, who opens a fountain which from time to time may give refreshment to man and beast.

Tenison then goes on to describe the Catholics with some vitriol, though the words can just as well be used to describe certain groups that have been causing destruction and terror in any age:

And this puts me in mind of still a worser sort of men, who by their inhumanity, make such desolations in their times, as late posterity can scarce repair. Their talent lies not in building and planting, but in plucking up and destroying. They are imitators of Apollyon the God of this world, whose delight is mischief, whose triumphs are barbarities. Fire and sword are the instruments of their glory: they spare neither the bodies of the living, not the monuments of the dead. They lay waste in a few hours, strong and beautiful cities, which were the fruit of the arts and labours of former times. One would think they anticipate Doomsday itself, if their force were equal to their pride and malice.

30th – Of Peace

Peace is the next in order, first in end;
As the most perfect state of Government,
Where Art and Nature each to other friend,
Enlarge the crown by giving men content;
And what by laws within and leagues without,
Leaves nothing but prosperity to doubt.

So that in her orb there is left for kings
Great undertakings, far beyond the flight
Or pitch, of any lower-feather'd wings:
The charge, care, council being infinite;
As undertaking range of Time, and seas,
Which tyrant-like, to ruin else finds ways.

Ordering of boats, and bridges to be placed
Upon advantage, for the trade of men,
Rebuilding monuments, or towns defaced,
Cleansing of havens, draining dry of fens,
Fitting out brooks, and mears for navigation,
All works of princely art, charge, reputation.

Such was the cleansing of Egyptian sluices,
Which got Augustus ornament and food,
For his Praetorian bands, and people's uses;
In this kind prov'd the Appian highway good;
Those public works which active states bring forth.

'Of Peace', *The Works in Verse and Prose Complete of the Right Honourable Fulke Greville, Lord Brooke,* Fulke Greville, 1870

Fulke Greville, 1st Baron Brooke, Elizabethan statesman and dramatist, died from gangrene on 30 September 1628, during the reign of King Charles I. His manservant, Hayward, stabbed him in the stomach before killing himself. Despite the treatments provided by his physicians, Greville died from his injuries. He had been a friend of the Elizabethan poet Sir Philip Sidney, who was a popular figure in the Elizabethan court.

OCTOBER

1st – John Blow

John Blow, an English composer of Baroque music, died on 1 October 1708, during the reign of Queen Anne. In 1700, Blow published *Amphion Anglicus: A Work of Many Compositions, for One, Two, Three And four Voices; with Several Accompaniments of Instrumental Music: and a Thorow-bass to Each Song, Figur'd for an Organ, Harpsichord, Or Theorbo-lute.* The piece was dedicated to Anne, Princess of Denmark (later Queen Anne).

2nd – Transactions at Sea

When I had completed these two Parts, which compose the Fourth and Fifth Books of the ensuing History, I began to reflect that, among the numerous Subjects which have been treated in the English tongue, (wherein scarce any in any part of learning hath been left untouched) no one hath hitherto undertaken to collect somewhat of a Naval History, or general Account of Wars on the Sea; whereof both ancient and modern Times have been so productive, that I know not any Subject which affords more ample circumstances ... As the Kings of England thought it necessary, from time to time, to increase their maritime strength, the French, and the States-General of the United Provinces have augmented theirs, especially in latter Days; but of those Princes, or Governments, who have been most formidable at Sea, from the remotest Times of Navigation, I shall be as particular as possible in the ensuing History, and will therefore confine my self in this Preface to what doth more immediately relate to the Royal Navy of Great Britain.

Preface, *A Complete History of the Most Remarkable Transactions at Sea*, Josiah Burchett, 1720

Josiah Burchett was a naval administrator who had begun his career as a clerk under Samuel Pepys. His book, *A Complete History of the Most Remarkable Transactions at Sea*, was a revised and expanded version of the work he had published in 1703, *Memoirs of Transactions at Sea during the War with France*. Burchett married thrice. He died on 2 October 1746.

*

It was also on this day in 1617 that Isaac Oliver, the renowned miniature portraitist, died. Formerly one of Nicholas Hilliard's pupils, the French-born Oliver became so talented in his work that he came to rival that great portraitist. His most famous works include: *Robert Devereux, 2nd Earl of Essex* (c. 1596–98), *Unknown Woman in Masque Costume* (1609), *Anne of Denmark* (c. 1610), *Henry Frederick, Prince of Wales* (c. 1612), *Charles, Prince of Wales* (1615) and *John Donne* (1616). Isaac's son, Peter Oliver (c. 1594–1647) became a sought-after painter in his own right.

3rd – Marcus Zuerius van Boxhorn

Daer is een seecker slach van menschen, die alles doorsnuffelen, ende welckers weetgiericheyt sich streckt van het Oosten tot het Westen, eertsklappers. Het is te vreesen dat haer werck dueren sal van nu aen af tot het eynde toe van de weerelt, van het welcke alleen sy voorgenomen hebben niet te sullen schrijven.

> *Bediedinge van de tot noch toe onbekende afgodinne Nehalennia,*
> Marcus Zuerius van Boxhorn, 1647

Marcus Zuerius van Boxhorn, a Dutch scholar, died on this day in 1653. He was born in 1612, and although he unquestionably possessed one of the most earworm-worthy names of the Stuart era, that was not what made him famous. As a professor at Leiden University in the Dutch Republic (now the Netherlands), Marcus Zuerius van Boxhorn is known for his work in the field of linguistics. His biggest contribution to this field was the theory that major languages such as Latin, Greek, and German came from a source language, which he labelled 'Scythian'. In 1650 he published *Commentariolvs De Statu Confoederatarum Provinciarum Belgii* (Commentary on the State of Confederate Provinces of the Netherlands). Linguistics aside, Marcus Zuerius van Boxhorn was also Professor of Rhetoric at Leiden from 1632 to 1648, as well as Professor of History and Politics, again at Leiden, from 1648 until his death in 1653.

4th – General Fleetwood

Dear Brother,

We stick still how to send you ready cash. There is but one way best, if we effect it; which is to be out of the exchequer money, which this half year past are to be paid, our excise and other revenues coming in so slowly, that we are much disappointed in our affairs. If we can get this it is much as at present we can have hopes of; but I hope very suddenly we shall have such a way, as will deliver you and us out of such intricacies. We have had very notable discoveries of the malignant designs, which I hope will convince all men that we have not pretended one, but that the thing was real. Suddenly the justice upon some of them will clear it up. In this Mr. Secretary's account to you will give a more full satisfaction. Clearly such providences are very signally teaching. The lord give us hearts rightly to improve the same, and to let us see how deceitful a thing it is to put a confidency in any outward arm of flesh, but to make him our strength and confidence, who never slumbers nor sleeps, but even then we are most secure and nearest danger, then is his wakeful eye of providence over us; a present experience whereof I am sure we have had in the prevention and discovery of this design; which, now through mercy, hath proved so abortive. The Lord give us hearts to own him in this, which that we may, is the desire of Your most affectionate brother and humble servant, Cha. Fleetwood.

Letter dated 13 April 1658, General Fleetwood to Henry Cromwell, Lord Deputy of Ireland, *A collection of the state papers of John Thurloe, Esq., secretary, first, to the Council of State, and afterwards to the two protectors, Oliver and Richard Cromwell*, 1742

Sir Charles Fleetwood, an English Parliamentarian soldier and former Lord Deputy of Ireland, died on 4 October 1692, during the reign of William and Mary. At the time of the English Civil Wars, Fleetwood was, in the words of the eighteenth-century historian Hume, 'a notorious fanatic', who encouraged radicalism in the troops he commanded. During the Irish campaign of 1649 to 1650, Fleetwood was one of three men – the others being Henry Ireton and Edmund Ludlow – who continued the campaign following Oliver Cromwell's return to England in May 1650. In terms of his private life, Fleetwood married Cromwell's daughter, Bridget, in 1651 – a mere six months after the death of her husband, Henry Ireton.

5th – An Italian Princess

Princess Maria Beatrice, known to history as Mary of Modena, was born on 5 October 1658. When Anne Hyde died from breast cancer in 1671, James, Duke of York, spent little time as a widower. Most people had frowned on his marriage to Anne because she was a commoner, and common sense would have told him to look for a Protestant princess. He soon began looking for his next duchess, but, unfortunately for him, he once again chose a wholly unsuitable bride. Mary of Modena was an Italian princess and a devout Catholic – so devout, in fact, that she had been planning on entering a nunnery. James was a Catholic himself, and for him to have chosen a Catholic bride was an antagonistic decision on his part, especially as the country was becoming increasingly Protestant. It would have been in his best interest to marry an English Protestant of high birth, and his marriage to Mary of Modena certainly did him no favours.

With the death of her brother-in-law Charles II in February of 1685, James ascended the throne – and Mary, if her Catholic religion could be overlooked, was the perfect queen consort.

In the summer of 1688 the course of Maria's life took another dramatic turn. She gave birth to a son – but his birth signalled the end for her husband. The aforementioned 'Immortal Seven' took matters into their own hands. They wrote a letter to James's nephew and son-in-law, William III of Orange, the Stadtholder of the Dutch Republic, and formally invited him to take James's throne. When James went into exile, she followed, and under the patronage of Louis XIV, they retained an exiled court at the Chateau de Saint-Germain-en-Laye.

In November, Maria and baby James fled. It was there in exile that Maria gave birth to a daughter, Louisa, whom James heaped with affection. It was indeed a source of solace for a man who had firmly believed that he had been stabbed in the back by his beloved elder daughters.

Maria's legacy is mixed. Popularly labeled a Catholic bigot who entreated her husband to flee during the revolution in 1688, the truth is less clear-cut. She loved her children and her husband, and considering James's own father was beheaded in 1649, it isn't improbable that she feared this was a very real possibility for James. In such dangerous circumstances, if Maria had indeed pushed him to go into exile, it is perfectly understandable. James died after a stroke in 1701; Louisa died from smallpox in 1712, aged only nineteen. Maria Beatrice died six years later in 1718 at their Château and place of exile.

6th – Dr Arbuthnot's Masquerade

They'll tell you Virtue is a Masque:
But it would look extremely queer

In any one, to wear it here.
Madam, says I, methinks you ramble;
What need we this your long Preamble?
Well then, as in the different Ages,
So Virtue in the different Stages
Of Female Life its Station alters:
It in the Widow's Jointure shelters;
In Wives, 'tis not so plain where laid;
But in the Virgin's Maidenhead.

'The Masquerade', *Miscellaneous Works of the Late Dr. Arbuthnot:*
Vol. 2, John Arbuthnot, 1770

Dr John Arbuthnot was a Scottish physician and polymath who lived from 1667 to 1735. He wrote several poems, the most famous of which was 'Know thyself' (1734). He appears to have been in favour of the unification of Scotland and England and wrote *A sermon preach'd to the people at the Mercat Cross of Edinborough on the subject of the union. Ecclesiastes, Chapter 10, Verse 27.* He was physician in ordinary to Queen Anne.

7th – Eastward Hoe

There's another affliction too. As I have two 'prentices — the one of a boundless prodigality, the other of a most hopeful industry — so have I only two daughters: the eldest, of a proud ambition and nice wantonness; the other of a modest humility and comely soberness. The one must bee ladyfied, forsooth, and be attir'd just to the court-cut, and long tail. So far is she ill natured to the place and means of my preferment and fortune, that she throws all the contempt and despite, hatred it self can cast upon it. Well, a piece of land she has, 'twas her grandmothers gift; let her, and her Sir Petronel, flash out that; but as for my substance, she that scorns me, as I am a citizen and trades-man, shall never pamper her pride with my industry; shall never use me as men do foxes, keep themselves warm in the skin, and throw the body that bare it to the dung-hill. I must go entertain this Sir Petronel. Goulding, my utmost cares for thee, and only trust in thee; look to the shop. As for you, Master Quickesilver, think of husks, for thy course is running directly to the prodigals hogs trough; husks, sirrah. Work upon that now.

Act I: Scene I, *Eastward Hoe*, John Marston, 1605

John Marston (1576–1634), an English poet, was baptised on this day in 1576, during the reign of Queen Elizabeth I. Marston was not an easy person to get on with, and he was often in disagreements with people, including fellow author Ben Jonson.

8th – Of the Roman Foot

That the Foot was the most received, and usual measure amongst the Romans, as the Cubit amongst the Jews, is a thing not controverted by any. For Polybius describing their scutum, makes it in breadth over the bend two (Roman) feet and a half, and in length four feet. Or, if it be of a greater sort, a palm more is to be added to this measure.

A Discourse on the Roman Foot and Denarius, John Greaves, 1647

John Greaves (1602–1652), an English mathematician and astronomer, died on October 8 1652. As we've learned in other sections of this book, astronomy and science began to flourish during the Stuart Era, and John Greaves was an early part of scholarly developments. Hampshire-born Greaves attended Balliol College, Oxford, and studied the astronomical texts of the ancients. He became a professor at that university, and later became Savilian Professor of Astronomy.

9th – Enemies in Both Kingdoms

Dear Sir,

I have spent most of the time since I received your last in rambling from place to place in this country, or else you had received my thanks sooner, for the news you sent me, which was as acceptable to my Lord as myself. He read your letter, was very much pleased with it, and enquired particularly after you. Pray let me hear from you again, and write me as much news as you can of state and court matters, and let me know what stories go of my Lord now. I know he hath enemies in both kingdoms that correspond, and I would fain know what they say of him now. I have now a long story to tell you of myself, which I know will subject me to the censure of the English world, and therefore I must desire you, as a faithful friend, to justify me as you have occasion.

Letter dated 9 October 1677, Dr Hickes to Dr Smith

The Dr Hickes who wrote the letter above was probably one Dr George Hickes (1642–1715), who was a Fellow at Lincoln College, Oxford, from 1664 to 1681. Hickes is best known not only for his research involving

Old Norse and Old English languages, but for his political views. He (and some of his family members) got into some difficulties during the reigns of both James II and William and Mary. During the latter reign, Hickes refused to take the oath of allegiance to the new monarchs to the throne which had been 'vacated' by James II. This wasn't an unusual situation, for many members of the clergy remained conflicted about pledging their allegiance to William and Mary when the sovereign they had pledged themselves to was still very much alive.

10th – A Scotch mile and an English mile

A Line, or length to be measured, whether it be distance, height or depth, is measured by a line less than it. With us the least measure of length is an inch not that We measure no line less than it, but because we do not use the name of any measure below that of an inch; expressing lesser measures by the fractions of an inch; and in this treatise, we use decimal fractions as the easiest. Twelve inches make a foot, three feet and an inch make the Scotch ell, six ells make a fall, forty falls make a furlong, eight furlongs make a mile. So that the Scotch mile is 1,184 paces, accounting every pace to be five feet. These things are according to the statutes of Scotland, notwithstanding which the glaziers use a foot of only eight inches, and other artists for the most part use the English foot, on account of the several scales marked on the English foot-measure for their use. But the English foot is somewhat less than the Scotch, so as that 185 of these make 186 of those.

A Treatise of Practical Geometry: In Three Parts, Vol. 2, Dr David
Gregory, 1745

David Gregory, a Scottish mathematician and astronomer, died on 10 October 1708, during the reign of Queen Anne. Gregory was born in June 1659. Twenty years later, in 1679, Gregory attended the University of Leiden in the Dutch Republic. Five years after that, he published his first work, *Exercitatio geometrica de dimensione figurarum*. He was friends with Dr John Arbuthnot and Archibald Pitcairne, two notable Scottish physicians.

11th – An Introduction to the Skill of Musick

Observe, that in the tuning of your voice you strive to have it clear.
Also in the expressing of your voice, or tuning of notes, let the sound come clear from your throat and not through the teeth, by

sucking in your breath, for that is a great obstruction to the clear utterance of the voice.

Lastly, observe, that in tuning your first note of your plain song, you equal it so to the pitch of your voice, that when you come to your highest note, you may reach it without squeaking, and your lowest without grumbling.

> *An Introduction To The Skill of Musick: In Three Books. The Grounds and Rules of Musick, according to the Gamut, and other Principles thereof, Vol. 1,* John Playford, 1683

The Stuart period had many 'how-to' books, including this one which would have been useful to musicians and singers of the time. John Playford was a well-respected music publisher, and his *An Introduction To The Skill of Musick* was revised by Henry Purcell in the twelfth edition in 1694.

12th – Sir Edmundbury Godfrey

On Saturday the 12th of this month was Sir Edmondbury Godfrey, a justice of peace of Middlesex, missing, and so continued till Thursday morning following, when he was found murdered on Primrose hill, near Hampstead; his stick and gloves sett up against the hedge, his money and watch in his pocket, and his sword sticking in his body, but not bloody (which is an argument he was run through when dead), and he had a livid circle round his neck, as if he had been strangled. His death caused variety of talk: but that which is most remarkable are the several reports that run about while he was missing; that he was gone into the country; that he was at a relations house in town, and lay secret there while he was courting of a lady. Others reported that he had really killed himself; which the posture he was found in confuted.

> *A Brief Relation of State Affairs, from September 1678 to April 1714,* Narcissus Luttrell, 1857

Sir Edmund Berry Godfrey died under very mysterious circumstances on this day in 1678. Some claimed he had committed suicide – but he had been strangled and impaled by his sword. Had he uncovered something that cost him his life? If so, what?

*

Also on this day in 1663 the Farnley Wood Plot was uncovered. This plot, one of many in the Stuart period, took place primarily in the Yorkshire area of northern England.

13th – 'Send me a Brussels Gazette'

Sir,

I return you very many thanks ... for the great kindness and care which you showed to my son in his travels. I am very glad if your short stay at Stratten was not unpleasant unto you. I am sure I received great satisfaction in your learned conversation. I confess I have always taken much delight ... and I find no great reason now in my old age to alter my resolution. I have now settled my son Robert in the noble college of Trinity; I hope he will take to learning, and become useful to his country and his relations. I dare not say to him, without a great allowance for my vanity, *Disce puer virtutem ex me, verumque laborem Fortunam ex aliis.* I give you many thanks for your intelligence as to news. I desire you to send me a Brussels Gazette, and be pleased to inform Mr. Vigures, a coffee man in the old palace in Westminster, how he may send one every week ...

I am, you most affectionate friend and servant, J. Cotton.

Letter dated 13 October 1686, from Sir John Cotton to Dr Smith

14th – The Birth of James, Duke of York

My Lord,

The solitariness of this place, and the daily increase of the plague in this city, invite me to entreat your lordship's furtherance of my speedy removal: that if coaches be not already sent for me, they may come with the first opportunity.

I understand by my servant Leigh, that there is consigned into your lordship's hands £600 for my use. I have formerly contracted diverse little debts for several necessaries, and now of late my servants have engaged themselves for the expenses of my household and stables, without which I had not means to eat: the particulars thereof my servant Charles May will show your lordship a note, for which purpose I now send him to attend your lordship. I shall be very loath to leave this town with the just cries of poor men against me: £200 will discharge all these. Let me desire you that these my debts may be discharged, and my honour preserved, wherein you shall do a favour which shall be readily acknowledged by,

My lord,

Your affectionate friend,

York

Letter dated 16 July 1646, from James, Duke of York, from *Memorials of the great civil war in England from 1646 to 1652*, London, 1842

James, Duke of York, later King James II, was born on this day in 1633 to Henrietta Maria and King Charles I. James grew up to become an exceptionally handsome man, as most of the Stuart men were, and his portraits clearly show this – all featuring the slightly haughty nose, the clear blue eyes, the full lips, and the strong Stuart chin. The letter above, so full of concern for doing the right thing by his servants, is commendable, but even more so when one considers the young age of the writer; James was only three months away from his thirteenth birthday when he penned the above.

James, much like his elder brother Charles II, engaged in adultery but was saddled then by a guilty conscience. This, however, did not stop him from carrying on long-term affairs with several women, most notably Arabella Churchill and Catherine Sedley. Where his brother sought the most beautiful women as his mistresses, James was different in his personal preferences. Early twentieth-century historian Muriel Nelson D'Auvergne summed it up best by saying, 'Plainness, unredeemed by brains, exercised a strong fascination over the Duke of York, as it did over his Hanoverian successors.' While this can be said about most of the women, including his first wife Anne Hyde, it cannot be said about his second wife, Mary of Modena, who was aesthetically pleasing by most accounts. The wedding suit he wore for his second match, now owned by the Victoria and Albert Museum in London, is surprisingly small in person.

15th – A Royal Visit

About the beginning of this month (October 1678), the Duchess of York, the Lady Anne, the Duchess of Monmouth, with their attendants, went for Holland, to visit the Princess of Orange. With the Duchess of York there went over several persons, and, as is said, some priests, on the first discovery of the plot, and who ('tis thought) were concerned therein.

A Brief Historical Relation of State Affairs: From September 1678 to April 1714, Vol. 1, Narcissus Luttrell, 1857

Luttrell is mentioning an important visit. The Duchess of York was Mary of Modena, James, Duke of York's second wife; she went with Lady Anne (later Queen Anne), and Anna Scott, who was the Duchess of Monmouth (the wife of James Scott, who would be beheaded in 1685). They visited Mary, Princess of Orange (later Mary II).

16th – A Peace with Pirates?

I. That from this day, and for ever forward, there be a good and firm peace between his Sacred Majesty the King of Great Britain, &c. and the Bashaw, Divan, and Governors of Algiers, and the dominions thereunto belonging; and the ships, subjects, and people on either party, shall not do or offer any offence or injury to each other, but treat one another with all possible respect and friendship; and any ships belonging to the King of Great Britain, &c. or any of his majesty's subjects, may freely come to the port of Algiers, and buy and sell as in former times; and also unto any other port that belongs to the government of Algiers, paying the custom of 10 per cent, as in former times ; and no man within the jurisdiction of Algiers shall give the subject of his said majesty a bad word, or a bad deed, or a bad action.

II. That all ships, as well those belonging to his Sacred Majesty the King of Great Britain, &c. and any of his majesty's subjects, as those belonging to Algiers, shall freely pass the seas, and traffic without any search, hindrance, or molestation whatsoever;

III. That all subjects of the King of Great Britain, &c. now slaves in Algiers, or any of the territories thereof, be set at liberty, and delivered up, on paying the price they were first sold for in the market; and for the time to come, no subjects of his majesty's be bought or sold, or made slaves of in Algiers, or its territories.

IV. That if any ship of Tunis, Tripoli, or Sally, or any other, do bring any ship, men or goods, belonging to any of the subjects of his Majesty the King of Great Britain, &c. into Algiers, or any of the ports thereunto belonging, the governors there shall not permit them to be sold within the said territories. V. That any merchant of the subjects of the King of Great Britain, &c. dying in Algiers, or its territories, his goods or money shall not be seized by the basha, aga, or any other minister, but remain with the English consul.

'Articles of Peace between his Sacred Majesty Charles the Second, King of Great Britain, France, and Ireland, etc. and the City and Kingdom of Algiers', from *A Collection of Scarce and Valuable Tracts, on the Most Interesting and Entertaining Subjects: Commonwealth (cont.) Reign of King Charles II*, London, 1812

Charles II, like several of the rulers before him, had a big problem with pirates. Naturally, he sought a solution. The Articles of Peace was a treaty created in 1662 which barely made a dent in the prevalence of criminals on the high seas. A lot of promises were made on both sides, but they weren't kept. Twenty years later in the 1680s, Charles II still had a great deal of trouble with pirates and their practice of abducting English men, women, and children (who were sold off and enslaved).

17th – At the King's Levee

I was with the Bishop of Oxford at the King's levee; where he having received notice of the King's pleasure by my Lord Sunderland that I should be consecrated before him (though confirmed after him by the contrivance of my Lord Chancellor, at which the King expressed his high displeasure), urged my Lord Sunderland to signify to the King that it would be a thing against all precedents and much to his dissatisfaction, whereupon his lordship (having consulted the King in his closet) signified to me that the King would take it kindly of me if I would waive my pretensions to seniority, which he acknowledged to be just, and that I should receive such a mark of his royal favour as would more than compensate my present claim. After this we went in the Archbishop's barge from the Privy Stairs to Lambeth, with the Bishops of Durham, Norwich, and Ely, and there met the Bishop of Rochester, who joined with the Archbishop in our consecration. Mem. The Archbishop fell flat on his pace as he passed with the Holy Bread from the south to the north side of the altar, his head to the place where he knelt; but being raised up by his two chaplains, Dr. Morice and Dr. Batley, he proceeded well to the end of the service. Mr. Lowth preached the consecration sermon. The Bishop of St. David's and I went that night to the King's Chapel at Whitehall to prayers, and after attended his Majesty, who was graciously pleased to send us word by his secretaries that we should be admitted to do our homage the next day. Sir John Lowther, Sir William Meredith, Sir Edmund Wiseman, Mr. Poultney, Mr. Thame, and Mr. Callis, visited me that night. We gave guineas a piece for our offering.

Diary entry for 17 October 1686, *The Diary of Dr. Thomas Cartwright*, Thomas Cartwright, Bishop of Chester, 1843

Cartwright, not to be confused with another clergyman of the same name who died in 1603, was a loyal servant to King James II, the king mentioned in the above excerpt. Northampton-born Cartwright lived from 1634 to 1689. His total loyalty to James II, even during William III's invasion, left him no choice but to flee the country.

18th – A Singular Remedy

The juice of the leaves drunk with the distilled water of horsetail, is a singular remedy for all manner of wounds in the breast, bowels, or other parts of the body, and is given with good success unto those who are troubled with casting, vomiting, or bleeding at the mouse and nose, or otherwise downwards. The said juice given in the distilled water of oaken buds, is very good for women who have their usual courses, or the whites flowing down too abundantly: it helps sore eyes. The leaves boiled in Oil Omphacine, or unripe olives, set in the sun for certain days, or the green leaves sufficiently boiled in the said oil, is made an excellent green balsam, not only for green and fresh wounds, but also for old and inveterate ulcers, especially if a little fine clear turpentine be dissolved therein. It also stayeth and represseth all inflammations that arise upon pains, by hurts or wounds.

What parts of the Body are under each Planet and Sign, and also what diseases, may be found in my Astrological Judgement of Diseases; and for the internal work of nature in the body of man as Vital, animal, natural, and procreative spirit of man; the apprehension, judgment, memory: The external Sences, viz. Seeing, Hearing, Smelling, Tailing, and Feeling; the Virtues Attractive, Retentive, Digeftive, Expulsive &c. under the dominion of what planets they are, may be found in my Ephemeris for the year 1651 in both which you shall find the chaff of suthors blown away, by the fame of Dr. Reason, and nothing but rational truths left for the ingenious to feed upon.

*The English Physician Enlarged: With Three Hundred, Sixty and
Nine Medicines, Made of English Herbs*, Nicholas Culpeper, 1666

Nicholas Culpeper, a major English physician, herbalist, and botanist was born on this day in 1616. During the Stuart period, a great many people – even the more educated – were into astrology, and so Culpeper is certainly a man of his time. Having read through many of Culpeper's remedies, I'm fairly certain most modern physicians would advise not to try them.

*

Also on this day in 1642, King Charles I stayed at Aston Hall, shortly before the Battle of Edgehill. Aston Hall is a sumptuous Jacobean stately home in Birmingham, England. The house – which is still standing – is a remarkably well-preserved building and chock full of Stuart-era style.

19th – 'Reproached for Doing What They Ought'

It is a very great Pain to hear Men speak ignorantly or wickedly, and not to have Liberty to controul or disprove them; no Suffocation can be more unpleasant than such a forc'd Silence; to hear virtuous and worthy Actions declaim'd and inveighed against, and virtuous and worthy Men censur'd, traduc'd and reproach'd for doing what they ought.

A Vindication of the Conduct of James Duke of Ormond: During His Long and Faithful Administration in Ireland, Edward Hyde, Earl of Clarendon, 1736

James Butler, 1st Duke of Ormonde, was born on this day in 1610. During the English Civil Wars, he was a loyal Royalist soldier. After the Restoration in 1660, Butler became a statesman.

20th – Sir Christopher Wren

After the most dreadful conflagration of London, in the fatal Year 1666, Dr. Christopher Wren was appointed Surveyor-General and principal architect for rebuilding the whole city; the cathedral church of St. Paul; all the parochial churches (in number fifty-one, enacted by Parliament, in lieu of those that were burnt and demolished) with other public structures.

The Life of Sir Christopher Wren, from the Parentalia,
Christopher Wren Jr, 1750

Christopher Michael Wren, one of the greatest architects in British history, was born on 20 October 1632. Wren lived through the tumult of the English Civil Wars, and saw first-hand what happened in Windsor Castle, where his father worked as a clergyman. His son Christopher Wren Jr recorded some interesting biographical information about Wren, however erroneously, in *Parentalia*.

There is often argument as to which is Wren's greatest architectural triumph. Was it St Paul's Cathedral, which loomed brilliantly over London's skyline for nearly 200 years? Or was it the Old Royal Naval College in Greenwich? Wren enjoyed an excellent formal education and attended the University of Oxford, from which he obtained his MA. Later on, he became Professor of Astronomy at Gresham College. Wren was also one of the founding members of the Royal Society – a learned body that continues to this day. In 1661, Wren was the top astronomer in the country when he was appointed Savilian Professor of Astronomy. This was a huge boost to his career. Like most of his colleagues, Wren attempted to solve the problem of longitude, but was unsuccessful. With the use of a telescope, Wren observed Saturn and the moon.

As an architect, he left us some truly masterful works of architecture, including St Paul's Cathedral, the Old Royal Naval College in Greenwich, and the Monument to the Great Fire of London. London after the fire saw the erection of fifty-one new churches designed by Wren. His work was heavily influenced by the architecture of the Italian Baroque architect Bernini, and Wren was very pleased to meet him when he travelled to Paris in 1665. Bernini's work at the Vatican and the Louvre speak for themselves, and it's no wonder that Wren drew inspiration from them. By the end of his life, London was very much Wren's London.

A man of his time, he enjoyed frequenting coffeehouses. Wren was also a family man. His first wife, Faith, gave birth to two sons but died from smallpox in 1675. In 1677, Wren married his second wife, Jane Fitzwilliam, who bore him another two children before she too died in 1680 from tuberculosis. He never remarried.

By the time of his death in 1723, at the then very old age of ninety-one, Wren had already firmly put his stamp on the world and upon London's skyline. He was laid to rest in St Paul's Cathedral – arguably his greatest architectural achievement. His tomb has the fitting epitaph, 'If you seek his monument, look about you.'

21st – Hermes Theologus

It was the complaint of the Emperor Adrian, when he lay a-dying; 'Many physicians have destroyed the Emperor'. Their contrary conceits, and different directions, he meant, had hastened his death, and cut him off before his time.

There are so many censurers and correctors, of our, not sick but sound religion, approved by the sacred Scriptures, and attested by the blood of the many faithful martyrs. There are so many reformers and rectifiers, of all ages, sexes, and degrees, of all professions and trades, that take upon them to order our Church, according to their several crooked imaginations; that they have reduced all things in it to a chaos, and confusion and defaced and spoiled one of the most complete Churches, if not the principal, both for doctrine and discipline, now extant, in the Christian world.

Hermes Theologus: Or, A Divine Mercurie,
Theophilus Wodenote, 1649

Theophilus Wodenote (another interesting name!) was a clergyman in the Church of England. Born in 1588, Wodenote studied at Eton College before moving to King's College, Cambridge, from which he received his BA degree in 1611. He died in 1662.

22nd – The Scilly Naval Disaster

The Scilly Naval Disaster of 1707 occurred on this day in 1707, killing some 1,550 sailors. This was one of the most catastrophic naval disasters in British history. The Scilly Naval Disaster of 1707 proved without a doubt the necessity for accurate navigation for seamen. On the way back from a mission in the Mediterranean, the British ships ran into a very nasty weather pattern; because they weren't able to accurately measure longitude, the ships ran aground on the rocks of the south-western portion of the Scilly Isles. Among the men killed were Sir Cloudesley Shovell, and several ships were destroyed. Later in 1707 a pamphlet, entitled *The Life and Glorious Action of Sir Cloudesley Shovell, Kt: Admiral of the Confederate Fleet in the Mediterranean Sea, who was unfortunately Drown'd upon the 22d of October, 1707, through his ship the Association, Splitting on the Rocks near Scilly, in her passage from the Straights for England*, described the disaster. With so many lives lost, and potentially many more at stake, Queen Anne's government passed the Longitude Act in 1714, which was an 'Act for providing a Publick Reward for such Person or Persons as shall discover the Longitude at Sea'.

23rd – The Battle of Edgehill

Upon the Saturday at night, after a very long march, for they came not in till 9 or 10 o'clock, the army came to Keynton; and die next morning, about 7, (though all that night there was news came that the king was going to Banbury) we had certain information he was coming down a hill, called Edge-hill, which hath some advantage by nature for forts and breast works, and such things as those are; and the king's army (that army which, being raised by his authority, goes under the pretence of being raised for him and the parliament, but really against the parliament) coming down the hill, my lord of Essex presently drew out into the field; and drew his army into a place of as good advantage as possibly lie could, though the other army had the advantage by the hill, which they were possessed of before; and, at the beginning of the day, the wind was against us, and was for the advantage of the other army. The preparation on both sides was for the making of them ready for fight, and the king's coming down the hill was so long, that there was nothing done till 4 in the afternoon.

And, gentlemen, I shall tell you the worst as well as the best, that you may know all and that when you have known the worst, you may find it in your judgments, to give the more praise to God for his mercy, after there was so little probability of any success. After we had shot 1 or 3 pieces of ordinance, they began for to shoot some of theirs; and truly, not long after, before there was any near execution, 3 or 4 of our regiments fairly ran away. I shall name you the particulars, and afterwards name you those that did the extraordinary service, where of you will find those of this city to have been very extraordinary instruments.

Cobbett's Parliamentary History of England, Comprising the period from the accession of Charles the First, in March 1625, to the battle of Edge-Hill, in October 1642, Vol. 2, London, 1807

The Battle of Edgehill, part of the First English Civil War, was fought on 23 October 1642. The encounter is notable because it was the first major battle of the civil wars. William Harvey, a royal physician to both James I and Charles I, observed the Battle of Edgehill and even ended up pulling some freshly killed bodies onto himself to keep warm. Sir Edmund Verney was among the many who were killed.

24th – Histriomastix

Of our impudent, brazen-faced Man-woman Monsters, who have banished all shows of modesty, of shamefastness from their sex; carrying the very characters of impudency, not only in their blushless looks; but likewise in their lascivious gestures, their audacious deportment, their obscene discourses, their whorish attires, their immodest fashions and complements, their painted faces; their prodigious shorn, frizzled locks and foretops, which outstare the very Laws of God, of Man, of Nature, (so unnaturally, and more then whorishly impudent, are many of our females lately grown) Whence is it, comes it but from Plays and Theatres?

William Prynne, English Puritan, author of the controversial 1632 work, *Histriomastix: The Player's Scourge*, died on 24 October 1669. Why was *Histriomastix* so controversial? Prynne held some extreme views and was strongly against the performance of plays, going on to say that plays were 'profane and poisonous'. He used the word 'whore' forty-seven times throughout *Histriomastix*. Thus, it was taken by some to be insulting to the queen. He was pilloried, his ears cut off, and his cheeks branded with a hot iron.

25th – Choked to Death

There was never any age before this, in which writing was so much in fashion, *Scribimus indocti de Clique*; so as it should seem, there is a certain lechery in scribbling; to which I fear Mr William Prynne of Lincoln's Inn Esquire, is not a little given. For how much paper he hath spoiled in this kind, I leave to the judgment of all men that are not (as he) pretenders only, to learning. When this disease first took him, he chose to make the Hierarchy his enemies, afterward the King, the Queen, and all the Court at a time; when neither his pen nor sufferings (were he the man he would be thought) could advantage the godly party. His books were then as they are now, stuffed with nonsense, railing, improper instances misunderstood, and misapplied authorities. Only he was ever most careful of a jingling title, as unlovely lovelocks, unhealthy drinking of healths, etc. And indeed, this may be said for him, his whole book is suitable to his title. For writing these books, he suffered very much, and truly (as I think) not altogether undeservedly.

> *A word to Mr. Wil. Prynn esq; and two for the*
> *parliament and army, reproving the one and justifying*
> *the other in their late proceedings*, Henry Marten, 1649

Henry Marten, regicide, died on this day – though not by being executed, but by choking on his dinner. Marten was born around 1601, attended the University of Oxford, from which he received a BA degree, before he then travelled the Continent. When he returned, King Charles I didn't like Marten's womanizing – as John Aubrey phrased, his 'wenching' – and referred to him as a 'whoremaster'. Marten didn't take too kindly to this; eventually he became one of the signatories on the king's death warrant. The above excerpt is from a work Marten wrote in which he humourously criticises William Prynne – who was the subject of yesterday's entry.

26th – A Kidnapping Turned Murder

They met at the door the General's Lieutenant, who conducted them up to his chamber, and told him, being in bed, that there were some gentlemen who had brought him letters from General Cromwell. Upon which, they delivered Rainsborow a packet, wherein was nothing but blank paper. While he was opening it, they told him he was their prisoner, but that not a hair of his head should be touched, if he would go quietly with them. Then they disarm'd his Lieutenant, who had innocently conducted them to his chamber, and brought them both down stairs. They had brought a horse ready for General Rainsborow, upon which they bid him mount. He seem'd at first willing to do it, and put his foot in the stirrup, but looking about him, and seeing none but four of his enemies, and his Lieutenant and Sentinel (whom they had not disarm'd) standing by him, he pull'd his foot out of the stirrup and cry'd, Arms! Arms! Upon this, one of our men, letting his pistol and sword fall because he would not kill him, caught hold of him, and they grappling together, both fell down in the street. Then General Rainsborow's Lieutenant catching our man's pistol that was fallen, Captain Paulden's Lieutenant was on horseback, dismounts and runs him through the body, as he was cocking the pistol. Another of our men run General Rainsborow into the neck, as he was struggling with him that he had caught hold of him; yet the General got upon his legs with our man's sword in his hand, but Captain Paulden's Lieutenant ran him through the body upon which he fell down dead.

> *Pontefract Castle: an Account, How it was Taken and how*
> *General Rainsborough was Surprised in his Quarters at*
> *Doncaster, Anno 1648*, Captain Thomas Paulden, 1702

In late October 1648, Leveller and major Parliamentarian army officer Sir Thomas Rainsborow (also Rainsborough) was murdered in a botched kidnapping attempt.

27th – A Brother's Death

To Dr. Molyneux.

SIR,

Death has, with a violent hand, hastily snatched from you a dear brother. I doubt not but, on this occasion, you need all the consolation can be given to one unexpectedly bereft of so worthy and near a relation. Whatever inclination I may have to alleviate your sorrow, I bear too great a share in the loss, and am too sensibly touched with it myself, to be in a condition to discourse with you on this subject, or do any thing but mingle my tears with yours. I have lost, in your brother, not only an ingenious and learned acquaintance, all that the world esteemed; but an intimate and sincere friend, whom I truly loved, and by whom I was truly loved: and what a loss that is, those only can be sensible who know how valuable, and how scarce, a true friend is, and how far to be preferred to all other sorts of treasure. He has left a son, who I know was dear to him, and deserved to be so as much as was possible, for one of his age. I cannot think myself wholly incapacitated from paying some of the affection and service that was due from me to my dear friend, as long as he has a child, or a brother, in the world. If, therefore, there be any thing, at this distance, wherein I, in my little sphere, may be able to serve your nephew or you, I beg you, by the memory of our deceased friend, to let me know it, that you may see that one who loved him so well, cannot but be tenderly concerned for his son, nor be otherwise than I am, Sir, etc.

> Letter dated 27 October 1698, from
> John Locke to Thomas Molyneux

Sir Thomas Molyneux was an Irish physician and Fellow of the Royal Society. Molyneux's brother, William Molyneux, a natural philosopher best remembered for the philosophical question commonly referred to as 'Molyneux's Problem', had just died on 11 October, so the grief was all too recent. Locke was friends with both brothers, and he would have lamented the forty-two-year-old's death. Thomas Molyneux died in 1733, whereas Locke died in 1704.

*

Also on this day in 1644, the Second Battle of Newbury was fought. The Royalist armies were led by the brothers Princes Rupert and Maurice, while the Parliamentarian forces were led by the earls of Manchester and Essex and Sir William Waller. There was no clear victory, but each side lost between 1,000 and 2,000 men.

28th – Of Power

All Men desire Happiness, that's past doubt; but, as has been already observ'd, when they are rid of Pain, they are apt to take up with any pleasure at hand, or that Custom has endear'd to them, to rest satisfy'd in that; and so being happy, till some hew Desire, by making them uneasy, disturbs that Happiness, and shows them that they are not so, they look no farther; nor is the Will determin'd to any Action, in pursuit of any other known or apparent Good. For since we find, that we cannot enjoy all sorts of Good, but one excludes another we do not fix our Desires on every apparent greater Good, unless it be judg'd to be necessary to our Happiness; if we think we can be happy without it, it moves us not. This is another occasion to men of judging wrong, when they take not that to be necessary to their Happiness, which really is so. This Mistake misleads us both in the Choice of the Good we aim at, and very often in the Means to it, when it is a remote Good. But which way ever it be, either by placing it where really it is not, or by neglecting the Means as not necessary to it; when a Man misses his great End, Happiness, he will acknowledge he judg'd not right. That which contributes to this Mistake, is the real or suppos'd unpleasantness of the actions, which are the way to this end; it seeming so preposterous a thing to Men, to make themselves unhappy in order to Happiness, that they do not easily bring themselves to it.

'Of Power', *An Essay Concerning Human Understanding*, John Locke, 1689

John Locke, English philosopher, died on this day in 1704. During the Glorious Revolution of 1688/9, Locke travelled from the Dutch Republic to England with the soon-to-be Mary II. He remained a staunch supporter of their reign. The impact of Locke's philosophy is readily apparent to those who have read both his writings and the Constitution of the Unites States of America. According to J. R. Tanner in his *English Constitutional Conflicts of the Seventeenth Century*, Locke took Hobbes' theory of contract and ran with it to argue the right of resistance. His major works, including *An Essay Concerning Human Understanding* (1689) as well as his *Two Treatises of Government* (1689) were two of the most influential on the Founding Fathers.

29th – Give the World the Lie

Go, soul, the bodies guest, upon a thankless arrant;
Fear not to touch the best; the truth shall be thy warrant:
Go, since needs must die, and give the world the lie.

'The Lie', Sir Walter Raleigh, *c.* 1592

Although he had escaped from the executioner before, Sir Walter Raleigh, English adventurer, was executed on this day in 1618. Raleigh's life had been one of worldly action – the stuff from which great adventure stories are made. Raleigh is credited with bringing potatoes and tobacco into England from America. He had been a favourite of Queen Elizabeth I, who gave him lands along with money and a knighthood (in 1585), and the positions of Lord Lieutenant of Cornwall, among others. That being said, he incurred her displeasure when he impregnated and secretly married Bess Throckmorton, the Queen's Gentlewoman of the Privy Chamber. Both Walter and Bess were sent to the Tower in punishment, but Bess was released after four months' imprisonment. Raleigh was eventually freed, but he would spend a few more stints in the Tower before his execution in 1618.

30th – The Real Robinson Crusoe

September 30, 1659. I, poor miserable Robinson Crusoe, being shipwreck'd during a dreadful Storm in the offing, came on Shore on this dismal unfortunate Island, which I call'd the Island of Despair, all the rest of the Ship's Company being drown'd, and my self almost dead. All the rest of that Day I spent in afflicting myself at the dismal Circumstances I was brought to, viz. I had neither Food, House, Clothes, Weapon, or Place to fly to, and in Despair of any Relief, saw nothing but Death be fore me, either that I should be devour'd by wild Beasts, murther'd by Savages, or starv'd to Death for want of Food. At the Approach of Night, I slept in a Tree for fear of wild Creatures, but slept soundly tho' it rain'd all Night.

Robinson Crusoe, Daniel Defoe, 1719

Sometime in October 1704, a man we know as Alexander Selkirk was marooned on a Pacific island in the Juan Fernández Archipelago of the Valparaíso region of Chile. Selkirk was born in the 1670s in Scotland, and became a privateer in the 1680s. Selkirk had noticed the poor condition of the ship the *Cinque Ports*, and kicked up a fuss about it. He proved so irritating to Captain Stradling that the latter decided to leave him alone on a nearby island. The island of Más Afuera was renamed Alejandro Selkirk Island, and Más a Tierra Island, which was the island where Selkirk was marooned, was renamed Robinson Crusoe Island. These Chilean islands suffered substantial damage during the 2010 earthquake and tsunami, and the local economy is heavily reliant on tourism. Selkirk's astonishing story became immortalised in popular culture with Daniel Defoe's novel, *Robinson Crusoe*. It is possible that Selkirk read this story, as he died in 1721.

31st – President of the High Court of Justice

Judge John Bradshaw, an English lawyer and politician, died on 31 October 1659. Bradshaw was born around 1602 in Cheshire and is believed to have attended schools in Cheshire and Lancashire. He became a lawyer in 1627, and later was chosen Council of State. Bradshaw was selected as President of the High Court of Justice during the trial of King Charles I, and his was the first signature on the king's death warrant – thus making him culpable of regicide.

An oft-repeated anecdote about Bradshaw is that he took preventative steps to avoid being assassinated. One of these steps involved the wearing of a special beaver hat which contained a steel framework covered by leather. This curious hat is now located in the Ashmolean Museum, Oxford, England.

*

It was also on this day in 1632 that the Dutch Golden Age painter Johannes Vermeer was probably baptised. His work includes some of the most popular and instantly recognisable works of art from the seventeenth century, among them *Girl With a Pearl Earring* (c. 1665–7); *Young Woman with a Water Pitcher* (c. 1662); *The Astronomer* (c. 1668); *The Guitar Player* (c 1670–1); and *The Milkmaid* (c. 1658–1661). Vermeer remains an elusive figure in history, for although his works remain popular, very little is actually known about their creator.

NOVEMBER

1st – A Catholic Martyr

May it please your Lordship to give me leave to speak one word. If I were a man that had no care of my conscience in this matter, I might have saved my life; for I was offered it by diverse people here, so I would but confess my own guilt, and accuse others. But my Lord, I had rather die ten thousand deaths, than wrongfully accuse any body. And the time will come when your Lordship will see what these witnesses are, that have come in against me. I do assure your Lordship, if I were a man that had not good principles, I might easily have saved my own life, but I had rather die ten thousand deaths, than wrongfully to take away one farthing of any man's goods, one day of his liberty, or one minute of his life.

The Tryal and Condemnation of Dr Oliver Plunket,
Titular Primate of Ireland, for High-Treason,
Oliver Plunkett, 1681

Oliver Plunkett, Irish Primate, was born on this day in 1625. During the bloodlust and hysteria surrounding the Popish Plot, Plunkett was accused and condemned. He was executed at Tyburn in 1681, and was the last high-profile victim of the anti-Catholic fervour that gripped the nation in the late 1670s and early 1680s. As he was seen as a martyr, Pope Paul VI canonized him in 1975.

*

It was also on this day in 1604 that William Shakespeare's *Othello:The Moor of Venice* is believed to have premiered. This tragedy follows Othello, the

Moor, who is married to Desdemona. The play's villain, Iago, is married to Emilia and is envious of Othello. He fills the latter's head with nonsense about Desdemona being unfaithful to him with Michael Cassio, and Othello, in a jealous rage, kills his completely innocent wife.

> It is the Cause, it is the Cause, my Soul.
> Let me not name it to you, you chaste Stars,
> It is the Cause. Yet I'll not shed her blood,
> Nor scar that whiter skin of hers, then snow,
> And smooth as monumental alabaster:
> Yet she must die, else she'll betray more men:
> Put out the Light, and then put out the light:
> If I quench thee, thou flaming minister,
> I can again thy former light restore,
> Should I repent me. But once put out thy Light,
> Thou cunning'st Pattern of excelling Nature,
> I know not where is that Promethean heat
> That can thy Light re-Lume.
> When I have pluck'd thy Rose,
> I cannot give it vital growth again,
> It needs must wither. Ile smell thee on the Tree.
> Oh Balmy breath, that dost almost persuade
> Justice to break her sword. One more, one more:
> Be thus when thou art dead, and I will kill thee,
> And love thee after. One more, and that's the last.
> So sweet, was ne're so fatal. I must weep,
> But they are cruel Tears: This sorrow's heavenly,
> It strikes, where it doth love. She wakes.

Act V: Scene II, *Othello*, William Shakespeare, 1604

2nd – Even Kings Get Seasick

King William is not come over yet from beyond sea that we hear of. 'Tis observable of him that he cannot stay or abide long under deck, it makes him so exceeding sick so that he is oftentimes forced to have a great chair tied above deck to the mast, and there to sit sometimes many hours with his nobles about him.

Entry dated 2 November 1698
The Diary of Abraham de la Pryme, antiquary, Abraham De la
Pryme

*

It was also on this day in 1636 that Edward Colston, English merchant, was born. He was very successful, and in his will he left money for several philanthropic causes, including almshouses and schools. In recent years, Colston has become a highly controversial figure, especially in the Bristol area, due to his wealth being largely made through the use of slave labour. In 1680, he became a member of the Royal African Company (RAC), a mercantile company that had started with the financial backing of King Charles II and his brother, James, Duke of York. The Colston Bun, named after him, is a sweet bread bun that contains candied fruit.

3rd – Evelyn's Father

This year my father was appointed Sheriff, the last, as I think, who served in that honorable office for Surrey and Sussex, before they were disjoined. He had 116 servants in liveries, every one liveried in green satin doublets; divers gentlemen and persons of quality waited on him in the same garb and habit, which at that time (when thirty or forty was the usual retinue of the High Sheriff) was esteemed a great matter. Nor was this out of the least vanity that my father exceeded (who was one of the greatest decliners of it); but because he could not refuse the civility of his friends and relations, who voluntarily came themselves, or sent in their servants. But my father was afterward most unjustly and spitefully molested by that jeering judge, Richardson, for reprieving the execution of a woman, to gratify my Lord of Lindsey, then Admiral: but out of this he emerged with as much honor as trouble. The king made this year his progress into Scotland, and Duke James was born.

Entry dated 3 November 1633, *The Diary of John Evelyn*

*

It was also on this day in 1698 that the Darien Colony was founded. The idea for the venture was that Scottish emigrants would travel to the New World, to an isthmus of Panama, the territory then named Caledonia. The main colony established in Caledonia was called New Edinburgh. Colonies had made other countries such as England, the Dutch Republic, and Spain very wealthy, and those in Scotland thought it was their turn to reap some colonial rewards. This scheme proved disastrous for several reasons; despite this, the Scottish felt a surge of national pride as their nation took on global ambitions of its own. Panama certainly was a viable place to create access between the Atlantic and Pacific oceans, but the necessary Panama Canal which finally made this possible wasn't created until the early twentieth century.

4th – William and Mary

So influenced the heart of our late King Charles the second of England, that in spite of the French Intrigues, and the secret Inclinations of the then Duke of York her Father, to the Contrary, and to the surprise and mortification of the French King, he be stowed upon Him in sacred Marriage, the no less Virtuous and Accomplished, than the beauteous princess his Niece; the Presumptive Heiress of the British Monarchy, an alliance of a much more dreadful prospect to the Aspiring Monsieur, than the loss of all his late Conquests in Holland, Flanders, Brabant and elsewhere, and which threatn'd France it self, with an unpleasant Retaliation (in due time) for all her notorious Violences. This illustrious alliance was solemnised on the 4th day of November, 1677 being the joyful Birthday of his illustrious Highness, at eleven at Night.

> *Constantinus redivivus, or, A full account of the wonderful providences, and unparallell'd successes that have all along attended the glorious enterprises of the heroical prince, William the 3d, now king of Great Britain, &c.,*
> John Whittel, 1693

The wedding ceremony between William III of Orange and Mary Stuart, Princess of York, took place on 4 November 1677, in St James's Palace, London. The date also happened to be William's birthday; but it was not a happy occasion. Mary, only fifteen, had wept continuously for two days after she was told that she was to marry her first cousin, and was a miserable sight. William, at twenty-seven years of age, was chronically asthmatic, had a slight hunch to his back, was considerably shorter than Mary, and appallingly unfashionable with no wig and plain Dutch clothes. In other words, he did not cut an attractive figure.

As Wout Troost states in *William III, the Stadtholder-King*, William wasn't just interested in a political union – he wanted to like Mary herself. Danby's reports, and William's subsequent meeting with Mary, were enough to make him want to proceed with negotiations. But this wasn't without trouble. James didn't like the intended match at all, preferring his daughter marry the Dauphin of France, but ultimately he had little say in the matter and Charles accepted William as a bridegroom for Mary.

The political repercussions of this marriage were huge. King Louis XIV was furious with Charles and refused to pay him the remainder of the subsidy – Louis had been paying Charles since the Treaty of Dover. He angrily wrote to James stating, 'You have given your daughter to my mortal enemy.' Shortly after arriving in her new country, Mary was finally alone with her new husband, and soon fell completely – and deeply – in love with him. She soon saw past his less handsome exterior and seemingly cold personality to his qualities. Sadly, the one thing Mary wanted more than anything else in her life – children – was to be denied her. Soon after their marriage, Mary became pregnant. Everything seemed fine until an unfortunate desire to be with her husband made her travel to Breda, where he was encamped with his army; she suffered a terrible miscarriage in the spring of 1678.

Their marriage, despite being plagued by the heartbreak of miscarriages and William's infidelity with Mary's lady-in-waiting, Elizabeth, was and is still considered a success. Their joint reign as William and Mary ushered in a new era of monarchy – the constitutional monarchy.

5th – The Gunpowder Plot

Remember, remember the fifth of November,
Gunpowder treason and plot.
We see no reason
Why gunpowder treason
Should ever be forgot!
Guy Fawkes, guy, t'was his intent
To blow up king and parliament.
Three score barrels were laid below
To prove old England's overthrow.
By god's mercy he was catch'd
With a darkened lantern and burning match.
So, holler boys, holler boys, Let the bells ring.
Holler boys, holler boys, God save the king.

And what shall we do with him
Burn him!

Traditional rhyme about the Gunpowder Plot

The Gunpowder Plot was thwarted on this day in November 1605. What were the conspirators planning to do? They planned nothing less than to blow up the Houses of Parliament, killing King James I, his son, Prince Henry, and all other MPs in attendance. They thought that with these people out of the way, they could place James's daughter, Elizabeth Stuart, on the throne, and Catholicism would come back to England.

The leader of the Gunpowder Plot was actually Sir Robert Catesby, whose family, like many others, had become disenfranchised under the harsh anti-Catholic laws. Catesby had several other co-conspirators:

Thomas Percy, Francis Tresham, John Wright, Christopher Wright, Thomas Winter, Robert Winter, Ambrose Rookwood, Sir Everard Digby, Robert Keyes, John Grant, and Guido Fawkes. They didn't want to abolish the monarchy, but instead install James's daughter Elizabeth as a Catholic queen (her elder brother Henry would probably be killed in the blast). The vaults which lay beneath the chamber were available to rent and the conspirators rented the space and began filling it with thirty-six barrels of gunpowder (hence the 'Gunpowder Plot').

Needless to say, things didn't go according to plan. Tresham's brother-in-law, Lord Monteagle, received a letter (probably sent by Tresham) warning him not to go to Parliament that day for 'they shall receive a terrible blow'. Alerted by the tip-off, guards went down to the vaults and had a look around. There, they found Fawkes right beside the barrels of gunpowder.

When the other conspirators found out that their plot had foundered, and Fawkes had been arrested, Catesby tried to rouse other Catholics to rise up with him. This didn't work out either, and he and the other plotters fled to Holbeche House. There, soldiers found them, a fight ensued and Catesby was killed. The others were hauled down to London to await their punishment. The men were all subjected to the traditional hanging, drawing, and quartering. It certainly was severe, but the crime – treason – was considered reprehensible. Fawkes, his body broken from torture, managed to jump off the scaffold, breaking his neck and thus saving himself from the excruciating agonies that were to follow.

*

On the 5 November 1688, William III of Orange landed in Torbay as part of the Glorious Revolution. During the so-called Glorious Revolution, William III sent his propaganda printers ahead of him, who printed his manifesto and circulated it widely. Propaganda wasn't just limited to the printed word, though – William gave due consideration to his image as well. Although he was physically rather puny and sickly, most of the historical depictions have him displaying a strong martial air. In William III's State Apartments in Hampton Court Palace, William chose to identify with the mythological hero Hercules, and the glorious staircase which leads to his apartments were painted by Antonio Verrio to powerfully convey this imagery.

6th – 'Our Rising Sun Is Set'

To tell you that our rising sun is set ere scarcely he had shone, and that with him all our glory lies buried; you know and do lament as well as we, and better than some do, and more truly; or else you are not a man, and sensible of this kingdom's loss.

Letter dated 23 November 1612, from Richard,
Earl of Dorset to Sir Thomas Edmondes

Henry Frederick Stuart, Prince of Wales, heir to the thrones of England, Scotland, and Ireland, died on this day in 1612. It was a shattering blow to not only his parents – James I and Anne of Denmark – but to the whole of the Three Kingdoms. Born in Stirling Castle in 1594, Henry Frederick Stuart was by all accounts the epitome of what an Early Modern prince should be: learned, athletic, intelligent, handsome, confident, fashionable – you name it, he had it. Henry was the beloved golden boy in the family and his staunchly Protestant, sober court put his father's to shame. His morals were much admired; swearing was a punishable offence and drunkenness frowned upon. In 1610, Henry commissioned Jonson to write a masque. The following year, *Oberon the Fairy Prince* was performed, with the prince himself in the title role. Inigo Jones's costume designs for this masque are sumptuous combinations of ancient Roman and Renaissance styles. Henry's mother, Anne of Denmark, was an enthusiastic commissioner and performer in masques as well. But despite the hype, Henry Frederick certainly wasn't perfect – he appears to have been a bit of a bully when it came to his younger brother, Charles. The young boy idolised his older brother, and his letters to him almost plead for the elder boy's love and respect. In late 1612, Henry suddenly came down with a terrible illness, which modern historians now believe to have been typhoid fever. The handsome, robust eighteen-year-old died. Indeed, the tragic prince's early and sudden demise sent shockwaves across the nation – for in him all hopes of future stability had depended.

*

It was also on this day in 1649 that Owen Roe O'Neill died in Cloughoughter Castle. O'Neill, born in the 1580s, was an Irish soldier who had fought on the Continent during the Eighty Years' War. He had also fought in the Nine Years' War.

Owen O Neal still continu'd his Affection to the English Rebels, and when he found that his Design of drawing the King's Army from Dublin could not succeed, he hasted into Ulster, and upon the Payment of two thousand Pounds in Money, some Ammunition, and about two thousand O Neal Cows, he rais'd the Siege of Londonderry, relieves the only considerable Place in that Province that held for the English Rebels, and which was even then reduc'd to Extremity by the

Lord Viscount Mountgomery of Ardes, and must in few Days have submitted to the King's Authority, if it had not been in that Manner reliev'd by the unfortunate Irish.

A Vindication of the Conduct of James Duke of Ormond: During His Long and Faithful Administration in Ireland, Edward Hyde, Earl of Clarendon, 1736

7th – A Restoration Actress

There was, it seems, so little hope of Mrs Barry at her first setting out, that she was at the end of the first year discharged (from) the company, among others that were thought to be a useless expense to it. I take it for granted that the objection to Mrs Barry, at that time, must have been a defective ear, or some unskilful dissonance in her manner of pronouncing. But where there is a proper voice and person, with the addition of a good understanding, experience tells us that such defect is not always invincible; of which not only Mrs Barry, but the late Mrs Oldfield, are eminent instances. Mrs Oldfield had been a year in the theatre-royal, before she was observed to give any tolerable hope of her being an actress; so unlike to all manner of propriety was her speaking! How unaccountably then does a genius for the stage make its way towards perfection! For notwithstanding these equal disadvantages, both these actresses, though of different excellence, made themselves complete mistresses of their art, by the prevalence of their understanding ... Mrs Barry, in characters of greatness, had a presence of elevated dignity; her mien and motion superb, and gracefully majestic; her voice full, clear, and strong, so that no violence of passion could be too much for her; and when distress or tenderness possessed her, she subsided into the most affecting melody and softness. In the art of exciting pity, she had a power beyond all the actresses I have yet seen, or what your imagination can conceive.

An Apology for the Life of Mr. Colley Cibber: Comedian, Colley Cibber, 1740

Elizabeth Barry, one of the first celebrated actresses, died on this day in 1713. At the Restoration of the monarchy, King Charles II made it legal for women to act upon the stage. During the Interregnum, not only were women not allowed to act, but theatres in general were closed down. Elizabeth Barry attracted the eye of the notorious libertine John Wilmot, 2nd Earl of Rochester, and a popular story involves him training her to become a good actress. The two became lovers, and Barry bore her aristocratic patron a daughter, Betty. According to Charles Collins in his *Great Love Stories of the Theatre: A Record of Theatrical Romance* (1911), when Lord Rochester died in 1680, he left an annuity of £40 per annum for their daughter. Barry afterwards became the mistress of Rochester's friend, George Etherege. Barry's speech delivery was so beautiful and powerful that she was asked to coach the young Princess Anne (later Queen Anne) – the latter indeed becoming recognised for her mellifluous voice.

8th – The Putney Debates

The Putney Debates came to an end on this day in 1647. There were quite a few Levellers in the New Model Army because the movement's aims were broadly in keeping with their views. The popularity of the Leveller ideology didn't sit comfortably with Cromwell and his associates, and so the Leveller's momentum triggered the Putney Debates of 1647. These debates were talks held at St Mary's Church in Putney, where members of the New Model Army discussed the future of the nation and officers listened to the concerns and grievances of the common soldiers – many of whom were owed pay. One of the Levellers' main speakers was Colonel Rainsborow, who said, 'I think that the poorest he that is in England hath a life to live as the greatest he.' Royalists murdered Rainsborow in 1648 (though some suspect Parliamentarian involvement as well).

*

It was also on this day in 1543 that Lettice Knollys, English noblewoman and granddaughter of Mary Boleyn, was born. Mary Boleyn was the older sister of Anne Boleyn, the mother of Queen Elizabeth I and the second wife of King Henry VIII. Mary was, according to several historians including Christopher Hibbert, the mistress of King Francis of France and also King Henry VIII. Mary is believed to have given birth to Henry's son, but his attentions waned and he moved onto her younger sister Anne. Mary then married Sir William Stafford with whom she had a daughter, Katherine. This lady, in turn, gave birth to Lettice. Lettice became a maid-of-honour to Elizabeth but is best known for marrying Robert Dudley, Earl of Leicester, who was the queen's greatest favourite. This marriage unsurprisingly proved fiercely unpopular with the Virgin Queen (who as we have mentioned would later become irate when another favourite, Sir Walter Raleigh, secretly married another maid-of-honour, Bess Throckmorton). Lettice gave birth to Robert Devereux in 1565; he lost his head in 1601. Lettice died in 1634, having outlived her first husband, with whom she was buried, and several of her children.

9th – The Scandalous Hortense Mancini

Tout le monde sçait les propositions qui furent faites à diverses reprises de me marier avec le Roy d'Angleterre & pour le Duc de Savoye, vous savez ce qui s'en dit au voyage de Lyon, & que l'affaire ne rompit que par le refus, où Monsieur le Cardinal s'obstina d'abandonner Geneve en consideration de ce mariage.

Les Mémoires De Madame La Duchesse De Mazarin,
Hortense Mancini, 1675

Hortense Mancini, a former mistress to King Charles II, died on this day in 1699, during the reign of King William III. She was one of the most colourful women of the Stuart period. Hortense was one of the gaggle of Cardinal Mazarin's nieces who were popularly referred to as 'the Mazarinettes'. Her sisters were Victoire, Olympe, Marie, and Marianne. Marie, one of the least physically attractive of the sisters, shocked the French court when it transpired that the young King Louis XIV had fallen in love with her. Hortense, on the other hand, was a very beautiful woman – considered to be the beauty of the family. Hortense was promiscuous and pleasure-loving. In the excerpt above, Hortense states that she received marriage proposals from Charles II (in the later 1650s, when he was still in exile) and the Duke of Savoy, but her uncle Cardinal Mazarin refused both. Mazarin instead married her off to the wealthy Duc de Meilleraye, but this match was anything but happy. With the handy excuse that she was visiting her cousin, Mary of Modena (James, Duke of York's wife), Hortense arrived at King Charles II's court and temporarily managed to sideline both of the king's mistresses, Nell and Louise. She was considered scandalous because she often crossdressed in men's clothing and began an affair with one of Charles's daughters. This put a damper on her affair with the king, and both relationships came to an end. It is sometimes suggested that Hortense may have also had a further liaison with the female Restoration playwright Aphra Behn.

10th – Annus Mirabilis

Sir,

I am so many ways obliged to you, and so little able to return your favours, that, like those who owe too much, I can only live by getting further into your debt. You have not only been careful of my fortune, which was the effect of your nobleness, but you have been solicitous of my reputation, which is that of your kindness. It is not long since I gave you the trouble of perusing a play for me, and now, instead of an acknowledgment, I have given you a greater, in the correction of a poem. But since you are to bear this persecution, I will at least give you the encouragement of a martyr; you could never suffer in a nobler cause. For I have chosen the most heroic subject which any poet could desire: I have taken upon me to describe the motives, the beginning, progress, and successes, of a most just and necessary war; in it, the care, management, and prudence of our king; the conduct and valour of a royal admiral, and of two incomparable generals; the invincible courage of our captains and seamen; and three glorious victories, the result of all.

After this I have, in the Fire, the most deplorable, but withal the greatest, argument that can be imagined: the destruction being so swift, so sudden, so vast and miserable, as nothing can parallel in story. The former part of this poem, relating to the war, is but a due expiation for my not having served my king and country in it. All gentlemen are almost obliged to it; and I know no reason we should give that advantage to the commonalty of England, to be foremost in brave actions, which the nobles of France would never suffer in their peasants. I should not have written this but to a person who has been ever forward to appear in all employments, whither his honour and generosity have called him.

The latter part of my poem, which describes the Fire, I owe, first to the piety and fatherly affection of our monarch to his suffering subjects; and, in the second place, to the courage, loyalty, and magnanimity of the city: both which were so conspicuous, that I wanted words to celebrate them as they deserve. I have called my poem Historical, not Epic, though both the actions and actors are as much heroic as any poem can contain.

John Dryden writing to Sir Robert Howard about his
poem, *Annus Mirabilis: The Year of Wonders, 1666*

Sir Robert Howard was an English playwright as well as a politician, so it makes sense that he would be corresponding with the likes of Dryden. Howard, who was a Royalist during the English Civil Wars, was knighted following the Battle of Cropredy Bridge in 1644.

11th – Advice to a Daughter

You must first lay it down for a foundation in general, that there is inequality in the sexes, and that for the better economy of the world, the men, who were to be the lawgivers, had the larger share of reason bestow'd upon them; by which means your sex is the better prepar'd for the compliance that is necessary for the better performance of those duties which seem to be most properly assign'd to it. This looks a little uncourtly at the first appearance, but upon examination it will be found, that nature is so far from being unjust to you, that she is partial on your side...You have it in your power not only to free your selves, but to subdue your masters, and without violence throw both their natural and legal authority at your feet. We are made of differing tempers, that our defects may the better be mutually supplied: Your sex wanteth our reason for your conduct, and our strength for your protection. Our wanteth your gentleness to soften, and to entertain us...You have more strength in your looks, than we have in our laws, and more power by your tears than we have by our arguments.

Advice to a Daughter, George Savile, 1st Marquess of Halifax, 1688

George Savile, 1st Marquess of Halifax, was born on this day in 1633, during the reign of King Charles I. Savile, an English statesman, was an important figure in the Late Stuart era. He was a Minister under Charles II, President of the Council for James II, and Lord Privy Seal under William III.

12th – Hypocrite Pride is the Reigning Sin

But in the hypocrite pride is the reigning sin. The praise of men is the air which he liveth in. He was never well acquainted with himself; and never felt aright the burden of his sins and wants and, therefore, cannot bear contempt from others. Indeed, if his corrupt disposition turn most to the way of covetousness, tyranny, or lust, be can the easier bear contempt from others, as long as he bath his will at home and he can spare their love, if he can be but feared and domineer. But still his pride is predominant and when it affecteth not much the reputation of goodness, it affecteth the name of being rich or great. Sin may make him sordid, but grace doth not make him humble. Pride is the vital spirit of the corrupted state of man.

Select Practical Writings of Richard Baxter:
With a Life of the Author, Richard Baxter, 1831

Richard Baxter, a controversial Puritan theologian, was born on 15 November 1615, during the reign of King James I. In 1685, Henry More, an English philosopher, published *Some Cursory Reflexions Impartially Made Upon Mr. Richard Baxter: His Way of Writing Notes on the Apocalypse, and Upon His Advertisement and Postscript,* under the striking pseudonym of Phililicrines Parrhesiastes (yes, really!). In this twenty-nine-page pamphlet, More sharply criticised Baxter's arguments from 1684.

*

Also on this day in 1684, Admiral Edward Vernon was born, during the reign of King Charles II. Although he became more of an important figure historically during the mid-eighteenth century, he nevertheless began his naval career during the Stuart Era.

13th – Edward Stillingfleet

It hath been well observed by some that those who look at a distance upon human affairs are apt to think that the good or bad success of them depends wholly upon the wisdom and courage of those who manage them; others who look nearer into them and discern the many intervening and unforeseen accidents which often alter and disappoint the counsels of men, are ready to attribute the events of things rather to chance than wisdom, but those who have made the deepest search and the strictest enquiry, have most firmly believed a Divine Providence which overrules all the counsels and affairs of men; and sometimes blasts the most probable designs, sometimes prospers the most unlikely attempts, to let us see that though there be many devices in men's hearts, yet the counsel of the Lord that shall stand.

We live in an age not overprone to admire and take notice of any remarkable instances of Divine Providence either in our preservation from dangers or deliverances out of them, for so great is the security of some men that they are unwilling to apprehend any danger till they fall into it, and if they escape will hardly believe they were ever in it, and such is the concernment of others to baffle all evidences of truth wherein their own guilt is involved, that they all agree in robbing God of the honour of his mercy, and ourselves of the comfort of his protection.

On this day in 1678, Edward Stillingfleet, Dean of St Paul's, and Chaplain in Ordinary to King Charles II, gave a sermon at St Margaret's, Westminster before the House of Commons. Stillingfleet was born in Dorset and educated in that area before attending Cambridge University, where he received his BA and MA degrees. Stillingfleet had his portrait, attributed to Mary Beale, painted in 1690.

*

It was also on this day in 1642 that the Battle of Turnham Green, part of the First English Civil War, was fought. This ended with the Parliamentarians blocking the Royalists from advancing into London.

14th – The Protestant Whore

Of a great heroine I meant to tell,
And by what just degrees her titles swell,
To Mrs. Nelly grown, from Cinder Nell.
Much did she suffer first on Bulk and Stage,
From the Black-Guard and Bullies of the Age;
Much more her growing Virtue did sustain,
While dear Charles Hart and Buckhurst su'd in Vain.
In vain they su'd; curs'd be the envious Tongue,
That her undoubted Chastity would wrong.
For, should we Fame believe, we then might say,
That Thousands lay with her, as well as they:
But, Fame, thou ly'st; for her Prophetic Mind
Foresaw her Greatness, Fate had well design'd;
And her Ambition chose to be before
A virtuous Countess, an Imperial Whore.
E'en in her native Dirt her Soul was high,
And did at Crowns and shining Monarchs fly;
E'en while she Cinders rak'd, her swelling Breast
With thoughts of glorious Whoredom was possess'd
Still did she dream (nor did her Birth withstand)
Of dangling Scepters in her dirty Hand ...

'A Panegyric Upon Nelly', Lord Rochester, 1714

'Pretty, witty' Eleanor (Nell) Gwyn (sometimes spelled, Gwynn or Gwynne), an orange-seller, Restoration actress, and most popular mistress of King Charles II, was born on 2 February 1650. An oft-told tale recounts how Nell, riding along inside her carriage, was stopped by an angry crowd who thought she was Louise de Kerouaille, the King's French Catholic mistress. Nell poked her head out and cried, 'Good people, you are mistaken! I am the *Protestant* whore!' Nell wasn't just a pretty face – she was pretty savvy. Fully aware that she had to make the most of the notoriously unstable position of royal mistress, Nell secured the freehold on both her London property and Burford House in Windsor – a feat of which many a modern-day Brit now can but dream. The town of Windsor, located by the River Thames in Berkshire, still has many associations with Nell Gwynn. Although Burford House is no longer standing as it was in Nell's day, there are several places named after Nell. When Charles lay upon his deathbed in the winter of 1685, he told his brother James (soon to become King James II) to 'let not poor Nelly starve'. Unfortunately for Nell, she didn't live much longer, dying on 14 November 1687. Thomas Tenison read out a sermon at her funeral. Oddly enough, Nell and her great rival died on the same day – except that Louise lived on for a few decades more, dying in 1734.

15th – A Doubly Deadly Duel

Dueling as a pastime took a decidedly deadly turn on this day in 1712, during the reign of Queen Anne. James Hamilton, 4th Duke of Hamilton, and Charles Mohun – both highly disreputable rakes – engaged in a formal challenge. Both were killed from their injuries.

What had transpired to bring these two men to violence? Well, Mohun at least had already been known for violence, for he had been involved in the brutal murder of actor William Mountfort and the attempted kidnapping of actress Anne Bracegirdle. A wealth of information about this can be found in *The Whole Lives, Characters, Actions and Fall of D. Hamilton and L. Mohun*, published in 1713. In this tract, we learn that the two men had had a longstanding lawsuit, with each having an attorney working on the case. On 14 November 1712, a meeting took place at Lincoln's Inn, with both the lawyers and their clients in attendance – not the best ideas by any stretch of the imagination. Mohun accused Hamilton of owing him a considerable amount of money; Hamilton was incensed by this. Later that evening, a challenge was sent – which one of the two instigated the duel is not made clear – but they were to meet on the morning of the next day, Saturday 15 November, in Hyde Park.

Mohun arrived at Hyde Park by Hackney carriage with his second, Major General Maccartney. When the driver realised what was about to happen, he tried to intercede. Mohun threatened to run him through if he didn't back off, and so the driver understandably did just that. The Duke of Hamilton soon arrived with his second, Colonel Hamilton, a relation, and the fight began. They sparred, the clang of their swords no doubt reverberating throughout the area. Suddenly, Mohun thrust his sword through Hamilton's body, and although seriously hurt, Hamilton pressed him to continue fighting. After a time, Hamilton delivered a sword thrust straight through Mohun's heart. He was killed instantly.

Or so at least the report published in 1713 claimed. The post-mortem, carried out by Dr Ronjat, and included in the 1712 publication, *The Case at Large of Duke Hamilton and Lord Mohun*, revealed that Mohun had suffered three injuries. The ultimate consequence of this doubly deadly duel led to changes in how duels were carried out.

16th – A Beau

Of the first rank of these is the Beau, who is one that has more learning in his heels than his head, which is better cover'd than fill'd. His tailor and his barber are his cabinet council, to whom he is more beholding for what he is, than to his Maker. He is one that has travell'd to see fashions, and brought over with him the newest cut suit, and the prettiest fancied ribbands for sword knots His best acquaintance at Paris was his dancing master, whom he calls the Marquis, and his chief visits to the opera's. He has seen the French king once, and knows the name of his chief minister, and is by this sufficiently convinc'd, that there are no politicians in any other part of the world. His improvements are a nice skill in the Mode, and a high contempt of his own country ...

He examines and refreshes his complexion by it, and is more dejected at a pimple, than if it were a cancer. When his eyes are set to a languishing air, his motions all prepar'd according to art, his wig and coat abundantly powder'd, his gloves essenc'd, and his handkercher perfum'd, and all the rest of his bravery right adjusted, the greatest part of the day, as well the business of it at home is over. 'Tis time to lunch, and down he comes, scented like a perfumer's shop, and looks like a vessel with all her rigging under sail without ballast. A chair is brought within the door, for he apprehends every breath of air as much, as if it were a hurricane. His first visit is to the chocolate house, and after a quarter of an hour's compliment to himself in the great glass, he faces about and salutes the company ...

A Beau, *An Essay in Defence of the Female Sex*, Mary Astell, 1697

Mary Astell (1666–1731) was one of several successful female writers during the Stuart period. Besides the above, she also wrote *A Serious Proposal to the Ladies, for the Advancement of Their True and Greatest Interest* (1694) and *A Serious Proposal, Part II* (1697). She was a keen proponent of women's education.

17th – The Pentland Rising

On the 16th, Stephen Irvine, Bailie of Dumfries, personally reported to the Privy Council the proceedings at Dumfries on the previous day. Rothes, the High Commissioner, was already on his way to court. On the 17th the Council sent him an account of what happened, and of the measures which they deemed necessary. In their opinion it was advisable 'that the heritors of the several countries, especially of the southern and western shires, and such other as his Majesty's council shall think fit, be presently required to sign the declaration concerning the covenant, and that such as shall delay or refuse, be secured and looked upon as enemies to his Majesty's authority and government.' On the same day, Dalziel was instructed to proceed to Glasgow, and to march thence 'to the place at which he shall hear the insurrection is come to any head.' A week elapsed before Dalziel was able to fulfill his instructions. From Carsphairn on 18 November the insurgents marched to Dalmellington. Their proceedings had roused elsewhere hopes of a stubborn demonstration against the detested Bishops.

The Pentland Rising & Rullion Green, Charles Sanford Terry, 1905

The Pentland Rising of 1666 was in full swing on this day in 1666, having begun four days earlier on 13 November. The uprising began in southwestern Scotland, when 900 Covenanter rebels decided they'd had enough of the government's continued attempts to impose Episcopalianism in Scotland. This was to be expected, as previous attempts to enforce or change aspects of Scotland's religion had usually ended badly. The Battle of Rullion Green took place a little over a week later on 28 November 1666, pitting the 900 Covenanters against the 3,000-strong Scottish Royal Army led by Sir Thomas Dalyell of The Binns (the Dalziel referred to in the excerpt above). Unsurprisingly, given the odds, the battle ended in a government victory, and the subsequent harsh treatment of the surviving Covenanters earned Dalyell the grim soubriquet of 'Bloody Tam'. In 1738, a monument was erected in honour of the Covenanters who were slain at the battle. The Pentland Rising inspired Robert Louis Stevenson to write an essay on the subject, 'The Pentland Rising', which was published in Edinburgh in 1866.

18th – A Wedding at Hampton Court Palace

Joy to Endymion!
For he has Cynthia's favour won,
And Jove himself approves
With his serenest influence their loves.
For he did never love to pair
His progeny above the air,
But to be honest, valiant, wise,
Makes mortals matches fit for deities.

'Two Songs on the Lord Fauconberg and
the Lady Mary Cromwell', Andrew Marvell, 1681

Oliver Cromwell's daughter, Mary, married Thomas Belasyse, 1st Earl Fauconberg, on this day at Hampton Court Palace. While Fauconberg (1627–1700) came from a very Royalist family, he was himself a Parliamentarian. In honour of the match, the poet and playwright William Davenant composed an epithalamion (a poem written for a bride and bridegroom) – sadly it has been lost. The couple lived in the former royal palaces of Hampton Court and Whitehall, but upon the Restoration they moved between their several homes throughout the country. Mary and Thomas did not have children, and appear to have had a happy marriage until his death in 1700. Mary died in 1713.

19th – Cromwell's Wife

He had matched, a little before, upon the account of this estate in Reversion, with a Kinswoman of Mr. Hambdens, and Mr. Goodwins of Buckinghamshire, by Name Elizabeth, Daughter of one Sir James Bowcher, whom he trained up and made the waiting Woman of his Providences, and Lady rampant of his successful greatness, which she personated afterwards as Imperiously as himself; so did the Incubus of his Bed make her partaker too in the pleasures of the Throne.

Flagellum, or, The Life and Death, Birth and Burial of Oliver
Cromwell, the late usurper, faithfully described, James Heath, 1669

Continuing on in the Cromwellian vein, Elizabeth Cromwell, wife of the former Lord Protector, Oliver Cromwell, died on this day in 1665. Elizabeth, born in 1598, had married Oliver in 1620; the couple had nine children. Much like a queen, Elizabeth Cromwell, Lady Protectress of England, Scotland, and Ireland, had her own retinue. When her husband became Lord Protector, they were given apartments in palaces previously inhabited by King Charles I and his family, such as Hampton Court Palace and Whitehall Palace.

20th – The Metamorphosis of Ajax

But here methink it were good to make a pause, and (as it were at a long dinner) to take away the first course, which commonly is of the coarsest meat, as powdered beef and mustard; or rather (to compare it fitter) fresh beef and garlic, for that hath three properties more suiting to this discourse: viz. to make a man wink, drink, and stink. Now for your second course, I could wish I had some larks and quails, but you must have such as the market I come from will afford; always remembered, that our retiring place, or place of rendezvous (as is expedient when men have filled their bellies), must be Monsieur AJAX, for I must still keep me to my teshe: wherefore, as I say, here I will make the first stop; and if you mislike not the fare thus far, I will make the second course make you some amends.

The Metamorphosis of Ajax: a Cloacinean Satire,
Sir John Harington, 1596

Sir John Harington, an English author and courtier during Queen Elizabeth I's reign, died on 20 November 1612, during the reign of King James I. His portrait from the 1590s shows an angular-faced man with a marked widow's peak forehead, and a mischievous expression. With that being said, Harington is now best known for inventing the flush water closet, which he wrote about in the 1596 work *The Metamorphosis of Ajax*.

21st – Henry Purcell

Henry Purcell, the great composer of English Baroque music, died on 21 November 1695. It was a great blow to music, for what other great work could he have left us, had he not died then?

Henry Purcell, whom we believe to have been born in 1659, remains one of the greatest of all English composers. However, we know surprisingly little about his personal life. Purcell was a child prodigy, able to play several instruments and compose music. He attended Westminster School and was a pupil of English Baroque composer John Blow; he was also for a time a chorister and then organist at the Chapel Royal. By the age of just twenty, he was Organist of Westminster Abbey. Purcell eventually found a royal patron in King Charles II, under whom he wrote many works.

The range of his musical composition was impressive. Purcell had the ability to convey the depths of tragedy ('When I am Laid in Earth' from *Dido and Aeneas*) to the comical ('I'm drunk' from *The Fairy Queen*). *The Fairy Queen* was based on William Shakespeare's comedy *A Midsummer Night's Dream*. *Dido and Aeneas* was an important work of English Baroque opera. Purcell wrote secular music and sacred music to a very high standard. He wrote incidental music for nearly fifty plays, including Aphra Behn's *Abdelazar: Or The Moor's Revenge*, for which he wrote the unforgettable *Rondeau*, which was later famously used in the television series, *The First Churchills*.

When James II came to power, Purcell appears to have taken a slight decline in popularity with the new king. Purcell was a Protestant, and the king was increasingly favouring Catholics in his reign. His popularity was once again in the ascendant when William and Mary came to the throne in 1689. In Queen Mary II, Purcell found a much more enthusiastic patroness. He wrote several birthday odes for Queen Mary II, including *Love's Goddess sure was Blind*. In 1692, he wrote *An Ode for St Cecilia's Day*, which was very popular. Arguably his greatest achievement, the *Funeral Music for Queen Mary II*, which was performed at her funeral in March 1695, has all the elements that would later make Mozart's *Requiem* so brilliant – stateliness, a haunting poignancy, and unforgettable melodies.

The Indian Queen proved to be Purcell's last and unfinished semi-opera, and was completed by his younger brother, another talented composer, Daniel Purcell. For some years tuberculosis was considered the probable cause, but Purcell's biographer Maureen Duffy suggests influenza, which in turn progressed to bronchitis or pneumonia. We may never know exactly what led to his death in 1695, but there were some rumours including a popular but probably apocryphal story that he came home late on a rainy night only to find that his wife, Frances, had locked him out of the house.

Purcell was buried in Westminster Abbey, where a fittingly elaborate monument was erected to mark his grave. Across the street from New Scotland Yard in London stands a modern art sculpture dedicated to Purcell, entitled, *The Flowering of the Baroque Mind.* Purcell's story also found its way onto the screen in the film *England, My England.*

Many of the portraits we have of Purcell are posthumous, or from the year of his death – the three most famous extant works being two oil paintings and a black and white chalk drawing by John Closterman.

22nd – The Efficacy of Prayer

In discoursing on these words, I proposed:

First, to endeavor to show what is comprehended in the gift of the Holy Spirit mentioned in my text, and how great a blessing and benefit it is.

Secondly, what kind of asking is here required.

Thirdly, To confirm and illustrate the truth of this proposition, that God is very ready to give the Holy Spirit to them that ask him.

Fourthly, To make some practical application of it to ourselves.

The three former of these I have dispatched, and shall now proceed to the Fourth thing which I propounded, which was, to remove an objection to which this discourse may seem liable; the removal whereof will conduce very much to the clearing of this argument, about which men seem to have had very confused apprehensions. The objection is this: that none can ask the Spirit aright, but they that have the Spirit; and if this be so, then this large declaration of God's goodness and readiness to bestow his Holy Spirit upon them that ask him comes to nothing, for a promise signifies nothing which confers a benefit upon a person, upon a condition impossible by him to be performed, unless he first have the benefit which is promised, and to use a familiar comparison, if this were the meaning of it, it would be like a father's jesting with his child, when he has fallen, and bidding him come to him, and he will help him up. Now if God thus promise his Holy Spirit to them that ask it, with this reservation, that no man can ask God's Spirit, unless he have it, then this promise amounts to nothing.

Sermon CCLIIO: The Efficacy of Prayer, for obtaining the
Holy Spirit: Luke XI. 13, John Tillotson

John Tillotson, an English clergyman and Archbishop of Canterbury, died on 22 November 1694, during the reign of William and Mary. Tillotson was born in Yorkshire in 1630 and attended Cambridge University.

23rd – Richard Hakluyt

Then taketh him to his charge John Fox, the gunner, in the disposing of his pieces, in order to the best effect, and, sending his bullets towards the Turks, who likewise bestowed their pieces thrice as fast towards the Christians. But shortly they drew near, so that the bowmen fell to their charge in sending forth their arrows so thick amongst the galleys, and also in doubling their shot so sore upon the galleys, that there were twice so many of the Turks slain as the number of the Christians were in all. But the Turks discharged twice as fast against the Christians, and so long, that the ship was very sore stricken and bruised under water; which the Turks, perceiving, made the more haste to come aboard the ship: which, ere they could do, many a Turk bought it dearly with the loss of their lives. Yet was all in vain.

Boarded they were, where they found so hot a skirmish, that it had been better they had not meddled with the feast; for the Englishmen showed themselves men indeed, in working manfully with their brown bills and halberds, where the owner, master, boatswain, and their company stood to it so lustily, that the Turks were half dismayed. But chiefly the boatswain showed himself valiant above the rest, for he fared amongst the Turks like a wood lion; for there was none of them that either could or durst stand in his face, till at last there came a shot from the Turks which brake his whistle asunder, and smote him on the breast, so that he fell down, bidding them farewell, and to be of good comfort, encouraging them, likewise, to win praise by death, rather than to live captives in misery and shame, which they, hearing, indeed, intended to have done, as it appeared by their skirmish; but the press and store of the Turks were so great, that they were not long able to endure, but were so overpressed, that they could not wield their weapons, by reason whereof they must needs be taken, which none of them intended to have been, but rather to have died, except only the master's mate, who shrunk from the skirmish, like a notable coward, esteeming neither the value of his name, nor accounting of the present example of his fellows, nor having respect to the miseries whereunto he should be put.

But in time, so it was, that the Turks were victors, whereof they had no great cause to rejoice or triumph. Then would it have grieved any hard heart to see these infidels so violently entreating the Christians, not having any respect of their manhood, which they had tasted of, nor yet respecting their own state, how they might have met with such a booty as might have given them the overthrow; but no remorse hereof, or anything else doth bridle their fierce and tyrannous dealing, but the Christians must needs to the galleys, to serve in new offices; and they were no sooner in them, but their garments were pulled over their ears, and torn from their backs, and they set to the oars.

'The Worthy Enterprise of John Fox, An Englishman, in delivering 266 Christians out of the Captivity of the Turks at Alexandria, the 3rd January 1577', *Voyager's Tales,* Richard Hakluyt

Richard Hakluyt, an English clergyman, geographer, and writer, died on this day in 1616, during the reign of King James I. Born around 1552, Hakluyt became interested in geography at an early age. In 1589, he published *The Principal Navigations, Voyages, and Discoveries of the English Nation.* The Hakluyt Society was established in 1846 and publishes scholarly editions of accounts of exploration, with an additional focus on general maritime history.

24th – 'Ye Ill State of our Coin'

Gentlemen,

The bill for farther regulating ye ill state of our coin being this day read ye 3rd time, I think myself obliged to acquaint you with ye passage of it in our house; and also to inform you with ye particular heads and clauses of it, which for your satisfaction and ye benefit of trading men I have abstracted from ye bill itself, and are as follows: viz. that all dipped or unclipped silver money brought into ye mints between ye 4th of November last and ye 1st of July next shall be received at ye rate of five shillings and four pence per ounce; that all collectors, receivers, etc. shall take ye said hammered money from November 14 instant till 1st February next at five shillings and eight pence per ounce for all loans and arrears of taxes and revenues due to that time, and shall receive ye said hammered money for all future aids and taxes till June 1st next after ye same rate of 5s.8d. per ounce ...

Letter dated 24 November 1696, *Hervey Letterbooks, Vol. 1,*
John Hervey, 1st Earl of Bristol

There was a huge problem with counterfeit money in the 1690s, with the Chancellor of the Exchequer at the time even enlisting Isaac Newton to sort the situation out (as we have covered previously). The currency in the

Late Stuart period was severely devalued and many coins were clipped, meaning people cut slivers off coins from around the sides, with these clippings melted down and mixed with inferior metals. These practices were severely devaluing the nation's currency. And so, in 1696, Newton became a Warden at the Royal Mint, then based in the Tower of London, from where he oversaw the production of new, state-of-the-art coins.

25th – Catherine of Braganza

The Queen arrived with a train of Portuguese ladies in their monstrous farthingales, or guard-infantes, their complexions olivader and sufficiently unagreeable. Her Majesty in the same habit, her foretop long and turned aside very strangely. She was yet of the handsomest countenance of all the rest, and, though low of stature, prettily shaped, languishing and excellent eyes, her teeth wronging her mouth by sticking a little too far out; for the rest, lovely enough.

Entry dated 30 May 1662, *The Diary of John Evelyn*

Catarina da Bragança, Infanta of Portugal, was born on 25 November 1638. She married King Charles II of England in 1662, and was known as Catherine of Braganza. This noble lady was brought up a Roman Catholic, but her very generous dowry quickly overcame the problem arising from her religion. Catherine had to put up with Charles's flagrant womanising, made worse by the fact that several of his mistresses were given positions within her household – most notably Barbara Palmer, who gave birth to several of the king's children. As Catherine had several miscarriages and was ultimately unable to have children of her own, this must have no doubt caused her great distress. Although he was met with the continual insistence of his ministers to divorce Catherine, Charles refused to do so. That being said, without a legitimate heir to his throne, the succession became a vexed issue. Charles's natural heir was his brother, James, but James also was Catholic. Others, especially the Earl of Shaftesbury, thought it best for James to be excluded and that the king's eldest bastard, the Duke of Monmouth, become his heir instead. Upon Charles's death in 1685, Catherine moved to Somerset House, where she lived up until the reign of William and Mary, at which time she returned home to Portugal. She died there on 31 December 1705.

26th – The Great Storm of 1703

His Mercies are great. Therefore he has Goodness to temper his Justice; that under the same severe Dispensation we may see God merciful as well as just; compassionate as well as angry. In the late awful Storm, some were surprised by Death, and more were as surprisingly saved. The Triumphs of Mercy were more conspicuous and wonderful, then the Slaughters of Justice. He did fly upon the Wings of the Wind to rescue, as well as to destroy. In the midst of Judgment he remembered Mercy. How much better then is it to fall into his Hands, than into theirs whose very Mercies are Cruelty.

> A Sermon Preach'd in the City of York, on Wednesday,
> January XIX, 1703/4: Being the Fast-day. Appointed for the
> Late Dreadful Storm, Thomas Clapham, 1704

The Great Storm hit Britain on this day in November 1703. During the freak event a very destructive hurricane cut across England, leaving chaos in its wake. Hundreds of houses and windmills were destroyed, and many lives – both man and beast – were lost. Henry Winstanley, the English engineer and artist, was killed in Plymouth when his great creation, the Eddystone Lighthouse, was toppled and obliterated by the waves and winds – with him inside. The sermon excerpted above was printed two months after the storm and gives very good insight into how people thought it was a punishment from God.

*

Also on this day in 1651, General Henry Ireton, an English Parliamentarian general during the English Civil Wars, died. He was Oliver Cromwell's son-in-law through his marriage to Bridget Cromwell, the eldest of the Cromwell children. Ireton was both politically and religiously radical. On Tuesday, 9 December 1651, the House of Commons discussed that the Council of State would decide how to transport Ireton's corpse to London and its chosen method of interment. At this same session, an Act for settling manors, lands, and tenements in trust for Ireton's widow, Bridget, was discussed. Ireton was interred in Westminster Abbey, where he lay in peace for several years. As for Bridget, she remarried shortly after his death, to Charles Fleetwood, another notable Parliamentarian figure. At the Restoration, Ireton's body was exhumed and subjected to a posthumous execution.

27th – Barbara, the 'Curse of the Nation'

Scottish historian and philosopher David Hume (1711–76) stated she was 'a woman prodigal, rapacious, dissolute, violent, revengeful'. John Evelyn referred to her as the 'curse of the nation'. Beautiful, calculating, and possessed of a fearful temper, she had both admirers and many enemies.

There is only one lady who fits these descriptions. Barbara Villiers, the notorious royal mistress of King Charles II, was born on this day in 1640. Villiers would marry Roger Palmer and become the exiled Charles's mistress. She accompanied him at the Restoration and grew to become one of the wealthiest women in the kingdom.

One would imagine that being mistress to a highly sexed monarch would be enough to satiate a lady, but that was not the case with Barbara Palmer. She was a volatile vixen and in one particularly violent episode, she threatened to bash her baby's skull against the floor if Charles did not do what she wanted.

Barbara infamously posed for Peter Lely as the Virgin Mary with one of her illegitimate sons as the Baby Jesus. Barbara had a knack for courting trouble her whole life.

Charles II's strong libido was not enough to gratify Barbara, and she took several other lovers to her bed – including her cousin, John Churchill (who later became 1st Duke of Marlborough). Charles even caught the two in Barbara's bedchamber. As an older woman, she married a much younger rake, Robert Fielding, who spent much of her money. To make matters worse, it transpired that Fielding was already married, thus making their union bigamous! Barbara died in 1709, at the age of sixty-three.

28th – The Royal Society

As for what belongs to the Members themselves, that are to constitute the Society: It is to be noted, that they have freely admitted Men of different Religions, Countries, and Professions of Life. This they were oblig'd to do, or else they would come far short of the largeness of their own Declarations. For they openly profess, not to lay the Foundation of an English, Scotch, Irish, Popish, or Protestant Philosophy; but a Philosophy of Mankind.

The History of the Royal Society of London, for the Improving of Natural Knowledge, Thomas Sprat, 1667

The Royal Society was founded on this day in 1660, although the exact origins are still a source of considerable controversy. The Stuart era was a remarkable period for scientific endeavour, in which human curiosity mixed reason and philosophy with experimentation. The Royal Society was founded during the reign of King Charles II and is undoubtedly one of the greatest contributions to the advancement of Western knowledge. Edmund Halley, Robert Hooke, William Petty, Robert Boyle, Isaac Newton, Elias Ashmole, Christopher Wren, were all part of a dream-team of physicists, natural philosophers, mathematicians, and brilliant minds. Now, some people are apt to disparage the inclusion of royals in this list, but it would be silly to omit them because Charles, James, and especially Rupert were great patrons of science; the latter proved to be one of the most active members of the Society. The Royal Society's first meeting took place at Gresham College.

The Royal Society debated a wide variety of scientific topics including ventilation, bees, planetary movements, and the properties of light. Although a small number of people tend to disparage the achievements of the gentlemen-scientists of the Stuart age, one must remember that gentlemen in this period were encouraged to take an interest in a wide variety of things, as opposed to our own age of increasing specialisation. Though they may have been the greatest minds of the era, that fact certainly didn't stop them from bickering among themselves. Newton had a few quarrels with his colleagues, especially Robert Hooke. Wren was so good-natured that he got on well with most of his colleagues.

29th – Prince Rupert of the Rhine

Prince Rupert of the Rhine, Duke of Bavaria, Duke of Cumberland, Earl of Holderness, died on 29 November 1682. Born in 1619 to Elizabeth Stuart and Frederick V of the Palatinate, his life was filled with action and adventure from the outset.

During the English Civil War, Prince Rupert was the Commander of the Royalist Cavalry. As captain-general of the Royalist army, he bravely (and some would say recklessly) led his troops into battle; the troops under his command were from most accounts undisciplined and often reported to be engaged in looting. Rupert was not only a skilled military leader, but also a scientist and artist. Another charming aspect of his personality included his inclusion of his dog wherever he went. Boye was a white poodle that Rupert trained to urinate on command every time he heard the word, 'Pym' (Pym was a major Parliamentarian figure). Boye was killed during the Battle of Marston Moor on 2 July 1644.

When he failed to defend Bristol from the Parliamentarians, Rupert faced his uncle's extreme displeasure. Charles had, according to historian Christopher Hibbert, got it into his head that Rupert was going to launch a coup against him. Rupert's younger brother Maurice is believed to have died in a shipwreck during a hurricane in the West Indies in 1652. This was a huge blow to the normally assertive man, and for years he continued to hope in vain that his brother was alive. Rupert's travels took him to the Caribbean, where he nearly died from the bloody flux (also known as the pale mare). Rupert also acted as godfather to the future Queen Mary II at her baptism in 1662.

Off the battlefield, Rupert was accomplished in a wide variety of things. A mezzotint of his, *The Great Executioner* (c. 1658), is generally recognised to be a skilled example of the form. (He also evidently had a considerably large and extravagant signature.) Rupert was a savant, and his innate curiosity led to his becoming one of the founders and most active members of the Royal Society. He had a natural curiosity for scientific experimentation, a fact which led to several discoveries and inventions, including his improvement of gunpowder, mine detonations and naval technology. Towards the end of his rather long life, Rupert lived in Windsor Castle, where he worked on a variety of scientific experiments in a laboratory.

He was by his mother's side when she died in London in 1662. With his dimpled chin and striking good looks, Rupert didn't have trouble attracting the ladies. Although rumoured to have been married to the court beauty Frances Bard, who bore him a son, he appears to have remained a bachelor. Towards his later years, Rupert did have a relationship with the actress Margaret 'Peg' Hughes. He lavished jewels and gifts upon Peg. In 1682, after a life of adventure, Prince Rupert died, aged sixty-three. He was buried in Westminster Abbey.

30th – A Tale of a Tub

For, courteous reader, you are given to understand, that zeal is never so highly obliged, as when you set it a tearing; and Jack, who doted on that quality in himself, allowed it at this time its full swing. Thus it happened, that stripping down a parcel of gold lace, a little too hastily, he rent the main body of his coat from top to bottom; and whereas his talent was not of the happiest in taking up a stitch, he knew no better way, than to darn it again with pack-thread and a skewer. But the matter was yet infinitely worse (I record it with tears) when he proceeded to the embroidery: for, being clumsy by nature, and of temper impatient; withal, beholding millions of stitches that required the nicest hand, and sedatest constitution, to extricate; in a great rage he tore off the whole piece, cloth and all, and flung it into the kennel, and furiously thus continued his career: Ah, good brother Martin, said he, do as I do, for the love of God; strip, tear, pull, rend, flay of all, that we may appear as un like the rogue Peter, as it is possible. I would not, for an hundred pounds, carry the least mark about me that might give occasion to the neighbours, of suspecting I was related to such a rascal. But Martin, who at this time happened to be extremely phlegmatic and sedate, begged his brother, of all love, not to damage his coat by any means; for he never would get such another: desired him to consider, that it was not their business to form their actions by any reflection upon Peter, but by observing the rules prescribed in their father's will: that he should remember, Peter was still their brother, whatever faults or injuries he had committed; and therefore they should by all means avoid such a thought, as that taking measures for good and evil, from no other rule than of opposition to him: that it was true, the testament of their good father was very exact in what related to the wearing of their coats; yet was it no less penal and strict in prescribing agreement, and friendship, and affection between them ; and therefore, straining a point were at all dispensable, it would certainly be so, rather to the advance of unity, than increase of contradiction.

A Tale of a Tub, Jonathan Swift, 1704

Jonathan Swift, an Anglo-Irish author, was born on 30 November 1667. Swift, although most famous for *Gulliver's Travels* (1726), wrote many others books, including *A Modest Proposal* (1729). According to Thomas Sheridan in *The Life of the Rev. Dr. Jonathan Swift* (1784), 'He had, early in life ... imbibed such a strong hatred to hypocrisy, that he fell into the opposite extreme.' In the excerpt above from *A Tale of a Tub* (1704), Swift satirises those who take religion to extremes.

*

It was also on this day in 1680 that the Baroque painter Peter Lely died, during the reign of Charles II. Lely was born in Germany to Dutch parents, and became van Dyck's successor with the Stuarts. His most famous works were the 'Windsor Beauties' of the mid-1660s, which were commissioned by Anne Hyde, Duchess of York. These paintings took as their subject the most beautiful women in Charles II's court. Late Stuart-era satirist Alexander Pope wrote, 'Lely on animated canvas stole / The sleepy eye that spoke the melting soul' (*The First Epistle of the Second Book of Horace, To Augustus*).

DECEMBER

1st – Jeremiah Clarke's Suicide

One Jeremiah Clarke, organist of St. Paul's, abruptly determined to leave the house of a friend he was visiting in the country, to return to London. His friend, observing his dejection, and his disappointment in love, furnished him with a horse, and a servant to take care of him. A fit of melancholy seizing him on the road, he alighted, and went into a field, and stood on the bank of a pond, debating with himself whether he should there end his days by drowning, or hanging himself on the trees on its margin. He could not determine, and therefore made Chance his umpire: he threw a piece of money into the air, which came down on its edge, and stuck in the clay. The determination seemed to forbid both methods of destruction, and, had his mind not been so disordered, might have brought him consolation. It broke off his purpose for the present: he returned, mounted his horse, and rode to London; but, alas! The irritation of his mind was too great to be calmed by reason or religion, and in a short time he shot himself.

Suicide and Its Antidotes, Simon Piggott, 1824

Jeremiah Clarke, an English Baroque composer, died on this day in 1707, after committing suicide. It was a shockingly tragic end for a man who was so successful and admired. In *Amphion Anglicus*, John Blow's 1700 publication of his songs, Clarke – whose first name is listed as 'Jeremy', wrote five paragraphs to his master, whom he addresses as his 'Honoured Master, Dr. John Blow'. Clarke's most celebrated piece is *March for the Prince of Denmark* (written for Queen Anne's husband, George, Prince of Denmark), often referred to as *Trumpet Voluntary*, and is often used on happy occasions such as weddings. Clarke himself never married, and it is believed by some historians that his deep unhappiness stemmed from an unrequited love for a lady of another rank. He shot himself in the head in St Paul's churchyard and died from his injuries the following day. Although he had committed suicide, he was buried in the crypt of St Paul's Cathedral. His untimely death remains one of the greatest tragedies in the history of Baroque music.

2nd – St Paul's Cathedral

St Paul's Cathedral was consecrated on 2 December 1697, during the reign of William III. The English Baroque masterpiece that is St Paul's Cathedral in London is one of the most iconic buildings in the world. It has been the venue for royal weddings (Prince Charles and Lady Diana Spencer) and state funerals (Winston Churchill), as well as the resting place for some of the nation's great military heroes (Admiral Nelson). Before the current building's creation in the late seventeenth and early eighteenth centuries, however, the medieval St Paul's Cathedral was just as awe inspiring. It was inside this St Paul's that the wedding of Arthur, Prince of Wales, and Catherine of Aragon took place. St Paul's was where John Donne gave his sermons, during his time as the Dean.

With the 1640s came the Civil War, and Parliamentarian troops used the cathedral as a place to stable their horses (the Roundheads did that quite often). It was so badly damaged and poorly maintained that at the Restoration there were plans to spruce it up and restore it to its former splendour. Christopher Wren proposed a design for a dome to rest atop the cathedral, topped by a strange amalgamation of a pinecone and a pineapple. All such plans came to a fiery end in the Great Fire of London in 1666. The cathedral had been a place where booksellers could store their books, but these caught fire and destroyed the cathedral. On 14 May 1675, Charles approved Wren's plans and construction began.

Construction work was not as straightforward as one might imagine. Although it was opened during the reign of Queen Anne in 1708, it was by no means finished. The creation of the cathedral ultimately spanned the reigns of five monarchs, and finally was completed during the reign of King George. Various mason-contractors were hired, including Thomas Strong, Joshua Marshall, Edward Pearce, and Edward Strong, among others. Master Baroque woodcarver Grinling Gibbons created the decorative features on the organ. The interiors of the cathedral were entrusted to James Thornhill, who also created the interior of the Painted Hall in the Old Royal Naval College, Greenwich. Approximately £1,000,000 was spent in the construction of the new St Paul's – a massive sum in the Stuart period!

3rd – 'The Maid's Tragedy'

Great Queen of Shadows, you are pleas'd to speak
Of more than may be done; we may not break
The Gods' Decrees, but when our time is come,
Must drive away, and give the Day our room.
Yet, while our Reign lasts, let us stretch our Pow'r
To give our Servants one contented Hour,
With such unwonted solemn Grace and State,
As may for ever after force them hate
Our Brother's glorious Beams; and wish the Night
Crown'd with a thousand Stars, and our cold Light:
For almost all the World their service bend
To Phoebus, and in vain my Light I lend;
Gaz'd on unto my Setting from my Rise
Almost of none, but of unquiet Eyes.

'The Maid's Tragedy', *The Works of Francis Beaumont, and
Mr. John Fletcher*: Vol. 1, 1750

John Fletcher, a Jacobean playwright, was born in December 1579. Fletcher collaborated often with other writers, especially Francis Beaumont (as above) and Phillip Massinger. A good deal of co-authorship went on in Jacobean theatre, and one such hotly contested play is *Double Falsehood*. This play, according to some, was written by John Fletcher and William Shakespeare but entitled *Cardenio*. Indeed, The Arden Shakespeare cautiously concluded that there was enough evidence for the Shakespeare link in this and published *Double Falsehood* in 2010. Fletcher died in August of 1625, from what John Aubrey attributed to plague.

4th – Leviathan

Hereby it is manifest, that during the time men live without a common power to keep them all in awe, they are in that condition which is called War; and such a war, as is of every man, against every man. For War, consisteth not in battle only, or the act of fighting; but in a tract of time, wherein the will to contend by battle is sufficiently known: and therefore the notion of Time, is to be considered in the nature of war, as it is in the nature of weather. For as the nature of foul weather lyeth not in a shower or two of rain, but in an inclination thereto of many days together. So the nature of War consisteth not in actual fighting, but in the known disposition thereto during all the time there is no assurance to the contrary. All other time is peace.

Whatsoever therefore is consequent to a time of war, where every man is enemy to every man, the same is consequent to the time wherein men live without other security, that what their own strength, and their own invention shall furnish them withal. In such condition, there is no place for industry; because the fruit thereof is uncertain: and consequently no culture of the earth; no navigations, nor use of the commodities that may be imported by sea; no commodious building; no instruments of moving, and removing, such things as require much force; no knowledge of the face of the earth; no account of time; no arts; no letters; no society; and which is worst of all, continual fear, and danger of violent death; and the life of man, solitary, poor, nasty, brutish, and short.

Leviathan: Or, The Matter, Forme, & Power of a Common-wealth Ecclesiastical and Civil, Thomas Hobbes, 1651

Thomas Hobbes, a major English philosopher, died on 4 December 1679, during the reign of King Charles II. Thomas Hobbes made a significant impact on modern philosophy, too; the term 'Hobbesian' now refers to the notion of Man's life, without laws or a power to keep them in line, as 'solitary, poor, nasty, brutish, and short'. In other words, we need to be ruled because that is in our best interest. As Kevin Sharpe stated in his *Remapping Early Modern England: The Culture of Seventeenth-Century Politics* (2000), Hobbes believed that political stability could be achieved only through the use of a common language. Hobbes was thoroughly admired during the Stuart period, and biographer John Aubrey wrote one of his longest and most detailed biographical entries for him.

5th – Impeachment

And, in Consequence of which most dishonourable and perfidious Counsels, the most execrable Hostilities, Burnings and Plunderings were committed upon them, throughout their whole Province, without sparing the effusion of Innocent Blood, and without the distinction of Age or Sex; and that unfortunate People were afterwards forc'd to undergo the utmost Miseries of a Siege, in their Capital City of Barcelona during which great Multitudes of them perished by Famine and the Sword, many of them have since been executed: And great Numbers of the Nobility of Catalonia, who, for their Constancy and Bravery, in Defense of their Liberties, and for their Services in Conjunction with Her Majesty and Her Allies, had, in all Honour, Justice and Conscience, the highest Claim to Her Majesty's Protection, are now dispersed in Dungeons, through out the Spanish Dominions;

and not only the Catalan Liberties extirpated, but, by those wicked Counsels of him the said Robert Earl of Oxford and Earl Mortimer, Catalonia itself is almost become Desolate.

All which Crimes and Misdemeanors were committed and done by him the said Earl, against our late Sovereign Lady the Queen, her Crown and Dignity, the Peace and Interest of this Kingdom, and in Breach of the several Trusts reposed in him the said Earl. And he the said Robert Earl of Oxford and Earl Mortimer was either Commissioner of the Treasury, or Lord High Treasurer of Great Britain, and one of Her Majesty's Privy Council, during the time that all and every the Crimes before set forth, were done and committed. For which Matters and Things, the Knights, Citizens, and Burgesses of the House of Commons in Parliament assembled, do, in the Name of themselves, and of all the Commons of Great Britain, further Impeach the said Robert Earl of Oxford and Earl Mortimer of other High Crimes and Misdemeanors in the said Articles contained.

And the said Commons by Protestation, saving to themselves the Liberty of exhibiting at any time hereafter, any other Accusations or Impeachments against the said Earl, and also of replying to the Answers, which the said Robert Earl of Oxford and Earl Mortimer shall make to the Premises, or any of or to any Impeachment or Accusation that shall be by them exhibited, according to the Course and Proceedings of Parliament, do pray, That the said Robert Earl of Oxford and Earl Mortimer be put to answer all and every the Premises and that such Proceedings, Examinations, Trials and Judgments may be upon them, and every of them had and used, as shall be agreeable to Law and Justice.

Articles of Impeachment: Of High-treason and Misdemeanors, Against Robert Earl of Oxford and Earl Mortimer. July 9. 1715. With His Lordship's Answer, Paragraph by Paragraph. To which is Added, A Short State of the Late War and Peace, Vol. 2

Robert Harley, 1st Earl of Oxford and Earl Mortimer, was born on this day in 1661, during the reign of King Charles II. Harley died in 1724, and was buried in Herefordshire.

6th – Pride's Purge

It was on this day, 6 December 1648, that over 200 MPs were forcibly barred from entering Parliament during 'Pride's Purge'. Named after Colonel Thomas Pride, Pride's Purge was a major political event, in which all MPs who were known to harbour sympathy for Charles I or were known to be in opposition to the Army, were forcibly removed from Parliament. Because of this, the few MPs who remained formed what has come to be known as the Rump Parliament. The Rump Parliament must not be confused with the Barebones Parliament that followed in 1653. The outcome of Pride's Purge was that, without being hindered by opposition, it paved the way for Charles I's execution.

7th – Execution of a Republican

Corruption will always reign most, where those who have the power do most favour it, where the rewards of such crimes are greatest, easiest, and most valued, and where the punishment of them is least feared...

Liberty cannot be preserved, if the manner of the people are corrupted, nor absolute monarchy introduced where they are sincere; which is sufficient to show that those who manage free governments ought always to the utmost of their power to oppose corruption, because otherwise both they and their government must inevitably perish...

'Tis also natural for all such monarchs to place men in power who pretend to love their persons, and will depend upon their pleasure, that possibly 'twould be hard to find one in the world who has not made it the rule of his government: and this is not only the way to corruption, but the most dangerous of all. For though a good man may love a good monarch, he will obey him only when he commands that which is just; and no one can engage himself blindly to do whatever he is commanded, without renouncing all virtue and religion...

Ill men may possibly creep into any government, but when the worst are placed nearest to the throne, and raised to honours for being so, they will with that force endeavor to draw all men to a conformity of spirit with themselves, that it can no otherwise be prevented, than by destroying them and the principle in which they live.

Discourses Concerning Government, Algernon Sidney, 1704

Algernon Sidney, an English politician and ardent Republican, was executed on this day in 1683, for his involvement in the Rye House Plot to assassinate King Charles II and James, Duke of York. Others implicated in this plot included the Earl of Essex and William, Lord Russell – the latter was posthumously exonerated during the reign of William and Mary. Sidney's much younger brother, Henry Sidney, was not as radical as his brothers;

he kept his head and gained wealth and a great position during the reign of William III. In 1659, Sidney had his portrait painted by John Hoskins, who did not depict his imperfections. His political beliefs became popular during the massive revolutions in the latter part of the eighteenth century, especially those in France and in the American colonies. His legacy has been somewhat mixed. In *The Anti-Jacobite Review and Magazine, Volume 17*, Sidney is described as being of 'very dubious character'. The Jacobins thought he was great, and his bust stood beside those of their other heroes, such as Rousseau.

*

It was also on this day in 1545, that Henry Stuart, Lord Darnley, was born, during the Tudor dynasty. He is an important figure for the Stuart era in Britain because he became the second husband of Mary Queen of Scots (she was widowed by her first husband, Francis I of France) and was the father of King James VI/I. Dissolute, handsome and reckless, Darnley was an unfortunate choice of spouse for Mary, who had previously been widowed by her first husband, King Francis of France. On the night of 9 February 1567, Mary attended a wedding whilst her husband stayed nearby at Kirk o'Field. Two explosions rocked the house and Darnley's dead body was found outside; the cause of his death is still a matter of debate – some historians state he was strangled, but new research offers the suggestion that he could have died as a result of the blast.

8th – John Pym

For if you can get these by peace, you will have great advantages by it; you will hinder foreign invasions from beyond the seas, you will quickly be able to master the rebels in Ireland, you will quickly be able to suppress the Papists that begin to rise in England, that you shall have a perpetual security, that they shall never be able to hurt you more. Therefore, if we can have such a peace, without further hazard and blood-shedding, we shall praise God, and esteem it as a great blessing; but if not, pray lay not down the same spirits, for we have the same hearts, and multitudes of spirits, and the kingdom inclinable to us; where the King has passed, many to save their estates and lives, have showed themselves but men ...

John Pym's speech, as found in *Two speeches delivered by the earl of Holland, and Mr. John Pym concerning a petition to His Majestie for peace, spoken in Guild-hall on the 10th of November*, London, 1642

John Pym, an English politician, died on this day in 1643. Pym is best known for being one of the Five Members that King Charles I unsuccessfully attempted to arrest in the House of Commons in 1642. It was largely Pym's influence that led to the Earl of Strafford's Attainder and execution.

Although the Royalists largely shed no tears for him, there were those, besides his family, who lamented his loss. Stephen Marshall, an English Puritan clergyman, preached a sermon before the House of Lords and the House of Commons at Pym's funeral. He read first from the Book of Micah, with the rest of the sermon dutifully filled with other quotes from the Bible, including excerpts from Proverbs, Job, Genesis, and Luke, among others.

He was not a man, who when he was called to the public service of his country, lay here to satisfy his lusts, spending his time in riot and wantonness, in gaming, drinking, whoring, &c. Take heed none of you be such.

Perhaps in a tone of accusation, Marshall continued:

He was not a man who prov'd a Traitor to God and country, and the cause of religion, which he had solemnly protested to maintain.

9th – Paradise Lost

Brought death into the world and all our woe,
With loss of Eden, till one greater Man
Restore us, and regain the blissful seat,
Sing, heavenly Muse, that on the secret top
Of Oreb, or of Sinai, didst inspire
That shepherd, who first taught the chosen seed,
In the beginning how the Heavens and Earth
Rose out of Chaos: or if Sion hill
Delight thee more, and Siloa's brook that flowed
Fast by the oracle of God; I thence
Invoke thy aid to my adventurous song,
That with no middle flight intends to soar
Above the Aonian mount, while it pursues
Things unattempted yet in prose or rhyme.
And chiefly thou, O Spirit, that dost prefer
Before all temples the upright heart and pure,
Instruct me, for thou know'st; Thou from the first
Wast present, as with mighty wings outspread
Dove-like sat'st brooding on the vast abyss,
And mad'st it pregnant: what in me is dark,

Illumine; what is low, raise and support;
That to the highth of this great argument
I may assert Eternal Providence,
And justify the ways of God to men.

Book I, *Paradise Lost*, John Milton, 1667

John Milton, English poet, political writer, and major Republican, was born on 9 December 1608, in a house on Bread Street, London. During the English Civil Wars, he was a staunch supporter of Parliament; when the monarchy was abolished and Cromwell took the role of Lord Protector, Milton worked as Cromwell's secretary. Milton was a brilliant propagandist. When the popular pro-Stuart propaganda *Eikon Basilike* (1649) was released just days after Charles I's execution, Milton countered with *Eikonoklastes* (1649). Although this was nowhere near as popular as the *Eikon Basilike*, Milton fared better in his *Defensio* two years later. He also wrote *Areopagitica, A Speech for the Liberty of Unlicensed Printing to the Parliament of England* (1644), for which (along with *Paradise Lost*), he is known. Called 'the sweet Puritan poet' by Dr John Doran in *Their majesties' servants: Annals of the English stage from Thomas Betterton to Edmund Kean* (1880), Milton died, impoverished and blind, in 1674.

10th – The Prince Who Became King George I

Georg Ludwig of Hanover was the eldest child of Electress Sophia, herself the daughter of Elizabeth Stuart, Queen of Bohemia. In 1701, William III knew he would not leave an heir and, for that matter, neither would his sister-in-law and heiress, Anne. Her many children had all died by then and a Protestant succession was mapped out. Dozens of potential heirs were found who were closely related by blood to the Stuarts; but all too often they turned out to be Catholics and so were denied from ascending the throne. One offshoot remained staunchly Protestant, and that was the line from James I through his daughter Elizabeth and into the royal houses in Germany. And thus, it was arranged by the terms of the Act of Settlement 1701, that following Anne's death, the thrones of England, Scotland, and Ireland would pass to Sophia of Hanover and her descendants – which, of course, included the aforementioned Georg Ludwig. Funnily enough, Georg was considered as a potential husband for Anne Stuart of York (who became Queen Anne), but they disliked each other and were married to other suitors – she to Prince George of Denmark, and he, to Sophia-Dorothea of Celle.

And so, the recently married Prince and Princess of Hanover took up residence in the Palace of the Leine, in Hanover (in present-day Germany) on 10 December 1682. Sophia-Dorothea's tale is one of the most tragic. Georg was a philanderer and a boor. After Sophia-Dorothea bore Georg two children – the future King George II and Sophia, Queen of Prussia – she fell in love with the dashing Philip Christoph von Königsmarck. They were not discreet enough, and her lover suddenly vanished; he was probably murdered and either thrown into a river or cut up and placed under floorboards. Georg beat Sophia-Dorothea so badly he had to be stopped by his attendants lest he kill her. Not content enough with getting rid of her lover and beating his wife, he ordered Sophia-Dorothea's imprisonment at the Castle of Ahlden for thirty-two years! During this time, the heartbroken woman was forbidden from seeing her children. This story of doomed love was beautifully translated onto the silver screen in 1948's *Saraband for Dead Lovers*, starring Stewart Granger and Joan Greenwood.

11th – First Encounter

An expedition was fitted out in the middle of December for the purpose of thoroughly scouring Cape Cod Bay ... Standish took care that the men were well armed, and that sufficient ammunition for all emergencies was stowed away in the boat. On setting off, the spray from the sea froze on the men's coats, and the first night of camping on shore was indeed a bitter experience. They sawe a few Indians, but were not disturbed.

In the morning they divided the company, some sailing along the coast, and others exploring on shore. The two parties met at night, and camped near a sheltered creek, making a barricade of boughs and logs, sentinels being placed on guard, as usual. Early in the morning, before daylight, some of the company took their arms down to the boat to preserve them from the moisture of the weather. On their return, just at the dawning of the day, the load, hoarse cry of the Indians was heard – 'Woach, woach, ha hach woach!' – Standish gave his orders, but had hardly spoken when arrows came flying amongst the company. The Englishmen fired two shots at random, and then Standish forbade further firing until the Indians approached nearer.

The Exploits of Myles Standish, Henry Johnson, 1897

The above, although taken from a nineteenth-century work that sometimes feels more historical fiction than fact, nevertheless describes the event which has come to be known as the 'First Encounter', which took place 11 December 1620, during the reign of King James I. Myles Standish was an Englishman, probably from Lancashire or the Isle of Man, who emigrated to the New World as a colonist on board the *Mayflower*. Standish became the leader of Duxbury, Massachusetts – a town that was settled in 1624 and incorporated in 1637. Standish died in the town in 1656; if he is not known as one of America's colonists, he is remembered in literary circles as a result of Henry Wadsworth Longfellow's epic poem *The Courtship of Myles Standish*.

12th – Anne of Denmark

Sir,

Your Majesty's letter was welcome to me. I have been as glad of the fair weather as yourself, and the last past of your letter you guessed right that I would laugh. Who would not laugh both at the persons and the subject, but more at so well chosen a Mercury between Mars and Venus. You know that women can hardly keep counsel. I humbly desire your Majesty to tell me how it is possible that I should keep this secret that have already told it, and shall tell it to as many as I speak with? If I were a poet I would make a song of it and sing it to the tune of 'Three Fools Well Met'!

Kissing your hands
Yours, Anna R.

Letter from Queen Anne to King James I

Anna, daughter of King Frederick II of Denmark, was born on this day in 1572, in Skanderborg Castle, Denmark. When she was fourteen, Anna married James VI of Scotland and became his queen consort. Theirs was a successful marriage – if not particularly loving – and Anna bore James an heir, Henry, followed by a spare, Charles, and a daughter, Elizabeth. Anna's brother back in Denmark, Christian IV of Denmark-Norway, was to become an important ally for James; and indeed, key to the ties between the House of Stuart and the House of Oldenburg. Upon the death of the English Queen Elizabeth in 1603, Anna became Queen consort of England, Scotland, and Ireland, but is best known in history as Anne of Denmark. Anna secretly converted to Catholicism. The death of her eldest son was a blow from which she never recovered.

13th – Prince Rupert's Dog

Since the unfortunate death of Mr Blake, I have, according to the direction of the two secretaries you named to me, had a strict eye upon Prince Rupert's dog called Boy; whom I cannot conlude to be a very downright devil, as is supposed, or a spirit sent to nourish division in Church or State (though I must confess the Irish Papists are very familiar with him in private) but certainly is some Lapland Lady, who by nature was once a handsome white woman, and now by art is become a handsome white dog, and hath vowed to follow the Prince to preserve him from mischief. Which I doubt not to indue you to believe, when I shall have delivered you my observations, first of his qualities, next to his behaviour to others, and lastly, of others' behaviour to him.

Observations upon Prince Rupert's white dog, called Boy, London, 1643

Prince Rupert's dog, Boy, was beloved of the Cavaliers and viewed with suspicion by some Parliamentarians – as you can well see from the previous excerpt. The dog was a poodle, and accompanied Rupert nearly everywhere, including the battlefield. Unfortunately, Boy was killed during the Battle of Marston Moor.

14th – Conway and Philosophy

Anne Conway, Viscountess Conway, an English philosopher, was born on 14 December 1631, during the reign of King Charles I. Born into the privileged Finch family, the voraciously curious Conway was interested in many intellectual subjects, exploring not only philosophy, but religion, too. She became drawn towards the Quaker movement and eventually became a Quaker herself. Her most notable tutor was Henry More, an English philosopher of the Platonist school, who is best remembered for *Some Cursory Reflexions Impartially Made Upon Mr. Richard Baxter: His Way of Writing Notes on the Apocalypse, and Upon His Advertisement and Postscript* (1685). A chronic sufferer of migraines since adolescence, she died on 18 February 1679, during the reign of King Charles II. In 1692, Conway's *Opuscula Philosophica Quibus Continentur Principia Philosophiae Antiquissimae Et Recentissimae* was translated and published as *The Principles of the Most Ancient and Modern Philosophy, Concerning God, Christ, and the Creatures.*

15th – 'An Elegy Upon the Death of My Brother'

Dear Brother,
The idea in my mind doth lie,
And is entomb'd in my sad memory,
Where every day I to thy shrine do go,
And offer tears, which from mine eyes do flow;
My heart, the fire, whose flames are ever pure,
Shall on Love's altar last, till life endure;

My sorrows incense strew, of sighs fetch'd deep;
My thoughts do watch while thy dear ashes sleep.
Dear, blessed soul, though thou art gone, yet lives
Thy fame on earth, and man thee praises gives:
But all's too small; for thy heroic mind
Was above all the praises of mankind.

'An Elegy Upon The Death of My Brother',
Margaret Cavendish, 1653

Margaret Cavendish, Duchess of Newcastle-upon-Tyne, an English writer and scientist, died on this day in 1673, during the reign of King Charles II. Originally Margaret Lucas, she was married to William Cavendish in Paris in 1645. The Cavendishes were an important aristocratic family during the Stuart era, and famously built and lived in Bolsover Castle in Derbyshire. In *The Description of a New World, Called The Blazing-World* (1666), a woman finds herself in another world, accessed via the North Pole. In this work, Cavendish gave us an early kind of science fiction. She not only enjoyed writing but was thoroughly interested in science. In the 1660s, she wrote *Observations on Experimental Philosophy* and *Grounds of Natural Philosophy*. Samuel Pepys referred to her as 'Mad Madge'.

16th – Situation, Trade, and Policy

Bad Land may be improved and made good; Bog may by draining be made meadow; Heath-land may (as in Flanders) be made to bear flax and clover-grass, so as to advance in Value from One to an Hundred; the fame Land being built upon, may centuple the rent which it yielded as pasture; one Man is more nimble or strong, and more patient of Labour than another; one Man by Art may do as much Work, as many without it; viz. one Man with a Mill can grind as much Corn, as Twenty can pound in a Mortar; one Printer can make as many Copies, as an hundred Men can write by Hand; one Horse can carry up on Wheels, as much as Five upon their Backs; and in a Boat, or upon Ice, as Twenty: So that I try again, this first Point of this general position, needs little or no Proof. But the second and more material Part of this Conclusion is, that this Difference in Land and People, arises principally from their Situation, Trade, and Policy.

Several Essays in Political Arithmetick, William Petty, 1691

William Petty, an English scientist and one of the founding members of the Royal Society, died on 16 December 1687, during the reign of King

James II. Petty was born in Hampshire in 1623, and was a precocious youth, displaying a particular aptitude for mathematics. In 1684, he was selected to be the first president of the Dublin Philosophical Society. He was certainly one of the great minds of the Stuart era.

*

It was also on this day in 1587 that John Selden, a legal scholar and historian, was born; he died in 1654. His most famous work is probably *Table-Talk*:

If the Physician sees you eat any thing that is not good for your Body, to keep you from it, he cries 'tis Poison; if the Divine sees you do any thing that is hurtful for your Soul, to keep you from it, he cries you are damned.

Table-Talk, John Selden, 1689

17th – Anthony à Wood

That the University of Oxford flourished after the going away of Grymbald and Preferment of other Professors, many there are, as I persuade myself, that doubt it not, especially during the Reign of King Alfred; and indifferently of King Edward senior, and Athelstan his Son, who, as Authors say, were both learned and good men. If Monies or Revenues were allowed from the King's Coffers for the maintenance of the Scholars at Oxford, which, as 'tis said, continued till the time of William the Conqueror, then doubtless there were not wanting those in Oxford that received it. By the presence of Ethelward the King's son, who was a Student there, as diverse Authors show, (especially Rouse and Leland, the last of which faith that he was *non insimus Isiacarum Scholarum Cultor*) an example thereby was showed to all the nobles of England and others of inferior rank to send their sons there. Which Ethelward, if he had lived to a competent age, would (as 'tis thought by some) have been beneficial to the muses of this place, but he dying and all hopes of him frustrated, was buried at Oxford as some say, others at Hyde Abbey by Winchester, causing thereby confusion between this and Ethelward junior, of whom, many things also are reported.

Ancient and Present State of the City of Oxford, Anthony à Wood, 1773

Anthony Wood, also known as Anthony à Wood, an English antiquarian, was born on this day in 1632, during the reign of King Charles I. Wood is best known for his *Athenae Oxonienses*; he also wrote *Historia et antiquitates Univ. Oxon.* Oxford was very important during the English Civil Wars, primarily because King Charles moved his court there, thus making it the de facto Royalist capital (as London was in the hands of the Parliamentarians). Wood seems to have fallen out with his friends, including fellow antiquarian John Aubrey, and does not appear to have ever had any romantic attachment to anyone. Wood increasingly became both deaf and sickly until his death on 29 November 1695, aged sixty-three. He was buried in the Church of St John Baptist in Merton College, Oxford.

18th – Plots and Union

We should commiserate others being of the same body and flesh hide not thyself from thine own flesh, we should contribute to their bodily necessities and this according to our capacity, according to the necessities of others and according to the opportunities put in our hands, giving freely, giving prudently, and giving thankfully. Because it is more a blessing to give than to receive. Again, we should show pity and compassion towards others, in forgiving their offences. And that by forgiving them fully, as we expect God should forgive us. Again, we should be merciful to the names of others, by not detracting from their good fame or virtues; an evil report.

A Sermon Preached Before His Grace James Duke of Queensberry and the Honourable Estates of Parliament in the Parliament House Upon Sunday the 24th Day of November 1700,
John Hamilton, 1701

James Douglas, 2nd Duke of Queensberry and 1st Duke of Dover, a Scottish politician, was born on 18 December 1662, during the reign of King Charles II. Queensbury was an important player in early negotiations for a union between England and Scotland. Unfortunately for him, he lost any semblance of credibility when the Jacobite plot was uncovered, which was subsequently named after him (the Queensbury Plot). That being said, things improved for him a few years later; for in 1708 Queen Anne created him the Duke of Dover. Queensbury died in 1711.

19th – 'On His Mistress, the Queen of Bohemia'

You meaner Beauties of the Night,
That poorly satisfy our Eyes,
More by your number, than your light,

You Common people of the Skies;
What are you when the Moon shall rise?

You curious chanters of the wood,
That warble forth Dame Nature's lays.
Thinking your passions understood
By your weak accents; what's your praise,
When Philomel her voice shall raise?

You violets that first appear,
By your pure purple mantles known,
Like the proud Virgins of the year,
As if the Spring were all your own;
What are you when the rose is blown?

So, when my Mistress shall be seen
In form and beauty of her mind,
By virtue first, then choice, a Queen,
Tell me if she were not design'd
Th'Eclipse and Glory of her kind?

'On His Mistress, the Queen of Bohemia',
Henry Wotton, 1651

Sir Henry Wotton, an English writer and diplomat, died sometime in December 1639. Wotton was born in 1568, and attended Winchester College and then the University of Oxford. He had a talent for languages, which came into good use for his career as a foreign diplomat; one of his ambassadorial jobs included moving to the Republic of Venice, beginning in 1604. Years later, and in need of money, Wotton worked as provost of Eton College from 1624 to 1639. When Queen Henrietta Maria gave birth to a son (who became Charles II) in 1630, Wotton composed a hymn, 'On the Birth of Prince Charles'.

20th – The Virginia Company

The first colony left the Thames on the 19th of December, but owing to unfavorable weather did not sail from the Downs until the first of January 1606-7. They were placed in three vessels, the Susan Constant of one hundred tons, with seventy-one persons, in charge of Christopher Newport the commander of the fleet, the God-Speed, of forty tons, Capt. Bartholomew Gosnold, carrying fifty-two persons, and the Discovery, of twenty tons, Capt. John Ratcliffe, carrying twenty persons. The Mercure Francois, published at Paris, 1619, says some of the passengers were women and children. Dissensions arose during the voyage, and on the 12th of February John Smith was suspected of mutiny. By the West India route they reached the Virginia coast on the 26th of April, and having entered Chesapeake Bay, on that night opened the sealed instructions. After some explorations in the small boats, they planted a cross at Cape Henry on the 29th, and took possession of the country in the name of King James, and on the next day the ships anchored at Point Comfort, now Fortress Monroe. The councillors designated by the London authorities were Edward Maria Wingfield, Bartholomew Gosnold, John Smith, Christopher Newport, John Ratclifle, John Martin, and John Kendall.

History of the Virginia Company of London,
Edward Duffield Neil, 1869

Despite the date indicated above, the general consensus is that the Virginia Company set sail from England on 20 December 1606 to create the first permanent English settlement in Virginia, during the reign of King James I.

21st – A New Queen

It is to their inexpressible grief, that Your Majesty's most dutiful Commons find any instances where they are unable to comply with what Your Majesty proposes to them; but they beg leave humbly to lay before your Majesty, the apprehensions they have of making a precedent, for the alienation of the revenue of the crown, which has been so much reduced by the exorbitant grants of the last reign, and which has been so lately settled and secured, by Your Majesty's unparalleled grace and goodness.

We are infinitely pleased to observe, by Your Majesty's late gracious acceptance of the Duke of Marlborough's services, that the only way to obtain Your Majesty's favour is to deserve well from the public; and we beg leave to assure Your Majesty, that whenever you shall think fit to reward such merit, it will be to the entire satisfaction of your people.

An Address presented before Queen Anne by the House,
London, 1743

The House of Commons presented an address before the newly ascended Queen Anne on this day in December 1702. Notice the dig at the previous

administration? William III, a foreigner, had not been popular and it was easy
to blame the deceased man for various things.

Anne responded to the address:

I shall always think myself much concerned to reward those who
deserve well of me, and of the public. On this account I bestowed some
favours on the Duke of Marlborough, and I am glad to find you think
they are well placed.

22nd – The World Conquered

Richard Alleine, an English divine, died on this day in 1681, during the
reign of King Charles II. Alleine was born in the early 1610s in Somerset
and grew up to become a rector. Several of his works have survived and
convey Alleine's strongly held views of spiritual matters. Alleine's *The World
Conquered, or A Believer's Victory Over the World* (1668) laments how many
people found excuses for, as he put it, 'neglecting Christ':

An excuse is a pretence to have reason for what we do: no man can
have reason to neglect Christ, no man can have reason to continue
in sin ... Though the drunkard can hardly say, I have reason to be
drunk; though the Adulterer can hardly say, I have reason to follow
Harlots; though the Swearer can hardly say, I have reason to swear, or
blaspheme; though the prodigal can hardly say, I have reason to waste,
and spend my Estate.

That Alleine may have looked down upon the king's proclivity for women
and general merrymaking is reasonable to assume, given the nature of his
work and opinions.

Believe it Brethren, when business gets the upperhand of duty, the
world hath gotten the upperhand of the Soul.

23rd – On the Twenty-Nine Regicides

The Prophet Isaiah denounces a Woe against them who call evil good,
and good evil; who put darkness for light, and light for darkness; who
put bitter for sweet, and sweet for bitter. And in the New Testament
we read of some, whose mind and conscience is defiled, who are led
by the spirit of error, who think they do God good service when they
murder his servants ...

Presently after the happy Restoration of the royal family and government, some of the most notorious regicides were seized on, and tried for the murder of their prince, and received the just reward of the treasons. Their trials were immediately collected together, and published by authority in the same year.

The indictment, arraignment, tryal, and judgment, at large, of twenty-nine regicides, the murtherers of His Most Sacred Majesty King Charles I, Heneage Finch, Earl of Nottingham, 1739

Heneage Finch, 1st Earl of Nottingham, an English politician, was born on 23 December 1621, during the reign of King James I.

24th – Death by Smallpox

Mary, Princess Royal and Princess of Orange, died on Christmas Eve of 1660, from smallpox. It was a cruelly ironic way to die. Her husband, William II of Orange, had died ten years before from this same disease; she had contracted smallpox at one of the happiest times in her life. Her brother, Charles II, had been restored to his throne and her family's fortunes had improved considerably as a result – and she had merrily left her son William III behind in the Dutch Republic to join with her family in England again. Mary had been born in St James's Palace, London, in 1631 and baptised shortly thereafter by William Laud.

She had had a miserable time in her adoptive country, which largely stemmed from a combination of her bad attitude and her mother-in-law Amalia van Solms-Braunfels's dictatorial manner. Mary's mother, Henrietta Maria, had probably not helped by having inculcated in her daughter that the Dutch alliance was decidedly beneath their family's dignity. This is very similar to Anne of Denmark's disapproval of her daughter Elizabeth's marriage to Frederick V of the Palatine. While that marriage was a relatively happy match, Mary had to battle against both her husband's mother, who reciprocated her young daughter-in-law's cold behaviour, and her highly sexed, philanderer of a husband, William II.

Her happiest times were when she was with her family. In 1654, her brother Charles left the court of Saint-Germain and spent time with Mary in Aachen and Dusseldorf. The Restoration had restored her family to their rightful place and they had been reunited. And, excepting the recent loss of their brother Henry, Duke of Gloucester, the Christmas period was supposed to be the happiest the family had known in many years. Alas, it was not to be, for Mary died, having dictated her will to her Nicholas Oudaert. Although she left no money to her son, William (later King William III), she requested that her brother King Charles II be his protector.

Mary was buried near her brother Henry Stuart in Westminster Abbey on 29 December 1660.

25th – Happy Christmas! (If You Dare)

Merry Christmas! The Stuart-era Christmas did not have Christmas trees, but there were certainly Christmas decorations, foods, and entertainments associated with the Christian holiday. (Stuart-era Christmas decorations were usually made from evergreens such as holly, ivy, and mistletoe.) But not everyone was filled with the Christmas spirit – the more radical Christians felt it was obscene to celebrate the birth of Jesus Christ. Indeed, in the 'Ordinance for the better observation of the monthly fast; and especially the next Wednesday, commonly called The Feast of the Nativity of Christ', from 19 December 1644, it was ordered by both Houses of Parliament that Christmas be kept as a fasting day and not a feast day because it gives 'liberty to carnal and sensuall delights'. That's your roast out the window, then! According to Godfrey Davies in his *The Early Stuarts 1603–1660*, soldiers were sent around to make sure people weren't cooking. If you were caught making a Christmas meal, you'd be in receipt of a fine and your meat would be taken away. Some people simply didn't accept this stricture, and pro-Christmas riots broke out in a few towns.

In his *Anatomie of Abuses* (1583), Calvinist Philip Stubbes complained, 'In Christmas time there is nothing else used by cards, dice, tables, masking, mumming, bowling, and such like fooleries; and the reason is, that they think they have a commission and prerogative that time to do what they like, and to follow what vanity they will ... Who knoweth not that more mischief is that time committed than in all the year besides?' From 1644 to 1656, the Puritanical Parliamentarians were so against the idea of Christmas that they were in session every Christmas day! Any Christmas decorations that were found were burned.

But things did not always stay the same. With the return of the monarchy in 1660, certain things that had previously been banned were again allowed, and indeed encouraged.

26th – An Enthusiasm for Books

Sir,

I am very much obliged unto you for yours of Dec. 26, containing so great a variety of mathematical news, and giving us hopes of shortly seeing so many admirable things. I hope it will not be long before we receive Dr. Pell's book, now in the press, but more particularly [we] long to see Kinckhuysen's Introduction to Algebra,

with those wonderful additions of Mr. Newton. In the meantime, to
keep us going, I must desire your assistance in procuring me these
books: *De Mensura perimetri Terrae*, which Mr. Oldenburg told me
was out before I came out of town, though as yet he hath not given
us any account of it in his transactions; for I very much long to see
it, upon several scores...I have the first two tomes of Descartes, his
letters, in French, but want the third; and this I must desire from you.
I had as lief have it in French as English. Another is Lucovici de la
Forge Salmuriensis M.D. notae in hominem Cartesii ...

A letter dated 4 January 1671/2, from Richard Towneley to Collins

Towneley's enthusiasm for the books he mentions in the above letter makes
for some wonderful reading. We all know someone who is a bibliophile
or very passionate about something or other, and the natural excitement
around that is rather infectious. Such was the case with Towneley, who was
an English mathematician and astronomer. No wonder he couldn't wait to get
his hands on the third volume of René Descartes and Gerard Kinckhuysen's
Introduction to Algebra! Richard Towneley was born into a wealthy Catholic
family in Burnley, Lancashire. He died in 1707, and some of his papers are
now in the Bodleian Library in Oxford. Towneley's ancestral home, Towneley
Hall, is a listed building and is now owned and managed by Burnley Borough
Council, who keep the building open to the public as a museum.

27th – John Dee and Queen Bess

All things which are, & have being, are found under a triple
diversity general. For, either, they are deemed Supernatural, Natural,
or, of a third being. Things Supernatural, are immaterial, simple,
indivisible, incorruptible, & unchangeable. Things Natural, are
material, compounded, divisible, corruptible, and changeable. Things
Supernatural, are, of the mind only, comprehended: Things Natural,
of the sense exterior, are able to be perceived. In things Natural,
probability and conjecture hath place: But in things Supernatural,
chief demonstration, & most sure Science is to be had. By which
properties & comparisons of these two, more easily may be described,
the state, condition, nature and property of those things, which, we
before termed of a third being: which, by a peculiar name also, are
called Things Mathematical. For, these, being (in a manner) middle,
between things supernatural and natural: are not so absolute and
excellent, as things supernatural: Nor yet so base and gross, as things
natural: But are things immaterial: and nevertheless, by material
things able somewhat to be signified. And though their particular
Images, by Art, are aggregable and divisible: yet the general Forms,

notwithstanding, are constant, unchangeable, untransformable, and incorruptible. Neither of the sense, can they, at any time, be perceived or judged. Nor yet, for all that, in the royal mind of man, first conceived. But, surmounting the imperfection of conjecture, weaning and opinion: and coming short of high intellectual conception, are the Mercurial fruit of Diancetical discourse, in perfect imagination subsisting. A marvellous neutrality have these things Mathematical, and also a strange participation between things supernatural, immortal, intellectual, simple and indivisible: and things natural, mortal, sensible, compounded and divisible. Probability and sensible prose, may well serve in things natural: and is commendable: In Mathematical reasonings, a probable Argument, is nothing regarded: nor yet the testimony of sense, any whit credited: But only a perfect demonstration, of truths certain, necessary, and invincible: universally and necessarily concluded is allowed as sufficient for an Argument exactly and purely Mathematical.

The Mathematicall Praeface to Elements of
Geometrie of Euclid of Megara, John Dee, 1570

John Dee (born 1527), a mathematician and astrologer, died in December 1609, during the reign of King James I. He is probably best remembered for his service for Queen Elizabeth I, to whom he had been presented soon after her accession by her favourite, Lord Dudley, and Lord Pembroke. Such was Elizabeth's belief in his knowledge of astrology that she agreed to the date he suggested for her coronation, 15 January 1559.

The Quene's Majestie came from Richmond in her coach, the higher way of Mortlake field, and when she came right against the church she turned down toward my house: and when she was against my garden in the field she stood there a good while, and than came into the street at the great gate of the field, where she espied me at my door making obeisance to her Majestie; she beckoned her hand for me; I cam to her coach side, she very speedily pulled off her glove and gave me her hand to kiss; and to be short, asked me to resort to her court, and to give her to wait when I came there; hor. 6¼ to meridie.

Private Diary of Dr. John Dee, And the
Catalog of His Library of Manuscripts, John Dee, 1842

In the above excerpt, Dee mentions his house in Mortlake. This was a town in Surrey that was a short distance away from Queen Elizabeth's Palace of Richmond.

*

It was also on this day in 1603 that Thomas Cartwright, an English clergyman, died, also during the reign of King James I. His views and actions proved so controversial that he incurred the wrath of Queen Elizabeth, who had him thrown into the Fleet prison, before placing him under house arrest.

28th – Smallpox Claims a Queen

Queen Mary II, who had been battling hemorrhagic smallpox for several days, lost her battle with the illness on this in December 1694, dying aged only thirty-two. Her distraught husband, King William III, had been by her side through her illness, and had even taken to sleeping on a camp bed nearby. It was a devastating blow. Only a few days before, hope had surged from a misdiagnosis; what had initially been thought to be smallpox was later said to be measles, and so the perceived risk was considerably less. It was not so, and in fact it was the more fatal strain of smallpox. William, overcome with intense grief, fainted and was expected to follow his wife.

Those thirty-two years had been extraordinarily varied and trying for Mary. Her birth heralded little joy because of her female sex, and her education consequently was neglected. It is sometimes remarked that, had she been born a hundred years before, she would have had a much better education. As such, Hester Chapman wrote of Mary as being 'naturally intelligent' and remarked on how much more learned she would have been, had that mind been given the education.

As Mary lay dying from haemorrhagic smallpox in December 1694, Anne tried to see her but was denied from doing so, either by Lady Derby or by William himself. Thus, the estranged Stuart sisters were never reconciled. Mary was unquestionably popular with her subjects both in Britain and in the Dutch Republic.

Mary was buried in a costly and extravagant funeral ceremony 5 March 1695 – something that she would not have liked. A grief-stricken William did not attend her funeral, but both Houses of Parliament (Commons and Lords) were in attendance. Henry Purcell's moving music flooded Westminster Abbey.

29th – Scorn the Sarcasms of Sciolists

Most learned Sir,

No physician hitherto, has attentively considered the force and influence of the atmosphere upon human bodies; nor yet lies he sufficiently ascertained the part it plays in prolonging human life. No one either hath noted the force it exerts in fermenting, altering, and circulating the blood. Finally, in respect to the manifold changes and alterations of its natural temperament, changes and alterations which you have properly called constitutions, both writers on medicine and writers on natural history have been so far from investigating them diligently, that they have hardly touched upon them.

Considering, however, that the air works its way into all parts of the body (even the most secret), it follows of necessity that such changes and alterations, which the atmosphere undergoes from matters with which it is impregnated, must also be communicated to the blood and juices of the body, and be impressed upon the same; so that such and such depraved dispositions of the blood originate in such and such depraved constitutions of the atmosphere. Well, then, have you, in your Medical Observations, considered the various constitutions of the different years and the different parts of years; since it is in these that the actions of the air upon the blood, juices, and especially the spirits are beheld. Indeed they may possibly be the matter of the spirits themselves. Little doubt have I but that the observation of the characters of fevers, as determined by the character of the year in which they prevail, constitutes the most useful (if not the only) way for establishing a method of practice. Proceed then in your Observations; and, if any still remain upon the fevers of the years lately elapsed, lay them before the public. So shall you consult the interests of humanity.

In the fifth chapter of the first section of your book, you have treated briefly on the use of the Peruvian bark, and the method of exhibiting it. For my own part, I know physicians of no small note, who give it in large doses often repeated. Others again contrive extracts and infusions; and then, out of the infusions, juleps and emulsions. Thus they profess to cure not only intermittent but continued fevers also. In the former the remedy is doubtless a great one. For twenty years (more or less) I have myself used the bark — in various forms, in manifold preparations, and with the greatest success. If however, you know anything peculiar in respect to its properties, or have been better taught by experience than myself oblige the world by proclaiming it. In the treatment of rheumatism you have proposed 'free and frequent bleedings'. I would ask whether some method less prodigal of human blood, and (at the same time) equally certain, may not be discovered.

I know, Most Worthy Sir, that you will experience the rebukes of malevolent men and the calumnies of the envious. These will attack your reputation, now as before. Liberal and candid men, however, whose nature it is to despise such detractors, will defend you. These they are who, if they wish to work out the history of fevers, as shown by long practice, their essences, their causes, their differences, and the true mode of treating them, will take you to lead them on their way;

since few or no other methods of investigation and treatment can be assigned to any one but yourself. Proceed then as you have begun. Scorn the sarcasms of sciolists. Excite the spirits of honest men. It is you who have pointed out the way. Let those who dislike it find a better. Farewell. Do this, and every physician will be beholden to you. No one more than your deservedly devoted friend,

   R. BRADY.

> Letter dated December 1670, from R. Brady to Dr Thomas
> Sydenham

Thomas Sydenham, an English physician, died on 29 December 1689, during the reign of William and Mary. Born around 1624, he and his brother William Sydenham joined the Parliamentarian forces during the English Civil Wars, during which time their mother was murdered. After that tumultuous period had ended, Sydenham turned once more to his studies and eventually became an esteemed physician. In 1688, Sydenham had his portrait painted by Mary Beale.

30th – The Diary of Thomas Burton

Mr. Secretary read the paper himself, in regard it was torn. He had read it three or four times, and desired he might read it. This paper was found the 6th of December last, where upon Sir Thomas Peyton was sent for, and all that he would say to it, is in this paper, which the clerk read. He con fessed such a paper came to his hand writ upon the top of it, the 30th of December. He conceived it to be of dangerous concernment. But how it came to him? It was by a porter from Blackfriars, as he believes, in regard he demanded monies for it. Mr. Secretary desired the papers back again, in regard they were the originals, which were delivered back. Mr. Secretary's report thus entered in the clerk's book. Mr. Secretary made a relation of a wicked design to take away the Lord Protector's life, and to fire Whitehall, and presented the examinations of John Cecil and John Toope, taken upon oath before Francis White and William Jesop, Esquires, two of his Highness's Justices of Peace for the liberty of Westminster, which was read.

> *Diary of Thomas Burton, Esq., Member in the Parliaments of*
> *Oliver and Richard Cromwell, from 1656 to 1659, ed.*
> John Towill Rutt, 1828

Thomas Burton was one of the lesser-known diarists of the Stuart era. Not much biographical information remains about Burton, such as when he was born, but his manuscript diary has become the go-to primary source for those studying the Protectorate parliaments. Burton died in 1661, having been knighted following the Restoration by King Charles II. Burton's name is often mentioned with that of Guibon Goddard, another parliamentary diarist.

31st – Oliver St John

My Lords, the Parliament, as it is best qualified and fitted to make this supply for some of each rank, and that through all the parts of the kingdom being there met, His Majesty having declared the danger, they best knowing the estates of all men within the realm, are fittest, by comparing the danger and men's estates together, to proportion the aid accordingly ...

And secondly, as they are the fittest for the preservation of that fundamental propriety which the subjects hath in his lands and goods, because each subject's vote is included in whatsoever is there done; so that it cannot be done otherwise, I shall endeavor to prove to your Lordships both by reason and authority.

My first reason is this, that the Parliament by the law is appointed as the ordinary means for supply upon the extraordinary occasions, when the ordinary supplies will not do it: if this in the writ therefore may, without resorting to that, be used, the same argument will hold as before in resorting to the extraordinary, of the ordinary, and the same inconvenience follow. My second reason is taken from the actions of former kings in this of the defence.

The aids demanded by them, and granted in Parliament, even for this purpose of the defence, and that in times of imminent danger, are so frequent, that I will spare the citing of any of them: it is rare in a subject, more in a prince, to ask and take that of gift, which he may and ought to have of right, and that without so much as a salvo, or declaration of his right ...

'Oliver St John's speech during the Hampden Case
(concerning Ship Money)', from *Constitutional
Documents of the Puritan Revolution*, S. R. Gardiner, 1906

Sir Oliver St John, an English judge and politician, died on this day in 1673 during the reign of King Charles II. In 1637, St John served as John Hampden's legal counsel during the Ship Money case, from which we have the above excerpt. During the English Civil Wars, St John was a Parliamentarian supporter and an Independent, much like his cousin Oliver Cromwell. On 17 January 1641, St John gave a speech to Parliament concerning 'the

Charge of Treason then exhibited to the Bishops, Formerly accused by the House of Commons'. It was St John who made a crucial speech to the Houses of Lords and Commons that Strafford was guilty of treason – not with any hard evidence, but just because there were suspicions enough to condemn him. Strafford had already gone through a trial, and had eloquently defended himself and been found not guilty. But when the Army Plot to break Strafford out of the Tower was uncovered, Pym and St John worked to get an Act of Attainder on Strafford. The earl was doomed. King Charles reluctantly signed his execution warrant and the man was executed in 1641. In an Ordinance dated 28 May 1644, St John was promoted from Solicitor General to having both that position and that of Attorney General.

GLOSSARY

Anabaptistism: a Protestant Christian movement from the sixteenth century, which, among other things, advocated adult baptism instead of the then-traditional infant baptism.

Anglican: can refer to the Anglican Church or a person who is a member of the Anglican Church. This was created in the 1530s during the reign of King Henry VIII, and is English and Protestant.

Antiquarian: someone who studies and/or collects objects/books from antiquity/ancient times.

Apotheosis: the elevation of a person to a status of divinity; or the apex or height of a person's career.

Arminianism: a Protestant movement based on the theological ideas formed by Jacobus Arminius, which opposed the idea of an absolute predestination and promoted free will.

Black Box: integral to the story that sought to legitimise the Duke of Monmouth. This box was believed to contain the marriage lines of his parents, Charles II and Lucy Walter.

Calvinism: named after the Protestant reformer John Calvin; a major offshoot of Protestantism.

Cavaliers: As with the term 'Roundhead' for those who supported Parliament, 'Cavalier' was used as a derogatory term for those who supported and/or fought on behalf of King Charles and his cause. John Evelyn called this term 'the invidious name'.

Covenanters: those who signed a Covenant as a result of King Charles I's attempt to impose a new Book of Common Prayer in Scotland.

Diggers: a radical political (and some say proto-Communist) movement during the 1640s.

Dutch Republic: present-day Netherlands; see also United Provinces.

Elizabethan: anything pertaining to the reign of Queen Elizabeth I, be it clothing, theatre, poetry, literature, etc.

Erastians: a doctrine loosely based on the work of Swiss theologian Thomas Erastus, which argues that the State should punish sinners, not the Church.

Fifth Monarchists: a political and religiously-motivated movement of English Dissenters from 1649 to 1660; these Millenarians awaited the establishing of the fifth (and final) kingdom under Jesus, King of Kings.

Five Members: The five Members of Parliament: John Hampden, Arthur Haselrig, Denzil Holles, John Pym, and William Strode. King Charles I entered Parliament with armed soldiers in an attempt to arrest these men, who had been informed and fled.

Free Will: the belief, in Roman Catholicism, that an individual's actions in life determine whether they will go to Heaven or Hell.

Immortal Seven: Seven of the most influential men in Stuart Britain in 1688, who together wrote an invitation to William III of Orange to invade England. These men were: William Cavendish, 4th Earl of Devonshire; Henry Compton, Bishop of London; Richard Lumley, Baron Lumley; Thomas Osborne, 1st Earl of Danby; Henry Sidney; Edward Russell; and Charles Talbot, 12th Earl of Shrewsbury.

Interregnum: Latin for 'in between kings', this term is used to describe the period between Charles I's death in 1649 and his son's restoration in 1660.

Jacobean: of or relating to the arts, architectural style, and literature under King James I of England (VI of Scotland).

Jacobites: those who supported James II and his descendants after the 'Glorious Revolution' of 1688/9.

Jacobins: a political movement in revolutionary France which was inspired by radical movements and figures during the English Civil Wars.

Levellers: one of the radical political groups that sprung up during the 1640s in England.

Lutheran: a branch of Protestantism named after Martin Luther.

Meridie: noon, midday.

Millenarianism: a belief that a Second Coming of Christ is imminent.

New Model Army: the highly efficient army created under Oliver Cromwell during the 1640s.

Nonconformist: the term used after 1662's Act of Uniformity for any Protestant who did not conform to the traditions of the Church of England (Anglican Church).

Papist: a disparaging term used to label a person who is a Roman Catholic.

Popish: another term for anything pertaining to Roman Catholicism.

Predestination: the belief that God has a plan for everyone and that in that plan, some are the elect (chosen to go to Heaven), while others are destined to languish in Hell.

Presbyterian: a Protesant Christian denomination that originated in the British Isles and based on Calvinism. Presbyterians are governed by presbyters (elders).

Providence: God's intervention in the world.

Ranters: a religious fringe group during the English Civil Wars.

Regicide: the killing of a king, or a person who commits the killing of a king.

Romish: another term for a person who is a Roman Catholic. *See also Romanish, Papist, Popish*.

Romanish: another term for anything pertaining to Roman Catholicism. See also *Romish*, *Papist*, *Popish*.

Roundheads: a term of disparagement, especially in the beginning of the English Civil Wars, for those who supported and fought for the Parliamentary cause. See also *Parliamentarian*.

Sciolist: someone who claims to be an expert in something, but in truth has only a superficial understanding of it.

Sennight (also spelled senet): 'seven nights' – a week.

Shallop: any kind of seventeenth- or eighteenth-century vessel used to row or sail on shallow waters.

Tories: one of two political groups that emerged in the 1670s.

United Provinces: the name, as with the Dutch Republic, of the country now known as the Netherlands.

Whigs: one of two political groups that emerged in the 1670s.

Williamite: those who supported William III of Orange during and after the Glorious Revolution of 1688–9.

SELECT BIBLIOGRAPHY

Primary Sources

A Complete History Of England: With The Lives Of All The Kings and Queens Thereof: From The Earliest Account of Time, to the Death of His Late Majesty King William III. London, 1706

A Discourse upon the Union of Scotland and England; Humbly submitted to the Parliament of Scotland by a Lover of his Country. Scotland, 1702

An Account of the Ceremonies Observed in the Coronations of the Kings and Queens of England: viz. King James II and his royal consort, King William III and Queen Mary, Queen Anne, King George I, and King George II and Queen Caroline. London, 1760

An Act for Laying Further Duties on Low-wines: And for Preventing the Damage to Her Majesties Revenue by Importation of Foreign Cut Whale-bone: and for Making Some Provisions as to the Stamp-duties, and the Duties on Births, Burials, and Marriages, and the Salt-duties, and Touching Million Lottery-tickets: and for Enabling Her Majesty to Dispose the Effects of William Kidd, a Notorious Pirate, to the Use of Greenwich Hospital. London, 1705

An Enquiry into, and Detection of the Barbarous Murther of the Late Earl of Essex, or a Vindiction of that Noble Person from the Guile and Infamy of having Destroy'd Himself. London, 1684

Articles of Impeachment: Of High-treason and Misdemeanors, Against Robert Earl of Oxford and Earl Mortimer. July 9. 1715. With His Lordship's Answer, Paragraph by Paragraph. To which is Added, A Short State of the Late War and Peace, Volume 2. London; 1727

Astell, Mary. *An Essay in Defence of the Female Sex*. London, 1697

Aubrey, John. *The Natural History and Antiquities of the County of Surrey: Begun in the Year 1673*. London, 1718

Baker, Thomas. *Reflections Upon Learning: Wherein is Shown the Insufficiency Thereof, in Its Several Particulars: in Order to Evince the Usefulness of Necessity of Revelation*. London, 1708

Bastard, Thomas. *Chrestoleros: Seven books of Epigrames*. London, 1598

Behn, Aphra. *Love-Letters between a Nobleman and His Sister*. London, 1712

Behn, Aphra. *The Plays, Histories, and Novels of the Ingenious Mrs. Aphra Behn: With Life and Memoirs. Complete in Six Volumes*. London, 1871

Birch, Thomas. *A collection of the state papers of John Thurloe, Esq., secretary, first, to the Council of State, and afterwards to the two protectors, Oliver and Richard Cromwell: in seven volumes: containing authentic memorials of the English affairs from the year 1638, to the restoration of King Charles II ... the whole digested into an exact order of time, to which is prefixed the life of Mr. Thurloe, with a complete index to each volume. Containing papers from the year MDCLVIII to MDCLX, Volume 7*. London, 1742

Blow, John. *Amphion Anglicus: A Work of Many Compositions, for One, Two, Three And four Voices; with Several Accompagnements of Instrumental Musick: and a Thorow-bass to Each Song, Figur'd for an Organ, Harpsichord, Or Theorboe-lute*. London, 1700

Boxhorn, Marcus Zuerius van. *Bediedinge van de tot noch toe onbekende afgodinne Nehalennia*. Leiden, 1647

Boyle, Robert. *A Disquisition about the Final Causes of Natural Things: Wherein it is Inquir'd, Whether, and (if at All) with what Cautions, a Naturalist Should Admit Them?* London, 1688

Brady, R. *Letter to Dr Thomas Sydenham*. 30 December, 1670

Bristol, John Hervey, 1st Earl of. *Letter-books of John Hervey, First Earl of Bristol: With Sir Thomas Hervey's Letters During Courtship and Poems During Widowhood*. Wells, 1894

Burchett, Josiah. *A complete history of the most remarkable transactions at sea: from the earliest accounts of time to the conclusion of the last war with France ... And in a more particular manner of Great Britain, from the time of the revolution, in the year 1688, to the aforesaid period*. London, 1720

Burnet, Bishop Gilbert. *The History of My Own Times*. Oxford, 1897

Cartwright, Thomas. *The Diary of Dr. Thomas Cartwright, Bishop of Chester: Commencing at the Time of His Elevation to that See, August M.DC.LXXXVI; and Terminating with the Visitation of St. Mary Magdalene College, Oxford, October M.DC.LXXXVII*. London, 1843

'Charles II: August 11-20, 1683', in *Calendar of State Papers Domestic: Charles II, 1683 July-September*, ed. F. H. Blackburne Daniell and Francis Bickley. London, 1934, pp. 277–311 http://www.british-history.ac.uk/cal-state-papers/domestic/chas2/1683-jul-sep/pp277-311

Chudleigh, Lady Mary. 'On the Vanities of this Life: A Pindarick Ode', *Poems on Several Occasions: Together with The Song of the Three Children Paraphras'd*. London, 1703

Clapham, Thomas. *A Sermon Preach'd in the City of York, on Wednesday, January XIX, 1703/4: Being the Fast-day. Appointed for the Late Dreadful Storm*. London, 1704

Clarendon, Edward Hyde, Earl of. *The Lord Clarendon's History of the Grand Rebellion.* London, 1717

Clarendon, Henry Hyde, Earl of; Rochester, Laurence Hyde, Earl of. *The correspondence of Henry Hyde, Earl of Clarendon, and his brother Laurence Hyde, Earl of Rochester; with the diary of Lord Clarendon from 1687 to 1690, containing minute particulars of the events attending the revolution and the diary of Lord Rochester during his embassy to Poland in 1676.* London, 1828

Cole, Christian. *Memoirs of Affairs of State Containing Letters.* London, 1733, p. 117

Cotton, Robert Bruce. *A Remonstrance of the Treaties of Amity and Marriage, Before time, and of late of the House of Austria and Spain, &c, Cottoni Posthuma: Divers Choice Pieces of that Renowned Antiquary Sir Robert Cotton, Knight and Baronet.* London, 1672

Cudworth, Ralph. *A Treatise Concerning Eternal and Immutable Morality.* London, 1731

De La Pryme, Abraham. *The Diary of Abraham de la Pryme: The Yorkshire Antiquary.* Durham, 1870

Durfey, Thomas. *The Comical History of Don Quixote.* London, 1694

Fairfax, Sir Thomas. *A Manifesto From His Excellency Sir Thomas Fairfax and the Army under his Command; Concerning the IX Member Impeach'd, in the name of themselves, and the Kingdome of England.* Cambridge, 1647. Courtesy of British Library, 102.b.34

Fanshawe, Anne Harrison. *Memoirs of Lady Fanshawe.* London, 1625

Gregory, David Dr. *A Treatise of Practical Geometry: In Three Parts. Volume 2.* Edinburgh, 1745

Halifax, Charles Montagu, Earl of. *The Works and Life of the Right Honourable Charles: Late Earl of Halifax, Including the History of His Lordship's Times, Parts 1-2.* London, 1715

Halley, Edmond. *Miscellanea Curiosa: Being a Collection of Some of the Principal Phænomena in Nature, Accounted for by the Greatest Philosophers of this Age. Together with Several Discourses Read Before the Royal Society, for the Advancement of Physical and Mathematical Knowledge, Volume 1.* London, 1705

Harley, Brilliana. *Letters of the Lady Brilliana Harley.* London, 1854

Harvey, William. *The Works of William Harvey.* London, 1847

Heath, James. *Flagellum, or, The Life and Death, Birth and Burial of Oliver Cromwel, the Late Usurper, faithfully described.* London, 1669

Herrick, Robert. *A Selection from the Lyrical Poems of Robert Herrick.* London, 1876

Hinman, R. R. *Letters from the English Kings and Queens, Charles II, James II, William and Mary, Anne, George II, &c: To the Governors of the Colony of Connecticut, Together with the Answers Thereto, from 1635 to 1749: and Other Original, Ancient, Literary and Curious Documents.* Hartford, 1836

Hobbes, Thomas. *Leviathan: Or, The Matter, Forme, & Power of a Commonwealth Ecclesiastical and Civil.* London, 1651

Holland, Henry Rich, 1st Earl of. *Two speeches delivered by the earl of Holland, and Mr. John Pym concerning a petition to His Majestie for peace, spoken in Guild-hall on the 10th of November.* London, 1642

Holles, Denzil. *The Long Parliament Dissolved.* London, 1676

The Petition of the Members of the House of Commons, Who are accused by the Army. London: 29 June 1647. Courtesy of British Library, 102.b.49

House of Commons, *Declaration and Impeachment Against the Duke of Buckingham.* 10 May 1626.

Ireton, Henry. *Sad Newes From Ireland.* London, 1650

Jones, Inigo. *The Most Notable Antiquity of Great Britain: Vulgarly Called Stone-Heng, on Salisbury Plain, Restored.* London, 1725

Law, John. *Money and Trade Considered: With a Proposal for Supplying the Nation with Money. First Published at Edinburgh 1705.* Glasgow, 1750

Lediard, Thomas. *Life of John, Duke of Marlborough, Prince of the Roman Empire.* London, 1743

Letters from Archibald, Earl of Argyll, to John, Duke of Lauderdale. Edinburgh, 1829

Life and Military Actions of His Royal Highness Prince Eugene of Savoy, With an Account of His Death and Funeral. London, 1739

Lister, Dr Martin. *A Journey to Paris in the Year 1698.* London, 1699

Malthus, Thomas. *An Historical Account of the Heroick Life and Magnanimous Actions of the Most Illustrious Protestant Prince, James, Duke of Monmouth.* London, 1683

Moore, John. *Sermon before the Lord Mayor and the Court of Alderman at the Guildhall Chapel.* London, 1684

Newton, Isaac. *Opticks, Or, A Treatise of the Reflections, Refractions, Inflections, and Colours of Light.* London, 1704

Orléans, Charlotte-Elisabeth, Duchesse d'. *Correspondance complète de madame duchesse d'Orléans née Princesse Palatine, mère du régent; traduction entièrement nouvelle par G. Brunet, accompagnée d'uné annotation historique, biographique et littéraire du traducteur.* Paris, 1855

Paulden, Captain Thomas. *Pontefract Castle: an Account, How it was Taken and how General Rainsborough was Surprised in his Quarters at Doncaster, Anno 1648.* London, 1702

Pearson, John (Bishop of Chester). *An Exposition of the Apostle's Creed, from the Holy Scriptures and Bishop Pearson.* London, 1704

Penn, William. *A brief account of the rise and progress of the people called Quakers.* London, 1769

Plunkett, Oliver. *The Tryal and Condemnation of Edw. Fitz-Harris, Esq; for High Treason ... and also the Tryal and Condemnation of Dr Oliver Plunket, Titular Primate of Ireland, for High-Treason.* London, 1681

Pope, Alexander. *The Works of Mr. Pope.* London, 1717

Queen Mary of Scots. *The Genuine Letters of Mary Queen of Scots to James Earl of Bothwell.* Westminster, 1726

Raleigh, Walter. *Poems by Sir Henry Wotton, Sir Walter Raleigh and Others.* London, 1845

Romney, Henry Sidney, Earl of. *Diary of the Times of Charles the Second by the Honourable Henry Sidney, (afterwards Earl of Romney) Including His Correspondence with the Countess of Sunderland, and Other Distinguished Persons at the English Court, Volume I.* London, 1843

Rowe, Nicholas. *The Works of Nicholas Rowe, Consisting of His Plays and Poems, Volume 1.* London, 1753

Rushworth, Jo. *A Declaration of His Excellency Sir Thomas Fairfax, and his Councill of Warre, on behalf of themselves and the whole army, shewing the grounds of their present advance towards London.* London, 1647. Courtesy of British Library, RB.23b.2029

Savile, George, Marquess of Halifax. *Advice to a Daughter from Miscellanies by the Right Noble Lord, the Late Lord Marquess of Halifax.* London, 1700

Savile, George, Marquess of Halifax. Letter, April 24, 1686. Savile Correspondence *Seasonable Queries Relating to the Birth and Birthright of a Certain Person.* London, 1704

Selden, John. *Table-talk, 1689, ed. by E. Arber. (Eng. repr.).* London, 1868

Settle, Elkanah. *The Character of a Popish Successor, and What England may Expect from such a One.* London, 1681. Courtesy of British Library. 101.d.25

Shadwell, Thomas. *The Libertine: A Tragedy.* London, 1676

Shaftesbury, Anthony Ashley Cooper, 1st Earl of. *A speech lately made by a noble peer of the realm.* London, 1681

Shaftesbury, Anthony Ashley-Cooper, 3rd Earl of. *Characteristicks of men, manners, opinions, times.* London, 1732

Shrewsbury, Charles Talbot, Duke of. *Private and original correspondence of Charles Talbot, duke of Shrewsbury, with King William, the leaders of the Whig party, and other distinguished statesmen; illustrated with narratives, historical and biographical.* London, 1821

Sidney, Algernon. *Discourses Concerning Government.* London, 1704

Smalridge, George. *A Sermon Preach'd Before the Right Worshipful the Court of Aldermen: At the Cathedral Church of St Paul, London, on Monday, January 31. 1708/9.* London, 1709

Smith, John. *The True Travels, Adventures and Observations of Captaine John Smith, in Europe, Asia, Africke, and America: beginning about the year 1593, and continued to this present 1629.* London, 1630

Sprat, Thomas. *The History of the Royal Society of London, for the Improving of Natural Knowledge.* London, 1667

Sprigge, Joshua. *Anglia rediviva: England's recovery: being the history of the motions, actions, and successes of the army under the immediate conduct of Sir Thomas Fairfax.* Oxford, 1854

Steele, Richard. *The Funeral: Or, Grief A-La-Mode.* London, 1735

Substance of All the Depositions Relating to the Duel Between Duke Hamilton and Lord Mohun. London, 1713

T. B. *Observations upon Prince Rupert's white dog, called Boy.* London, 1643

The Case at Large of Duke Hamilton and the Lord Mohun. London: 1712. Courtesy of British Library, 501.b.31

The Lives of Those Eminent Antiquaries John Leland, Thomas Hearne, and Anthony À Wood: With an Authentick Account of Their Respective Writings and Publications, from Original Papers, Volume 1. Oxford, 1772

The Whole Lives, Characters, Actions and Fall of D. Hamilton and L. Mohun. London, 1713. Courtesy of British Library, 899.d.19

Thornhill, James. *An Explanation of the Painting in the Royal Hospital at Greenwich.* London, 1730. Courtesy of British Library, 787.g.19

Tillotson, Dr John. *Sermon CCLIIO, The Efficacy of Prayer, for obtaining the Holy Spirit.* Edinburgh, 1748

Udall, William. *The Historie of the Life and Death of Mary Stuart Queen of Scotland.* London, 1636

Vaughan, Henry. *The Sacred Poems and Private Ejaculations of Henry Vaughan.* Boston, 1856

Webster, John. *The Dramatic Works of John Webster, Volume I.* London, 1857

Whittel, John. *Constantinus redivivus, or, A full account of the wonderful providences, and unparallell'd successes that have all along attended the glorious enterprises of the heroical prince, William the 3d, now king of Great Britain, &c.* London, 1693

Whittie, John. *An Exact Diary of the Late Expedition of His Illustrious Highness, The Prince of Orange (Now King of Great Britain) from his Palace at the Hague, To his Landing at Torbay.* London, 1689

Wilmot, John. *The Works of the Right Honourable John Earl of Rochester, Consisting of Satires, Songs, Translations, and other Occasional Poems.* London, 1718

Wood, Anthony à. *The History and Antiquities of the Colleges and Halls in the University of Oxford.* Oxford, 1792

Wood, Anthony. *The Life of Anthony À Wood: From the Year 1632 to 1672, Written by Himself, and Published by Mr. Thomas Hearne. Now Continued to the Time of His Death from Authentic Materials.* Oxford, 1772

Wotton, Henry. 'On His Mistress, the Queen of Bohemia'. *Poems by Sir Henry Wotton, Sir Walter Raleigh and Others.* London, 1845

Wren Jr, Christopher. *Parentalia.* London, 1750

Wycherley, William. *Plays Written by Mr. William Wycherley: Containing The Plain Dealer, The Country Wife, Gentleman Dancing Master, Love in a Wood.* London, 1731

Zouch, Richard. 'The Dove', *The Dove: or Passages of Cosmography. Reproduced, with a memoir and notes, collected by R. Walker.* Oxford, 1839

Secondary Sources

Ackroyd, Peter. *The History of England Volume III: Civil War.* London, 2015

Adamson, J. *The Noble Revolt.* London, 2007

Archer, Jeremy. *A Royal Christmas,* London, 2012

Ashley, Maurice. *The Battle of Naseby and the Fall of King Charles I.* Stroud, 1992

Baxter, Stephen. *William III.* London, 1966

Beard, Geoffrey. *The Work of Grinling Gibbons.* London, 1989

Begent, Peter J. and Chesshyre, Hubert. *The Most Noble Order of the Garter: 650 Years.* London, 1999

Betcherman, Lita-Rose. *Court Lady and Country Wife: Royal Privilege and Civil War, Two Noble Sister in Seventeenth-Century England.* Chichester, 1995

Birch, Thomas. *George Villiers' Letter to Secretary Winwood, as found in Birch's Life of Sir Walter Ralegh.* Oxford, 1829

Bowen, Marjorie. *The Third Mary Stuart: Mary of York, Orange, & England – Being a Character Study with Memoirs and Letters of Queen Mary II of England, 1662–1694.* London, 1929

Braddick, Michael. *God's Fury, England's Fire: A New History of the English Civil Wars.* London, 2008

Brown, Alan, ed. *Festivals in World Religions.* London, 1986

Brown, F.C. *Elkanah Settle: His Life and Works.* Chicago, 1910

Burrows, Donald; Helen Coffey; John Greenacombe; Anthony Hicks, eds. *George Frideric Handel: Collected Documents, Volume 1, 1609–1725.* Cambridge, 2013

Campbell, John. *Lives of the Admirals and Other Eminent British Seamen, Volume 1.* London, 1750

Cervantes, Miguel de. *Don Quixote de la Mancha.* London, 1837

Chapman, Hester W. *Mary II: Queen of England.* London, 1953

   Chapman, Hester W. *Privileged Persons: Four Seventeenth-Century Studies.* London, 1966

   Chapman, Hester W. *Queen Anne's Son: A Memoir of William Henry, Duke of Gloucester, 1689–1700.* Tonbridge, 1954

Churchill, Winston S. *Marlborough: His Life and Times, Book One.* Chicago, 2002

Clifton, Robin. *The Last Popular Rebellion: The Western Rising of 1685.* London, 1984

Collins, Charles. *Great Love Stories of the Theatre: A Record of Theatrical Romance.* New York, 1911

Coward, Barry. *The Stuart Age: England 1603–1714.* Harlow, 1994

Cruickshanks, Eveline. *The Stuart Courts.* Stroud, 2009

Davies, Godfrey. *The Early Stuarts 1603–1660.* Oxford, 1985

Davies, J. D. *Blood of Kings.* Shepperton, 2010

Duckitt, Mabel and Harriet Wragg. *Selected English Letters (XV–XIX Centuries).* London, 1913

Day, Gary and Jack Lynch. *The Encyclopedia of British Literature 1660–1789 Set, Volume 1.* Chichester, 2015

Dolman, Brett. *Beauty, Sex, and Power: a Story of Debauchery and Decadent Art at the Late Stuart Court, 1660–1714.* London, 2012

Doran, John. *Their Majesties' Servants: Annals of the English stage from Thomas Betterton to Edmund Kean.* New York, 1880

Duffy, Maureen. *Purcell.* London, 1994

   The Passionate Shepherdess: The Life of Aphra Behn, 1649–1689. London, 1977

E. H. *The History of the Warr of Ireland from 1641 to 1653: A British officer of the regiment of Sir John Clottworthy.* Dublin, 1873

Erickson, Carolly. *Great Harry.* London, 1980

Evenden. Doreen. *The Midwives of Seventeenth-Century London.* Cambridge, 2000

Ferguson, James. *Astronomy explained upon Sir Isaac Newton's Principles: and made easy to those who have not studied mathematics: to which are added, a plain method of finding the distances of all the planets from the sun, by the transit of Venus over the sun's disc, in the year 1761: an account of Mr. Horrox's observation of the transit of Venus in the year 1639.* Philadelphia, 1806

Fraser, Antonia. *Love and Louis XIV: The Women in the Life of the Sun King.* London, 2007

   The Weaker Vessel, Woman's Lot in Seventeenth-Century England. London, 1984

Gilfillan, Revd. George. *The Poetical Works of John Dryden, Vol I With Life, Critical Dissertation, and Explanatory Notes.* 1855

Hepworth Dixon, William. *Robert Blake, Admiral and General at Sea: Admiral and General at Sea.* London, 1856

Herissone, Rebecca, ed. *The Ashgate Research Companion to Henry Purcell.* Manchester, 2012

Hibbert, Christopher. *Charles I.* London, 1972

Hibbert, Christopher. *The Virgin Queen: Elizabeth, Genius of the Golden Age.* Reading, 1991

Hill, Christopher. *God's Englishman: Oliver Cromwell and the English Revolution.* Harmondsworth, 1970

Hill, Christopher. *The Century of Revolution 1603–1714.* London, 1961

Hind, Arthur M. *Wenceslaus Hollar and His Views of London and Windsor in the Seventeenth Century.* London, 1922

Hodges, George. *William Penn.* New York, 1901

Holmes, Richard. *Marlborough: Britain's Greatest General.* London, 2009

Hopkins, Graham. *Constant Delights: Rakes, Rogues, and Scandal in Restoration England.* London, 2002

Hume, David. *The History of England, From the Invasion of Julius Caesar to the Revolution in 1688.* London, 1789

Johnson, Henry. *The Exploits of Myles Standish.* New York, 1897

Keates, Jonathan. *Handel: The Man and his Music.* London, 1985

Keeble, N. H. *The Cultural Identity of Seventeenth-Century Women: A Reader.* Oxford, 1994

Kenyon, J. P. *The Stuart Constitution: Documents and Commentary.* Cambridge, 1986

Kightly, Charles. *The Customs and Ceremonies of Britain: An Encyclopaedia of Living Traditions.* London, 1986

Kishlansky, Mark. *Charles I: An Abbreviated Life.* London, 2014

A Monarchy Transformed: Britain, 1603–1714. London, 1997

Lediard, Thomas. *The Life of John, Duke of Marlborough, Prince of the Roman Empire, Volume I.* London, 1743

Lynn, John A. *The French Wars 1667–1714: The Sun King at war.* Oxford 2002

MacDonell. *The Closet of Sir Kenelm Digby Knight Opened.* London, 1910

MacLeay, Kenneth. *Historical Memoirs of Rob Roy and the Clan Macgregor: Including Original Notices of Lady Grange: with an Introductory Sketch Illustrative of the Condition of the Highlands, Prior to the Year 1745, Issue 1.* Philadelphia, 1819

MacLeod, Catharine. *The Lost Prince: The Life and Death of Henry Stuart.* London, 2012

Marah, William Hennessey. *Memoirs of Archbishop Juxon and his times.* London, 1869

Marshall, Rosalind K. *The Winter Queen: The Life of Elizabeth of Bohemia 1596–1662.* Edinburgh, 1998

McCall, Colin. *Crime, Cash, Credit and Chaos: A Brief History of the Life and Work of John Law (1671–1729) the Father of Credit Systems.* Matlock, 2007

McClain, Molly. *Beaufort: The Duke and his Duchess, 1657–1715.* New Haven, 2001

Melville, Lewis. *The Windsor Beauties: Ladies of the Court of Charles II.* London, 1928

Miles, Clement A. *Christmas Customs and Traditions: Their History and Significance.* New York, 1976

Miller, John. *A Brief History of the English Civil Wars: Roundheads, Cavaliers, and the Execution of the King.* London, 2009

Miller, John. *James II.* New Haven, 2000

Miller, John. *William and Mary.* London, 1974

Milton, Giles. *White Gold: The Story of Thomas Pellow and North Africa's One Million European Slaves.* London, 2004

Morley, Iris. *A Thousand Lives: An Account of the English Revolutionary Movement 1660–1685.* Tonbridge, 1954

Mottley, John. *The Life of Peter the Great, Emperor of All Russia, Volume I.* London, 1755

Mundill, Robin R. 'England's Jewish Solution. Experiment and Expulsion, 1262-1290', http://www.history.ac.uk/reviews/review/70 (Accessed 15 January 2016)

Neil, Edward Duffield. *History of the Virginia Company of London.* London, 1869

Oman, Carol. *Mary of Modena.*

Oman, Carol. *The Winter Queen.*

Opher, Philip. *A Brief History of Oxford: The Evolution of the City from 900 AD to 2000 AD.* Heritage Tours Publications, 1997

Parker, John Henry. *The Ashmolean Museum: Its History, Present State and Prospects: a Lecture Delivered to the Oxford Architectural and Historical Society, November 2, 1870, Volume 19.* Oxford, 1870

Parry, Graham. *The Seventeenth Century: The Intellectual and Cultural Context of English Literature, 1603–1700.* Harlow, 1989

Piggott, Simon. *Suicide and Its Antidotes.* London, 1824

Plowden, Alison. *Henrietta Maria: Charles I's Indomitable Queen.*

Powell, Roger. *Royal Sex: The Scandalous Love Lives of the British Royal Family.* Stroud, 2013

Prebble, John. *Glencoe: The Story of the Massacre*. Aylesbury, 1974
Purkiss, Diane. *The English Civil War: A People's History.*

Ramsey, R. W. 'Elizabeth Claypole'.*The English Historical Review* 7 (25), 1892
Reynolds, Graham. *Fitzwilliam Museum Handbooks: British Portrait Miniatures.* Cambridge, 1998
Roberts, David. *Thomas Betterton: The Greatest Actor of the Restoration Stage.* Cambridge, 2010
Royle, Trevor. *Civil War: The Wars of the Three Kingdoms, 1638–1660*

St. George, C. *A civil and ecclesiastical history of England, to 1829: Volume 1.* London, 1830
Sandars, Mary Frances. *Princess and Queen of England: Life of Mary II*. London, 1913
Sharpe, Kevin. *Remapping Early Modern England: The Culture of Seventeenth-Century Politics.* Cambridge, 2000
Shawe-Taylor, Desmond and Quentin Buvelot. *Masters of the Everyday: Dutch Artists in the Age of Vermeer.* Royal Collection Trust/Mauritshuis, 2015
Somerset, Anne. *The Affair of the Poisons: Murder, Infanticide, and Satanism at the Court of Louis XIV.* London, 2003
Spencer, Charles. *Cavalier: Prince Rupert of the Rhine*. Oxford, 2007
Spencer, Charles. *Killers of the King: The Men Who Dared to Execute Charles I.* Oxford, 2014
Starkey, David. *Crown and Country: The Kings and Queens of England*. London, 2011
Strong, Roy. *Coronation: From the 8th to the 21st Century*. London, 2005
Stubbs, John. *Reprobates: The Cavaliers of the English Civil War.*

Tanner, J. R. *English Constitutional Conflicts of the Seventeenth Century 1603–1689.* Cambridge, 1952
Terry, Charles Sanford. *The Pentland Rising & Rullion Green*. Glasgow, 1905
Tinniswood, Adrian. *His Invention So Fertile: A Life of Christopher Wren.*
Tinniswood, Adrian. *The Verneys.*
Troost, Wout. *William III, the Stadtholder-King: A Political Biography.* Aldershot, 2005

Watson, J. N. P. *Captain-General and Rebel Chief: The Life of James, Duke of Monmouth.*
Wedgwood, C. V. *Thomas Wentworth, First Earl of Strafford, 1593–1641: A Revaluation.* London, 1961
Wilson, Derek. *All the King's Women: Love, sex, and politics in the Life of Charles II.* London, 2003

Womack, Pamela J. *An Illustrated Introduction to the Stuarts.* Stroud, 2014
Womersley, David. *James II: The Last Catholic King.*
Woodward, Gertrude L. and James G. McManaway. *A Check List of English Plays 1640–1700.* Chicago, 1945
Worsley, Lucy and David Souden. *Hampton Court Palace: The Official Illustrated History.* London, 2005

Zimmerman, Franklin B. *Henry Purcell 1659–1695: His Life and Times.* New York, 1967
Zimmerman, Franklin B. *Henry Purcell: A Guide to Research.* New York, 1989
Zuvich, Andrea. *The Stuarts in 100 Facts.* Stroud, 2015

ACKNOWLEDGEMENTS

This book, like *The Stuarts in 100 Facts* before it, could only have been made with the support of fellow historians, friends, and family. With immense gratitude, I would like to acknowledge my first editor, Sarah Kendall, for initially contacting me about writing books about the Stuart period for Amberley Publishing. I would also like to thank my editors Aaron Meek and Annie Campbell for their help and support in the writing of *A Year in Stuart Britain*, and the rest of the team at Amberley, including Phillip Dean and Sarah Greenwood.

I would like to thank historian J. D. Davies, who has kindly given his time to read my work and provide much-needed feedback. Thanks as well to those who have helped, supported, and/or inspired me in a variety of ways over the past few years: Alexandra Kim, Sarah Levine, Sarah Seale, Samuel McLean, Patrick Baty, Catherine Curzon, Fahran Wallace, Jacqueline Reiter, Ed Abrams, Stephenie Woollerton, Robin Rowles, Josh Provan, Kate Morant, Anna Belfrage, Fiona Orr, Alison Stuart, Jayne Smith, Leslie Smith, Adrian Tinniswood, Elaine Chalus, Richard Foreman, Kris Martin, and Mike Paterson.

Thank you as well to DenRon Pugh-van Randeraat, Oscar Meijer, Patric Aalders, and Henri van Oene for their help translating Marcus Zuerius van Boxhorn's seventeenth-century Dutch writing.

A big thank you to the helpful and indefatigable staff at the UK National Archives, Paleis Het Loo, Historic Royal Palaces, Castle Howard, Blenheim Palace, the Monument to the Great Fire of London, National Maritime Museum, Westminster Abbey Library, Aston Hall, the British Library, and the various local libraries and Record Offices I've visited throughout the UK.

Of course, a person cannot devote so much time to historical personages unless some love is involved, and I do love the Stuart era very much. This time period, at least during my schooling, was severely overlooked and I hope that the work which I (and other historians of this time period) have done will ameliorate this situation.

Many thanks to my fans – especially those on Facebook, Twitter, Goodreads, and on *The Seventeenth Century Lady* who have supported me over the past few years – you know who you are, and how much I appreciate your encouragement.

Quiero dar las gracias también a mi familia por su apoyo: Edelmira, Visnja, y Milka – las quiero mucho.